THE JEWISH FAMILY BOOK

THE BANTAM JEWISH BOOKSHELF

THE JEWISH ALMANAC
  Richard Siegel & Carl Rheins, Eds.
WORLD OF OUR FATHERS
  Irving Howe
A TREASURY OF JEWISH FOLKLORE
  Nathan Ausubel, Ed.
LEO ROSTEN'S TREASURY OF JEWISH QUOTATIONS
  Leo Rosten
CHILDREN OF THE HOLOCAUST: *Conversations with Sons and Daughters of Survivors*
  Helen Epstein
WAR AGAINST THE JEWS 1933–1945
  Lucy L. Dawidowicz
HOLOCAUST YEARS: *Society on Trial*
  Roselle Chartock & Jack Spencer, Eds.
THE NEW BANTAM MEGIDDO HEBREW AND ENGLISH DICTIONARY
  Reuben Sivan & Edward A. Levenston
THE ART OF JEWISH COOKING
  Jennie Grossinger

THE JEWISH FAMILY BOOK

SHARON STRASSFELD
& KATHY GREEN

PHOTOGRAPHY BY BILL ARON

BANTAM BOOKS
Toronto • New York • London • Sydney

FOR OUR FAMILIES

for our parents, who nurtured us and helped us carve out a Jewish space . . .

for Art and Michael, our partners, who gave freely of their support and love and who shared our search . . .

for Hannah Leah, Kayla and Noam, whose presence in our lives makes us ask the questions

and with the hope for us all that
v'shavu lev vanim l'avot v'lev avot l'vanim
"the hearts of the children shall turn toward the parents and the hearts of the parents shall turn toward the children."

Grateful acknowledgement is made to the publishers named below for permission to reprint the following excerpts.

Jewish Publication Society, excerpt from *Hebrew Ethical Wills*, translation by Israel Abrahams, copyright 1976
Doubleday & Co., Inc., excerpt from *A Bintel Brief* by Isaac Metzker, translation and introduction copyright by Isaac Metzker
New York University Press, excerpt from *God's Presence in History* by Emil Fackenheim, copyright 1970
Chapter 28, Talking With Our Children About Sex, copyright © 1980 by Estelle and Eugene B. Borowitz.

THE JEWISH FAMILY BOOK

A Bantam Book / December 1981

Library of Congress Cataloging in Publication Data

Main entry under title: The Jewish family book.

Includes index.
1. Family—Religious life (Judaism) 2. Jewish religious education—Home training. 3. Jews—United States—Social life and customs. I. Strassfeld, Sharon. II. Green Kathy.
BM 723.J47   296.7'4   81-66703
AACR2

ISBN 0-553-01339-4

Published simultaneously in the United States and Canada

Bantam Books are published by Bantam Books, Inc. Its trademark, consisting of the words "Bantam Books" and the portrayal of a rooster, is Registered in U.S. Patent and Trademark Office and in other countries. Marca Registrada. Bantam Books, Inc., 666 Fifth Avenue, New York, New York 10103.

—Since this is a family book, it is not accidental that there are several family relationships represented among the contributors.

ROBERT ABRAMSON is the headmaster of the Hillel School in suburban Detroit. He received his doctorate in education from Columbia Teachers' College and was ordained by the Jewish Theological Seminary. He and his wife Charlotte are the parents of two children. Bob likes to see himself as born and bred in Brookline, Massachusetts.

ANITA BELT sees herself as a "freelance generalist and community resource consultant." She is a long-time resident of Brookline, Massachusetts, where she lives with her sons Jonathan and Eitan.

ESTELLE BOROWITZ is a psychoanalyst in private practice, serves on the faculty of the Center for Modern Psychoanalytic Studies, and is an editor of the journal, *Modern Psychoanalysis*. She is the wife of Eugene Borowitz.

EUGENE BOROWITZ is a professor of education and Jewish religious thought at Hebrew Union College—Jewish Institute of Religion in New York. He edits *Sh'ma: A Journal of Jewish Responsibility*. He is the author of *Choosing A Sex Ethic, A Jewish Inquiry*. His most recent book is *Contemporary Christologies, A Jewish Response*. He is the husband of Estelle Borowitz.

RACHEL FALKOVE works as program director with older adults in the Philadelphia Jewish community at the Jewish Y's and Center's David Neuman Senior Center. She is one of the founders of the Germantown Minyan in West Mt. Airy, where she lives with her husband Michael Masch and her son Solomon.

RUTH PINKENSON FELDMAN is a doctoral candidate in early childhood education at Temple University. She holds a masters degree in the field from the Banks Street College of Education and is the director of a progressive program for children between the ages of six months and seven years at the Germantown Jewish Centre. She is also an early childhood consultant on the staff of Woodmere Associates.

EVA FOGELMAN is a doctoral candidate in social and personality psychology at the Graduate Center of CUNY, a psychotherapist in the group project for Holocaust survivors and their children, and a research associate at Brandeis University.

AUDREY FRIEDMAN MARCUS is the vice president of Alternatives in Religious Education, Inc. She has served as editor and publisher of Alternatives Magazine. A lecturer, author, and educational consultant, she lives with her family in San Jose, California.

SIDNEY GREENBERG is the spiritual leader of Temple Sinai of Dresher, Pennsylvania. He is an author, anthologist, and columnist for *The Philadelphia Inquirer*. He has edited numerous volumes including *Li'Krat Shabbat* and *The New Mahzor*.

EARL GROLLMAN is the rabbi of Beth El Temple Center in Belmont, Massachusetts. He is the author of more than twelve books, among them *Talking about Death* and *Living when a Loved one has Died*.

PAULA HYMAN is dean of the Seminary College of Jewish Studies and associate professor of history at the Jewish Theological Seminary of America. She is a founding member of Ezrat Nashim and a member of the New York Havurah. She lives with her husband and daughters in northern New Jersey.

ALISA ISRAEL is majoring in anthropology at Barnard College. In addition to her academic work, she is a gourmet caterer.

RICHARD J. ISRAEL is the executive director of the B'nai Brith Hillel Council of Greater Boston. He also keeps bees, runs marathons, and raises four children with his wife Sherry. Their daughter Alisa is one of our contributors.

ARTHUR KURZWEIL is a writer and lecturer and the author of *From Generation to Generation: How to Trace Your Jewish Genealogy and Personal History.*

RICHARD LEVY is the executive director of the Los Angeles Hillel Council. He helped found the Westwood Free Minyan and Bet Tzedek Legal Services, and was on the editorial board of the Guide to Jewish Los Angeles. Richard lives with his family in Los Angeles.

DANIEL J. MARGOLIS is senior consultant of the Bureau of Jewish Education in Boston. He is the director of its resource center as well as Patty's, Ariel's, and Hadassah's favorite husband and *abba.*

HERSHEL MATT is the rabbi of Temple Har Zion in Mt. Holly, New Jersey. He is the author of numerous articles on Jewish theology and has served as chaplain in nursing homes and hospitals. He is both a father and grandfather.

BELLA SAVRAN is a psychiatric social worker in the mental health field currently living in Bloomington, Indiana, with her husband George and son Chanan. The family plans to make aliyah to Israel in the near future. Bella is one of the originators of therapeutic awareness groups for the children of Holocaust survivors.

SHOSHANA SILBERMAN is Educational Director of the Norristown Jewish Community Center. She is a doctoral candidate in elementary education at Temple University. One of the founders of the Germantown Minyan, she lives in West Mt. Airy with her husband Mel, her children Steven, Lisa, and Gabriel, her dog Megillah, one guinea pig, five gold fish, her brother Elliot Ribner, and countless plants.

MARILYN SLADOWSKY has been in and around Jewish camps since 1948. She is now the administrative director for the Department of Youth Activities of the United Synagogue of America.

ESTHER TICKTIN is a clinical psychologist in private practice in Washington, D.C., where she is a member of Fabrangen, and where she lives with her husband Max. They have three daughters and one grandson.

MAX TICKTIN is a Jewish teacher whose vocation led him to serve as a Hillel director and national Hillel staff member for thirty years. After retirement from Hillel, he chose to become an assistant professor of Hebrew and Yiddish language and literature at George Washington University. He, like his wife Esther, is a member of Fabrangen in Washington. They have three daughters and one grandson.

GILA VOGEL works in the field of Jewish education, concentrating on special education. She lives with her husband and two children in Israel.

SHEILA WEINBERG works as the Director of Program Department and Extension Services of the Jewish Campus Activities Board of Philadelphia. She is also a member of the Germantown Minyan and lives in West Mt. Airy with her daughter Abby and son Ezra.

DAVID ZISENWINE is a lecturer in Jewish curriculum development at the School of Education, Tel Aviv University. Prior to his move to Israel with his family, he was the rabbi and educational director of Congregation Tifereth Israel in Columbus, Ohio.

CONTENTS

INTRODUCTION

Kathy Green/Sharon Strassfeld

We began our work with a commitment to raising Jewish children and a question: How? We began with a conversation, a dialogue between two old friends who were new mothers. Out of that conversation, which has continued for years now, emerged a book. In fact, the book has undergone innumerable changes, from minor revisions to radical reorientations. At each step along the way we have reached out for help to others too numerous to name. We have invariably met with encouragement on the part of these concerned Jews, eager to share their hard-earned knowledge. Some contributed articles which fell by the way as the direction of this book changed. Others read, re-wrote, commented, saw favorite sentences changed in the editing of what appears below. Still others shmoozed with us at great length. All have exercised great patience and generosity. We wish to express our heartfelt appreciation.

Photographers remind us that a picture only captures a fleeting moment; and we feel that the same is true of this book, that the finished product distills only a moment in the process of Jewish parenting, or perhaps more accurately, a moment in our ongoing conversation about parenting. But the process of people talking with one another about raising children is as old as our history. Perhaps it began with a discussion between Adam and Eve about the rivalry they perceived between their sons. We believe that as long as parents inhabit the earth, the conversation will not end. We hope that this book will serve as another vehicle through which we can join together to continue that tradition.

Those articles that are unaccompanied by name were written by Sharon and Kathy. All other articles are identified by their authors. More information about these contributors can be found on pages v–vi. We hope that as you read on and react you will join with all of us in the process of this book, the ongoing exploration of raising a Jewish family.

PART ONE
BEGINNING

CHAPTER ONE

IN THE HOSPITAL WAITING ROOM

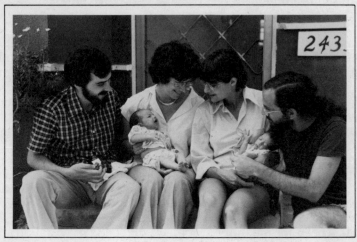

To my (as yet) unborn child:

It is late. Though expectant fathers are supposed to be nervous, I am more restless than worried and wish you would already arrive.

Observing the children of friends, it is my impression that it may be some time before I will once again have the opportunity to address you in as much quiet as I have available this evening. Since talking to you at this time in the waiting room would merely raise questions in the nurse's mind about my potential competence as a stable parent, I shall commit this address to writing, to deliver it at some presently unknown and undesignated time.

I am full of expectations for you. Not about your sex. I don't have the least interest in whether you are a girl or a boy. Five or six children from now, if the law of averages treats us shabbily, I might have some feelings about the question, but I don't now.

There are other matters that seem far more significant. It is, for example, very important to me that you be fun, not so that you should keep me amused, though I wouldn't mind that, but, more significantly, that you should be joyful. It appears that whatever you turn out to be, you are likely to be named after my father, who was an Isaac ("Yitzchak," from "laughter"), so that somehow your name will have to do with laughter or happiness, and that seems right. I do not commend earnestness to you as your chief virtue.

That does not mean that I don't want you to care about others. I want that very much. May you be able to be either kind or angry for others' sakes. You will know which is appropriate when the time comes. Even more, may you be willing from time to time to risk doing something that may turn out to be foolish, for the sake of a wise concern.

Tonight, I am particularly conscious of our responsibilities to make the world a better place, since it is with mixed feelings of guilt and relief that I am now sitting in the hospital rather than driving to Montgomery, Alabama, with Bill Coffin and John Maguire (they drove off without me) in pursuit of what seems like a very important cause. (Someday, if you like, I'll tell you about them and what their adventure turned out to be.)

I write all this to warn both of us that I shall try not to live out my deficiencies through you but at the same time that I do not plan to abandon all goals and aspirations for you just because they happen to be mine, too. One goal that I think I shall not give up is that I want you to be clearly and irrevocably Jewish. I do not know if my way will be your way, but your way must be a real way, and a serious way. I won't give an inch on that one. It is perhaps a sign of our (or at least my) time that I am already taking a defensive posture on this issue. Perhaps for you, being Jewish will be an easy and relaxed thing, not the struggle and effort it has been for me, but I don't feel compelled to wish you an easy time of it. Valuable things usually cost quite a bit. Perhaps part of your struggle will be with me.

I want you to be happy, caring, and Jewish. How am I going to get you to be any of them—ah, now the anxiety begins. I don't have the vaguest notion of what it means to be a parent or how one goes about the task. Doing what comes naturally is clearly no panacea. People have been doing that for years, and we can see what the results have been. But then what alternatives have I but to promise you that I will try hard and hope that you won't have to pay too much for my on-the-job training. If you try to forgive my mistakes, I'll try to forgive yours. We are both going to make them—lots.

But, alas, my noble sentiments are rapidly leaving me as I am slowly becoming engulfed by the desire to sleep and my impatience for you, or at least for Dr. Friedman, to appear with joyous tidings. The Almighty is clearly helping me to practice parenting even before your arrival. I am not sure that I am grateful for His concern in this area at this moment. In any event, my wishes for you and the Messiah are the same at this moment. May you both come speedily.

With love of unknown and untested quality,
Your expectant father
Richard Israel

CHAPTER TWO

ON HAVING CHILDREN

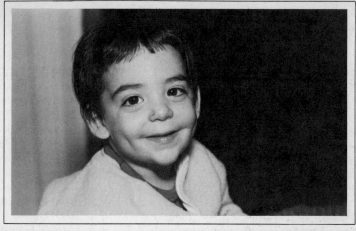

There's no getting around the fact that it used to be much easier to decide to have a child. In fact, who decided? The assumption was that after a suitably brief period of couplehood, the next step was to begin a family. Husband would continue his career, wife would stay home with children, and the world would continue in its natural order.

The last fifteen years have seen the end of that era. For many couples, the decision is no longer when but whether to have children. Since there is no longer the assumption that *everyone* will have children, couples, aware of the sacrifices they will have to make for children (privacy, money, freedom, couplehood, etc.), assess whether such sacrifices are appropriate for them.

The truth is, it is hard to raise children. In some ways, it is even harder for us than it was for our parents, both because we have greater awareness and sensitivity to children's healthy psychological development and because we don't have the benefits of extended-family situations that effectively distributed tasks of child care among a greater number of adults.

In addition, the women's movement has acted powerfully on all of us, even on those of us who don't see ourselves as feminists. The two-career family is here to stay, if not because we've learned that women have a right to fulfillment, then because economic conditions dictate the necessity of a second income. Once both members of the couple are climbing the career ladder, the decision to get off that ladder, even temporarily, is hard and becomes harder with each successive child. Such a decision, also of necessity, is one that affects the woman more than the man, since it is she who will have the pregnancy, go through the birth, and, if she is breast-feeding, be tied to the child for some months. As Michael Waterman put it, "We knew that we cared about the value of sharing child care. Lisa planned to go back to work soon after Mitchel's birth, and we had tried to anticipate the logistical problems of that decision. But the plain truth was that since it was Lisa who was breast-feeding, it was she who ran home from the office for feedings, got up in the middle of the night, etc., and somehow my taking over the household tasks to even the work balance only made *me* feel like the frustrated housewife."

It would have been harder twenty-five years ago, but today it is possible to say, "I don't think I *want* to have children. I've got a good career; I'm successful in what I do. I do not feel an instinctual need to have my own children, and, frankly, I don't think I'd be a good parent. I'm really just not interested." Today, we think no one would deny that it is legitimate to feel this way and legitimate to make the decision not to have children based on such feelings.

But then how does one balance such concerns with Judaism's emphasis on the importance of having a family? Indeed, the first *mitzvah* (commandment) in the Torah is *pru u-rivu* (be fruitful and multiply). We are told that fulfillment of this *mitzvah* is equal to fulfillment of all the other *mitzvot*. In addition, we who live after the Holocaust must also consider seriously the impact of the loss of six million Jewish lives on the Jewish people. For both these reasons and because Jewish life is so very family centered (Shabbat, Passover Seder, Hanukah), couples can be faced with trying to weigh contemporary liberal notions of the self and the needs and mandates of Judaism and the Jewish community. Trying to respond to both claims on one's allegiance, both parts of one's identity, places heavy psychic demands on the individual. Moreover, the individual's decisions affect the future of the Jewish community, perhaps in more far-reaching ways than one may realize.

It ought to be unnecessary, but it is probably still important to say, "You who feel ambivalent about having children, who are pretty sure but feel guilty because of (a) your parents, (b) the Jewish people, (c) your friends and neighbors, should perhaps try to take a long-range look at your life. Do you not want children *now*, at this particular moment in your life, or do you not want them forever? Is it possible you will regret a decision not to have children when you are fifty?"

If the fully honest answer to these questions is that you really do not think (now or ever) that you will want children, then you probably ought not to have them. Having said that, you do not want to feel guilty about such a decision. Childbearing is not the kind of life decision you should arrive at out of duty or guilt or a vague feeling of "it's my responsibility." It's hard enough to raise children when you want to; imagine the task if you did not want to.

What about if you're uncertain? Probably this is the most common feeling. You *think* you'd probably like to have kids sometime, but you're just not sure. You're frightened by how much having a child will change your relationship with your spouse, financial position, life-style, and you have no deep yearning for a child but sometimes feel as though you'd like to begin a family eventually. The best advice anyone can offer you is to go hang out with a family. Try to find a couple with a six-month-old child. (By then, the baby is usually sleeping through the night, and the parents are settled into a more workable schedule and have had the time to discuss between themselves how their lives have changed.) It's good to talk to parents who've just had their first child. It's also good to talk to families with more than one child. Don't talk only to the parents, however. Spend a weekend with the kids, too. Let the parents go away for an afternoon, and baby-sit. Play with them. You won't know what it's like to have your own child, but you'll at least have a better sense of childhood. Such experiences can be helpful in trying to figure out if you want to be a parent yourself.

JEWISH GENETIC DISEASES

There are a number of Jewish genetic diseases that you should investigate before you get pregnant. While some, like Gaucher's, Niemann-Pick, and dysautonomia, are not well known, Tay-Sachs disease is an easily determined disorder for which every Jewish couple should be alert. A simple blood test can determine if a person is a Tay-Sachs carrier. If both parents are carriers, the fetus can be tested in utero to determine if it has Tay-Sachs disease. With that knowledge, parents can then make an informed judgment about whether or not they will elect to have an abortion if their child has the disease. Given the fact that Tay-Sachs is a lethal disorder that invariably results in death by the age of five years old, it behooves all parents to discover if they are, indeed, carriers. (Keep in mind that it takes two carriers to produce a Tay-Sachs baby.) Contact your local physician or hospital for information on where you can have a Tay-Sachs test performed in your area.

Also, as Fran Wolf puts it, "It's important to keep an open mind. When I was twenty-six, you couldn't have paid me to get pregnant. Michael and I were quite sure, from observing our friends who had just begun to have families, that we did not want children. But ten years later we felt (and did) differently. We had changed our minds, our lives were in different places, and we were ready—in fact, eager—to have a family."

For parents who are ready to make the decision to have children, a number of issues become central:

WHERE TO LIVE

Choosing a neighborhood can make the difference between a supportive environment for raising children and an alienating one. You might ask yourself some of the following questions about the place you choose to live:

1. Are there other kids whose ages coincide with your kids' (as in play groups, baby-sitting cooperatives, car pools, support groups, etc.)? If there are no kids nearby, at least make sure your immediate neighbors don't feel about children the way certain condominium retirement villages feel—the ones that ban children from the premises!
2. Is there a playground or other play facilities nearby?
3. Is the neighborhood within reasonable distance of day care centers, community centers, nursery schools, libraries, grocery shopping, and any other communal facilities that are important to your life style?
4. If there is no day care group, and you are interested in creating one, is there a communal institution in the neighborhood that could house it?
5. If you don't have a car (or if you have one car and will be negotiating with your spouse for use of it), is public transportation reasonably accessible?

In terms of Jewish needs, you might also ask:

1. Are there other Jews with whom you could share Jewish holidays and Shabbat in the neighborhood? Is there a *chevrah* (a group) with whom you'd be comfortable?
2. If you prefer walking, are you within walking distance of a synagogue, Hebrew school, or Jewish community center?
3. Are Jewish resources (e.g., kosher foods, Jewish book stores, restaurants) readily accessible?
4. What are the values and levels of ritual observance of the Jews in your neighborhood? Will you and your family Jewish life-style fit in?

What happens when you are ideologically or professionally committed to living in a place where there are no other Jewish families (i.e., you're committed to living off the land; or you can't afford a house in the middle-class "Jewish neighborhood"; or you're a government worker in a town that has a residency requirement). One solution is to try to bring people along with you to the new neighborhood. It's possible that among your friends are those who have a certain flexibility in their mobility; three households can create enough of a *chevrah* that you needn't feel Jewishly isolated.

PARENT SUPPORT GROUPS

The demise of the extended family has spelled the end of not only a variety of physical supports within the family but also of emotional support. Thirty years ago, if your friend Bella called you up to let you know Macy's was having a one-day sale on bedspreads, you could drop Junior off at your mother's house two blocks away and make a spontaneous excursion to Macy's. Similarly, if Junioress was up all night shrieking, it was your mother who was able to tell you about teething times and how children act out their misery on such occasions.

Now most of us don't live within the bounds of extended families, and we have to rely more heavily on our doctors for advice on health. It is crucial, however, for parents to feel that they have other parents to turn to—as a sort of substitute family—for advice, empathy, emergency help, etc. Such informal arrangements sometimes get formalized into weekly parent-support groups or baby-sitting cooperative groups. Sometimes an informal *shmooze* (chat) at the playground while the kids are playing is enough. Whatever your situation, though, such support systems can be essential in letting you know that other people will be there for you and that you can be there for them. They are also impor-

tant for doing Jewish things with your kids. It's much more fun for several three-year-olds to get together to bake *hallah* than to do it alone with your own child. (See Chapter Ten for more suggestions.)

However you manage it, try to make sure you give yourself the time and space necessary to stay in touch with your own needs as well as the needs of your child. We know of at least one person who claims that her parent-support group saved her life. Laurie Posen says, "I was drowning in my own tears after Steven was born. I couldn't keep the house clean or him or me together. I was exhausted, hysterical, and out of control. And the worst of it was that I had *chosen* to get pregnant and quit my job. I really believe I might have sailed out the window in my own tears if I hadn't met a woman while I was standing in line at the supermarket one day who invited me to her support group. I haven't needed a box of Kleenex in ages now!"

CHAPTER THREE

STEREOTYPES: ON BECOMING A JEWISH MOTHER

Paula Hyman

When asked what attracted them to Judaism, many converts will cite the possibility of belonging to a close-knit family and community. Certainly, the stereotype of the Jewish family has always been a positive one, that of a mutually concerned and emotionally involved unit. The stereotype of the Jewish mother has not been treated quite so kindly.

When I was growing up, the last thing I wanted to be was a Jewish mother. Not that I planned to be childless. It was just that I feared that as I acquired children I might also acquire the characteristics of the stereotypical Jewish mother—in particular, a domineering personality and a neurotic over involvement with my children, a kind of obsession with mothering that American culture found alternately ludicrous and destructive.

I resolved my "Jewish mother problem" in a double process: first, by becoming a mother myself and, almost simultaneously, by studying the history of Jewish women and the emergence in the past thirty years of the very stereotype of the Jewish mother that had so appalled me. Confronting that stereotype—as well as other unflattering images of Jews, from the Jewish American princess to the materialistic, vulgar, and stingy Jews of anti-Semitic lore—is an important process for Jewish parents.

These stereotypes affect us as parents in several ways. Most obviously, we seek to protect our children from them. We want our children to develop a positive sense of themselves as Jews, free from the defensiveness or self-hatred that negative stereotypes engender. And we want to prevent them from being hurt. In this, we share the goals of all minority parents living in cultures that have limited our powers of self-definition. I, for one, would like to spare my children the experiences I had as a child of being chased away from a skating pond by a group of older children screaming "kike" after me. But we Jewish parents do have to prepare our children for the possibility of anti-Semitic incidents, as rare as they may be in the circles in which we move. And, at a later stage, our children will have to try to understand why Jews have been, for so much of our history, the victims of hatred and the models for denigrating stereotypes.

Some of this discussion can occur only once the children are of school age. As the mother of two very young daughters, I rarely have focused on the subject of anti-Semitism with them. Yet, on a certain level, even a young child learns that Jews have not been universally appreciated. Telling the stories of Hanukah and Pesah, for example, must of necessity introduce the element of Jewish oppression. However, in my experience at least, it has always been possible to neutralize the persecution of the Jews or turn the subject into a teaching device about the dark underside of intergroup relations. Hanukah and Pesah, after all, do celebrate Jewish triumphs; and it is the opponents of the Jews who can be dismissed for their brutality and intolerance.

More difficult for parents is the way our own reactions to Jewish stereotypes influence our behavior. It is easy to deal with the Hanukah and Pesah stories; it is even easy to deal with the existence of anti-Semitism. It is far more difficult to come to terms with stereotypes toward which we ourselves feel ambivalent.

The "Jewish mother" stereotype is a case in point. It is only in the past

THE LITTLE GIRL AND THE KIPPAH

What should you do when your daughter announces that, like her brothers and father, she is going to wear a *kippah* (skullcap)? Or, alternately, how should you react when your little girl informs you that, unlike her mother and sisters, she will not wear a *kippah* while davvening in your egalitarian *minyan?*

Don't laugh: that is the first rule. Beyond that, let's think seriously about the problem of Jews covering our heads. The problem of when and how to cover our heads goes beyond fashion esthetics. The rationale for men covering their heads has to do with expressing respect and humility in the divine presence; for women, customs of concealing their hair originally had more to do with modesty before men. For feminists who live outside of communities where established norms are firmly entrenched and who themselves are attracted to the rationale that has traditionally been associated with men's respect of God, what to do is a real question.

If the issues are real for you, it makes sense to investigate the problem further. A good starting point is the article by Dr. Meir Ydit on head covering in the *Encyclopedia Judaica*, vol. 8, pp. 1–6. Knowing the history of

(Continued)

generation that the Jewish mother has emerged as a derisive character. In eastern Europe and in the immigrant centers of America, she was celebrated by her children in song and story. The precipitous decline of her image reflects first and foremost a shift in the criteria for evaluating what makes a good mother. It is according to middle class, midtwentieth century American standards that the Jewish mother fails to meet the test. At the very least, we must recognize that our acceptance of the stereotype implies a rejection, perhaps unconscious, of traditional Jewish family values in favor of middle-class American norms. Certainly in the case of the authors and comedians who exploited the stereotype, fixation with the faults of the Jewish mother signaled a deep-seated sense of not being fully at home in American society. What better way to compensate (or overcompensate) for this unease than to lay the blame for incomplete assimilation at the feet of their Jewish mothers?

The Jewish mother stereotype arose only in part from the application of American standards to traditional Jewish cultural behavior. It also originated in the social situation of a second generation of Jewish mothers in America. While they patterned their intense life style of mothering after their immigrant mothers, they lived in an environment

covering our heads will enrich the inevitable conversations that we will have with our families, our communities, and Jewish professionals.

Through such discussions we may discover that for some of us the when and how of covering our heads (all the time, in synagogue with a skullcap, a hat, a scarf, nothing at all, a bit of lace?) has tremendous emotional significance. In fact, the intensity with which some of us respond to these issues is shocking. ("That *yarmulke* on that woman looks ugly!" "They made my uncle wear a hat to my cousin's bar mitzvah, and I wouldn't walk into that synagogue again!")

Regardless of "what people will say," the logical next step is experimentation, trying on different modes of headdress for size. Our very best recommendation is to explore all these issues seriously but not earnestly. Humor can redeem the most sober debate. If you feel that your deliberations have become too earnest, we recommend study of the illustrations of past ways in which Jews have resolved the issue of how to cover their heads. These illustrations can be found in the *Jewish Encyclopedia*, vol. 6, 1904. A glance at the once-stylish pointed beany favored by Medieval Jews will convince you: you should not laugh at your daughter's concern, but certainly you should laugh at yourself.

that made fewer demands on their time than had their mothers' more straitened economic circumstances. And there were few acceptable outlets for their energy other than concern for home and children. Paradoxically, the "Jewish" intensity of the mother-child bond may thus have been heightened at the very time when many American Jews were most anxious to feel themselves fully American and least Jewish or immigrant in their behavior. Hence, the extreme sensitivity to neurotic aspects of the Jewish mother.

The popularity of the particular comic stereotype lies in its recognizable kernel of truth. Eastern European Jewish culture did foster an intense style of mothering, which was reinforced by the physical and psychological insecurity of life in the *shtetl* and later in the immigrant ghettos. Not only was it a style of mothering appropriate to its surroundings, it also served to equip the children for survival, even for success, in an environment that was often hostile. Whatever the merits of this mothering style, to a generation of women raised on a combination of popular Freudianism and feminist concepts of self-fulfillment, the "Jewish mother" is hardly a model to emulate. On the one hand, she damages her children, denying them the independence necessary for healthy development, at least as defined by our psychologists. On the other hand, apart from her role as mother, she has no sense of worth, at least as defined by contemporary feminism. Intellectually and emotionally, then, it is hard for us *not* to accept the partial truth of the stereotype. But it is important to realize that the stereotype is exaggerated and divorced from the cultural context in which our Jewish mothers and grandmothers functioned. In assenting to that exaggeration, we alienate ourselves not only from our past as history but also from our past as source of cultural continuity. The stereotype makes us self-

conscious: since we don't want to be "Jewish mothers," we hold ourselves back from the kind of behavior satirized in the caricature. When we find ourselves, despite our best intentions, behaving "just like a Jewish mother," we condemn ourselves for doing so. The stereotype can thus influence our relationship with our children as well as our self-evaluation as parents.

Another stereotype that crops up increasingly as the two-career family comes into its own is the 'Eyshet Hayil' stereotype, or, in American terms, the superwoman image. The poem 'Eyshet Hayil' (which many traditional men recite to their wives on Friday night before *Kiddush*) praises the "Woman of Valour" who is a successful businesswoman, nurtures and feeds her family, sews their clothes, gives charity, and dispenses wise advice. The question for many of us who are participating in a two-career family is how to provide healthy models for the family work distribution. We are in a time of transition in which we are not satisfied with the roles our mothers played and have not yet fully discovered how to do the thing better. All too often when women decide to embark on a career, it simply means that now, instead of being responsible for the housekeeping, laundry, cooking, clothes buying, and general welfare of their families, they are also responsible for their new careers AND the housekeeping, laundry, etc. How does a couple truly share household tasks? How does a couple convey to their child the notion that men and women can share nurturing roles as well as housekeeping responsibilities? How can we avoid, for ourselves, in our own minds, the eyshet hayil stereotype? Certainly, what we don't want to do is trade in the Jewish mother stereotype for the 'Eyshet Hayil' stereotype.

Understanding the sources of the stereotype prepares the way for a reexamination of traditional Jewish mothering, for a liberation of the real Jewish mother from the stereotype. To paraphrase a truism in immigrant history, what the child wants to forget, the grandchild is eager to remember. If the Jewish family has been a source of stability in Jewish life as well as the launching pad for Jewish social mobility, the nature of Jewish involvement with children has been at the center of the family. Only when the stereotype of the Jewish mother is exposed as the caricature it is can we recognize and integrate into ourselves the positive aspects of the Jewish mother. Her warmth, her involvement with her children, her ability to convey to them that they are marvelous and special, are talents that we would do well to foster in ourselves. These are characteristics that we can develop even if we reject the limitation of the Jewish mother's role to mothering and choose to combine mothering

with a career. They "travel well," whatever our social circumstances. We are fortunate to live at a time when ethnic and cultural differences are celebrated rather than suppressed. If, as Jewish parents, we are, in fact, more exuberant, more aggressively involved with our children than others, we need not despair. The culture of Jewish parenting is still basically a healthy one in which we take pride and which we can present to the world as a model for others to emulate.

CHAPTER FOUR

ADOPTION

After considering whether or not to have children, some of us have been able to decide in the affirmative only to discover that we are unable to bear children. As we begin to deal with our own infertility, where can we turn to fulfill our desire for children?

While abortion clinics struggle to help women with undesired pregnancies, the specter of infertility looms large in the lives of increasing numbers of American (and therefore American Jewish) couples. Couples since Abraham and Sarah have experienced difficulties in conceiving offspring. Only within the last twenty years has medical science developed sophisticated techniques that sometimes help childless couples. Ironically, new levels of medical sophistication also are accompanied by new heights of anxiety on the part of couples who want children. Infertile couples often undergo emotionally and physically stressful procedures and periods of tragically frustrated hopes as they work on a monthly basis with doctors in the struggle to become pregnant. Recently, in fact, support groups have begun to spring up in an number of cities to help infertile couples cope with life-styles that become interwoven with medical consultation.

Sometimes modern medicine appears to work miracles, and like the Biblical matriarchs, God "turns the barren housewife into a happy mother of children." For others it becomes a question of at what point (of increasingly serious medical procedures) do we draw the line and stop trying? And once a couple has stopped trying, what are the options? Childlessness is one alternative; the other is adoption.

Adoption presents its own series of alternatives and difficulties. One mode of adoption is to seek an infant or child who, for reasons of the social realities of our imperfect world, needs more than others to be adopted. Such children include the handicapped, the older child, the racially mixed or nonwhite child, and children of underdeveloped nations.

We believe that the adoption of these children represents a unique *mitzvah*. We also acknowledge the many difficulties that they and their adoptive parents encounter. The Jewish community has an obligation to be supportive of such adoptions. First, our community must be willing to accept people who are racially or physically different; second, the adoptive parents must assume potential responsibility to help the adopted child resolve issues of his/her own identity when that child is clearly an offspring of another and well-defined culture. For example, it is not easy to evolve an identity as both a Vietnamese and a Jew.

These children, whom our society sees as deviant, are most available for adoption. Another mode—adopting a healthy white infant as close as possible to the moment of birth—presents the prospective parents with the greater difficulty of finding a child to adopt. Such adoptions seek to approximate the biological experience—of receiving a baby from the moment of birth or soon thereafter. Because of the desirability of these babies, the increased effectiveness and acceptance of birth control methods, the availability of abortion, and the increasing social acceptance of the unwed mother, these neonates are terribly difficult to find. While a variety of agencies are eager to help the prospective parent find a "difficult-to-adopt" child, neonates are generally not accessible through agencies. In fact, Jewish social service agencies, which, in the 1950s, were in the business of placing such infants, have generally redefined their communal roles and now fulfill a variety of other family social work tasks. Therefore, the couple usually has to seek a child through private adoption—and nonagency sources.

The first intelligent move such couples should make is to tell everyone they know that they want to adopt a child. Occasionally, word of mouth bears fruit; for example, a friend who has a friend who is an obstetrician has a patient . . . This happy scenario is very unusual. Often such couples end up entering the "gray market," in other words, legally adopting a baby through a lawyer who has secured the infant from a secret source. Such adoptive parents generally pay large sums of money to the lawyer. Ostensibly, the money is going toward the biological mother's prenatal care; actually, the adoptive parents have no way other than their trust in the lawyer to verify that the money was dispersed ethically. It must be pointed out that all private adoptions are not gray-market adoptions; private adoption simply means that, for better or worse, an agency was not involved. (Legally adopting the child of a deceased relative is a private adoption.) The advantage of privately adopting a neonate is that the adoptive parent can receive the baby closer to the point of the actual birth; from what we know from contemporary psychologists about bonding and attachment, any shortening of the time between birth and contact with the parents is advantageous for both the infant and the parents.

Let's say that a wide range of difficulties has been overcome and that a Jewish couple has managed to find a child to adopt. What are some of the directly Jewish issues that may be relevant to the couple? A couple concerned with issues of Jewish law might prefer to adopt a child whose biological parents were not Jewish, thereby circumventing any question of Jewish law about incestuous marriage when the child grows up. (Jewish law is concerned that an adopted child may unintentionally marry a sibling within the Jewish community.) Once adopted, a child should receive a *brit milah* (circumcision) or be named according to practices of the Jewish community. In general, according to Jewish law, an

> We wanted to have children, lots of them. The decision "to have children" was not well thought out. It represented a natural progression in our marriage and was probably based on all kinds of romantic dreams. I had this vision of myself as a mother of many children living in a rambling house in Berkeley and baking bread and weaving and wearing Marimekko dresses. We started to try to conceive a child. The process of trying to have a child took a long time, with lots of tests and medical consultations and delays. Trying to have a baby became an obsession, and each menstrual period became a secret tragedy. By the time we decided to adopt, we had lost all perspective. We were older and more set in our ways, and it might have made more sense simply not to have had children; but when we reached the point of adopting a child, not having children was not an alternative.
>
> Our son came to us through crazy channels of the gray market, suddenly, with about two weeks' warning. I see how friends prepare for nine months for the birth of a baby. When our son was nine months old, my husband said, "Now we are ready." Our son has given us new life; there are dimensions of my life that I would never have explored without him. Who I am today has so much to do with him. I love him more than life itself, and yet I know my life is much more complicated because of his presence as part of our family. And I know that it will take years of analysis before I really understand the meaning of the loss of that old dream of lots and lots of children in the rambling house in Berkeley.

adopted child is named "so and so the son or daughter of Abraham our father and Sarah our mother." The reason for this is that, mythically, Abraham is seen as the father and Sarah the mother not only of the Jewish people but also of all converts, because they themselves were the first Jews, indeed the first converts to Judaism, and because in the biblical tale they reached out to all people. According to the *midrash* (Jewish folktale), their tent was open on four sides so that guests could enter from all directions. Since the non-Jewish child who is adopted—even adopted at birth and knowing no other religion—is, in fact, a convert, the child must, like all converts, go to the *mikvah* (ritual immersion) before the child reaches maturity, that is, twelve for girls or thirteen for boys.

In naming a child the son or daughter of Abraham and Sarah, we are giving the child the name by which he or she will be called up to the Torah and the name which will appear on any legal Jewish documents (such as his/her eventual marriage contract). We sense in the custom of giving all converts the same ancestry both wisdom and pain. Perhaps Jewish law was promulgating a kind of honesty and avoidance of self-deception by insisting on the adopted status of the child in his or her name. On the other hand, many parents who truly see the adopted child as their own as well as adopted children themselves must find the constant reminder of adoption difficult. According to a *teshuvah* (responsum) discussed by Rabbi Seymour Siegel, the Rabbinical Assembly maintains adopted infants should receive the patronym of their adoptive parents. This view, presented by the Rabbinical Assembly Law Committee, is based on Talmud Megillah 13A.

Another problem that some Jewish adoptive parents experience has to do with the Jewish community's acceptance of adoption *per se*. Adoption of a child who was not the child of a deceased relative was generally unheard of in Eastern Europe. Occasionally, grandparents who themselves are closely tied to Eastern Europe need time and persuasive conversations before they accept an adopted grandchild. It is also true that these grandparents, in accepting this grandchild, are also admitting the unlikelihood of a grandchild's being conceived through the biological process. They may initially react negatively to an adopted grandchild whose biological mother may not have been Jewish. Their vocabulary may strike us as racist, but it is important to keep in mind that with their words comes the pain of accepting their own genetic mortality.

It is also perhaps significant to realize that adoption as we know it in America is a relatively new phenomenon. Biblical examples of adoption are ambiguous and rare. Perhaps the nicest is the sense conveyed in Psalm 2:7–8 that the People Israel were the adopted child of God. "Let Me tell of the decree: The Lord said to me, 'You are My son, I have fathered you this day.' " In other instances, the sense of adoption is more vague. For example, we find the very beautiful statement that Bilhah, Rachel and Jacob's servant, gave birth "onto" Rachel's knees. We know that adoption ceremonies practiced by other ancient European and Asiatic peoples included placing the child to be adopted on the knees of the adoptive parent. The idea of placing a child on the adoptive parents' knees hints at the beautiful moment that perhaps could be incorporated in a modern naming or *brit* ceremony. On the other hand, other stories in Genesis relating to Rachel, Jacob, and the children of Bilhah argue against this actually being a situation of adoption and suggest rather a primitive posture or position in which the woman giving birth straddled the knees of the midwife, who thus received the baby. Throughout Genesis, we can find hints of situations that we might want to interpret as adoption, but in each instance we can also find information that argues against that understanding. Perhaps it is more useful to think in metaphorical rather than specific terms. Thus, we can enjoy the sense of rebirth or new birth suggested by the passage from Psalms about how Israel is born again this day as the son of God (Jeremiah 3:19, 31:8, and Hosea 11:1). Certainly, as a religious community, if we think of all children as gifts of God, how much more so the adopted child?

A difficulty all adoptive parents must eventually confront is talking with their children about their adoptions. No matter how the child is told, the adoptive parent will ultimately have to help the child deal with the reality that the biological parents did not want him or her. This must be one of the most basic pains any individual will ever be called upon to accept. It is not a pain to be dealt with in a brief bedtime intimacy. It is a part of the life of an adopted child, a pain and an understanding that takes on different guises and forms at different life stages. For some adopted children, such pain is translated into fear when the adoptive parent is late picking up the child at school. For another, it may assume the guise of anger. Whatever the form of the child's anxiety, the demand placed on the parent is one of patience. No book is adequate, but two helpful possibilities for sharing with adopted children are *The Adopted One* by Sara Bonnett Stein (Walker and Co., 1979) and *Why Was I Adopted* by Carole Livingston (Lyle Stuart, Inc., 1978).

Some adopted children become obsessed with curiosity about their biological parents and have entered into searches for them. We believe that the sealing of records, thereby creating extreme obstacles for adopted children in search of biological parents, is absurd. On the other hand, we would advocate respect for the needs of all parties concerned, not only those of the adopted child and adoptive parent but also those of the biological parent, who may or may not want to be found. Perhaps an adopted child's search for his or her biological parents has to be undertaken alone; sometimes such searches can involve the adoptive parents, thus uniquely allowing the adopted child to feel the support of his or her adopted family.

There are no easy answers, only the optimism engendered by the love shared by adoptive parents and adopted children. Judaism adds a dimension of potential difficulty for adopted children, for it asks them not only to accept their adoptive parents but also to accept their history; we are asking them to say, like Ruth (and like other converts): "Your people will be my people."

A PLEA FOR SENSITIVITY

Our child has blond hair and blue eyes and was adopted. We, her parents, have dark-brown hair and eyes. Middle-aged and older Jews, responding to our child's very real beauty, say: "What a beautiful *shiksa!* Where did you get such a beautiful *shiksa!*"

*　　　*　　　*

We are Ashkenazi Jews living in Israel. Our last name sounds decidedly German. Our adopted daughter's sparkling eyes and jet-black hair convey her Sephardic ancestry. A while ago, I asked our daughter to leave a pair of sandals at the shoemaker's shop to be repaired. Our daughter reported that when she told the shoemaker her name, the man said, "No, that is not your name; that is the name of an Ashkenazi."

*　　　*　　　*

Imagine how the parents and children feel when they have to respond regularly to these casual and often well-meaning remarks. Like the psalmist, we plead, "O Lord, guard my tongue from speaking evil and my lips from speaking guile."

CHAPTER FIVE

THE JEWISH SINGLE PARENT
Anita Belt

Being a parent is not easy, but being a single parent is doubly hard. Our friend Anita Belt writes personally about herself and her family, and voices the concerns of ever increasing numbers of Jews who are raising children without the help of a spouse.

I have two sons, two cats, two boarders, a two-family house, two jobs, one automobile. I am Jewish and one of a growing number of single parents.

In the last decade, the ratio of the number of divorces to the number of first marriages has risen sharply, while the ratio of the number of remarriages to the number of divorces has begun to drop. This continued trend implies a substantial rise in the number of formerly married people who remain single. An important consequence is the rising number of children under eighteen who are living in single-parent homes. There are estimates that nearly one-third of all American children born over the next five years are likely to be raised in single-parent homes. In the Greater Boston Jewish community, for example, Hebrew schools, community centers, and summer camps are reporting that their enrollment of Jewish children from single-parent homes has reached 25 percent. Who are these parents? What are the particular problems they face as Jews? What are the problems of the parent who does not have full-time rearing responsibilities for his/her children?

Harry Keshet, the director of the Divorce Resource and Mediation Center, Inc. (Cambridge, Mass.), has studied male parenting and finds that there are two main functions of parenting: the decision-making function and the child-rearing function. He explains, however, that "decision making does not necessarily mean that you are rearing the children on a daily basis but that you have rights to and are actively involved in the decisions affecting their lives." If we consider this distinction, it becomes clear that single parenting refers not only to the parent living full time with the children but to the "visiting" parent as well.

The degree to which a single parent feels burdened with the decision making and child rearing is directly related to how the role of single parenting limits his or her daily life. If there is joint cooperation between the former spouses where, for example, the children live half the week with mommy and half the week with daddy, then both are single parents with a great deal of flexibility and free time to pursue their own interests. If, however, one parent has full custody and the absent parent rarely visits (or there is a widowed single parent), the single parenting burden is *full time*, with only occasional opportunities for intermissions, interludes, vacations, and the like. There are also all kinds of permutations of the above arrangements, but regardless of the individual arrangements, the daily planning and the interdependence of the schedules of all the parties involved become complex.

As one single parent put it: "I heaved a sigh of relief when Philip moved out of the house. I'd lived with the tension and pain so long that I was eager to get on with my life and begin to do all the things that had been simmering on my back burner. But suddenly the reality of child custody hit me. I was responsible—all by myself—for the physical and emotional well-being of our two children. Even though Philip cared about the children, when David woke up in the middle of the night with an earache, I was the one who had to sit by his bed. It took a while to sort out my feelings toward the children, Philip, and this new responsibility in ways that don't make me constantly feel harassed and victimized (even though those feelings still are there at times)."

There are few parents who would refute the statement that child rearing is among the most difficult tasks of their lives (if not *the* most difficult). Certainly, it is both physically and emotionally draining. While many of the problems encountered are precisely the same whether the child is being raised in a single- or two-parent family, the child of a single parent actually has suffered a loss. The intensity of the child's feelings regarding the loss varies greatly depending on whether the loss is permanent (due to the death of one parent) or whether the parent simply moved to another household. How much the absent parent is available to the child certainly diminishes but never dissipates the feelings of loss.

Moreover, the single parent himself or herself is always aware of "going it alone." You are one person doing what the world has really programmed two people to do—and the task can be overwhelming. Many single parents, because of the seriousness and endlessness of these demands, refuse to face the fact that their new singleness is not simply temporary.

To such parents I can offer what it took me a while to learn.

You can face the reality of your singleness with a sense of balance coupled with occasional minor panic, or you can face this reality with an orgy of self-pity. In a similar vein, either you can act as if your life situation is entirely transitory as you wait for your heartthrob to appear on the scene, or you can act to create a stable environment for yourself and your children, one where you put down roots and make decisions based on the stability of those roots. Keep in mind that if your children feel that something is missing from their lives, they will suffer. It is very human to hold back creative energy if you feel you are in transition.

Whether you want to remarry eventually or not, your position should not have to affect the stability and "wholeness" of your family now.

THE JEWISH COMMUNITY

A man leaves his father and mother and cleaves unto his wife, and they become one flesh.

GENESIS 2:24

He who has no wife lives without good, without help, without blessing . . . he is also without life, . . . he is also not a complete man . . . and some say that he also (thereby) diminishes the divine image.

GENESIS RABBAH, XVII, 2

Tradition maintains a negative position toward the "unmarried state." Clearly, the rabbis felt that God in His infinite wisdom had created the perfect *shiddukh* (match) for every person and that only the misfit or the stubborn person did not marry. This position has been and continues to be alienating to single parents. It has been said, and rightfully so, that Judaism is a family-centered religion, that our communal institutions were not, as a result, set up to cope with singles and the single situation.

As a result, the need for community professionals, rabbis, and congregants to accept and welcome single parents to their communities and institutions becomes all the more crucial. The single parent is often already so isolated that further isolation from their Jewish heritage and community can prove devastating. Furthermore, a commitment to Jewish life only creates more complications in lives that are already sometimes unbearably complicated.

As one parent commented: "I needed to go to Friday night services with the kids like I needed another car pool in my life. All my rabbi could understand was the dictum 'the family that prays together stays together,' and all I could understand was Suzi's Monday dance lessons, my Tuesday therapy appointment, Mark's Wednesday karate class, and their Thursday gym program. Who needed to tie down my Friday night or Saturday morning life, too?"

But despite such feelings, Jewish needs do exist. Some of the issues that become important to many single-parent families are:

Holiday Observance

Who gets the kids?

How or what do I observe with the children?

What will *I* do if the children are with him or her?

How can I readjust my attitudes toward holidays and learn to enjoy them again?

How can I make the holiday meaningful when I don't know how to do anything?

How can I sufficiently rid myself of the stereotyped perfect Jewish
family holiday celebrations that I carry in my mind to enjoy my own
holiday celebrations?

Life-Cycle Observances
(weddings, funerals, bar/bat mitzvahs)

My ex-mother-in-law died! Shall I go to the funeral?

My ex-sister-in-law is getting married and invited me to the wedding.
What will I do?

How do I handle all the social arrangements for my child's bar/bat
mitzvah?

Who will walk down the aisle with my child at his or her wedding?

Jewish Education and Identity
My children are not in Hebrew school. My ex-husband doesn't want
them to go. What shall I do?

How much time can be committed? (Their time is so fragmented now
due to the fact that they must share their time between parents in
two households.)

Do I date only Jews?

Do I go to synagogue with the children on Friday nights or go to a
singles' party to try to meet someone?

These are only some of the issues and questions that plague Jewish single parents. The problem is that few Jewish organizations are concerned with providing answers to these questions. It is only recently that some—a very few—Jewish social service agencies are beginning to form single-parent support and outreach groups. Other organizations—like the Jewish Big Brother and Big Sister Associations—which fulfill some important needs of the single-parent family are pitifully small and underfunded. And most synagogues appear indifferent to the plight of the Jewish single parent, claiming that their facilities and programs are open to all and that no special provisions need be made for single-parent families.

The truth is, the possibility of being able to attend a single-parent family retreat or of joining a single-parent *havurah* (fellowship or community) would be greeted with joy by many single parents. Indeed, the simple act of designating a category of synagogue membership fees for single-parent families would reflect some commitment toward recognizing the plight of the single-parent family. (Jay Klein claims that he joined his local synagogue only because when he was initially approached to join and refused, citing the financial obligations incurred by being a single parent, the board of the congregation met to vote in a new fee schedule. He was so impressed by this act of caring that he did join that synagogue.) An added benefit would be the creation of more situations where sex-role stereotyping could be deemphasized to allow single women to share in synagogue ritual or leadership roles.

Not all the answers to the Jewish questions that arise in single-parent families can be provided in institutions. Some of these issues are particularly personal or private ones and can be addressed only by the parent or family alone. Most single parents agree, for example, that celebration of the Jewish holidays creates situations that are particularly painful. With whom will the children spend the holidays? What kind of holiday environment can you, on your own, create when you feel unsure about your own observance, embarrassed that you aren't better versed in Hebrew language and Jewish ritual, afraid that your children's memories of their holiday celebrations will fall woefully short of your own warm and nostalgic ones?

The parents in the support group to which I belong have evolved their own individual ways of handling these problems. Some people urge you to consider celebrating holidays with another single-parent family or perhaps with a two-parent family with whom you and your children are particularly close and comfortable. It is important that there be other adults present. A single parent wants to be able to celebrate the holiday, too; a Rosh Hashanah dinner for one parent and one child can be a sad affair.

Discuss with the children any ideas they might have for observing the holiday. Ask if there has been anything in the past that they didn't like or perhaps something they remembered as "very special" (maybe a new ritual created by and for your family—see Chapter Ten). Use the fact that the family situation is different in a positive way as an opportunity to create new models. The first year of my divorce, conducting a Seder in "my style" was indeed a new vehicle for expressing my Judaism. It was very different from the old way, when I prepared huge quantities of food that I dispensed with inevitable Jewish-mother warmth and hospitality. It was nice to feel I could free myself of a role that had only caused me fatigue and resentment.

If you are a parent celebrating without your children, you, too, must plan for yourself—far in advance—to be sure that *your* needs will be adequately met. This may be even more difficult. Feelings of being left out can be overwhelming and depressing. Feelings of being totally free of any obligations and responsibilities might lead you to avoid the holiday. Ask youself if you want to be with a large group of people; if so, look for a possible community setting. If you are interested in a smaller gathering, you can create one by seeking out other single parents or couples without children who want to share a holiday. Or you can use the holiday as a time to visit and celebrate with old friends in another city. I usually do the latter, as I find old friends serve as extended family members, especially where the friendships have a long history.

All of the above-mentioned ideas require advance planning. If, however, you take the time to assess your needs and are willing to create new models for holiday observance, then you will be able to establish patterns that permit you truly to celebrate Jewish holidays.

The life of the single parent is a complicated and difficult one. The Jewish community—and parents themselves—can help to pave the road. Below are some suggestions:

Community professionals should

Create outreach to the single parents and form support groups.

Invest in intensive outreach to male parents.

Produce a resource directory describing local services for singles and single parents.

Develop workshops and seminars to bring together rabbis, educators, and parents.

Expand or create Big Brother/Big Sister programs.

Organize and develop day-care centers.

Create weekend family programs for socializing and study.

Develop a single-parent hotline.

Rabbis and educators should

Sensitize and educate your congregants and boards to the issues facing single-parent families.

Create or expand opportunities for family observance of holidays.

Aid in developing single-parent *havurot* (fellowships) in your community.

Consider the role of family mediator.

Help create comfortable situations for socializing.

Expand the nursery-school hours to meet the growing need of working parents.

Organize holiday-observance programs.
Expand scholarship programs for summer camps and for trips to Israel.

Parents should

Think positively.
Plan ahead; be creative.
Check out all community resources.
Organize family *havurot*.
Practice rituals to gain confidence.
Study together with your children.

HOW DO SOME JEWISH SINGLES FEEL?

"I wish someone would outreach me from the synagogue. I'm sure I would respond, but I just don't have what it takes or enough energy after working all day and then coming home to face the kids alone, to make it a priority and go after the resources. It takes an effort to survey the community and see what I might like. I would also feel uncomfortable showing up at a synagogue as a single."

"I would feel comfortable with more family programming situations, especially ones which would help educate parents like myself and let us learn together with our children."

"I am more comfortable with the idea of discovery and learning in small groups in homes where I don't feel threatened or out of place."

"I am unaffiliated, uneducated Jewishly, but I want to do something . . . where do I go?"

"I had no background as a child; my mother was married to a non-Jew. One trip to Israel (as an adult) created in me a desire to learn . . . My kids are in Hebrew school now, but there is no comfortable place for me as a single. I would like to find other people like myself with whom to learn and to celebrate holidays."

CHAPTER SIX

WHEN ONE PARENT IS NOT JEWISH

Intermarried couples who raise their children as Jews face difficulties that make the difficulties of families in which both parents are Jewish pale by comparison. Initially, intermarried couples face the Jewish community's question as to whether their children can be considered Jewish. According to the legal opinions of both Orthodox and Conservative Judaism, a child is Jewish if his or her mother was Jewish (either because her mother, in turn, was Jewish or because she participated in a ritually correct conversion). Reform Judaism maintains that children are Jewish if one parent is Jewish.

In fact, most intermarried couples care little about their children's Jewish legal status and are more concerned with the realities of how they will raise their children. Thus, partners in an intermarriage confront the question, Will we raise our children to be Jews? Responding in the affirmative to this question does not end the discussion but leads to further questions. What if one partner deeply wants to raise children to become knowledgeable and committed Jews and the other is indifferent or hostile to that goal? It is not that uncommon to find the non-Jewish spouse more actively involved in exploring Judaism and supporting children's evolving Jewish identities than the Jewish member of the household. In fact, many people who have never formally converted to Judaism consider themselves Jews.

Ann P. maintains that "as far as we're concerned, Ron is Jewish. Oh, he may never have been converted formally, but he *feels* Jewish, so why should *we* not see him as Jewish when he sees himself as Jewish?"

Another friend points out, "I didn't marry Margo *because* I wanted to be Jewish. I married her because I loved her. But after we were married, I found myself more and more drawn to wanting to be a part of 'the Jewish family'—the warmth, the kinship. Oddly enough, Margo resented my growing interest, and as we talked about it, what emerged was her feeling of 'it's mine. I rejected it, and maybe that's part of my marrying a *goy*, but it still belongs to me. So you keep your hands *off* of it!' Now that we have children, we are struggling to work out a Jewish life-style that doesn't take her farther than she wants to go but does let me pursue my ever-growing interest in and connection to the Jewish people."

Caution: There may (or there may not) come a time in your children's lives when the fact that one parent is not Jewish will vitally affect their future. We can envision a scenario where your child falls in love with a traditional Jew or with an Israeli who wants to live in Israel. In either case, the genealogical history of the child—whether the parent's or child's conversion was in accordance with Jewish law—will then matter to your child and to the child's future spouse.

Intermarried parents trying to raise Jewish children face many of the practical problems of couples in which both partners are Jewish, but have a whole host of additional problems. For example, the question will arise about how the children can and should relate to their non-Jewish grandparents. Will they visit on Christmas? Will they attend non-Jewish places of worship with their grandparents? Will they temper their own Jewish observance when those grandparents come to visit? Will they attend family or institutional religious celebrations with their non-Jewish relatives?

To such questions there can be no easy answers. The goal is to help children love and respect their non-Jewish relatives while teaching them that they themselves are Jews and that Jews live their lives in ways that are different from non-Jews. Not better. Different. Whatever can be done to lessen the confusion in children's minds about why they are different from their grandparents or why one set of grandparents is different from the other should be a priority for the parents. Allowing young children to attend non-Jewish places of worship or to celebrate non-Jewish holidays, even in a nonparticipatory fashion, is almost always a mistake. At best, it can lead a child to feel confusion about his or her own religious tradition. At worst, it can nurture conflicts in the child who may see him or herself as betraying beloved relatives by having allegiance to a religion other than theirs. As difficult as it is, it may be better not to visit non-Jewish grandparents at Christmas or Easter. Such a decision will be painful to grandparents who always expected to share their holiday traditions with their grandchildren and are denied this pleasure. Yet most parents would agree that grandparents are, in general, better equipped to handle disappointment than children are able to handle value confusion; and so the children's welfare probably ought to come first in making such decisions. What happens in cases where the non-Jewish parent is actively hostile toward allowing his or her children to be raised as Jews? Certainly, whether or not to raise the children as Jews is an issue that ought to have been decided before the couple had children. And, in most cases, there has been discussion and prior agreement. But the fantasy of "how we'll raise the kids" before one *has* kids is always different from the reality of "Yipes! What do I do now?" Once the child's existence is fact, issues that may have formerly seemed clear become muddled. The birth of a child revitalizes family bonds and loyalties that may have been subsurface before. And so the non-Jewish partner who blithely, albeit sincerely, agreed to raise his or her children as Jews may experience a sense of shock at his or her son's *brit milah* or at the absence of a Christmas tree once December rolls around.

A LETTER TO A FELLOW TRAVELER

You consider yourself Jewish, for you feel with the Jewish people and participate in our life; but I must tell you that while I accept you as a friend, I do not yet accept you as a Jew. In the same way that others have spent time in France and learned the language and culture so well that they feel themselves to be French, you have come to know us and feel yourself to be one of us. The fact is that until a temporary resident applies for and is granted French citizenship, he or she has neither the rights nor obligations of that nationality. So, too, it is with Judaism. Until you fulfill the laws of citizenship of the Jewish people, you remain a beloved fellow traveler, a close friend of the family, but not a relative.

As Ron put it: "Everything was going along well until we actually put into practice an agreement we had both made—not to have a Christmas tree after Jennifer was born. When mid-December came and there were no Christmas plans afoot, I began to feel edgy. As the time grew nearer, my edginess increased. And all the while I wasn't able to define my problem. Finally, when Christmas Eve arrived, it hit me like a ton of bricks. I was going to raise a child who would never participate in or understand an important part of who I am and how I was raised. It staggered me and took me a long time to come to accept." Such feelings must be taken seriously and worked through as soon as possible. Lamenting that a spouse has changed the rules of the game midquarter can be fruitless and destructive. The two worst things to do are to ignore the problem or to make concessions to the spouse's feelings in an (often subconscious) attempt to allay that spouse's fears with the thought that whatever ground is conceded initially can be recovered later on when the spouse is less adamant or frightened. It is *not* reasonable or indeed fair to assume that you can give in and have a Christmas tree or not have a Passover Seder this year and then be able to change that pattern next year. Precedents, once established, have lives of their own.

What about the spouse who is passively or actively hostile to the whole enterprise of raising the children as Jews? Frequently, in such situations, the children become the pawns in a game of the parents' fashioning called, "Let's use the kids to act out our hostilities." It's a fairly useless enterprise to tell such parents about the harm they do their children by making Judaism, or indeed anything else, the cause around which to conduct marital warfare. Parents who are having fundamental disagreements about how to raise their children should seek help from trained professionals, whether a good rabbi or a counselor or therapist. Rare is the couple who can end such warfare independently.

What about parents who are indifferent to whether or not their children are raised as Jews? Such indifference is really not a mask for hostility or passive aggression but is rather the true indifference of someone who is not particularly interested in Judaism or any religion but is perfectly ready to have the children raised as Jews. When such a situation arises, it's a good idea for the committed Jewish partner to introduce Jewish ritual into the family's life in carefully thought out and talked through segments. For instance, the non-Jewish partner may not feel intruded upon by the introduction of limited rituals around the Friday-night meal. A full-blown Shabbat dinner, however, may feel oppressive and will ultimately produce exactly those kinds of negative feelings both partners are anxious to avoid. In other words, for such couples, consultation and cooperation can be the key to harmony. Neither partner should be trying subtly to coerce the other into believing that she or he is "right" to want or not to want to be Jewish. Rather, the whole area should be defused emotionally into a what-rituals-make-sense-for-our-particular-family kind of discussion that tries to be open and fair to both sides without unduly abusing either's trust.

Being an intermarried couple is not easy. Certainly some of the more successful intermarriages we know have been between people who knew when the time had arrived to seek professional help in negotiating their lives. But it is true that in America it is possible for intermarried couples to have healthy Jewish commitments that involve their children and their own lives. Possible, and yet inevitably, difficult.

1906

Dear Editor,

For a long time I worked in a shop with a Gentile girl, and we began to go out together and fell in love. We agreed that I would remain a Jew and she a Christian. But after we had been married for a year, I realized that it would not work.

I began to notice that whenever one of my Jewish friends comes to the house, she is displeased. Worse yet, when she sees me reading a Jewish newspaper her face changes color. She says nothing, but I can see that she has changed. I feel that she is very unhappy with me, though I know she loves me. She will soon become a mother, and she is more dependent on me than ever.

She used to be quite liberal, but lately she is being drawn back to the Christian religion. She gets up early Sunday mornings, runs to church and comes home with eyes swollen from crying. When we pass a church now and then, she trembles.

Dear Editor, advise me what to do now. I could never convert, and there's no hope for me to keep her from going to church. What can we do now?

Thankfully,
A Reader

ANSWER:

Unfortunately, we often hear of such tragedies, which stem from marriages between people of different worlds. It's possible that if this couple were to move to a Jewish neighborhood, the young man might have more influence on his wife.

From Isaac Metzker, ed., *A Bintel Brief*. New York: Doubleday, 1971.

Part Two
CELEBRATING

CHAPTER SEVEN

GIVING NAMES

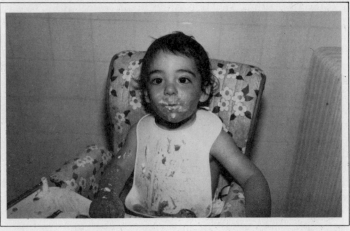

From the beginning of recorded history, we Jews have been concerned with names. Calling out to one another, bearing the right name, sowing the seeds of identity in the names we give our children—all point to the tremendous importance of naming.

The pattern of naming in the Bible is interesting. In the very beginning, God creates through names, through words, and through letters. He calls the world into being by saying, "Let there be light," "Let there be firmament." And as God creates through names, so, too, does He create distinctions: between day and night, earth and sea, sunlight and moonlight. His creature Adam follows suit. His task is to name the birds and beasts and creatures of the world.

As we continue our reading of Genesis and Exodus, we notice how varied are the names of God. We know that biblical commentators have been very concerned about these different names and have sought to identify attributes or qualities of God with corresponding Hebrew names of God. *Eloheinu,* for example, is seen as suggesting qualities of ruling or reigning, while *Rahum* implies mercy.

Moses wants desperately to know the name of the God with whom he has dealt for so long. Moses' struggle to learn God's essential name prompted the great Protestant theologian Paul Tillich to observe that the name participates in the reality of the being. In other words, to know the name is to know something essential and intimate about the being. It is not by chance that according to our traditions we knew in the ancient Temple in Jerusalem how to pronounce God's most secret name. Since the destruction of the Temple, we only know the letters of the name, Yod-Heh-Vav-Heh; we no longer remember how to put the letters together to pronounce them as an entire word. According to tradition, only in Messianic times will we once again recall how to say God's name.

The Torah tells us not to "take the name of the Lord your God in vain." Again, we are reminded of the importance of a name. It is especially interesting that in being commanded *not* to do something, we are credited by implication with the capacity to do it. By being commanded not to take God's name in vain, we realize that we have the power to do just that and must be careful.

From our own very human experiences, we realize that to know another's name is to have at least a modicum of power. "Hey, you" shouted out in a crowd cannot evoke the response that a name can. A schoolteacher who knows all thirty children's names is in a more powerful position than one who doesn't. Remember seeing a nurse calling out the name of a patient just emerging from an anesthetic? It is as if the patient's first name has the power to reach deep into his or her consciousness.

We Jews have long treasured names and traced our history through our names. The Torah carefully records generations of names ("And these are the names of Israel . . ."). A *midrash*, which explains the Passover story, reminds us that one of the reasons we merited redemption from Egyptian bondage was that we did not adopt Egyptian names but retained our Jewish identities through the years with our Hebrew names. The irony of this statement is that our leader in liberation was Moses, whose name quite probably was of Egyptian origin.

Elias Bickerman, the great Jewish historian, was able to glean insights about the Jews' sojourn in Babylonia through tracing names. He noted that while Jews assumed Babylonian names, the generation that anticipated return to Zion gave its children Hebrew names. Therefore, in the last generation of Babylonian exile, it is not unusual to find individuals whose names follow the pattern of a Hebrew name accompanied by a Babylonian patronym.

It is not uncommon for scholars of all periods of Jewish history to trace relationships and approximate dates on the basis of patronyms and matronyms. We may figure out, for example, that the author of a medieval manuscript was the grandson of another author on the basis of both writers' names.

Many of us have read stories of Israel Baal Shem Tov, the great Hasidic master who roamed the Carpathian Mountain region during the first half of the eighteenth century. But how do we understand the man's name? Actually, Israel was his first name and "Baal Shem Tov" described his profession and reputation, for the words mean "master of the good name." Many contemporaries of Israel were called Baal Shem, referring to amulet writers who knew the correct names of both God and the angels to protect the wearer from harm. But a Baal Shem *Tov* refers to someone who was especially good at writing effective amulets. Thus, we see an example of how Jewish piety used names for protection and also how the very act of writing down names became a name in itself.

In the twentieth century, our names assume a special poignancy. With the destruction of whole families and communities at the hands of the Nazis, we sometimes find that the only record of an individual is his or her name on a document in a file at Yad VaShem, the Holocaust memorial in Israel, or in a particular city's memorial volumes. One way of experiencing the power of these names and beginning to realize the lost lives each represents is to stand quietly in Yad VaShem's archive room in Jerusalem, knowing that you're in the physical presence of as many names as researchers have been able to write down.

When we give a name to another or when we explore the significance of our own names, we realize that the name may be a living memorial to a dead relative or friend. For some of us, this kind of memorialization provides a beautiful continuity or entryway into our pasts. For others, the implications seem too complex. ("I never liked my grandfather; and I do not want to convey any of his unpleasant character traits to this innocent baby. As a matter of fact, there is no way in which I want my son to remind me of Zeide.")

For all of us, naming is not a casual affair. What are some intelligent guidelines for giving a name, whether that name be for a newborn baby or for an adult who never had a Hebrew name and now wants one—perhaps to be called up to the Torah?

First of all, must a Jew have a Jewish name? Of course, we can find acceptable "Hebrew" names that are not Hebrew in origin. As we pointed out earlier, Moses is probably an Egyptian name. Alexander, a name by which many have been called to the Torah, is clearly Greek. Names were sometimes borrowed from other languages and integrated into Jewish languages. But today, whether a name is Hebrew, Yiddish, Ladino, or Aramaic, the use of Jewish names that resonate through our past should be encouraged. Living as we do in the second half of the twentieth century, we believe it incumbent upon each of us to reach out and reclaim names that our tradition preserves. Of course, in our choices of specific names, we must be sensitive and flexible; but our searches for names should be through Jewish sources.

We realize that we must be honest in our perceptions of family dy-

namic. We all know those stories: Tante Pesha Sora did not speak to Uncle Dovid Gershon for fifty years after he went to *shul* and announced their daughter's name after *his* mother rather than *her* mother. We also understand that widowed or orphaned grandparents have emotional investments in names that may not appeal to us. Potential for family conflict and the accompanying demand for sensitivity is enormous. We can only recommend that you try not to use name selection as a metaphor for fighting other battles; that you try to be aware of the feelings of others and explore creative compromises; and, finally, that you recognize that it is you, the parent and your child, who will have to live with the name and that you therefore have the right to be firm in your conviction.

Next, try narrowing the field of potential names. Must the name be the same as that of a grandparent? Will you have to adapt a name? For example, will you try to make a masculine name into a feminine? Will David become Davida or Gabriel become Gabriella? Will you translate a Yiddish name back into Hebrew; for example, will Gittel—which means "good"—become Tova, or Kriendl—meaning a "small crown"—be transformed into Ateret or Atarah? Some of us face the dilemma of wanting to name a child after a relative whose name simply does not appeal to us. ("I would love to name my baby after my grandfather Shlomo, but we just don't like the sound of the name, and Solomon sounds like something out of the 1920s.") In such situations, we often try to preserve the name as the Jewish name and give the child an English name that conveys the initial sound of the Jewish name. This practice does perpetuate the positive Jewish custom of naming for our ancestors. On the other hand, as we search for viable English names, we find that, sadly, we are attaching ourselves to popular names without any Jewish historical association whatsoever. In the best of all possible worlds, we want to encourage the use of one Jewish name; short of this ideal, we hope that any name chosen resonates in some way with our Jewish past rather than with the past of the Welsh or Irish or French.

Some of us, rather than struggling with names of family obligation, find ourselves free to choose any name in the world. Where can we begin to look for names? Should the name be from the Bible? Must it be the name of a biblical personality, or could it be the name of a quality or attribute? What about names of animals and plants that are described so poetically in the "Song of Songs"? Consider names that come from postbiblical literature, for example, the names of angels, of rabbis who appear in the Talmud, of characters in stories by Agnon.

Where can you go for help? The best existing reference to the history of Jewish names is the glossary at the back of the great Hebrew dictionary by Evan Shoshan. If your Hebrew is not yet good enough to use Evan Shoshan, we suggest enlisting the aid of a friend whose Hebrew is better. The dictionary itself can be found in any good Judaica library. Try also *The Name Dictionary: Modern English and Hebrew Names* by Alfred J. Kolatch, published by Jonathan David, New York, 1967. People may prove invaluable resources. Asking questions about names can open the door to interesting dialogue with Jewish professionals in your community. Asking older relatives about the history of a name that occurs in your family may elicit fascinating information about your past.

Once you have decided on a name, consider exploring its history. If, for example, the name is biblical, look it up in the *Encyclopedia Judaica*, in Ginsberg's *Legends of the Jews*, or in a biblical concordance. Consult a local Jewish scholar for ways of researching the history of a name. How might you use the fruits of your research? At the very least, your own understanding of the name will be enriched. Other possibilities include writing up your research and giving the document as a gift to a family with a new baby or using your information to create a *d'var Torah* or unique *midrash* (commentary) to use at a naming ceremony or *brit milah*.

Many of us struggle with feelings of the inappropriateness of names. How often have we heard a new parent say, "Such a long and pompous name for such a little baby"; how often have we known an individual whose name did not appear to our outsider's eye to fit at all? Remember the 250-pound matron who was called Birdie? Or the ugly lady named Yaffah (pretty)? Remember the children who seem to be victims of their parents' ideologies: they go through life with seven names strung out on their birth certificates or evocations of historical characters like Theodor Herzl Jabotinsky Goldberg. While we can only be awed by the sincerity of the parents of Shekhinah Schwartz, we must caution that a great deal of a child's personality is formed by the ways in which others react to him or her. A contemporary study of children in a large urban public school system showed that teachers tended to be less comfortable calling on children with unusual names and that these children often did less well than their peers with more ordinary names.

Consider where the child will use the name. Will the child be comfortable with the name in a public school in the United States? Will the child feel better about the name in a Jewish day school? Will it be an object of derision in a *gan* (kindergarten) in Israel? How confident are you of your Hebrew? Will anyone who knows Hebrew cringe upon hearing a grammatical mistake in an inaccurate attempt to transform a masculine word into a feminine?

The process of how an infant somehow becomes his or her name and how we as adults relate to our own names or even choose names remains mysterious. Yet often we find elements in our names that make us experience them as uniquely appropriate. Our relationship to our names may be so intimate as to be invisible to outsiders.

How and where are Jewish names used? We hope that ours is a generation in which the answer to that question is increasingly "Everywhere." Our hope is that our children will be able to use one name in more than one culture and that the need for an English name and a Jewish name will be seen as symptomatic of a particular social circumstance in our past.

In Jewish liturgical life, your name (with patronym and/or matronym) is used at rites of passage and on legal documents. The use of your parents' names is for identification. In a society that did not encounter last names until fairly recently, parents' names simply gave more identifying data. Traditionally, patronyms were used, except when praying for someone who was ill or when sending a petitionary note *(kvitel)* to a Hasidic master, in which case the matronym was used—perhaps as a more intimate and pleading form of identification. Recently, many of us have chosen to use both our parents' names (_____, the child of father and mother). It has been argued by the heterodox to Orthodox rabbis that on such a document as a marriage contract in which each partner is identified by his or her father's name, including the mother's names simply improves or extends the identification. (It also makes the document more egalitarian.) In any case, we are first identified by our new names at naming ceremonies or upon entering into the covenant of the Jewish people. Next, our names are used when we are called to the Torah at bar or bat mitzvah. At our weddings our *ketubot* (marriage documents) bear our names, which may also appear on documents when we fulfill the role of witness or if we divorce a spouse. When we are ill, we are prayed for by name, and there is even a custom that a mortally ill person's name can be changed in order to fool the Angel of Death and save a life. Finally, when we die, our names are mentioned in the El Molai Rahamim prayer. If we are Ashkenazim, after death our names may be given to a descendant. If we are Sephardim, we may even live to hear children called by our own names.

Our names are an intimate and public part of us all the days of our lives. We struggle not only to gain insight into the roots of our own names and identities but also to make a name for ourselves in the world. The rabbis (in *Pirke Avot*) taught: "There are three crowns: the crown of the priesthood, the crown of Torah, and the crown of kingship; and the crown of a good name exceeds them all." Thus, while concerned with our pasts in our names and with our futures in the names we give our children, we also struggle to fulfill our names and maintain our good names in our own present.

> I couldn't bring myself to name my child "Max" after my father. It seemed like such an old-fashioned name that I changed it to "Matt" and retained the "Moshe" in Hebrew.
>
> How do I feel now about the name "Matt"? I don't know. Everyone is going back to old-fashioned names, so "Max" is chic again. Maybe if I had to do it over now, I'd choose "Max," even though Matt became Matt and I love him with that name.
>
> PETER RAPAPORT

Franz Rosenzweig wrote:

One thing is certain, I have no real feeling about my first name. I can only guess why this is. It seems to me that it may be because my parents gave it to me without any particular feeling, simply because they "liked it" (and why did they like it? because at the time it was "different"; only later were there other Franzes in the Jewish community of Cassel). It's as though my parents had seen it in a window shop, walked inside, and bought it. It has nothing traditional about it, no memory, no history, not even an anecdote, scarcely a whim—it was simply a passing fancy. A family name, a saint's name, a hero's name, a poetic name, a symbolic name, all these are good: they have grown naturally, not been bought ready-made. One should be named after somebody or something. Else a name is really only empty breath.

I had wanted to name my child "Adin" if it was a boy. It seemed like such a gentle name—it means "sensitive" in Hebrew—that I fell in love with it the first time I heard it.

But when, during the birth, my son came surging forth from my body in an incredibly violent flow of energy, I knew instinctively that Adin was not the right name. I named him, instead, Chaim—meaning "life"—and I've never regretted the choice.

JEAN GOLDSTEIN

My English name is Nancy; I never had a Jewish name. When I got involved in Jewish things, I found myself wanting to own my own Hebrew name. So I "shopped around" until I found the name. And, at the age of thirty-four, I hired a tutor to prepare myself, and I had a bat mitzvah, during which I chose the Hebrew name Talya. And I feel now that in choosing my name and having (finally) a bat mitzvah, I finally did come of age as an adult Jew.

NANCY MICHAELS

CHAPTER EIGHT

BRIT AND NAMING

Rachel Falkove and the Editors

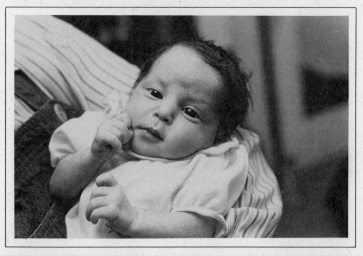

This is My Covenant which you shall keep . . . every male among you shall be circumcised . . . that shall be the sign of the Covenant between Me and you. At the age of eight days every male among you shall be circumcised throughout the generations. . . . And the uncircumcised male . . . shall be cut off from his people; he has broken My Covenant.

GENESIS 17:10–14

The word *brit* (*bris* in Ashkenazic communities) means covenant, a pledge of obligation between two parties, which is generally accompanied by a token exchange or a symbolic act. *Brit milah* refers to the covenant between God and the Jewish people and is symbolized by the act of circumcision. Our father, Abraham, circumcised himself and so was the first to participate in this covenant with God, who, in return, promised that Abraham's seed would inherit the land of Canaan.

Procedurally, *brit milah* is a simple operation that involves the removal of the foreskin covering the glans of the penis. The ceremony takes place on the eighth day of the child's life, generally in the morning, and is performed by a *mohel* (a person trained in Jewish ritual as well as the operative procedure). A *minyan* (a quorum of ten people) of family mem-

To me, *brit milah* has a lot to do with sexual imagery. It is the sanctifying of the sexual organ, a way to state the commitment to procreate. When I invited people to Solomon's *brit milah*, many of them said to me that they thought it was great that Rachel and I were bringing another Jewish child into the world. I couldn't relate to that. The *brit* doesn't transform the baby into a Jew. For me, it marked the end of one process—my maturation as a Jew—and the beginning of another—imparting the tradition to my child. It was the fulfillment of a process that began at my bar mitzvah. No, I wasn't afraid of hurting our baby. I had a *brit*, and I don't remember anything about it. It couldn't have been that traumatic.

MICHAEL MASCH

We didn't announce our baby's name until the *brit milah*. At the *brit*, he became Shalom Zvi (after my father)—an authentic Jew with a name—a part of the community of Israel. During the ceremony, I was thinking about my father, wishing that he could be here, feeling anger that he wasn't able to be part of the *simkha* (celebration). I spoke about my father at the *brit*, and Michael spoke about the names we had chosen. We then recited El Molai Rahamim (remembrance prayer) for my father.

GRACE MILLER

Brit milah is very important. It's an act of faith about being a Jew, and that in itself overshadowed any medical fears that I might have had. To me, *brit milah* is the continuity of identity and history, an especially important responsibility I have because I live after the Holocaust. The Holocaust is very much part of my Jewishness. *Brit milah* is like most Jewish ceremonies—if you really try to think about them on the rational level, very few of them make any sense.

MICHAEL MILLER

bers and friends is often invited to attend the ceremony. It is at the *brit* that a male child is named.

A feast or symbolic celebratory meal is held afterward, followed by a special *birkat hamazon* (grace after meal) for the occasion. Although it is possible to have a private *brit* in the hospital, performed by a physician, the feeling of communal celebration and a spirit of the Jewish community welcoming its newest member will probably be lacking. We urge everyone to consider, whenever possible, having the *brit* at home with relatives, friends, candles, wine, food, song, personal blessings, dance, and celebration—letting our children know right from their beginnings how much we care about them, need them, and welcome them not only to our nuclear family but to the Jewish people, too.

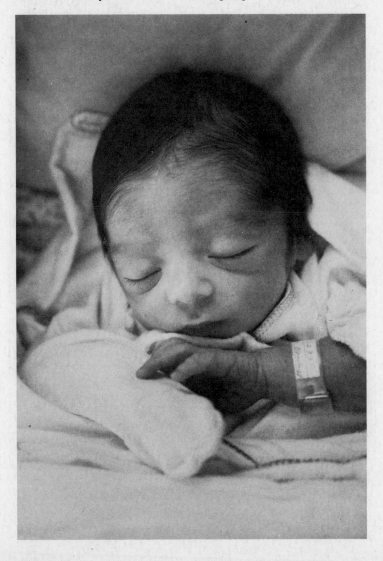

I realize now that our daughter's naming was a moment for which I had waited my whole life. She was our first child and certainly not the child of our youth. It was a sunny spring day. The house was decorated with flowers, and even now when I think of the sunshine and flowers I recall lines from the Song of Songs, lines about buds appearing in the fields. Our daughter was two weeks old and very tiny. We had gotten little sleep the night before the naming and my husband was determined that the naming should occur in the context of a morning *shaharit* service in our living room. I remember feeling utter physical exhaustion at seven o'clock in the morning before guests began to arrive. I really felt ill with nervousness. Unlike mothers of boys, I had no fears about our baby's physical well-being. The impact of the event was overwhelming. I am by trade an intellectual, but I could not begin to intellectualize or isolate my feelings at the naming. My husband and I carried our daughter to the Torah and named her and recited some appropriate biblical passages. After *shaharit* my friends served the hundred or so guests a bagel and lox *kiddush.* We made *hamotzi* (the prayer over bread) and when it was time to say the grace after the meal friends gave creative Torah teachings or blessings for the baby. One friend provided us with a magnificent midrashic commentary to our baby's name; he had created the commentary himself. It was an interpretation we had not thought of in naming her.

In the intervening years we have attended many ceremonies initiating boys and girls into the Jewish community. When our daughter was small, we explained *brit milah* and naming ceremonies as parties for babies which were like the party we made for her. In fact, I realize now that each ceremony is different, reflecting the individuality of the parents and the situation. Inevitably they are touching. When we planned our daughter's naming ceremony we were concerned that it equal that of a boy. Did we succeed? The emotional impact of circumcision, the power of thousands of years of tribal history, has to make *brit milah* unique. Naming ceremonies are different but no less important. One of the guests at our daughter's naming ceremony taught us an important lesson when he explained, "There I was trying to decide if I could afford the time and the airplane ticket to come here today. I said to my wife that if it had been a boy I would not have hesitated and then I realized that because of that statement it was important for me to come. Thank heaven for little girls!"

IT'S A GIRL!

Traditionally, a new baby girl is welcomed to the community by being named in the synagogue after birth. The father is called for an *aliyah* (a going up) to the Torah and afterward recites the naming formula for his new daughter.

With increased concern about an equal place for women in the Jewish community, many new parents have spent time and effort in devising new home ceremonies to welcome their daughters to the Jewish people. (See *The Second Jewish Catalog* for suggestions and examples.) It is worthwhile to explore such alternatives (preferably *before* your child is born, since waiting until afterward can put a lot of pressure on new parents, who will need to be ritually creative when a new baby is absorbing much time and energy) so that we can convey with honesty our priorities and values to ourselves, our family and friends, our other children, and our new daughters.

PARENTS' REFLECT

There I was, a mother of a baby boy born only one hour before, and in the middle of my euphoric exhaustion the horrifying thought struck me—my God! I've got to plan the *bris!* Something about the sound of the word made me incredibly anxious. My perfect little baby with his carefully counted ten fingers and ten toes was not ready for a *bris.* (Actually, it was his mother who was not ready for this *bris!*)

I found myself jealous of my Christian hospital roommate. I watched her as the smiling nurse walked into our room to take her little boy for his "circ." My roommate cheerfully handed him over to her and went back to watching the soaps on TV. *Why is it that we Jews have to do everything in as traumatic a way as possible?* I wondered to myself.

In a way, during the last few months of pregnancy, I had attempted to prepare myself for the idea of a *bris.* I'd fantasized about the ceremony, my reactions, my heroic child, and his heroic mother. Certainly, I never considered not having a *bris* if my baby were a boy, since it is one of those central rituals in the life cycle of a Jew that is so "bottom line" that there's really no room for picking and choosing.

Lying there holding my baby, knowing that no nurse would come to relieve me of the responsibility of confronting and being present at my son's *bris,* I felt myself bursting with questions. True, the Covenant of circumcision was clearly more than a style of penis. But it seemed like such a frighteningly primitive way of welcoming a baby boy into the Jewish community. Why *was* it so important to do? How would it make him Jewish? What feelings was I supposed to experience during the ceremony?

When the day of our baby's *brit milah* came, all the preparations were complete. The day dawned bright and sunny. We had decided to hold it in our friends' house, which was bigger than ours; our guests brought

At both of my sons' *britot*, I felt tremendous emotion, a great sense of being with friends and family, almost like a wedding. There were ninety people at one, and sixty-five at the other. And setting aside the barbaric quality of the circumcision, I had a real sense of continuity, a very special continuity because we named the children after people who were important to us. Joshua was named after Sheila's father. Eli Mordechai is after my grandfather. We gave a *derash* (a talk) at both *britot* about the names we had chosen and the people after whom we were naming our children. (I guess I was more nervous at Eli's *brit milah* because I was the one making the speech.) It's very important to add a special *derash* about the name. It makes the ceremony more personal. When I think about it, the *brit* was our *mitzvah* (commandment), our welcoming a child into the fold. At Eli's *brit*, Joshua's presence made it extra special, because it was the three of us doing the welcoming. Joshua was celebrating the Jewishness of it along with me and Sheila.

DAN SEGAL

I have very positive feelings about *brit milah* and wish that more people could approach it without fear. To me, it is all about joy and renewal. At both our sons' *britot*, I felt enfolded by the warmth of our families and friends when I walked into the room. Perhaps people are often tense at a circumcision because traditionally the mother has often been kept away from it. They probably surmise that if it's something that the mother is to be protected from, then it must be pretty scary. But for most people, circumcision is bottom line to being Jewish. They do it in spite of their fears.

Telling Joshua (our four-year-old) about the ceremony before Eli's *brit* was a real issue for us. I was afraid that if he heard that the baby would be "cut," he would think, *Oh, my God. This is terrible. Being Jewish must be terrible.* So I knew that he must be told in a very careful way. We talked with a friend who had a baby boy six weeks before us. A psychiatrist told them that in no way should their older child be told. It would leave a traumatic mark on his life even if it were explained in a positive way. But our style is more direct. Finally, we told Joshua that the *mohel* was taking away an extra piece of skin. I felt good about that explanation, and Joshua handled it just fine.

SHEILA SEGAL

food and wine to share, and the house began to feel crowded and full of love, energy, and excitement. Perhaps because the *mohel* had a very calm way about him, our baby hardly cried during the ceremony. We named him Solomon after my father, and although I was not able to watch the circumcision, I closed my eyes, experiencing feelings of some confusion but intense joy as well.

Several months later, I have only begun to understand the importance of the *brit milah* ceremony. Talking to other parents who shared their children's *brit milah* experiences with me and thinking about our own ceremony, I find myself strangely moved by and very supportive of the *brit milah* ritual which became for me that day a ceremony about joy and the renewal of Judaism.

PLANNING A BRIT CEREMONY

While you're pregnant

Even before giving birth to your baby, you should begin planning for a *brit*. For a girl, you should spend time tracking down new ceremonies, talking with friends, rabbis, relatives, etc., about what kind of ceremony you'd like to have. If it's a boy, remember that when you arrive at the hospital, you will probably be asked to sign a series of forms. One of these forms states that you give the hospital permission to medically circumcise the baby. Do not confuse this with ritual *brit milah*. If you want a ritual *brit milah*, do not sign this form. Medical circumcision is done by a doctor. Ritual circumcision is performed by a *mohel*.

Finding a mohel

If you live in a large city, chances are that there will be a *milah* board, a committee of rabbis and medical physicians who supervise, certify, and recommend the local *mohelim*. You can probably locate the *milah* board through the local board of rabbis, but if your town does not have a board of rabbis, ask the local rabbi to help you find a *mohel*. Also, speak with friends who have used the local *mohelim* to get their recommendations.

Choosing a Place

Most *mohelim* prefer to perform the *brit milah* at your home, although they generally will agree to work in the hospital. If you need to use the hospital, speak with the administrative office to make arrangements for a room where invited guests can gather. At most hospitals, there is room for only a handful of guests. Only the Jewish hospitals have special facilities for a *brit milah*.

For a girl's *brit* ceremony, there is probably no reason for you to reserve space in the hospital, and you'll want to think about a home ceremony. If your own home is not suitable, consider asking friends to "lend" their home or else use Jewish institutional space.

I felt very proud and a little angry at Ariel's *bris*. Proud—because it was the first public Jewish thing asked of me since my wedding. I was glad to do it and felt a real connection to the Jewish people. I was participating in something that thousands of Jewish people have participated in. Angry—because I couldn't understand why this happens to a little baby who can't say anything or make that choice with me. After the circumcision, Ariel peed all over the *mohel*. I laughed and thought, *Good for you, kid!*

REBECCA COLLIS

January 1980

It took us a whole week to prepare for Ami's *brit milah*—his *bris*—getting the *mohel*, adding our own readings to the traditional ceremony, buying and cooking the food. As I put Ami to bed the night before the *brit*, I looked at our week-old son, and the fact that the next day we were going to inflict a wound on him overcame me. I suddenly desperately wanted to cancel the *brit*.

The day dawned bright and warm, and friends and family began to arrive very early in the morning. Ami squirmed and looked so very small and helpless in his white gown as he was cradled and passed along a chain of selected friends and relatives until he was placed on the little table on which the circumcision was to take place. All time and all space condensed in the few minutes it took the *mohel* to perform the most primitive of initiation rites. The room was filled to overflowing with joyous tension as everyone strained to see or to avoid seeing the circumcision. After the *mohel* had finished, I announced our son's names as Amnon Sar and explained whom he had been named for. Suddenly, I found myself choked with tears as I realized that my son had just been joined in a covenant that united him with every generation of Jewish males that had ever existed. I knew that the *brit milah* had forged a powerful bond between him and me.

ROBERT L. BLUMENTHAL

Planning the Ceremony

For a boy, the *mohel* usually takes care of the entire ceremony, but you may want to consider doing some additional things that will personalize the event. For example, you might want to involve the mother as well as the father in making the *brit milah* blessings. For either a boy or a girl, you'll probably want to involve relatives and friends by assigning special readings, talking about the significance of your child's name, reading a relevant psalm or poem, including a favorite song, or asking invited guests to bless the child after the *birkat hamazon* (grace after the meal). If a *mohel* is involved, be sure to clear such additions with him in advance. He might not be as flexible as you would like. Also, be careful not to go overboard in making additions, especially around the time of the actual circumcision. Many people are tense then, and adding too much may only prolong the tension. (See also Chapter Twelve.)

If you have other children

Spend time talking with them about the ceremony and ritual you will be following. Depending on the age and personality of your other child(ren), you may or may not want them to be there for a *brit milah* ceremony. Similarly, you may or may not want them to have a special role in the ceremony (carrying the wine glass, reciting a poem/blessing, singing a song, etc.). Talk with your physician and other friends to get advice on how best to handle such situations. Finally, use your own instincts to make a decision about your own child; ultimately, no one has better access to information about your child than you do.

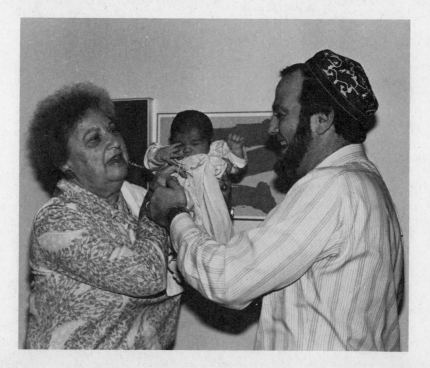

SHIR L'CHANAN

After months at anchor,
submerged in half-light and muted sounds,
after months alone with your secrets,
you opened your mother's womb
and burst into a room
of bright lights and stark silence.

Torn from your mooring,
with your first cry
you became one with all life.
Today you are joined by cutting
to a people
who would repair
the universe

Chanan,
will you now
take up our task
of salvaging the secrets
of rahum v'hanun
lost in the passage
from womb to world?

SUE ELLIS
(for Chanan Shalom Savran),
September 15, 1980

CHAPTER NINE

INTRODUCING YOUR CHILD TO YOUR JEWISH LIFE

Parents of yet unborn children generally sound sure about how they will raise their children. They know what they would or would not permit. ("I would never let *my* child whine during *kiddush* the way *they* did last night.") Prospective parents also sound more self-conscious about modes of ritual observance and what they would do "for the child" than most parents who are involved with real, live, breathing, kicking, squirming children. ("I have not put on a *tefillin* in years, but maybe if we have a son, I should. Oh, my God, what if it's a girl? What should I do about a *kippah* (skullcap) if it is a girl?" or, "I hate the commercialism of Hanukah; it's really such a minor holiday, but with children around maybe I should make a big deal of it; what do you think?")

Removed from the real-life situation of interacting with a young child, this kind of questioning and self-consciousness about your own modes of Jewish observance are good ways for prospective parents to clarify and share your own thinking and values. Such questioning, though, does not take some things into consideration. While participating in these theoretical conversations, we lose awareness that our behavior with a spouse is different from our behavior when there are three people present. For example, even though your commitment, let's say, to reciting the grace after meals remains constant, your manner or style of saying those blessings for food might vary depending on whether you had eaten alone, with a spouse, or with a few or many friends. The same is true as children join parents in any Jewish observance. Another neglected consideration is the child's level of development. Clearly, whatever a child learns from participation in a ritual moment must be appropriate to his or her age. A three-year-old does not understand the concepts that underlie the Shema prayer, but may learn to recite the words of the Shema at bedtime. A five-year-old may neatly chant *mah nishtanah* (the four questions) at the Passover Seder with no comprehension while a four-year-old cousin unconsciously knows what it means when he grabs a piece of matzah and asks, "Hey, why are we eating matzah tonight?" (In fact, a four-year-old may understand the question much better than the proud but complicated answer his parent is trying to formulate about how "we" were slaves in Egypt.)

Noam: It's not only the right but the *duty* of a parent to impose his Judaism on his child. Judaism starts in the home and nowhere else. If a child is not given a basic exposure to Jewish ideals and ritual at home, there is nowhere else he can effectively pick it up. If he does learn about Judaism somewhere else, the home must reinforce his learning with fundamental and practical applications of what he has learned.

Stuart: Although my parents sent me to a Jewish school, none of what I learned was ever acted out in the house. When I came home, they might ask me what I did and what songs I learned, but very rarely did they question me further or ask me to teach them the Passover song or ask to hear the Hanukah story. As a result, I don't remember any Jewish songs, can barely recall any Jewish tales, and my Hebrew is in very bad shape. If I were a parent, I would try not to let my children forget what they learned. For me, it is too late, as a lot of my Jewish knowledge is gone.

Missy: Parents shouldn't impose Judaism on their kid but they should try to practice it—kind of advertise it—with the kid. The kid should see that they're not imposing it just to be a bother.

A child learns, acquires skills, and evolves his or her Jewish self-understanding in the context of ritual moments. The importance to the child of an adult sharing a moment of strange and magical words cannot be overestimated. Yes, we serve as role models; and yes, as parents we may bring to such moments self-conscious agendas of what we want our children to learn. Yet as we enter into the moment we are affected by other priorities; we, like our children and anyone else who is present, become participants in a sacramental act. We recite the blessing and hope that we are thereby fulfilling the *mitzvah*, the commandment. Our actions may speak more loudly to our children than our words (or melodies). Beyond the content or form of liturgical acts, as we participate with our children, we are exposing our children to our Jewish selves. Sometimes our feelings in such moments are contrary to the warm, smiling illustrations in Hebrew-school textbooks; sometimes our feelings are painful or ambivalent. Perhaps we try to censor, to avoid revealing the depth of our pain to our young child. Yet happy or sad, we value that exposure of our Jewish selves to our children and seek opportunities to share with children Jewishly. Will it matter if I sing *zemirot* (*Shabbat* table hymns) to my baby? Will it keep her within the fold? That question has no answer. I do not know that my songs will in any direct way enhance my daughter's Jewish identity. I do know that by sharing my songs I am exposing a part of myself to my child that goes beyond both the words of the songs and my inability to carry a tune.

That *learning* comes naturally is obvious, especially to anyone acquainted with a young child. That *teaching* or sharing may not come as naturally is also apparent. For most of us, there are Jewish experiences we can share effortlessly with our children. The sharing is irrelevant to where we come from Jewishly; it can cut across lines of our Jewish educational backgrounds. On the other hand, we all have areas that are problematic. The classic example of the person who finds such sharing problematic is the parent who came from an assimilated Jewish background, in college was challenged to think about his Jewish identity, and moved into an adult circumstance that led him to accept the notion that he and the family should try some mode of Jewish observance. This person who rightly perceives himself as unskilled Jewishly then sends his child to a synagogue-related nursery school. At the third *Shabbat* party of his child's nursery-school class, he resolves to try to orchestrate some kind of Friday-evening observance at home. Perhaps he says to himself that he should support and reinforce his child's learning. Perhaps he would say that he feels somewhat pushed by his child. Yet he is open to being pushed. He is a little like the mother with the child at the circus who admits that she loves circuses and is grateful that her child provides an excuse to attend.

Having resolved to try out some home *Shabbat* ritual, the problems for such a parent have just begun. Perhaps he has seen highly skilled communal leaders make *kiddush*, light candles, sing *Shabbat* table hymns. These leaders were so skillful as to be inaccessible role models. As Dan Finkelstein put it: "Sure my kids pushed me to consider where I was at Jewishly. But I was ready for it. The problem for me was that I didn't

know how to do anything, was afraid I'd make an ass of myself, and was too embarrassed to ask for help from the rabbi or cantor." Such parents are beset by a variety of difficulties. Some typical problems might vary from gaining the consent or participation of other family members to learning how to speak the appropriate words or sing the melodies or deal with feelings of embarrassment or awkwardness or unsureness of how his beliefs relate to what he is doing, or . . . The list goes on. Rather than being paralyzed, consider ways of overcoming the difficulties:

1. Learning—a basic way of becoming comfortable with a ritual is to become skilled in its performance. That means learning how to do it. And that can mean finding someone to help you. Where do you find such a teacher? Sometimes a friend or relative can show you how. Sometimes a professional, like the nursery-school teacher in the example above, is happy to help. A rabbi can be either a direct teacher or can act as a matchmaker by putting you in touch with someone who knows more.

2. Getting support—Jews enjoy celebrating together. What is more natural than inviting friends over for a meal? If that meal is a Friday-night *Shabbat* dinner, then friends who are joining you in the enterprise may prove helpful, especially if, like you, they are eager to learn and experiment with modes of experiencing *Shabbat*. Do exercise caution; you want to invite supportive friends, not people with whom you will be more uncomfortable. A book you may find helpful is *A Shabbat Haggadah* compiled by Michael Strassfeld and published by The American Jewish Committee, 1981. When you know more, you may want to invite another novice to your home so that he or she can learn from you. Now may be the time to accept (or even ask for) invitations to learn from others with a bit more experience than you.

3. Realizing the limits of your commitment—you are learning and exploring but not making lifetime commitments. Sometimes a great deal of anxiety can be alleviated simply by seeing yourself as someone in a clothing store trying something on for size. A shopper only tries on clothes he/she likes, but, on the other hand, if the clothing does not fit, the shopper either does not buy or has it altered. Taking the metaphor even further, have you ever debated whether to buy something on the basis of how costly or dramatic the alterations would be? The same approach can apply to trying on a ritual. Does it fit? Would it grow more comfortable with wear? Could simple alterations help? Perhaps the alterations required are too extensive to make it worthwhile.

4. Going slowly—neither Rome nor Jerusalem was built in a day. Although some find it inspirational to enter into, for example, an intensive *Shabbat* experience in the form of a retreat or a visit to a Hasidic family organized by Lubavitch, experimenting in your own home is different. Many people find it helpful to limit themselves at the beginning, taking a step at a time and not being overwhelmed by too much too soon.

We know of one family who began by having a traditional Friday-night meal together. They did nothing else together in a Jewish way except Friday night for about six months. They then decided to do *havdalah* (the ceremony that marks the end of *Shabbat*) together. As one of the children put it, "It felt a little weird to bring in the Sabbath together and to end the Sabbath together with nothing in between, but we weren't ready to go the whole way." Slowly, the family has expanded, modified, and reformulated their Jewish observance so that their Jewishness grew organically in their lives.

5. Finally, consider written and recorded resources that are available. A visit to a good synagogue library or Jewish book store may yield treasures of helpful material—from Jewish books and games to records and tapes of *Shabbat* songs.

All of these suggestions are addressed to you, the adult, for obvious reasons. Also, they assume that you will be able to make some contact with other Jews or with an existing Jewish community.

But what if your problems in sharing with your children have to do not with knowing too little but with knowing too much? What if, for example, you came from an intensely traditionalist home and attended *yeshivot* and have now moved away from that life-style? We have many friends who, as adults, now describe their *yeshivah* training as psycholo-

Heidi: I was never forced into my religion. It was there for me, and I took it. I love it. Jewish parents who feel strongly enough about their Judaism to try to pass it on to their children are, in some way, very serious about their religion. The ways they try to reach us are very important because we are not always discriminating enough to distinguish between the way they ask and the thing they ask. That is, if your parent wants to stress the importance of a clean room, he or she would do best to set an example by keeping his or her own room neat and then by helping you learn how to keep your own room neat until you knew how to do it yourself and wanted to because you saw how nice your parent's room was and liked your room so much when it was clean. If your parent yelled at you once a week to keep your room clean and vacuumed her own but never cleaned off the desk, you would be upset that she yelled at you, and you would probably forget how gross you'd thought her desk looked and refuse to clean your room because she had yelled at you.

gically damaging and who say that for their own emotional health they have moved into other areas of intellectual and personal development. University degree and professional training in hand, such people have families and life-styles independent of their own parents; and they have overcome adolescent anger or agnosticism and want, in some non-Orthodox fashion, to be involved within the Jewish community, sharing experiences with their children. In other words, as a friend wrote, "I don't want to throw the baby out with the bathwater, and as I grow older, I realize that there are aspects of *Yiddishkeit* I love. It's just that I can't go home again." If you find yourself identifying with our friend, you probably have considered:

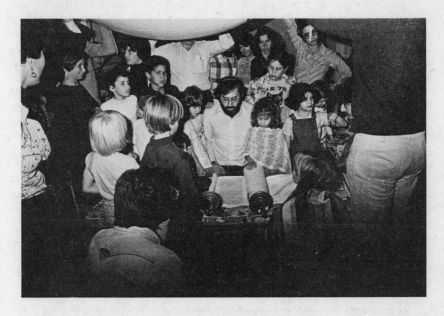

1. The necessity of dealing with your own anger. This process can, and for many does, take a lifetime. (Are you rejecting *davening* [praying] or the person who made you *daven*?)
2. Accepting as valid other varieties of being Jewish. A problem many face is that the Orthodox community has taught them that the only way to be Jewish is to be Orthodox. Such people, who can no longer be *frum* (religious), still have problems accepting the validity of heterodox and non-*halakhic* modes of expression. ("I won't go to my parents' *shul*, but neither can I accept what happens down the street in non-Orthodox synagogues.") Obviously, this is an attitude that must be overcome in order to be free to move in other directions.
3. The underlying difficulty of dealing with *halakhah* (Jewish law). What happens if you no longer view Jewish law as binding? Can you see the *mitzvot*, the commandments of Jewish law, as voluntary rather than compulsory? You react positively to the notion that

now you can perform a ritual act because you want to rather than because you are compelled to. While embracing such freedom of choice in observance ("After all, isn't it better that I make *kiddush* because I really want to?"), you will probably also feel obliged to establish some pattern of observance on which your child can rely. A child's need for consistency juxtaposed with a voluntary attitude toward *mitzvot* can produce serious questions. Dialogue with Jews who come from more liberal communities than the one you were raised in may prove helpful; they have more experience than you with these issues.

4. What price might you have to pay for consistency and perhaps for peace between generations? Will you have to be more consistent than you might otherwise choose for your children's peace of mind? How will you negotiate with your more traditional parents? Often these issues get symbolized by or expressed in food. What happens when your son or daughter tells one of your parents about a gastronomic adventure in a *treif* (nonkosher) restaurant? These are painful issues. As in the case of those struggling to learn Jewish ritual, help sometimes comes best from supportive friends, although you must beware of friends who support negative and neurotic attitudes rather than challenging you in your struggles not to throw out the baby with the bathwater.

Another pitfall is "child-centered Judaism"—infantilizing and trivializing a ritual even for the children. A good example is the sight of adult Jews prancing about on Simkhat Torah with flags and apples for the children, who, like their parents, are bored and out of touch with any deeper meaning of the holiday. The futility of the enterprise is

---

Rona: I feel a parent has the right to impose his belief on his child as long as he is consistent. As a child, I felt that my parents restricted me more than themselves. They didn't let me go out on Friday nights, but they could if they felt it was important. I was also angry and resentful because I couldn't understand why Friday night was made so important (as being Shabbos) and Saturday I could do anything. One way for parents to impress upon their children the importance of their religion is by, so to speak, keeping their rooms clean all the time. That is, the more positive religious, educational, and social Jewish experiences a kid has, the more likely he is to begin to consider Judaism a positive and important part of life.

While bedtime rituals vary from dramatic renditions of *Goodnight Moon* to Yiddish lullabies, generations of Jewish parents have included saying *Shema:* Hear, O Israel: The Lord is Our God, the Lord is One. *"Baruch Shem k'vod malchuto l'olam va'ed."*

Zalman Schachter has suggested another approach to the *Shema*. Instead of reciting "Hear, O Israel," try saying "Listen _____" The name to fill in might be your own, your child's, your parent's or spouse's—anyone to whom you would like to direct the words. So it might go, "Listen, Jack, the Lord is Our God; the Lord is One!"

obvious. You want to involve children in what interests you; if your only motive is that it's for the sake of the children, then is it worthwhile?

What about situations in which you want to teach your children very specific skills? Children profit from the involvement expressed by parents who help with Jewish school homework, and the parents learn at the same time. A child who can show off what he or she learned by delivering a *"d'var* Torah" (a teaching) at a meal is receiving various kinds of reinforcement and positive feedback. On the other hand, there are dangers. Sometimes a teacher who is an outsider to the family can be less threatening and more effective in teaching a skill than a parent, no matter how skillful and knowledgeable that parent may be. We also hope our children will be exposed to a wide range of positive Jewish role models and people who may vary their approaches to texts and skills. In the end, we must tread lightly, cautiously. What could be more touching than to teach your child how to put on a *tefillin?* What could be more frustrating than listening to the child scream that he or she does not want to finish the passage you are trying to drill?

In the end, our struggle as Jewish parents is for completeness or wholeness. And out of that wholeness we seek to share, to share ritual moments, stories, songs, intellectual insights, and feelings that defy articulation. Sometimes we are privileged to share the beautiful and the unproblematic. Sometimes we can only convey our ambivalences and our constraints. Often what we are sharing is only mundane. We cannot compartmentalize or subdivide ourselves. We cannot label one part of ourselves as Jewish and another as not. As we live with our children, we give of ourselves to them. We reaffirm our authenticity as we share our Jewish lives. As the Psalmist said, "Generation to generation praises Your deeds" (Ps. 145).

CHAPTER TEN

DEVELOPING JEWISH RITUALS FOR YOUR FAMILY

Shoshana Silberman

Wedding ceremonies begin marriages: brit *and naming rituals begin families. Certainly* brit *and naming ceremonies not only initiate our children into the covenant of the Jewish People, they also represent our own initiation into parenthood. What comes next? Shoshana Silberman, a Jewish educator and parent of three children, talks about developing Jewish rituals for our own families.*

If you were asked to list your three most memorable Jewish experiences, what would you list? It would not surprise me if one or more were family experiences. Although these experiences may have occurred in the past, the warmth and pleasure associated with them can easily be recalled.

My fondest Jewish memories are of the Passover *sedarim* at my maternal grandmother's house. So many relatives were crowded into one tiny room! As we chanted the Haggadah, the heavenly aroma of the festive meal permeated the small space. My cousins and I loved to sing the holiday songs, especially those with many verses. We plotted and planned our strategy for hiding the *afikomen* and for bargaining for our reward upon its return. The highlight for all of us was the moment my grandmother began to sing Yiddish songs from the "old country." She would tell us about life in Russia under the czar and why she and her husband came to America. The meaning of Passover, with its message of freedom, was dramatically brought home to us.

In talking with adults who have had few or no positive Jewish family experiences but who were excited by attending a Jewish camp, being involved with a Jewish youth movement, or going on a trip to Israel, I've often heard their regrets about not having had a richer Jewish home life. They sense that they have missed something special, something that they do not want to deny their own children.

For me, being a Jewish parent means facing the responsibility and the exciting challenge of creating Jewish family experiences. Celebrating Jewish holidays and life-cycle events has woven us together. Family

rituals have given us a focus for communicating issues, ideas, and feel-ings, helping us understand ourselves and our needs.

Since my children have fewer relatives than I or my husband did, and all of them live far away, long ago we sought out other families to celebrate with us and create a sense of "community." We formed a *havurah* (fellowship or community) with other families and came together, with our children, in our celebrations. In this informal and close-knit community, we were able to affirm Jewish traditions as well as create new modes of expression without being hindered by ideological labels.

Although many of the experiences we've shared as a *havurah* have been child centered, others have not. Certainly, if children see and hear their parents "doing Jewish," they will both sense its significance and consider exploring it seriously with a model for doing so. Planning only child-centered activities makes Judaism seem childish. It is our goal to present Judaism as a way of life, with room for the growth and develop-ment of every person.

At times, traditional observances have met our needs. At other times, we've wanted to enrich Jewish observances or rituals to make them more personalized. The ideas in this chapter are ways our family has tried to make our Jewish family life meaningful to us. Included also are suggestions from other families. (In this short space, I cannot explain the meaning of Jewish holidays or life-cycle events but will include some resources at the end of the chapter.)

What follows is our smorgasbord of ideas. Important to remember, however, is that every family has its own dynamic. There are things you will or will not be comfortable doing with your family. There are things

ON LEARNING TO TIE YOUR OWN SHOELACES:
A CREATIVE RITUAL

How can a four-year-old celebrate learning to tie her own shoelaces (making bows *and* double knots)! After the child has gained some confidence in making bows but as soon after the first gleeful success as possible, the child's parents should request hagbah and gleelah in *shul*. In other words, *Shabbat* morning the parents should receive the honor of raising up the Torah scroll, dressing it in its mantle, and holding it. Part of the job of hagbah and gleelah is wrapping a belt-ribbon around the Torah and tying it in a bow before dressing the Torah in its mantle. The child should go forward with the parents for the honor and should get to tie the bow! Hannah Leah adds, "If the kid is scared to go up in front of all those people in *shul*, she shouldn't have to do it, even if it is a nice idea, Uncle Zalman."

ZALMAN SCHACHTER and
HANNAH LEAH GREEN

you'd be interested in trying but are afraid your child(ren) will balk. Leave them. Start as naturally as you can with whatever seems simplest to you and will blend most harmoniously with your family's dynamic. This is not to say that you shouldn't risk in this venture. You are trying to add new dimensions to established life patterns. That's a difficult, risk-taking, sometimes scary enterprise. Family members become accustomed to relating to each other in certain established patterns, and whatever jeopardizes those patterns can be threatening if only because you are, ultimately, asking those same family members to reach beyond what they already know, are sure and confident about. Your ten-year-old *knows* that if she asks to stay up until ten o'clock on a school night, you will say no. She may ask, but there's a security in the knowledge of how you will respond. Suddenly, on Friday night, at nine-thirty, you're not only willing to let her stay up, you'd like to take a walk and have a talk with her. The rules of the game have changed, and she's not sure she's pleased about it. So go slowly.

The only other rider worth mentioning here is a serious one. You are not trying to create the Jewish *Good Housekeeping* family. You may think to yourself, "Gee, this is a wonderful family picture, all of us sitting around the Shabbos table in our best clothes with our gleaming china and silver, having a real *family* celebration." Beneath the veneer, however, one of your children may be beginning to run a temperature, another may be deeply resentful of having to spend time with his family when his best friend is having a party that night, and a third may be in her own dream world, totally out of touch with whatever else is happening. The point is, you are not creating someone else's image of the beautiful Jewish family. You are trying to recognize what your family is and what kinds of forces operate within it. Build on the foundation you have, striving for honest celebration rather than superficial illusions.

What follows, then, is a sharing of some of our family's sacred moments together.

FAMILY CONSCIOUSNESS

To give us an idea of our immediate Jewish roots, we long ago made a family tree. Accompanying it, we hung a "gallery" of framed photographs of our nuclear family, grandparents, great-grandparents, and even great-great-grandparents. We've not only learned about who these people were, we've also come to understand why they and others of that generation came to America. We have a booklet of treasured family stories and favorite family recipes. We've put together a photo album of our extended family that we enjoy reviewing together.

Shabbat, by the way, is a wonderful time to look at family albums. Besides old family pictures, we enjoy looking at pictures of our own nuclear family—a wonderful way to recall Jewish experiences that we've shared. The children are always delighted to see pictures of themselves lighting a *menorah*, dressing up in Purim costumes, baking *hallah*, or building a *sukkah*. For us, pictures lead to "remember when" reminiscences.

SHABBAT

Our most important family time is Shabbat. Both my husband and I have hectic schedules, and we welcome this unpressured time to relax and enjoy each other and our three children. Once every month or so, we spend a Sunday afternoon baking and freezing *hallah*. The children especially like braiding the loaves and sprinkling sesame or poppy seeds on top, and everyone agrees that ours is better than the store-bought version.

Even very young children appreciate a beautifully set table. Long ago, my daughter said to me, "You must think Shabbat is special to go to all this trouble, and you must think we're special to let us use the best dishes and all our other good things." We do try to communicate that Shabbat is worthy of our best efforts.

One family ritual we've created that is a highlight of our Friday-night meal is our blessing of the children. Each week, my husband and I give the children a different blessing. Often, it is based on that week's Torah portion. For example, on the appropriate week, we might say, "May you be like our father Abraham, who was kind and gracious to people."

Another week's blessing might be "May you be like Miriam the Prophet who could express herself in dance and write songs to God." Sometimes we focus on a prophet in the *haftarah* of the week, a Jewish personality in the news, or a Jewish poet or artist who has touched us. Often, our blessings are prepared with remarks to a child about how his or her behavior reminded us of the person in the blessing. For example, we might say something like, "You try hard to solve conflicts without violence. Therefore, we hope you'll always be like Moshe, who first tried to work things out with Pharaoh." Or, "You write so beautifully. May you be able to write a poem like Hannah did when she thanked God for giving her a child." Often, during the meal, we continue to discuss the blessing and our reasons for choosing it.

Although it is not our custom, it has been suggested that parents may wish to bless their children by presenting them with a Shabbat gift (something sweet or artistic or even a kiss), since one of the connotations of *berakha* (blessing) is gift. Howard Bogot suggests that one could also write the blessing before Shabbat; then after it is read, the blessing could be placed in a child's private "treasure box" of blessings for later reading and rereading.

Every Shabbat, a different person in our family is responsible for planning a "Shabbat event." Perhaps someone will tell a favorite Shabbat story or teach a new melody for a Shabbat song. Maybe there's a new game someone bought or made. Occasionally, there's a mini-play or Jewish charades. Once we even had a magic show. There are times when someone brings up a serious subject for discussion. This custom has given the children a sense of ownership about our Shabbat experience. They like having input and feel validated when we follow through with their suggested events.

Of course, family activities will vary according to the ages of the children (and maybe even the ages of the parents!). When our two older children were small, we would motivate them to learn *zemirot* (Shabbat songs) by letting them play rhythm instruments at the table and by dancing with them on our shoulders. Now we don't need the triangles and cymbals anymore for motivation. The two older children are *"zemirot mavens"* and the little one has learned from them. What we did learn is that Shabbat experiences must be geared to children's age levels and needs.

For those who ride on Shabbat, consider taking trips that can be tied to Jewish content on Saturday afternoons. For example, go to the zoo

and look for animals mentioned in the Bible. Discover paintings by Jewish artists at a museum. Some libraries have a Judaic section where you can take out books of Jewish interest.

For those who do not ride on Shabbat, I heartily recommend a family walk. Let the children choose the destination. If your children are like our children, they probably will choose to end the walk at another family's house where both families can get together to share Shabbat time.

We have found that enjoying Shabbat with friends enriches our Shabbat. We often invite other families to join us. We also invite both younger and older adults (single and married) to be our guests. Our children have learned to relate to adults and have also learned that everyone does not have the same life-style.

If your family has a wonderful Shabbat, consider sharing it with a family that does not. No books or lectures can substitute for the experience. You just might motivate someone else to make Shabbat. When our *havurah* first started, few families really knew how to make Shabbat for themselves. By sharing, every family now not only knows the basic rituals but is also committed to making Shabbat in their own homes.

HOLIDAYS

The Jewish year is punctuated by holidays, each with a different theme. They offer families a way of focusing on these themes and making them personally relevant.

It is the custom in our neighborhood for all the *havurot* to gather together on the second day of Rosh Hashanah to walk to a nearby stream for *tashlikh*. We fill our pockets with pieces of bread that symbolize our sins and later toss them into the water. Each year our family spends time discussing what traits we'd like to discard and what changes in ourselves we'd like to make. These are serious, sometimes painful discussions that needn't always be group parties. Family members can seek each other out for private talks about their relationships, weaknesses, and strengths.

We love receiving New Year's cards! They are displayed in our living room and then saved to be used as *sukkah* decorations. We also enjoy making our own New Year's cards. Each person contributes to the design, which we transfer to a ditto master. This is an inexpensive but lovely way to send greetings to families and friends.

There's no more exciting family activity than building a *sukkah*. At first, our *havurah* had one communal *sukkah*, but now many families build their own. Those who, for whatever reason, cannot build one often join families who do. Their help in building and decorating the *sukkah* is always welcome and creates a communal activity for what would otherwise be a long, hard task. Families often take *sukkah* walks, visiting the different *sukkot* and admiring the ingenuity of the creators. Many of the children in the local religious school make miniature *sukkot*, and those, too, are proudly displayed.

Our family follows the traditional custom of inviting "selected ancestors" to our *sukkah*. Every year each family member chooses an ancestor to invite and makes a sign to welcome that person. We then discuss the choices. This has been an interesting learning experience for all of us. I can recall the time I "invited" Mira Weinstein, a teacher of children in the Warsaw ghetto. Everyone was deeply moved by her story. It sparked an interest in learning more about the Holocaust, which we later pursued together as a family.

Around *sukkot*, several friends usually go apple or berry picking in the country. We've sampled the results: fresh apples or applesauce and delicious jams or jellies that we serve for our *sukkot* meals. We also usually set aside a day to visit a local arboretum where the fall colors are breathtakingly beautiful.

We feel very fortunate that our synagogue has a tumultuous Simhat

Torah celebration. People dance in winding circles around the Torahs. It is an occasion for great rejoicing, especially because our synagogue has several small Torahs for the children to take turns carrying. The last few years, I have come while the celebration is in progress. (I first go to the synagogue where I am the educational director.) When my children greet me, they proclaim excitedly, "I got a turn! I carried a Torah!" I strongly urge all synagogues to obtain small Torahs; they have been a meaningful and worthwhile investment for us.

I also urge parents to take their children to a Simhat Torah rally for Soviet Jews. Besides showing our support for their human rights, it creates a feeling of *K'lal Yisrael*, teaching us that we, as a people, are responsible for one another. If your community does not have such a rally, perhaps you can spearhead the organization of one.

Hanukah, with its candle lighting, gift giving, *dreidel* playing, and latke making, is a happy time for Jewish children. If you haven't tried making the Israeli Hanukah treat *sufganiot* (doughnuts), you're missing something delicious. We have a *menorah* for every person in our family, which not only avoids arguments about who will light the *menorah* but adds a touch of splendor to our celebration.

Hanukah provides a wonderful opportunity to give Jewish gifts. There's a large variety of items from which to choose: Jewish books or records, posters, games, a new *kippah* or *mezuzah* for a child's room. These items can be found in synagogue gift shops or most Hebrew book stores. Hanukah cookie cutters and decorations are also sold there. Other gifts and decorations can be homemade. (See Chapter Twenty-five.) These are often less expensive and far more fun.

On Tu b'Shevat, it is traditional to plant trees in Israel or give money to the Jewish National Fund for planting trees there. Trees can be planted in honor of a special person or in memory of someone who died. The selection of the person to honor or remember has been an important family decision for us. We lovingly share stories of deceased relatives (often looking at their pictures in our "gallery" or in our album). We talk of family and friends who are dear to us and why we cherish our relationships with them. Last year we chose a beloved aunt to honor. The children wrote an inscription on her tree certificate. Her emotion-filled thank-you letter taught the children the reward of doing a *mitzvah*. Recently the ancient Sephardic custom of holding a Tu b'Shevat Seder has been revived. Although the ones I've seen are not very suitable for home use (but rather for a school setting or a group of adults), they can easily be adapted for a family Tu b'Shevat experience. You can obtain a Tu b'Shevat Seder from the following sources:

> *Tu Bishevat Haggadah*, prepared by Sy Hefter, Jewish Community Center, 60 S. Boulevard Street, Wilkes-Barre, PA
> *A Seder for Tu B-shvat*, Neot Kedumim Youth and Education Dept. of the J.N.F., 501 Fifth Avenue, New York, NY 10017

Both have similar themes but use different texts.

There are several planting activities that families can do at home for

Tu b'Shevat: planting bulbs, planting peas or beans, or making a terrarium. It's also a nice time to discuss plans for a summer garden. This is the time of year to remember the birds. Since it is hard for them to find food in the winter, it's helpful to make a bird feeder.

On Purim, families in our *havurah* gather in our kitchen (it's very large) for a Purim bake-in. Even the youngest children participate. We compare recipes and triangle-making tips. As the *hamantaschen* are baking, we sing Purim songs. There's plenty of *hamantaschen* to nosh as well as to take home.

Each year our family also makes a large quantity of *hamantaschen*, which we package with candy or fruit and personal Purim greetings and tie with gaily colored ribbon. The children "map out" our delivery route. As we drive about the neighborhood, they pop out at the appropriate stop and deliver the *shalah manot* with a "Happy Purim" greeting. Purim is also a time to remember the poor. Our family has been inspired by the work of a local Jewish organization called Mazon that distributes funds to organizations that provide food for the needy. The last few years we've sent them our Purim *tzedakah* (charity). You might organize such an effort in your own town.

Making *groggers* (noisemakers), wearing costumes (the adults in our family dress up for Purim, too), reading the Megillah accompanied by the whirl of the *groggers,* makes Purim a splendid time for children and the young at heart. It is a time to affirm Jewish survival and our need to live freely as Jews.

Our observance of Pesah is very traditional. To make the holiday important to the children, we involve them in the preparations. This includes the cleaning of their own rooms, helping to kasher the kitchen, polishing silverware, and shopping. (Shopping, by the way, is a wonderful way to learn about what's kosher or not kosher for Passover.) It's also important to get their input in planning a Seder. Be sure to include melodies with which they are familiar. They will be honored if you use their handmade Seder plate or matzah cover at the Seder. Junior cooks can be called on to make *charoset,* matzah balls, or chicken soup. A visit to a matzah factory to see how matzah is made can also be a fascinating experience.

Before bedikat chametz (the final search for leaven, traditionally done with a feather and spoon), let the children have a popcorn party, followed by a thorough sweep-up. It's a fun way to dramatize the last farewell to *chametz.*

Before Pesah begins, we pack our *chametz* (leaven) in a carton and bring it to a central place. Mazon collects these packages in our neighborhood and distributes them to non-Jews in need of food. This custom has become so much a part of the holiday now that I can't imagine Pesah without it.

While attending an inter-*havurah* retreat, we learned of another *tzedakah* project suggested by Rob Agus that has since become an important family ritual for us and many other families in our community. From the second night of Pesah until Shavuot (fifty days), Jews in ancient times counted the *omer* by setting aside a measure of wheat. Today, we count verbally, for example, "Tonight is the fifth day of counting the *omer.*" Rob suggested that we add the counting of coins for *tzedakah* money as well.

Our family made an "*omer* box," and we put in a coin for *tzedakah* each night. Since the original *omer* was a food substance, it is appropriate to

When Rabbi Noah, the son of Rabbi Mordechai, assumed the succession after his father had died, his disciples noticed that there were a number of ways in which he conducted himself differently from his father. They asked him about this, and he replied, "I do just as my father did. He did not imitate. And I do not imitate."

donate the money to an organization that distributes funds for food distribution to the poor or elderly. Many communities have a "Meals on Wheels" program for the elderly and would welcome your contribution. Even better would be your volunteering to make a few "deliveries" as a family.

Counting the *omer* and seeing the coins mount up daily heightens the excitement about the approach of Shavuot. Our family looks forward to Shavuot, especially because we join others in our community for a retreat in the country. Since Shavuot was originally an agricultural festival, it is most appropriate to focus on the beauty of the natural world and the bounties of the earth.

Of course, Shavuot is also the time traditionally celebrated as the season of our receiving the Torah. This is an appropriate time for parents and children to study a section of the Torah together. The selected text could be written on a little scroll. Illustrations, poetry, or creative *midrashim* (interpretations) can also be included. These can be collected over the years and reread on Shavuot.

For those who cannot organize a family retreat, consider returning to the spot you visited on *sukkot* (e.g., the arboretum). Revisiting in early summer will be a delightful contrast.

Since Shavuot teaches that we have a covenantal relationship with God, we also can explore the making of family covenants. The family is more than the sum of its parts; it is a system that needs maintenance to thrive and flourish. Shavuot calls for our commitment to a Jewish way of life. If we believe that families are an important part of a Jewish lifestyle, then we must be committed to strengthening and nourishing them. Shavuot night is a traditional time to study Torah. Consider reading children a favorite Jewish story. Topped with a blintz dinner, what could be a nicer evening?

Between Pesah and Shavuot is Lag B'Omer. There is an old custom of coloring eggs for Lag B'Omer (shades of Easter; but who's borrowing customs from whom here?). This is based on the legend of Rabbi Shimon Bar Yochai, who, with his son, lived in a cave for eleven years to hide from the Roman soldiers enforcing laws against the study of Torah. Once a year (on Lag B'Omer) his students visited him. To avoid suspicion, they dressed as hunters. When Bar Yochai was finally able to leave the cave, a splendid rainbow appeared as a sign.

Coloring eggs will invite many questions from curious children and provide a pleasant time to share legends of Shimon Bar Yochai as well as the famous Rabbi Akiba. These eggs can be included in the picnic basket for a Lag B'Omer outing. Invite other families to join you and enjoy a day of family sports.

Tisha B'Av, the day on which we remember the destruction of the Temple, is not an easy time in which to involve children. It helps to have them think of things or people they have lost so that they can get in touch with their own sadness. Their witnessing our sadness can also help them learn that adults, too, have a wide range of emotions and that we create rituals to help us express and deal with our feelings. Perhaps we can share with them those things in our lives that make us sad as

well as listening to what makes them sad. This can be strengthening and supportive for all involved.

In modern times, two special days have been added to the Jewish calendar: Yom haAtzmaut (Israel Independence Day) and Yom ha-Shoah (the day of remembering the Holocaust). There are usually many community-wide events to commemorate these times. Certainly, they offer much content for family discussions. We don't have any family rituals to share but hope that those who do will be kind enough to share them with us. My fantasy family ritual is to take the family to Israel each Yom haAtzmaut as a pilgrimage.

CALENDAR

Of course, if there's no Jewish holiday to celebrate, create one! Rosh Hodesh (the beginning of a Jewish month) can be a wonderful family time. Have the children make their own Jewish calendar. Include every Rosh Hodesh. This is a good time to explain the difference between the solar and the lunar calendar. Prepare a special dinner or party. How about crescent-shaped cookies (suggested by Judith Saypol and Madeline Wikler in *My Own Jewish Calendar*)? A Jewish gift for the family can be selected or made. Each person should make a wish for every member of the family for the coming month.

This year, for the first time, we looked up our Hebrew birthdays and decided to celebrate them. Our older son, who is a birthday-cake-decorating *maven*, has volunteered to decorate the cakes with our Hebrew names. Although we are a family unit, it's nice to be individually recognized and validated. This is a wonderful opportunity to "bombard" the birthday person with positive attributes (e.g., you always make us laugh, you know so much about Jewish history, you are very kind and generous. Everyone needs attention and recognition.

For families with musical talent, compose a *niggun* (melody) in honor of the occasion. If you're not skillful in this area, let the birthday person choose a song that is designated his or her special song for that year.

Of course, *niggunim* can be written for other life-cycle events. There are several articles about creative life-cycle rituals in the *Jewish Catalog*, vol. II, that all who are interested should be sure to read.

There are endless ideas for enriching Jewish family life. My goal is to share some of our family rituals and customs with the hope that others will be motivated to share those they've created or learned. The result will be an assortment of ideas from which to choose. Of course each family will need to adopt rituals that meet its needs. Often one idea leads to another, which is what creativity is all about. May all our sharing enrich our Jewish family lives.

Blessed are you, God, Ruler of the world, who has given us the joy of living together as a family.

> When we acquire new clothing, what do we say? Traditionally, we may recite the blessing "Blessed are You, O Lord our God, Who clothes the naked." Alternately, we could recite my grandmother's benediction, "You should tear it to pieces in good health."

SELECTED RESOURCES AND REFERENCES

BELLOW, SAUL, ed. *Great Jewish Short Stories*. New York: Dell, 1963.

BELTH, NORTON, ed. *The World Over. Story Book*. New York: Bloch Publishing Company, 1952.

BRODIE, DEBORAH, ed. *Stories My Grandfather Should Have Told Me*. New York: Bonim Books, 1977.

GOLD, DORIS. *Stories for Jewish Juniors*. New York: Jonathan David, 1967.

GOODMAN, PHILIP, ed. *Holiday Anthology* (series). Philadelphia: Jewish Publication Society.

GREENBERG, IRVING. *Holiday Guides*. New York: National Jewish Resource Center, 250 W. 57th St. New York, NY 10019

HIRSH, MARILYN. *Could Anything Be Worse?* New York: Holiday House, 1974.
———*Where Is Yonkela?* New York: Crown Publishers, Inc., 1969.

HOWE, IRVING, AND GREENBERG, ELIEZER, eds. *A Treasury of Yiddish Poetry*. New York: Holt, Rinehart and Winston, 1969.

LEVIN, NORA. *The Holocaust—The Destruction of European Jewry 1933–1945*. New York: Schocken, 1975.

MILLGRAM, ABRAHAM E. *Sabbath—A Day of Delight.* Philadelphia: Jewish Publication Society, 1952.

NARKISS, BEZALAL, ed. *Picture History of Jewish Civilization.* New York: Harry N. Abrams, Inc., 1970.

RAPHAEL, CHAIM. *A Feast of History—Passover Through the Ages as a Key to Jewish Experience.* New York: Simon and Schuster, 1972.

ROSKIES, DIANE K., AND ROSKIES, DAVID G. *The Shtetl Book.* New York: Ktav, 1975.

SCHLOSS, EZEKIEL, AND EPSTEIN, MORRIS, eds. *The New World Over Story Book.* New York: Bloch Publishing Company, 1968.

SHULMAN, ABRAHAM. *The Old Country—The Lost World of East European Jews.* New York: Charles Scribner's Sons, 1974.

SIEGEL, RICHARD, STRASSFELD, MICHAEL, AND STRASSFELD, SHARON, eds. *The (First) Jewish Catalog.* Philadelphia: Jewish Publication Society, 1973.

SIEGEL, DANIEL, AND SUGARMAN, ALLAN. *And God Braided Eve's Hair.* New York: United Synagogue of America, 1976.

SOLIS-COHEN, EMILY, *Hanukah—The Feast of Lights.* Philadelphia: Jewish Publication Society, 1965.

STADTLER, BEA. *The Holocaust: A History of Courage and Resistance.* New York: Behrman House, 1973.

STRASSFELD, MICHAEL, AND STRASSFELD, SHARON, eds. *The Third Jewish Catalog.* Philadelphia: Jewish Publication Society, 1980.

STRASSFELD, SHARON, AND STRASSFELD, MICHAEL. *The Second Jewish Catalog.* Philadelphia: Jewish Publication Society, 1976.

SUHL, YURI. *An Album of the Jews in America.* New York: Franklin Watts, Inc., 1972.

ZBOROWSKI, MARK, AND HERZOG, ELIZABETH. *Life Is With People—The Culture of the Shtetl.* New York: Schocken Books, 1952.

ZIM, JACOB, ed. *My Shalom, My Peace.* Tel Aviv: Sabra Books, 1975.

Records for the Whole Family

(For information on where to obtain records, see Chapter Fifty)
"Ye Shall Rejoice On Your Festivals," sung by Shimon and Ilana, Rotona Records
"Chanukah Songs for Children," sung by Shimon and Ilana, Elite Records
"Chassidic Song Festival Records," Hed-Arzi
Records by Rabbi Shlomo Carlebach:
  Zimra Records, The Greater Recording Company, CBS (Emes Records)
  Zimrani Records
"Pirchei Sings," Tikva Records
"Israeli Folk Dancing Medley," Tikva Records
Records by Chabad, Nochoah Records
"Shepherd of the Highway," Jeff Summit, Mt. Moriah Music Co. (2412 Vera Ave., Cincinnati, OH 45237)
"Theodore Bikel Sings Jewish Folk Songs," Electra Records
Tov Lanu Lashir, UAHC Camp Songs
"Shabbat and Chassidic Songs"
Nira Rabinowitz, Shlomo Nitzan—Hed-Arzi
Ruach and Ruach Revival (their own production)
Hassidic and Shabbat Songs, Litraton Records
Songs of Israel (El Al Flight Entertainment Program), Hed-Arzi

CHAPTER ELEVEN

KASHRUT:
HOW DO WE EAT?

Sheila Weinberg

Jewish preoccupation with eating fits right in with contemporary obsessions about food. The wealth of our nation has gone hand in hand with a proliferating food economy, creating a dazzling array of synthetic foods and assembly-line eating establishments as well as gourmet sophistication and health awareness.

Food relates to every aspect of human interaction and every phase of the parent-child relationship. Food serves as pacifier and punishment, as reward and celebration. It is used to bestow love and to inflict guilt, to escape anxiety and to compensate for defeat.

Food theories and practices are almost cultic in our society—signs of prestige and snobbery. "You never heard of tofu?" "Don't you use a mushroom brush?" Every week publishing houses mass-produce diets to prevent disease, cultivate glamour, and bestow serenity.

Eating forms the basis of what pass for ritual acts in our secular world, from the first-date ice cream soda to the farewell banquet, from the martini lunch to the wedding dinner.

Food, too, is an ethnic badge. It is the lowest-common-denominator identity gimmick. Flip through sample brochures of Jewish organizations and notice how often the word *bagel* appears. If a Jewish group wants to have a program, be it Hadassah, Hillel, or the Jewish War Vets, the easiest way to fulfill the obligation to the tribe is by eating a knish. The same is true for Italians and Poles and other groups. (A cross-cultural experience is a pizza bagel.)

Family life continues to revolve around the kitchen (if not the television). Dinner time in most households is the ultimate together time. Parents often use acts related to eating as vehicles for teaching responsibility to children. How many relationships have faltered over taking out the garbage and doing the dishes?

One may even modestly propose that the refrigerator and McDonald's are to blame for the alarmingly accelerating divorce statistics. The refrigerator allowed for infrequent shopping, thereby cutting women off from the warmth and support of regular marketplace companionship and isolating them in supermarket suburbs. The frustration of this loneliness put undue pressure on husbands, wives, and children, contributing to the breakdown of marriages.

Meanwhile, fast foods have given mothers and fathers an escape hatch. Either parent can go it alone, just pop a TV dinner in the oven or buy a bucket-to-go. Traditional patterns of defined, mutually respected and accepted parental roles are no longer viable.

Even within stable family settings, moments of greatest joy and deepest sorrow are enhanced or relieved by communal feasts. How many about-to-wed couples spend more time deciding on the caterer and planning the menu than contemplating their future relationship? It is true that parental insecurity, sibling rivalry, and child-parent testing often revolve around issues of eating. The anxious mother asks herself: "Why do I have such a fussy eater (thin child, fat child)?" We hear the tears and screams because "he" or "she" got a larger portion. How often do we grit our teeth and ponder whether or not to serve that apple pie before they finish the carrots? Some of these parenting dilemmas are exacerbated by proliferating theories in popular journals and books offering varying but always so-simple solutions to deeper questions of respect and autonomy.

One can go on endlessly about the madness of contemporary life. In the midst of it all, however, we are trying to raise Jewish children and choosing to cope with an inherited set of rules or practical teachings regarding eating as a Jew, namely *kashrut*.

In the bewildering maze of modern times, who needs this archaic and bizarre system? Does it have something to offer that we can transmit with integrity to our children? We start with the assumption that only if we can personally value this system and make a wholehearted commitment to it can we hope to relay its educative spirituality to the next generation. Therefore, we ask ourselves what basic lesson we are learning from eating in accordance with the laws of *kashrut* and if the lesson is worthy and capable of being transmitted to our children.

Samuel Dresner, in a short, eminently readable, and eloquent discussion of *kashrut* (*The Jewish Dietary Laws* by Samuel Dresner and Seymour Siegel [New York: Burning Bush Press, 1959]), asks what is the primary concern of *kashrut*. He responds by quoting the source:

> In Leviticus (11:44–45), after we are told which animals, fowl, and fish are permitted and which forbidden, the reason for this long series of laws is at last given: "I am the Lord your God; sanctify yourselves therefore and be *holy*; for I am holy . . . For I am the Lord that brought you up out of the land of Egypt to be your God; ye shall therefore be *holy*." In Deuteronomy (14:21) we read: "Ye shall not eat anything that dieth of itself . . . for thou art a *holy* people unto the Lord thy God. Thou shalt not seethe a kid in its mother's milk." In Exodus (22:30): "And ye shall be *holy* men unto Me; therefore ye shall not eat any flesh that is torn of the beasts of the field; ye shall cast it to the dogs." Each of these passages deals with a different aspect of *kashrut* and yet in all of them the same word is repeated again and again: *Kadosh*, holy. This, then, is clearly the purpose and goal of the kosher laws: not *health* but *holiness* (p. 13).

How do we understand this meaning of *kedusha* (holiness)?

Modern science, communication, and transportation have heightened our awareness of the unity of our planet and the interdependence of its human and natural resources. A recent, very popular vegetarian nutrition book and cookbook is called *Diet for a Small Planet*. The authors ask us voluntarily to consider the shrinking world food supply to population ratio in developing our personal diets. We are being asked to make a commitment to a reality that transcends our own wishes and preferences, although not our own nutritional needs.

There is a theological assumption in *Diet for a Small Planet* that may provide a contemporary key to understanding the educational and spiritual function of the laws of *kashrut*.

Eating is a common denominator of all life. However, eating is only one side of the process of reciprocal maintenance that sustains the universe. We eat, and we feed. We are ultimately bound to replenish what we take. In today's idiom, "There is no such thing as a free lunch." This is a painfully learned lesson of maturity that we try to communicate to our children. We are part of an intricately woven and interconnected system of life levels on earth. As human beings, created in the image of God, we alone are endowed with the vision to glimpse this truth. We are capable of expanding our awareness to detect purpose and plan—the fragile balance of relationships. We can also choose to live with that awareness and manifest it in our most mundane, daily, habitual, yet universal behavior—eating. We can hallow our acts—try to live a holy life.

This awareness—of life as an ecosystem, of the human created in God's image, of our duties on earth—*underlies* the ancient idea of *kedusha* and the practice of *kashrut* as well as the pattern of blessings associated with different foods and meals in Jewish law. By voluntarily and lovingly accepting this practice, we are invoking the most profound and eternal mysteries. We are remembering ourselves and our God.

The ultimate Messianic ideal is a world of vegetarian humans and vegetarian animals. Life will be so sacred that in the verses of Isaiah (11:6–9):

> The wolf shall dwell with the lamb,
> The leopard lie down with the kid;
> The calf, the beast of prey, and the fatling together,
> With a little boy to lead them.
> The cow and the bear shall graze,
> Their young shall lie down together;
> And the lion, like the ox, shall eat straw.
> A babe shall play
> Over a viper's hole.
> And an infant pass his hand
> Over an adder's den.
> In all of my sacred Mount
> Nothing evil or vile shall be done;
> For the land shall be filled with devotion to the Lord
> As waters cover the sea.

Slaughter and bloodshed will vanish from the earth. Not one nation or one species will seek its self-preservation through the destruction of another creature. Redemption and the end of days are our goal and purpose but not our present reality. Therefore, we are enjoined to withdraw from the vegetarian ideal toward a highly regulated system of meat eating. The *kashrut* laws invoke the sacredness of life as they remind us of our connection with all nature. Blood is the symbol of life; hence, we must be certain to drain all blood from our meat. We are forbidden to eat predators or prey. We must separate the meat (of which we partake with hesitation) from the milk (the perfect food—source of life and nourishment). We must not slaughter a kid and mother goat on the same day. Our tradition haltingly concedes our need to eat the flesh of animals in order to derive the protein we need to survive and prosper.

We recall, too, that our forefathers were shepherds and cattle raisers. Perhaps vegetarianism is the fulfillment of *kashrut* in our day, when we know how to develop a nutritionally sound vegetarian diet and hunger stalks the planet. However, let us remember that we have not yet been redeemed. Perhaps a slice of meat, now and again, slaughtered and prepared according to those ancient laws, may guard us from this enticing delusion. Many Jewish laws remind us that we are living between creation and redemption. Ours is the task to complete the work of creation. It is a difficult one. We are often prone to imagine that by embracing an enticing new and simple ideology we are telling of the Messiah's coming.

There is a big price to be paid for failure to lead a life marked by acts of holiness as manifest in a diet that respects all life and cultivates planetary consciousness. The biblical warnings of disobedience in accepting the yoke of the commandments resemble the ecological disaster predictions outlined in *Diet for a Small Planet*. Deuteronomy (11:17–18) tells us the earth will not yield its fruit. Analysts of world food supply warn us that we will perish if we destroy the delicate balance of nature. This means the life layer coating planet earth. Perhaps not in our generation but in our children's or their children's. It will ultimately catch up with us.

We will have descended through our failure to see to an inability to see. We will become like the dumb brute or inert stone, static and immobile, if we allow narrow interests to dominate and fail to act in accord with transcendent purpose and commitment.

When we sit down to dinner, we hold hands and say a simple verse:

> Blessed are You, Lord Our God, King of the Universe, Who brings forth bread from the earth.

This verse is a prayer with several components:

> Blessed: *We expand beyond ourselves and open our senses to the blessings of the world around us.*
>
> You, Lord Our God: *We make personal contact; we establish a direct link with the ineffable.*
>
> King of the Universe, *Master of the World: We remember creation and the Creator. We acknowledge the existence of a source of power and purpose beyond ourselves. The world is a unity—indeed a small planet—beneath the Sovereign's reign.*
>
> Who brings forth bread from the earth: *The Infinite Unifier stands behind the production of this ordinary slice of bread. The bread comes from the earth, nourished by organic and inorganic generations of matter. It has passed through stages from seed to fruit. It has passed through many hands and lands. It has been planted, reaped, threshed, and ground into flour, transported, baked, packaged, distributed, purchased. It has been touched by men and women, some fat, some thin, some black, some white, some wise, and some foolish. Before we take a bite, we remember them all and recall our duty to return the gift, to return the energy about to be created, to build, to care and to serve.*

The priests are gone, as they were destined to depart from the Jewish scene. Why else were we called upon to be a "nation of priests"? It is our task to cultivate the awareness of God's presence in every act. The dinner table is our altar, the prayer our sacrifice. We wash our hands. We are silent. We sprinkle salt on the offering.

Can we really play the role of ancient priest at the dinner table? We may respond to the theory. The laws of *kashrut* do present us with a system for cultivating a holy approach to life. But each time we wait three or six hours after a meat meal to indulge our desire for an ice cream cone, can we recall that we are sanctifying life? Isn't it natural to apply these rules in a mechanical or compulsive manner? We are facing one of the central religious problems of form and content, fixed observance and intention, ritual and rote. There is no glib solution to this eternal dilemma.

If we have cultivated a reciprocal learning-teaching relationship with our children, we can hope that their questions about our ritual behavior will challenge us to a recollection of our intent. If we are growing, questing parents, we can search the tradition and ourselves for ever deeper responses to the meaning beyond the acts.

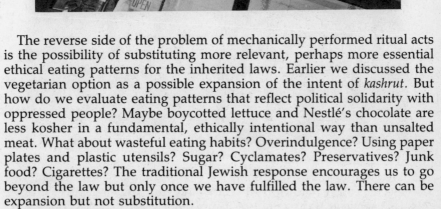

The reverse side of the problem of mechanically performed ritual acts is the possibility of substituting more relevant, perhaps more essential ethical eating patterns for the inherited laws. Earlier we discussed the vegetarian option as a possible expansion of the intent of *kashrut*. But how do we evaluate eating patterns that reflect political solidarity with oppressed people? Maybe boycotted lettuce and Nestlé's chocolate are less kosher in a fundamental, ethically intentional way than unsalted meat. What about wasteful eating habits? Overindulgence? Using paper plates and plastic utensils? Sugar? Cyclamates? Preservatives? Junk food? Cigarettes? The traditional Jewish response encourages us to go beyond the law but only once we have fulfilled the law. There can be expansion but not substitution.

We are not given any more precise reasons for the practice of *kashrut* than the cultivation of holiness. To touch and taste holiness, to bring

holiness into our lives, is a goal of all our days and deeds. We can search for the reasons, but we cannot grasp them fully. We cannot substitute practices that this year seem to coincide more clearly with the reasons we suppose underlie the law. We commit ourselves to *kashrut*, which is one very clearly articulated system. We may commit ourselves to a multitude of other noncontradictory eating practices. They may be inspired by principles we associate with various parts of Jewish tradition.

There is another crucial dimension that leads us as Jews to embrace this specific eating pattern. To become holy human beings, ever moving toward a sense of transcendence, is indeed a goal of *kashrut*. But we are Jews who as a collective entity have entered a covenantal relationship with God. We have accepted our membership in this collectivity as another transcendent reality that binds us to the tradition, community, and destiny of Israel. There are indeed other *sancta*, other methods of aspiring to holiness that belong to other human communities. As Jews, however, we have received the laws of *kashrut*. Do we casually ignore them or substitute for them without losing a dimension of ourselves, without severing a horizontal and vertical link with our family? The horizontal connection is in space. It is the bond that ties us to Jews in every corner of the globe. The vertical link goes back and forward in time. It returns us to our ancestors in Hellenistic Egypt, to Marranos in the Inquisition, to Jews of Yemen and the Polish *shtetl*, and forward to unborn generations. We can perceive this bond of blood as a leaden chain that confines us. Or we can accept it as a glorious golden strand that deepens our experience. It can remind us that we do not begin the world anew. It can release us from the future shock of our world of disposable ideas and products. It can make us see our existence as a product of words and deeds long ago cast on the ocean of history.

In considering *kashrut* and family life, we can touch briefly on several other constellations of dilemmas. One relates to consistency of practice, as manifested in the classic questions: Is it hypocritical to eat nonkosher food out when you have a kosher home? How do we relate to graded levels of observance? Is there a sliding scale of *kashrut*? Can we accept the basic laws without maintaining absolute strictness? In other words, how kosher is kosher? How kosher can we be or should we strive to be?

A second set of conflicts concerns sensitivity to others with varying values and practice. What happens when the grandparents aren't kosher and it's Passover or Thanksgiving? Within the same family, perhaps mother or father has a different standard or attitude toward *kashrut*. This may be a source of confusion for children, as one parent— even unconsciously—undermines the other.

A third serious issue revolves around determining a child's own responsibility for *kashrut*. What happens if, after a certain point, the child develops significantly more or less stringent *kashrut* requirements than the rest of the family?

We conclude our discussion with questions, although they are of a different dimension from the questions with which we began. We have seen that as Jews we have inherited a guide to developing an understanding of the reciprocal nature of existence. We are reminded that all life is nourished and nourishing, all reality is in the process of transformation, giving and receiving again and again. If we appropriate this guide, we must struggle with it, probe it, and even play with it. If we make this guide our own, we then possess a link to a unique culture and tradition.

The situational dilemmas remain, but we possess an abiding context from which to approach our education as parents and enhance our appreciation of life.

The pursuit of holiness is an aim of a lifetime. It is not an easy path, for it requires wakefulness, discipline, humility, flexibility, and patience. *Kashrut* is a gift that can help guide a Jew on this path.

SUGGESTIONS FOR FUTURE READING

The Concise Code of Jewish Law, compiled by Gerson Appel, vol. I (New York: Ktav, 1977), has two major sections, "Blessing and Grace After Meals" and "Kashrut: Holiness and Jewish Identity," summarizing rabbinical development in these areas. Another concise source for the fundamentals of *kashrut* may be found in *To Be a Jew*, by Hayim Halevy Donin (New York: Basic Books, 1972).

There is an endless array of kosher cookbooks, from the *Kosher Trilogy* providing kosher adaptations of Chinese, Italian, and French cuisine to *Jewish Cooking Around the World: Gourmet and Holiday Recipes* by Hanna Goodman (Philadephia: Jewish Publication Society, 1973). This cookbook is a reliable and authentic guide to traditional Jewish foods, spanning a broad range of history and geography. The *Jewish Holiday Kitchen* by Joan Nathan (New York: Schocken Books, 1979) is another recommended source. Lubavitch has published an outstanding and comprehensive cookbook with explanations on how to set up a kosher kitchen called *The Spice of Life,* available from all local Lubavitch centers.

Hundreds of kosher cookbooks are available offering advice and inspiration, just as there is a plethora of handsome volumes dealing with child rearing. We found good practical suggestions about diet, junk food, and raising kids in the chapter "Food and Nutrition" in *Kids: Day In and Day Out,* edited by Elisabeth L. Scharlott (New York: Lonesome Sparrow Press, 1979).

A rich man once came to the Magid of Koznitz. The Magid asked him what he was in the habit of eating. "I am modest in my needs," replied the man. "All I need is bread, salt, and a drink of water."

"What do you do!" reproved the Magid: "You must eat roast meat and drink wine like all rich people." And he would not let the man go until he had promised to do as he had said.

Later, his Hasidim asked him why he had insisted on such an odd request.

The Magid replied, "Not until he eats meat will he realize that the poor man needs bread. As long as he himself lives on bread, he will think that the poor man can live on stones."

CHAPTER TWELVE

PLANNING A SIMKHA:
or
HOW TO HAVE A JEWISH AFFAIR

WHAT IS A SIMKHA?

Jews come together for a variety of reasons: to pray, to collect and distribute *tzedakah*, to mourn, to celebrate. Frequently, these gatherings are celebrations, formal parties given by the parents of a newborn child of a bar or bat mitzvah, or of a wedding couple. Sometimes such celebrations are less formal, like Hanukah or Purim parties, children's birthday parties, Passover *sedarim*, or anniversary celebrations. How to plan a celebration that is esthetically pleasing, logistically viable, and Jewishly sensitive is a topic of concern to all of us who have ever hosted one.

The most important thing to remember as you begin to plan a *simkha* is this: a truly Jewish celebration is not a big bash thrown by Jewish hosts. A truly Jewish celebration is a group of Jews coming together to celebrate *as a community*. This is a subtle and very important distinction. There is, for example, a *mitzvah* to be *misame'ah hatan v'kalah*—to bring joy to the bride and groom. This *mitzvah* places the responsibility for the celebration squarely on the guests. It is *our* responsibility to create a Jewish celebration—not the responsibility of the hosts to give us a nice party.

Thus, the role you as host perform is that of creating the setting for Jews to come together to celebrate. Jewishly, such celebrations have two time-honored ingredients without which no *simkha* is complete. First, there is the concept of *seudat mitzvah*—the celebratory *mitzvah* meal. A Jewish celebration is incomplete without this meal, and it must therefore be planned carefully. Second, in the words of *Pirkei Avot*, "If three have eaten at a table and have not spoken words of Torah, it is as if they have eaten from the altars of dead idols. But if three have eaten at a table and have spoken words of Torah, it is as if they have eaten from the table of God." Thus, the custom arose to include words of Torah at every gathering of Jews. Such words can be observations and metaphors about the occasion itself; *midrashim* (interpretations) about the Torah portion for that week; an analysis of a biblical character of event; spiritual reflections

JETHRO REJOICED AT ALL THE GOOD (EXOD. 18)

For ordinary people, the joy of all good things does not come together. For there are various kinds of joy. For example, when people come to a wedding, there are those who are happy because of all the good food they eat: meat, fish, and all the rest. Others are happy over the music; others, about various other things that go on. Then there are those who are happy about the wedding itself: the immediate families, for example, who care nothing about the food and drink. And so there are various kinds of joy. But there is no one who is happy for all good things at once. And even if someone is happy about all these things, surely all those joys are not simultaneous, but rather follow upon one another. And there are those at the wedding who have no joy at all, neither from food nor drink, nor anything that is provided. On the contrary, they are jealous and upset, sorry that this one is marrying that one.

But the wholeness and fullness of joy belongs only to one who can rejoice in all things at once. And this cannot be done except by him who looks upward at all the good, seeing to its root. For in this root from which all good things come, everything is one. Then, in looking at the root, he can rejoice in all things at once; that joy is truly great, shining with the brightest light. For as one joins the joys to one another, the very process of their meeting increases the light. As more joys are brought together, the light becomes ever brighter and brighter. The light keeps getting brighter from the sparks that are set off each time one joy meets another. So the more they are joined, the brighter the light of those many sparklings.

So when one rejoices for all good things together—when all joy becomes one—that light is really very great, due to all the sparks that are flickering into one another. This is how Jethro rejoiced for "all the good"; he looked upward to "the God," to the root. There all is one, and all the joys are joined together, so he could rejoice in them all at once!

NAHMAN OF BRATSLAV,
LIQUTEY MOHARAN II, 2:34

and insights or tales of wise people. They can be given by anyone, even those who have never done it before. But do not unfairly ask someone to speak without preparation. You have to ask people in advance to teach something at your *simkha*, and you have to plan the appropriate moment to introduce the *divrei* Torah (insights derived from Torah). (Choosing that moment requires sensitivity to liturgy.)

A variation of offering *divrei* Torah is giving *berakhot* (blessings) to the new baby, the bar or bat mitzvah, or the bride and groom at the *sheva berakhot* meals, traditionally planned for them by friends and relatives for the seven evenings after their wedding. These blessings can take the form of formal *berakhot*—Blessed Are You, Lord Our God—but most often are simply the prayers or wishes of the guests. Some guests may be comfortable spontaneously offering their wishes to those honored, since that can be less difficult or threatening than spontaneously giving a *d'var* Torah.

A WORD ABOUT JEWS AND DRINK

A generation ago, the claim could be made that "Jews don't drink." For better or worse, those days are gone; feet firmly planted in America, Jews most certainly do drink now. In fact, in typical Jewish exuberance of spirit and flesh, Jews sometimes drink to excess! Twenty-five years ago, you would not have expected to find guests getting drunk at a bar mitzvah party. Today, there are few celebrations where at least some of the guests are not distinctly high. It is worth noting that long ago Jews found an occasion for which it was (and is) appropriate to get roaring drunk. That occasion was *not* a bar mitzvah or a wedding but Purim. As host, your desire to provide a bar replete with professional bartender and every conceivable liquor, mixed drink, and liqueur should be confined to whatever Purim parties you decide to throw. No Jewish *simkha* would be complete without a *le-hayyim* toast, but to feature a bar as an important element of your *simkha* is simply to subvert the true nature of the occasion you have brought people together to celebrate. It is not that we should not drink, but we should not elevate the bar to the position of an altar at our celebrations.

PLANNING THE SIMKHA

There is a great difference (which will be discussed later) between planning a large-scale party that "is so big we'll have to hire a hall" and planning a party in your own home. Still, a few things apply to both. (1) For invitations, you needn't necessarily feel bound by the artistic limitations of a printer. For formal parties, you can have a calligrapher do an invitation to your specifications. For less formal parties, anything you or your children or friends or relatives can draw can be reproduced—in vivid color—by a Xerox machine. (You may have to scout around in your city to find out where there is a color Xerox machine, but the vibrant color is well worth the effort.) (2) If you know how to make wine, do it. If you don't, you might want to learn. Wine has always accompanied every Jewish *simkha:* serving your own wine at a *brit* or naming ceremony, bar or bat mitzvah, or wedding enriches the occasion. If you do make your own wine for the birth of your child, put some bottles away for the bar or bat mitzvah and wedding.

FOOD

In planning the food for a *simkha*, you have three choices: a caterer, a modified caterer, or home cooking.

If you choose to use a caterer, you would do well to be concerned with issues other than simply the menu and the quality of food. Such issues as unobtrusiveness of the caterer and serving staff (far too many caterers see themselves as Ye Old Genial Hoste); lack of ostentation in serving (do you *really* want him to light up each individual duck flambé?); and willingness to provide sufficient yet not overlarge portions of food. *You* must plan the *simkha* you want. Plaintive remarks about how "*everyone* chooses the forty-three piece smorgasbord rather than the nine-piece, which is, shall we say, tacky?" should leave you unmoved. If it's so tacky, why does he offer it as an option and, anyway, who *needs* more than nine things to eat before the meal even begins? Remember, the caterer is in the business of urging you to be more ostentatious or lavish than you want or need to be. You have to be prepared to fight for the quiet elegance or natural simplicity that you want at your *simkha*.

A variation of the caterer is the modified caterer. This can take two forms: the you-buy-prepared-food-from-a-caterer-or-restaurant-and-arrange-to-serve-it-yourself variety, or the accommodator-cook variety. In the latter version, you hire a cook who prepares the food in his or her own home, in your home, or in a synagogue or hall, and you arrange to serve it yourself. In both cases, you can control how much food is prepared as well as how it is served. On the other hand, you will either have to serve it yourself (with your friends) or hire waitresses to serve it for you. Finally, there is the do-it-yourself home-cooking method. Here you do all the cooking yourself or solicit help from your friends. If your friends help, you can do a prepared menu or a potluck meal. There are some bits of advice we've gleaned over the years about potluck meals that can be helpful to you.

The basic worry about a potluck meal is that you will end up with eighty-three desserts and no main dishes. So do a little structuring.

Figure out how many people you expect, and divide by ten or fifteen. Then call your friends and give a general specification such as, "Please bring a vegetable that will serve fifteen people." That way you *know* if you've covered main dish, starch, vegetable, salad, dessert, *hallah*, and liquid refreshments; you'll have a complete meal. Always specify, incidentally, whether the meal is a dairy or meat meal so people can cook appropriately.

The other way to plan a dinner is to control the menu. Here you work out the menu you want to serve and then ask all the people making a starch to make mashed potatoes. All your guests will have the same food to eat, made by different people.

CENTERPIECES

At my wedding, an enormous amount of money and esthetic planning was devoted to the cut-flower centerpieces. Now, years later, it seems a waste of time and money, since I don't really care for cut flowers, anyway. I've seen people substitute a cluster of small plants, which the guests took home later, simple elegant candles, and individually made *hallah* covers. At one of the nicest bar mitzvahs I have attended, the centerpiece was a simple folded note that read, "The money which would have been used to purchase flowers has been donated by David in your honor to the Jewish Home for the Aged."

BANDS

Choosing a band for those *simkhas* where music is appropriate is not very difficult. Always ask to hear a band before you hire it. Then you can make sure that the band leader knows he's a musician and not a master of ceremonies and that the band really does know how to play Jewish music (other than "Fiddler on the Roof" and "Hava Nagilah"). It's useful to make sure that the band leader is sensitive to the changing moods of the guests. There are moments, even during a *simkha*, when quiet, reflective music is appropriate.

CONTENT

Below are some content ideas for specific kinds of celebrations.

Brit or Naming Ceremony

The birth of a new child has always been an event celebrated joyously in the Jewish community. (For suggestions on gifts, see Chapter Twenty-five.) The *brit* ceremony for a boy principally centers on the circumcision itself, although various blessings and readings can be added.

Elaborations of the naming ceremony for a girl are sufficiently new so that you can feel free to improvise. Write to the Jewish Women's Resource Center (c/o YMHA, 92nd St. and Lexington Ave., New York, NY 10024) for advice and suggestions. Also consider designing a ceremony that initiates a girl baby into the Covenant, redefined to her sex.

For either gender, an interesting new custom that has arisen is the use of the Jewish "birth certificate." Such a certificate is simply an illuminated document that begins with an appropriate *pasuk* (verse). For example:

> *U'bnei Yisrael paru va'yishritzu.* (And the children of Israel multiplied and grew in number.) *Hodu laShem ki tov ki l'olam hasdo.* (Give thanks to the Lord for He is good; His mercy endures forever.)

This is followed by the following words:

On _____ the community of Israel gathered to welcome
(Date)
into its midst_____
(Hebrew name)
Who was born to_____
(Mother's name)
And_____
(Father's name)
On_____
(Date)

> Just as this child has been introduced into the Covenant, may this child be brought to the Torah, to the wedding canopy and to a life of good deeds.

Space is left at the bottom for all those present to sign their names as representatives of the community of Israel. Such certificates can become part of the family genealogical documents to be passed down from one generation to another. (Also see Chapter Thirty-four.)

Bar/Bat Mitzvah

Instead of using the ready-made grace-after-meals booklets, consider putting your own booklet together and including your family's favorite songs and *zemirot* (*Shabbat* hymns). (For more ideas, see Chapter Thirteen.)

Hanukah Party

Since adults as well as children celebrate Hanukah, plan a party to which both can come. For the children, provide *dreidels* and Hanukah *gelt* for gambling. The adults might want to put on an informal play or puppet show for the children. Everyone should light the *menorah* together, and adults and children can join together in singing holiday songs.

Purim Parties

Definitely encourage everyone to come in costume. A *grogger*-making preparty activity, coupled with a Purim *shpiel* (play), which should be planned in advance (by adults with or without kids), can be fun.

Anniversary Parties

You might want to reexamine the *sheva berakhot* (seven blessings) that are recited at the wedding ceremony and use these as a jumping-off point for writing new *berakhot* or rediscovering the old.

Weddings

For wedding ideas, see *The Jewish Catalog* (Siegel, Strassfeld, and Strassfeld, Jewish Publication Society, 1973) and *The Jewish Marriage Anthology* (Philip and Hanna Goodman, Jewish Publication Society, 1965).

Siyyum

A *siyyum* is *the* authentic Jewish party, which has fallen into disuse outside the Orthodox community. It is the celebration held at the completion of studying a book or section on Torah literature. It is always accompanied by a meal and *d'var* Torah. Frequently, the *d'var* Torah is based on the completed text and is a further exposition of the material studied. How might you revive this celebration of your own cycle of study?

Seder

Although it is a little strange to think of a Passover Seder as a *simkha*, since the ritual is so firmly a part of the meal and since the entire holiday is so firmly a family celebration, it would feel incomplete to omit it. The single most important thing to remember at a Seder is that to do it right, you must be willing to spend as much time thinking about the issues you'd like to raise, the readings you'd like to add, and the textual contradictions and ambiguities you'd like to discuss as you do planning the menu. The Seder is an elaborate play, and the text has to be carefully examined in order to find the themes and resolutions that speak to you. They will differ from year to year. Think also about which text of the Haggadah you want to use and how best to involve the children.

Finally, there are a host of other moments that can serve as legitimate *simkhas*—whether they are really "Jewish" occasions or not. In this context, we think both of Thanksgiving, which, in our family at least, had a distinctly Jewish flavor, and of our family circle meetings (see Chapter Thirty-four), which were nothing short of a joyous Jewish celebration. Both these occasions in our family's history of sharing *simkhas* have served, over the years, to convince me that it is possible to make our *simkhas* honestly Jewish, truly joyous occasions if the right values and esthetics are allowed to prevail.

Rabbi Meyer Hurwitz of Tiktin heard that a dozen distinguished rabbis, all of them his grandsons, planned to pay him honor by attending a family gathering in celebration of his birthday. The aged rabbi immediately sent a messenger to halt their plans, and enjoined him to deliver the following word: "From the children that the Lord has granted me, I expect delight in the World-to-Come, not in This-World."

CHAPTER THIRTEEN

BAR/BAT MITZVAH

Bar or bat mitzvah plans preoccupy Jewish parents, sometimes for years before the event; at times, unfortunately, preparation can become a central focus of children's Jewish education.

What does bar or bat mitzvah mean? Literally, *bar* means son and *bat* means daughter. (It is, incidentally, a Hebrew linguistic atrocity to say someone was "bar mitzvah'd." A person *becomes* a bar or a bat mitzvah.) To become a bar or bat mitzvah means that a child has entered the adult Jewish community and is responsible for fulfilling *mitzvot* (commandments) of Torah. The event of a child attaining a majority occurs for boys on their thirteenth birthday and for girls on their twelfth and is publicly acknowledged by calling the individual to Torah with an *aliyah* (a "going up" to recite blessings). Other ways of ritually marking the occasion are often observed. Some *bnai* or *bnot* (the plural form) *mitzvah* read the entire Torah portion and chant the *haftarah* section. Others fulfill the ritual moment of an *aliyah* simply through reciting the appropriate blessings. But all stand both before Torah and in relationship to their communities on the day that they become bar or bat mitzvah and begin to relate to new responsibilities as adult Jews. (For descriptions of bar and bat mitzvah ceremonies, see the articles under that heading in the *Second Jewish Catalog* (Jewish Publication Society, 1976) and the *Encyclopedia Judaica* (Keter, 1971).

An old joke that circulates in the Jewish community defines contemporary bar mitzvah as an event that is long on bar and short on mitzvah. Crass and ostentatious examples abound. We all know stories of desperately conspicuous consumption—from bringing Disneyland to Forest Hills to helicoptering to the top of Masada. Out of our opposition to these perversions and our desire to add depth and meaning to a potentially important experience, we propose some alternative ways of preparing for bar and bat mitzvah.

Jews understand preparation as central to religious experience. Remember that before the People Israel could approach Mt. Sinai to receive Torah, they prepared themselves for three days. A Hasidic commentator has pointed out that through that three-day process each of the people actualized or realized Torah within themselves, and it was only for future generations that the Torah needed to be written down at Sinai. Preparation can and should be an integral part of any religious event. It goes without saying that by talking about preparation we do not mean

calling the caterer. A general preparatory program as conducted by many synagogues has the child attending Hebrew school and meeting for special sessions with the cantor or tutor. How long before the actual date of bar or bat mitzvah the child begins this program will vary from synagogue to synagogue. Also, the content of these sessions varies, from children who learn to perform the assigned parts from tape recordings to children who explore content and meaning of the section of Torah read on their bar or bat mitzvah. Concerned parents will investigate the nature of bar or bat mitzvah preparation in their synagogues. Some will be pleasantly surprised by the high educational standards; others will be dissatisfied and want to explore alternatives.

One alternative to the standard synagogue program is arranging that the child be tutored by a family friend or relative who is knowledgeable. In this situation, part of the significance of tutoring lies in the unique nature of the relationship. To be able to say that your grandmother taught you the family melody for lighting *Shabbat* candles that she heard and learned as a child is very special. Another alternative is to hire an especially knowledgeable, qualified tutor who will both teach and act as a resource person to the child and family. Qualified tutors can be found, usually by personal referral. (Try calling your local Hillel director or Hebrew school principal.) They are generally paid on a scale commensurate with foreign-language tutors and must be interviewed in advance. You will, for example, want to feel that you will be able to work well with the tutor and that the tutor understands your expectations. Tutoring should not, of course, be limited to preparing the young person to perform at a ceremony and need not necessarily end with that ceremony.

Designing a curriculum (in other words, the content that tutor and child will work on together) can in itself be a learning experience in which parents have an opportunity to clarify their own values and thinking. What do you as a parent believe important for your child to know upon attaining "majority" within the Jewish community? What of your own Jewish heritage do you want to share? What skills will help your child function as a Jew? The process of designing a curriculum should include all concerned parties and should be part of the learning experience.

Skills to perform effectively in a synagogue on the day of the bar or bat mitzvah are the same skills the child will continue to use during the rest of his or her religious life. It is important for the post-bar or post-bat mitzvah to have further opportunities to use new skills in reading Torah or leading the congregation in prayer. Opportunities for a young person who has mastered these synagogue skills to help tutor or train another child can be important.

Inevitably, what is planned for a bat/bat mitzvah will reflect the values and attitudes of your family. Not to decide is to decide. Going along with an established pattern in a synagogue or trying to insert your own family traditions into that synagogue's system or hiring a tutor privately and reflects *"davvening shaharit* or *minhah"* in your living room value decisions. It is important to realize that a family that is far removed from synagogue participation can design bar or bat mitzvah ceremonies of personal meaning. We remember a secular Yiddishist family who, through intense consultation with a tutor, were able to affirm both a current concern with Torah and involvement in their own history. Thus, their son's bar mitzvah included not only the child's reading and explicating a section of Torah but also family members' reminiscences, which helped the child feel he was truly entering the adult Jewish community and being accepted by adult family members. Important in this example is the realization that the young man actually studied significantly more than many of his Hebrew school-attending counterparts. Our fear, however, is that not all Jewish families are as seriously committed to the enterprise; they may use creative and private modes of bar mitzvah as a way of avoiding more stringent synagogue requirements. (Interesting to note that the United Synagogue of Great Britain will not accept a child for bar mitzvah ceremonies who cannot pass a written, standardized examination of Hebrew language skills and general Jewish knowledge.)

Families sometimes choose unique places for a bar or bat mitzvah, from the Western Wall in Jerusalem to their own back yards. We attended a bar mitzvah in a Jewish old age home in New Jersey, which was touchingly arranged to permit a ninety-seven-year-old great-grandfather to attend. The celebration was a special moment for the other patients in the home, who were among the honored guests.

It is worth considering scheduling a bar or bat mitzvah for a Monday or Thursday morning or a *Shabbat minhah* (afternoon service) rather than the usual *Shabbat* morning. These changes in time expand possibilities. For example, a *minhah* bar or bat mitzvah lends itself to a *seudah shlishit* (the third, late-afternoon meal of *Shabbat*), during which the child can deliver a *"d'var* Torah" and other guests may also share teaching or Torah or *berakhot*. By the same token, scheduling the ceremony for a Monday or Thursday morning removes any *Shabbat* prohibitions and suggests the possibility of rejoicing in the first public occasion when the child wears *tefillin*. An additional benefit of any of these "different" times is that they further separate you from any similarity to the objectionable *Shabbat*-morning extravaganza to which so many of us have fallen victim.

Consider the underlying meanings of bar or bat mitzvah. Does it represent a rite of passage to a new life stage for you, the parent, a moment of welcoming the child into the adult Jewish community, or . . .? Your careful consideration of underlying meanings may affect your plans for celebrating the moment. For example, we know of an Israeli kibbutz where bar and bat mitzvah is seen as a rite of passage; twelve- and thirteen-year-olds are challenged to survive arduous camping expeditions alone, coming back to reenter their communities with new-found maturity. Steve Stroiman in *The Second Jewish Catalog* (Philadelphia: Jewish Publication Society, 1976) wrote of creating a "leaving home" ritual for older teenagers; consult his article for ideas on your own adaptations for bar or bat mitzvah. If you see bar or bat mitzvah as a way in which the Jewish community welcomes its new members, how else might that welcome be acted out in addition to the ceremony? We know of a family in which a bar mitzvah chose to donate a portion of the money he received as gifts to American Jewish communal charities—to *tzedakah*. The experience was further enhanced by the fact that the boy had to make his own decisions concerning which charities would be most worthwhile recipients of his money. Another example comes from a family living in a middle-sized Jewish community. In that community, the mother took very seriously the *mitzvah* of *bikur holim* and regularly visited the sick in a local hospital. When her daughter became twelve, the mother began to take her along on hospital visits, sharing the *mitzvah* with her and conveying the message that the child had come of age.

(Continued page 106)

AN ALTERNATIVE/TRADITIONAL BAR MITZVAH

Our son Steven's bar mitzvah did not seem "alternative"; it all felt so simple, so natural. Yet, on second thought, I realized that it had aspects that were atypical and worth sharing with others who might be planning this life-cycle event.

Our first "alternative decision" was not to hold the bar mitzvah in the main sanctuary of our local synagogue. The large room, the formal pews, the great space between the *bimah* (altar) and the congregation created an atmosphere that lacked the warmth and intimacy we wanted. Also, we could not imagine a rabbi or cantor leading the ceremony.

And so we arranged to have the bar mitzvah in the auditorium, which our friends decorated with plants and flowers. Chairs were arranged in a semicircle, close together. We hung a parachute over the reading table, which gave the effect of a *hupah* (wedding canopy) or, as someone else suggested, a portable *mishkan* (tabernacle).

Several months before the bar mitzvah, Steven selected a teacher with whom he could review Torah *trop* (notes for chanting) and discuss his *parshah* (Torah portion of the week). This was an exploration he thoroughly enjoyed. His father taught him *haftarah* (*haftarah* refers to the prophetic passage read at the end of the Torah service) *trop,* and I reviewed *shaharit* (the morning service) with him. The rabbi in our synagogue also met with Steven to discuss his *parshah* and its meaning.

Steven was not only a learner but a teacher as well. He taught my husband and me how to read Torah *trop.* For the first time we read one *aliyah* at his bar mitzvah. As it happened, it was the verses where Moses turns his authority over to Joshua—most appropriate for the occasion!

Another "first" was that Steven's grandmother and aunt both received their first *aliyot* at his bar mitzvah.

Steven's speech was an especially wonderful moment for us. He spoke about his own thoughts on his *parshah* and about his bar mitzvah. His *parshah,* Nitzavim-Vayeleh, contained the verse "I have set before you life

(Continued)

and death, blessing and curse, therefore choose life that both you and your seed may live." So much of our family's discussions about his *parshah* had focused on this verse and the whole subject of responsibility for choosing a life of positive values. This had led us to thinking about an old custom of reciting the blessing *"baruch shepetarani me'ansho shel zeh"* (blessed are you who remove this burden—i.e., responsibility for the spiritual well-being of this child—from us) after the bar mitzvah is called to the Torah. We decided to do it, but instead of the usual translation, we said, "Blessed is God who releases us from the responsibilities that have now become Steven's."

What we meant by our translation was that we were not "washing our hands" of Steven. We felt that as parents we still wanted to guide him and be close to the new ways of Jewishness he would be developing. We also felt that we were prepared to "let go," to give Steven the responsibilities for which he was ready and give him increasing independence afterward. His answer to us was, "It is now my duty to keep the commandments and become responsible for my own actions." He then said, "Shema Yisrael . . ." In this way, he announced his willingness to assume these responsibilities.

This recitation was the most emotionally charged part of the bar mitzvah. As he finished reciting the *Shema*, the congregation called out, *"Mazal Tov!"* and showered him with candy. Everyone surged forward to lift Steven up into the air and dance around the *bimah* with all of us.

It is written in Proverbs, "My son, hear the instructions of your father and forsake not the law of your mother." An so my husband and I each shared with Steven some teaching, some Torah. I don't know if he'll remember the content (though I hope he will), but I think he'll always remember that we cared enough to give him a piece of our deepest selves at his bar mitzvah. I also know that he feels it was truly *his* bar mitzvah, for his needs guided us in all our planning and celebration—all in all, a good way to enter the adult community of Israel.

SOSHANA SILBERMAN

Preparing for a bar or bat mitzvah includes preparing not only the child and family but also the guests. This preparation should not be limited to convincing Aunt Sophie not to wear silver-lamé toreador pants. Letting people know in advance what to expect can circumvent a variety of problems. Involving guests in the celebration also helps them feel included in the extended family and may defuse judgmental attitudes. The nicest gift that you can ask anyone to bring to a bar or bat mitzvah is a *d'var* Torah or a *berakha*. These kinds of gifts are discussed further in Chapter Twelve.

Recently, some friends began the practice at each *simkha* (and after *Shabbat* when the event occurs on *Shabbat*) of asking all participants to make a "collection" or collective contribution to an organization fighting world hunger. By these donations, we are acknowledging that in the midst of our gastronomic plenty we must not forget the hungry of the world.

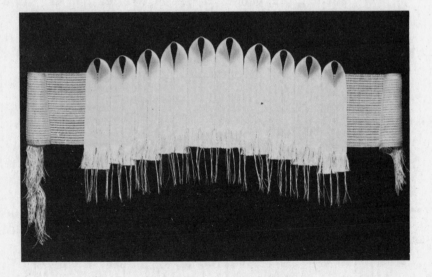

Finally, consider the possibility of adult bar or bat mitzvah celebrations, of calling people to Torah who are already grownups. Grownups who have experienced adult bar or bat mitzvah rituals they missed when they were younger describe their experiences as deeply meaningful. (In particular, Rabbi Albert Axelrad of Brandeis University Hillel Foundation has experimented in working with adults who want to acquire adult Jewish skills and experience bar or bat mitzvah.) It should be noted that the Reform movement's initiation of confirmation ceremonies at age sixteen was designed both to postpone a rite of passage like bar or bat mitzvah until the individual was closer to real physical and psychological adulthood and also to try to extend the number of years of required Jewish education.

A bar or bat mitzvah is a *simkha*. And most twelve-and thirteen-year-olds want their *simkha* to resemble those of friends that they have attended. They do not want to be *that* different. That is why preparing for a bar or bat mitzvah must be a family experience involving the boy or the girl, the parents, and perhaps other siblings. Yes, there are values that cannot be compromised, but the party can be planned more for the child than for the parents. What does the child really want? Odds are that the boy or girl does not care whether there is an elaborate bar, complete with professional bartender.

CHOOSING A BAR/BAT MITZVAH GIFT

How well you know the person who is about to become a bar or bat mitzvah and how clearly defined his or her Jewish interests are will affect your selection of a gift. What follows are some ideas that may help:

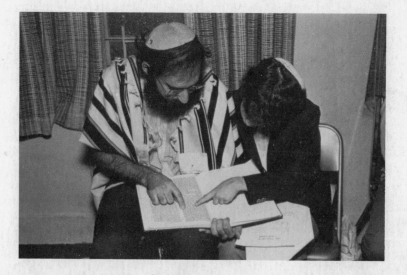

1. *Ritual objects. Tallit, tallit* bag, *tefillin, kiddush* cup, candlesticks, *shofar.* Traditionally parents and/or grandparents have equipped a son for his future prayer life with *tallit* and *tefillin,* which he would not use until bar mitzvah. Today, many will want to similarly equip daughters. Ways of providing these objects range from purchase (through Jewish book stores and hand weavers) to making what you can yourself. Needlepoint experts sometimes produce beautiful *tallit* and *tefillin* bags and collar bands for *tallitot.* (See *Jewish Catalogs* or *Work of Our Hands* for ideas.) Some ritual objects might be reserved for wedding presents, since they suggest less individual responsibility than family sharing: *hallah* covers, *havdalah* sets, Seder plates, etc. Again much depends on the individual child. Also, see Chapter Thirty-four for suggestions on recycling ritual objects.

2. *Gift subscriptions to a Jewish book club* (for example, the Jewish Publication Society, 117 South Seventeenth St., Philadelphia, PA 19103; Enjoy-a-Book Club, 25 Lawrence Ave., Lawrence, NY 11559; or The Jewish Bookshelf, P.O. Box 434, Teaneck, NJ 07666), or give gift certificates to Jewish book stores. (For listings of Jewish book stores, see *The Jewish Catalog* or *The New Jewish Yellow Pages* by Mae Shafter Rockland [New York: SBS Publishing Inc., 1980]). To spend such gifts (whether subscriptions or certificates) the recipient will have to look at the options and make decisions.

3. *Books of Jewish interest* again depend largely on your perceptions of the child. Books can vary from *seforim* (Hebrew texts) to novels dealing with Jewish themes. Sometimes you will want to give a bar or bat mitzvah a book that is really too mature for now or a reference that she or he will use in later study. The young person with well-defined interests makes your task easier. It was easy, for example, to buy Lawrence Kushner's *The Book of Hebrew Letters* (Harper & Row, 1976) for a young person interested in calligraphy.

4. *Subscription to* The Jerusalem Post for someone interested in current issues facing Israel; subscription to a simplified Hebrew language newspaper for a budding Hebrew scholar.

5. *Membership in a local Jewish museum* in your area (New York, Philadelphia, Chicago, Los Angeles, Berkeley).

6. *Tickets to a Jewish cultural event*, a play, a concert. Be sure the event is appropriate and will not be a "turnoff" for the young person.

7. *A kit to make a Jewish object*. Commercially prepared needlepoint kits are available. You might also assemble your own kit, supplying materials to make a *dreidel*, a *grogger*, a *menorah*. See the first *Jewish Catalog* for instructions.

8. *A family heirloom of your creation.* Consider assembling recipes of favorite relatives or a family photo album or genealogical tree.

9. *Calendars.* Jewish calendars are indispensable for living a life of traditional observance. (It is crucial to know the date of Pesah or the proper time to light *Shabbat* candles.) Calendars can be appreciated on a variety of levels. A seven-year-old can enjoy leafing through the individual days of the week recorded in the Hebrew-English calendar called "Seven Days Make a Week" published by Lion the Printer of Tel Aviv. An older child (or adult) might enjoy Jewish art calendars; for example, Lion the Printer also publishes the Israel Art Calendar, which contains reproductions of works by

contemporary Israeli artists. The "Jewish Calendar," published by Universe Books, New York, offers another alternative of interesting illustrations and information about important (and not so important) dates in Jewish history and experience. Also see "For Children," a Turnowsky Art Calendar, which won top prizes at the Stuttgart annual calendar design competition. The Turnowsky calendar was created in Israel and features figures on each page which can be cut out and made into three-dimensional dolls. Any of these calendars could prove useful and informative for bnai or bnot mitzvah who want to number their days.

What does it mean to be thirteen? The night before my son became a bar mitzvah, I decided that I would say good night and "tuck him in," something that I had not done for years. I went to his room and found that he had already fallen asleep with his light on. As I tiptoed in to turn off the light, I saw that under one arm he clutched his old teddy bear, and in the other he held a copy of *Playboy* magazine. That's what it means to be thirteen.

Part Three

LEARNING

CHAPTER FOURTEEN

THE WORKING PARENT

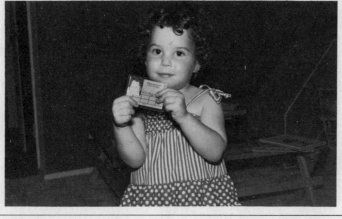

Parents do not usually consider sending their children to infant day-care programs unless both parents work. The decision about child-care is almost invariably linked to questions of career. ("If I work, who will take care of my child; if I don't work, who will take care of me?") It makes sense to talk about career issues that emerge once parents feel they are "coming out of the woods" with their infants (i.e., the baby is finally sleeping through the night and the parents are finally feeling like human beings again).

No matter how many or how few children you have, whoever is doing the primary home nurturing (and that is still usually the woman) begins to think about returning to work and begins to confront questions of whether, when, how much time, how much money.

Some people who need to work can arrange their schedules so successfully—either because of supportive families, neighbors, or nearby day-care centers—that they feel few ambivalences about going back to work almost immediately. Other people feel the opposite need, to be at home full time with their children until the children are at the age where they can be enrolled in a nursery-school program.

As one young mother put it, "Before I had even given birth, I made the decision that I wanted to quit my job as a social worker and stay home with the baby. I expected to feel ambivalent about that decision after having worked for ten years. But both Fred and I believe in the

113

importance of early nurturing, and I thought that I'd at least try to be the one giving it.

"Instead of feeling ambivalent, though, I find myself reveling in being at home with Sarah. My pace of life has changed, my interests have grown, and I've never felt so wonderful. I love spending time with Sarah, but since I make sure to have some outside babysitting help, I am also getting a chance to do some of the things I never could before. I've taken a course in Zionism. I've learned how to bake bread, which Sarah loves to do with me. I've gotten a chance to read more. I'm beginning to learn quilt making. All of these things have enriched my life, and I don't at all feel that staying home with Sarah deprives me of my career. I feel more that I worked for ten years, and I'll probably want to do it again later. But it's wonderful, really wonderful, to have this time with Sarah now, to watch her grow and develop and to be part of that. We have a special kind of closeness that I wonder whether we could have if we didn't spend this much time together. I'm grateful to the women's movement, which helps me appreciate Fred, who had to be willing to *not* get off his 'career ladder' so that I had the option to get off mine. I didn't know it at the time, but I believe now that my decision to stay home with Sarah was the best one, for both of us, that I ever could have made."

Still other people, however, are less clear in their needs. They want to be at home with their children, yet they find full-time parenting a draining experience and miss their careers. Or they need to work, and miss their children.

This is another of those areas where ultimately you have to decide for yourself when you and your child are ready for you to go back to work. Regardless of the quality of substitute care you arrange, regardless of whether you *like* to be at home all day with your child, it is painful to leave your child and go back to work. You will feel (as I have) guilty, lonely, bereft, angry, and unfulfilled. I've come to think that this is the inevitable and inescapable price we pay in trying to be part of two worlds, both of which we care about and both of which we need. As Ruth Strauss said: "I want it all. And I can't make peace with the reality that I can't have it all. I want to be the one to pick up my kid when he falls down, to hear the new words he's trying out, to laugh at his crazy antics. I also went to law school, edited the law review, and got a job in a good firm. My job gives me a channel for my own personal ambition and I can't give up work that gives me such enormous satisfaction. I live with a certain type of frustration that many of my women colleagues and I have shared. The sharing vents the frustration, but we all know that we live in a no-win situation. We lose if we stay home. We lose if we pursue our careers."

Keep in mind, though, that our job as working parents is to provide the best substitute care we can for our child, and make sure our career provides us with some kind of self-fulfillment. All of us will simply have to live with ambivalent negative feelings, realizing that part of being an adult is knowing that it can't go all our own way, that we have to make tradeoffs that feel sensible to us, and that we have to learn to accept and live with the consequences of the tradeoffs.

ON NEEDING A PUSH

There are two syndromes that should be mentioned. One is the "I'd feel guilty leaving my baby, but I hate to be at home" syndrome. People with that feeling are often immobilized by their own misery and can't make the decision to seek substitute child care and return to their careers. Generally speaking, although it is good to understand both sides of the question, the answer to the dilemma is clear. It will probably be a huge relief to both parent and child if the parent goes back to work. Helping the parent to see this fact can be a great *mitzvah* (good deed).

The other syndrome is the "I wasn't so excited about my job, anyway, and I love being at home with my child." Such people continue to stay at home with successive children, feeling perfectly content until the last child starts school. Then the empty-nest syndrome strikes, and the parent, who hasn't worked in years and feels insecure about reentering the job market, is left bewildered and miserable. Here, too, the person may need a gentle nudge in the direction of career retraining or job hunting techniques.

HAVING MADE THE DECISION

Once the time element is decided (i.e., I will go back to work when Leah is six months, one year, or three years), you have to negotiate the practical ramifications of your decision.

Interestingly enough, the Jewish community, which has been loud in its condemnation of "selfish" young couples who won't make the sacrifice necessary for having children (more children, any children), has, thus far, put little money into making the job of parenting any easier. It is a fascinating comment on the community that the care of the elderly has been seen as an essential priority in ways that children have not. (Now wait a minute, this is not to say that the elderly should not be regarded as a priority.) But if the community really sees itself as having a vested interest in Jews having children, then it is surprising that it invests so little in creating structures to facilitate child care.

> Must what happens in day care or preschool programs be Jewish? Is there a Jewish way to change a diaper? Might my child learn more about the Jewish value of *menschlichkeit* (interpersonal decency) at a humanistically oriented preschool with a teacher trained by Bank Street College of Education rather than at a Jewish school where the teacher yells at the kids to color their *menorahs* neatly? These are questions which plague us. Generally we are forced to compromise, to choose between a few imperfect alternatives. Yet in the best of all possible worlds we dream of having it all, of early childhood programs which integrate the lessons learned from developmental psychology, the best insights of such particular approaches to teaching as Montessori and Dewey and others with Jewish content. For a taste of what is possible see Chapter Fifteen.

The truth is, your feelings about going back to work will also be much less painful if you have some confidence in the quality of the day-care programs to which you are committing your child. For infant day care (usually up to eighteen months), there probably should be no more than three children per worker. Different states have different laws, and you should familiarize yourself with those in your locale. The space provided ideally ought to be well lit, airy, and spacious, with plenty of play equipment and toys. Accessible outdoor space is also desirable. In addition, there should be a separate room equipped with cribs or mattresses to accommodate infant nap schedules.

For toddler day care (eighteen months to three years), outdoor play space becomes a necessity, as well as large, indoor play areas and plenty of recreational and "vehicular" equipment. Clean, well-maintained toddler toilet facilities are also important.

Where can you find such day-care centers? It's sad to admit, but probably the best place (at least for infant children) is the local church.

Certainly, you should first try your local Jewish community center or synagogue. But the odds are that you'll find yourself being forced, in looking for an established day-care center, to look outside the institutions of the Jewish community. Other places to try include YMCAs and community centers. In addition, it is quite likely that there are some people in your neighborhood who are running their own (probably unlicensed) daytime play groups. The best way to find out about such groups is by word of mouth from friends or by asking parents at the local playground, pediatrician's office, or library.

Before you enroll your child in any such program, of course, you should check out carefully the facilities, the equipment, and the personnel. Ask for references from the day-care worker and call at least two or three parents. It can be a good idea to call at least one parent whose child has already "graduated," since such parents are freer to speak openly about the program than parents whose children are still enrolled. Also, if at all possible, try to schedule a visit while the children are there. The time investment is worthwhile.

IF ALL ELSE FAILS

You've looked around and (a) can't find any infant day care or (b) can't find a program that will suit your child. The next step, for some, could be starting one yourself. There are a number of possible scenarios,

which range from the less complex, less professional model to the more complex, most professional model:

Scenario 1: You work part time and set out to discover other parents who do the same or who do not work at all but need some free time. You arrange a simple swap schedule. If you work from nine to twelve every day, the other parent can take that as his or her responsibility while you take either another three-hour daily time slot or compensate in some other way (bartering a skill either you or your spouse possess, trading a half share in your second car, etc.).

Scenario 2: You get together a number of other working parents and arrange to pay an at-home parent to start a play group to fit your working hours.

Scenario 3: If you have the space in your home, you can hire someone and arrange to split the cost with a number of other working parents who are in the same situation you are.

Scenario 3A (a variation on the above): If you have even more space in your house, you can arrange to "rent out" a bedroom to a local student, artist, etc. (anyone who only wants to work part time) in exchange for child-care help for your child (and perhaps other neighborhood children as well). So as not to rip off the resident student-artist, the financial details of such arrangements should be explicitly negotiated.

Scenario 3B: If *you* have no room in your house, perhaps someone else does. (Renovated attic or cellar space is fine for such purposes.) Then you could arrange some other form of you-put-up-the-day-care-worker-and-I'll-provide-the-play-space barter.

Scenario 4: You negotiate with your local synagogue or center to give you space for a day-care program at a nominal charge. (It helps if you and the other working parents are members of that synagogue or center.) You then go about hiring a trained, certified day-care worker whose job it will be to pull together a program. This is somewhat tricky, since you've presumably undertaken a salary commitment to someone before you're quite sure you have all the planning pieces in place. To minimize this, you might want to line up as many children as possible and then hire a director.

FINDING OTHER CHILDREN FOR YOUR GROUP

There are a number of good places to find kids for your group. In general, it's best to try places where kids/parents hang out. Put up signs in your local library, community center or Y, pediatrician's office, playground, supermarket, or parents' organizations. Call all the parents you know to start the grapevine growing. Put a notice in your local newspaper. It's almost inevitable that you'll discover a reasonable number of parents who have just been waiting for someone like you to come along.

1910*

Dear Editor,

Since I do not want my conscience to bother me, I ask you to decide whether a married woman has the right to go to school two evenings a week. My husband thinks I have no right to do this.

I admit that I cannot be satisfied to be just a wife and mother. I am still young and I want to learn and enjoy life. My children and my house are not neglected, but I go to evening high school twice a week. My husband is not pleased and when I come home at night and ring the bell, he lets me stand outside a long time intentionally, and doesn't hurry to open the door.

Now he has announced a new decision. Because I send out the laundry to be done, it seems to him that I have too much time for myself, even enough to go to school. So from now on he will count out every penny for anything I have to buy for the house, so I will not be able to send out the laundry any more. And when I have to do the work myself there won't be any time left for such "foolishness" as going to school. I told him that I'm willing to do my own washing but that I would still be able to find time for study.

When I am alone with my thoughts, I feel I may not be right. Perhaps I should not go to school. I want to say that my husband is an intelligent man and he wanted to marry a woman who was educated. The fact that he is intelligent makes me more annoyed with him. He is in favor of the emancipation of women, yet in real life he acts contrary to his beliefs.

Awaiting your opinion on this, I remain,

Your reader,
The Discontented Wife

ANSWER:

Since this man is intelligent and an adherent of the women's emancipation movement, he is scolded severely in the answer for wanting to keep his wife so enslaved. Also the opinion is expressed that the wife absolutely has the right to go to school two evenings a week.

*From Isaac Metzker, ed., *A Bintel Brief*. New York: Doubleday, 1971.

HOUSEHOLD HAVOC

Do you know the old story* of the overcrowded family who sought help from the rabbi? The rabbi suggested they take a goat into the house. Asked the harried *baal habayit* (householder): "Rabbi, will taking a goat into the house really help?"

Replied the rabbi, "No, but things will definitely improve when you get rid of the goat."

Commented our friend Joanne Schindler of Gainesville, Florida: "The question here is not when will the goat leave; but given that we will always live with one manner of goat or another, the real question is how quickly do goats multiply?"

*See Chapter Twenty-four.

CHAPTER FIFTEEN

PRESCHOOL EDUCATION
Ruth Pinkenson Feldman

Regardless of how young our children are when they begin their "formal educa-
tion" in day-care centers or nursery groups, we know that as parents we are their
first and primary teachers. If we've never taken a college education course, where
do we begin, especially if we want to be effective teachers contributing to our
children's Jewish education? Ruth Pinkenson Feldman, a friend who is an early
childhood specialist in the Jewish community, has shared her thinking and
advice. We hope that many of her ideas will prove directly useful to you in
working with your children. You may also want to bring some of these ideas into
your local Jewish preschool group.

Advice about preschool children tends to be somewhat ambiguous.
On the one hand, we're told, "Don't treat them like babies," and on the
other, "Don't expect them to act like adults." Preschool children,
roughly the three- to five-year-old segment of the population, are in a
rather unique developmental stage. While they are no longer toddling
about communicating their needs with gestures and coos, they are still
far from being totally rational. It's not just that these young folks are

Commenting on our responsibility to tell our children the story of our Exodus from Egypt, a Talmudic sage maintained, "The parent should teach the child on the level of the child's understanding." (*Pesahim* 116a)

shorter than the rest of us or that they know less than we do; rather, it's that they think in a manner quite their own.

Jean Piaget uncovered a system of beliefs about the world and a logical structure peculiar to childhood itself and outlined a progression through stages in the development of intelligence. If we look at some of the characteristics of young children's thinking, and if we take these characteristics into account when planning appropriate educational expectations, we will probably be better able to support children's efforts to be themselves. The role of the preschool parent (or teacher) is *not* to teach a child to be an adult but to help the child to live life fully as a child.

So, *nu*, what's life like for a child? Basically, it's a world devoted to finding out what adults do. Many of us learned to be Jewish by being with other Jews and by living Jewishly. Learning to be Jewish these days may be very different from what some of us learned from "other Jews" when we were young. Maybe the child's mother wears the *tallit* in the family. Maybe there is no father to say *kiddush*. Maybe the grandparents celebrate Christmas. All these role models are real in the lives of Jewish children today and make learning what it means to be a Jew a complex matter in a changing world.

Children integrate. They fit each new bit of information into what they already know, and change their own thinking to incorporate each new bit of information. Each child is unique, with a personally constructed matrix of understanding built upon his or her unique experiences. When we talk about children's Jewish education beginning around their third birthday, it is important to remember that each of them already has a three-year history reflecting the language, values, interests, and humor of the family. Even when a child is only three, the preschool home (or classroom) reflects a broad spectrum of learning styles and personal meanings.

Children learn through an interaction between themselves and their environment. They learn *who* they are as they come into contact with others. They learn what they can do by seeing the results of their actions. It's crucial that they have an active relationship to both the physical and social world. An ideal learning situation is one that tries to match what is new with what is familiar. For instance, suppose you want to teach children about Hanukah candles. Begin by encouraging them to talk about other candles they have known and loved. How are these Hanukah candles the same as or different from *Shabbat* candles or birthday candles? True, this will not help children to understand anything about the Syrians; it will enable them to construct a meaningful understanding of Hanukah candles, based on their own observations, seen in relation to what they already know about candles.

Children are intensely interested in their environment. They are naturally curious. They both delight in make-believe and are intensely interested in the real world. In fact, it is the real world that makes up the stuff of their active fantasy lives. It's both the pleasure and responsibility of the preschool parent to infuse the child's environment with the elements of the Jewish world. Sounds calculating? Well, let's face it: education is an intervention. We can make the most of it by carefully planning an interesting and appropriate Jewish environment for the child. It's up to us to bring within the sight (and reach) of each child every range of Jewish experience. So if you want your children's block building to reflect a religious motif, do not (only) send for blocks marked "Made in Israel." Take the children to tour the synagogue in your neighborhood, examine the *bimah* (altar) of several different *shuls*, or visit a bakery making *hallah*, a book bindery, a local artist, a hospital, a neighbor, or a relative preparing for a holiday. Don't just point to an old synagogue as you ride past on your way to the zoo. Go inside! The more familiar the child is with the real elements of his or her Jewish world, the more easily it will be to incorporate it into the child's repertoire of thoughts and play. And *play* is the mechanism through which children try on and learn about their world.

Our aim is to combine the transmission of knowledge about Jewish life with the ongoing development of the child's thinking and social skills. The teaching of Jewish life, attitudes, and values needs to be enmeshed with the day-to-day activities of the child. Realizing that "thinking" for young children consists of seeing similarities and differences, learning problem solving, seeing relationships, and organizing experiences, we try to create situations (activities, games, materials) that reflect the content of what we want to teach with the thinking skills we want to support.

At the same time, we want to combine the growth of a child's feelings of Jewish identity with the ongoing development of a concept of self as a competent, learning person. For instance, suppose it is Purim and you are making *hamantaschen* with your three-year-old and his friend. It is far more important for the child to feel a sense of mastery and accomplishment in his or her own creation than for the parent to "correct" the child's production. True, your child's creation of a three-cornered hat may look much more like a pinched circle than a triangle. However, for him to feel positively about activity, you should validate his attempt at the process. In other words, do not confuse the learning process with the finished product. And don't feel that you've failed if your child hasn't produced a perfect replica. Not only don't all children like to bake *hamantaschen*, some don't even like to taste them! (And that's OK, too.)

You will never be able to teach the holidays just by playing Lotto with pictures of *hamantaschen* and *shofrot*. While it's true that it's a good idea to teach a child to recognize and label a picture of a *shofar* or to discriminate between the word *shofar* and the word *sukkah*, that's not all there is to teaching the symbols of different holidays. A symbol is only a symbol if it has meaning. Although some of children's learning and thinking reflects their need to label, classify, and discriminate objects, much of their learning reflects a deep desire for a personal sense of meaning. They want to know how they fit into the universe and just how that universe works. Children need to act on their environment in order to master it—*if* they are to understand it. In the case of the *shofar*, it's not enough to recognize a picture. They need to feel a real one, hear the blasts, have the opportunity to make (or try to make) it sound. There should be discussion of what the sound makes the child think of or how the *shofar* is like a bell, a siren, or a flashing light. Children want to find out which other animals have horns and which other kinds of horns make noise. Each symbol we present to the child must be "given" to the child to understand in his/her own terms. Each ritual object or symbol comes alive to the degree that it can be played with, found out about, and given meaning.

"LET EVERY LIVING THING PRAISE GOD"

For a young child, anything that moves is real. Piaget has called this tendency to attribute life to inanimate objects "animistic thinking." Did you ever watch a child bump into a door and yell, "That dumb door"? (Or an adult scream at the car to get it to start?) Once, while I was teaching, a four-year-old girl fell off a chair and came over to sit on my lap. "I'm not hurt," she assured me, "the chair's hurt. That's because a chair's real. That's because you sit on his lap. I sit on you, you sit on him. Chairs are called hims. They're boys. God makes girls, girls. And He makes boys and boy chairs. Chairs are real."

Children are very busy finding out what's real and what isn't. They want to know what makes something alive. The best way to find out is by examining the world of the living: animals, people, and plants. By learning about life, the young quickly and naturally learn about death.

The study of the life cycle of people and plants is an excellent and exciting way to begin to lay the foundation for meaningful *tefillah* (prayer) as well as appreciation of the holidays. Young children first need to learn the effects of rain on the earth before a prayer for rain can make much sense. And they need to know which things are alive if they are ever to know how each living thing can praise God. So if your children are learning about the animals, ask them how a giraffe or a fish might praise God. And don't let your own embarrassment get in the way of creative thinking. Remember, to be creative means to "make it new," so if you've never thought how every living thing might praise God, start now, with you!

Many programs for young children abound in growing things, from lima beans to vegetable gardens. Take advantage of this with your child and try to instill a sensitivity not just to the new foliage but to creating *berakhot* (blessings) for each state in the planting cycle. Holidays that celebrate harvests, first fruits, and seasonal changes are all the more meaningful to children who have a sense of what it's like to see a first fruit or leaf that they've planted and watered. Don't worry if the harvest in your home doesn't correspond exactly to the Jewish calendar year. What you want is to give the children real experience in their own lives to which they can refer in order to understand other external experiences. Children need our active help in orienting themselves to the world of time and seasonal changes. We can assist by helping them to record their experiences and to make predictions. Through the use of clay, paint, and blocks, children can attempt to interpret their own experience. After all, it is through an ever-growing system of symbols, both verbal and nonverbal, that people communicate. Children need the opportunity not only to "take in" their world but also to "pour out" (always cover the floor!) images of that world. Free expression lets them clarify what they've seen. Remember, you, the parent, structure the initial experience, but you must then be accepting. What you will probably find is that what is meaningful to your child is not always exactly what you had hoped for in planning the experience. So even though *you*

took the children to the *sukkah,* do not be surprised if the child draws a picture of bees in the *sukkah* or of a fire hydrant that he passed on the way to the *sukkah!* The ability to use symbols is the basis for human communication. So the next time your three-year-old tells you those crayon marks on the paper are "a man," smile. If you are the questioning sort, ask if the "man" has a name. Do not ask why he doesn't have a *kippah* (skullcap).

Egocentrism is the name given to the uniquely childish form of thought most prevalent between the ages of four and six. Often the results of children's thinking will be in agreement with adult thought: what differs is *how* the child reasons. Adults basically reason deductively; one thought leads to another. Most are careful to differentiate what's real from what isn't; many can tell the difference between personal opinion and fact and try not to contradict themselves. Generally, when given the opportunity, adults are only too glad to give "proof" for their opinions.

Not so with children. Young children's thinking is intuitive. They reason on the basis of individual facts. There is no process of deduction. The child believes in what she or he thinks and therefore feels no need for proof. By being continually able to juxtapose propositions, the child can contradict him or herself without feeling any logical inconsistency. It's much like the story of the Rebbe, who, after deciding in favor of both parties in a dispute, was asked, "But Rebbe, how can they both be right?" The Rebbe looked at the man and said, "He's right, and he's right, and you're right, too!"

Language, like all of experience, is set into a personal matrix of the child's own construction. Even though you may think you know what you're talking about, children understand it according to what they think it to mean, which may be very different from what *you* had in mind. In the struggle to communicate, the issue is what is understood, *not* what was meant. This doesn't mean that adults should stop talking to children. What it does mean is that children's understanding of language is based on their own experience. So make your language concrete and help broaden your children's range of experiences so that you and they have shared both the experience as well as a meaningful, intensive, and common language to describe it. When you tell a Jewish story, if you want to know if your children understand something, ask them to talk about it—out loud! Take the time to find out what things mean to them. Sure, it takes much longer. But the goal is to get the child to think as much as for the adult to be heard!

(Incidentally, beware of the highly verbal child! What could please "the people of the book" more than the child's first words? Children learn that talking pleases, but the adult must not confuse words with reason. A child who has learned the vocabulary of emotion [e.g., I *need* that] has not necessarily developed the emotional controls to go along with the words.)

Young children need to be supported in their efforts to make themselves understood. Too often, the adult steps in to stop a fight or to solve a problem before the child has a chance to express his or her thoughts and feelings. How often do parents say, "Stop crying, tell me what happened." Let the tears come, and comfort, and then let the child tell what happened. Language is useful as an expression of experience, *not* as a substitute for it. Children begin to use language only as it begins to have as much meaning for them as the actions and feelings of their own bodies.

We have already spoken of the child's developing sense of self and of an ever-elaborating meaningful system of symbols with which we learn to communicate. But most crucial in terms of a child's development as a competent Jew is the learning of Hebrew. For Jews to communicate with other Jews and to partake of the knowledge and heritage written over the course of our history, they *must* know the language. There is no more important way to communicate the meaning of things that are Jewish than in the language of the Jewish people. Children who learn the word *mitzvah* (commandment) as they learn and do the *mitzvot* have no need to learn the translation; the meaning is real. Just as all of language is based on meaningful experience, a child's Jewish experience and the understanding of the Hebrew language can and need to be inextricably meshed together.

To name is to know. Children who are learning to talk will walk about, saying, "What's that? What's that?" They want to know what things are called. Once children have a name for something, it has meaning. So if their desire to learn Hebrew is only limited by what you the parent know, well, there's no better time than now to learn more Hebrew yourself. Learn *with* your child.

Regardless of the most elaborate educational environments we can

create, it is the family that gives real psychological coherence and meaning in a young child's life. The most successful Jewish preschools pay more than lip service to parent participation. They know that the home and school must function as reciprocal reinforcing Jewish environments. The success of a child's Jewish identity depends in part on the willingness of the parents and teachers to present a united positive image in the eyes of a child.

The preschool can also function as a mechanism for a beginning relationship between the family and school. There is much that the parents can teach the school and much that they can learn there, too. Only when the child's images of family and school are linked by their common Jewishness can we begin to succeed to educate the *whole* Jewish child.

Here is a list of types of games appropriate for young children. Parents can make appropriate games for each of the different holidays, changing the content to reflect the symbols, vocabulary, activities and customs, foods, etc., for each.

Remember that regardless of which particular developmental task is stressed (e.g., eye-hand coordination or visual discrimination), the whole child participates. Each activity has a personal-social aspect and a language component, resulting in the child's continual emergence as a learner.

Seeing Similarities and Differences

- Card games—use pictures of Jewish objects from catalogues, magazines (*Hadassah, Moment*, etc.).
- Matching picture card games (like Concentration, Old Maid).
- Double picture cards—are the two pictures the same or different?
- Find the same picture—construct a board or a strip of paper using several similar or a few very different pictures. Hand the child a picture of one of the pictures on the board and have the child find the match.

Seeing Relationships

- Patterns—make a set of picture strips using ritual objects, food, familiar faces, toys. Have a duplicate set of individual pictures for the child to arrange in the same order as the original set of pictures.
- Follow the pattern—set up a strip of pictures or use real objects or miniatures. Repeat a pattern or have the child complete it: "What comes next?"

Board Games

(These are particularly good for cooperative learning.) Substitute familiar and new objects for the colors in games such as Candyland or Chutes and Ladders. The object is for the child to recognize the picture, know the Hebrew vocabulary (*hallah*), activities represented on the board. Try to make the games reflect the interests as well as the developmental levels of the children.

- Lotto (can be adapted to Jewish content)
- Bingo with pictures

Dramatic Play

- Create holiday boxes. Fill clear plastic shoe boxes with the ritual objects for different holidays or *Shabbat.* Include miniature people, furniture, or empty boxes from spices used in familiar recipes.

Classification

- Sorting objects. What makes a *kiddush* cup different from a "regular" cup? Allow the children to put objects, or pictures of objects, together according to what the *child* sees as the organizing principle. It might be interesting to hear a child's ideas of appropriate work/ *Shabbat* activities.

Organizing Experience

- Take dictation from the children to record *their* stories. Tell them *your* stories. How do *you* celebrate *Shabbat?* What do *you* do as a Jew?
- Self-made books by parents or children.
- Personal books, reflecting activities, trips, or shared adventures.
- Picture books of drawings, paintings, or photographs.
- Stories written by the child. Display the stories to visitors to your home.
- Recipe books—exchange your children's favorite recipes with those of children in other families. Let the parents know which parts of the recipe the children can do by themselves. Send along a "pinch" of a particular spice attached to the child's favorite recipe.
- Tape recordings—record your child singing or telling stories.

Problem Solving

- Jigsaw puzzles—create your own by gluing large pictures to boards and covering with contact paper, then cutting them up on a jigsaw. If you have access to a laminating machine, use it. Use pictures of things your child has seen or would like to see, or enlarged pictures of Jewish celebrations.
- Sequence puzzles—three, four, or five separate pictures showing the sequence of an activity—the different stages of a cooking experience or stages in preparation for *Shabbat.*

CHAPTER SIXTEEN

EVALUATING SCHOOLS

Daniel Margolis

Whether it is a day care center or a Hebrew high school, as you seek a good setting in which your child will learn and grow, you'll find yourself necessarily evaluating educational institutions. Friends may recommend schools or programs, but you know that the burden of choice rests on you. Where do you begin? What constitutes a good school for your child?

What follow are some ways of sorting out your reactions as you visit and explore different kinds of Jewish educational programs.

While only a few items on this list are important, the lack of many of them or their inaccessibility to you ought to raise questions in your mind.

ATMOSPHERICS

The atmospherics of a school (camp, youth program or other educational enterprise) can be important and include the physical design of the school and of each classroom; the appearance of students and staff; the rules and regulations and how they are enforced; the tone of the written material; the availability of staff to talk with you (are they there before and after school for any length of time?); maybe even how the kids enter the school (how quickly they leave is never a serious or reliable indicator); and the condition of the textbooks, furniture, and equipment. While there are some "intangibles" in this category, subject to any one person's own interpretation, it should be clear that we are not referring to concerns about the "happiness quotient" of students and staff. Happiness is not, despite observable appearances, a readily determinable or evaluable criterion. What you are looking for is the ambience of the school as manifested in its atmospheric elements.

PEOPLE

Another major source of information is the people involved in the school—students and staff, lay people and professionals. Lay people should have considerable opportunity for influencing the direction and operation of a school, whether they are officially charged with that responsibility (e.g., school committee or board of directors) or not (parents). Having the opportunity to make oneself heard or simply to advise on the operation of the school is very different, however, from having the opportunity or the right to run the school. There is a very fine line between behaving as a responsible lay person in a school setting and behaving as a professional in "lay clothing." Professionals, too, must exercise their authority, responsibility, and expertise and be prepared to be evaluated for their efforts. This is not as tangential an issue as it might seem. All the documents and feelings a school generates will not tell where the real authority or power lies. Knowing who is ultimately responsible is important to you as you go about gathering information and drawing conclusions.

You will want to use both objective and subjective information to learn about the people in the school. You have to rely on your own (and the other people's) ability to separate fact from feeling, but you will be looking for answers to such questions as: What are the goals and expectations of the individuals you talk to—for themselves and for others? What has their experience been? Even the custodian or the owner of the candy store around the corner will have insights into the school that, at the very least, might be of interest. In short, get as much information as you can.

OBSERVATION

I cannot urge strongly enough that you visit the school to observe it in action. Although one visit is seldom enough for a complete judgment, it's the best index you have. Plan to spend at least two hours (or one full day's schedule) in the school to get an accurate impression, plus any more time needed for personal interviews and reviewing printed materials. Calling ahead and setting up an appointment is the correct thing to do; surprise "dropping in" is almost always considered unfair and inappropriate.

WHAT DO YOU LOOK FOR
WHEN YOU OBSERVE A SCHOOL?

The temptation is often to skip the prosaic elements of observing a school setting in favor of the more "seductive" areas of philosophy, goals, and decision making. When observing the school, however, remember to notice the day-to-day aspects of the program, including the physical space and layout of classrooms, the daily program, the staff's relationships to the students, and other very mundane issues.

PHYSICAL SPACE AND LAYOUT

Is it reasonably clean?
Can everyone get out in the case of an emergency?
Are there any physical hazards or obstacles anywhere in the building or on the grounds?
Are the bathrooms clean?
Are the children crowded?
Do the classrooms or study areas provide sufficient space for various kinds of learning experiences: large and small groups, individuals, tutoring sessions, etc.?
Is the plant in good repair? Well lit? Attractive? Decorated well?

THE DAILY PROGRAM

Is there a daily plan of the educational experience? Weekly? Monthly? Yearly? Does each day seem to include some experience that is important, exciting, or interesting? Are there any arts experiences planned on a fairly regular basis (music, art, drama, etc.)? Does the daily program seem to be varied in content and method? Are the transitions from one activity to another smooth? What goes on when the kids arrive at and leave the school? Is the environment and the daily routine essentially active or passive for the students?

RELATIONSHIPS BETWEEN STAFF AND STUDENTS

A competent staff can make up for other lacks in the program, materials, or surroundings. Recognizing that "good" teaching can include any number of basic approaches and styles, we would urge you not to jump to prejudicial conclusions about the "appropriateness" of a given school simply because the teachers seem to have only one way of teaching. ("Who is wise? He who learns from all people"; Pirkei *Avot* IV:1.) Still, some guiding questions might help you observe the interpersonal relationships.

Do the professionals seem to like the children?

Do teachers converse with the students or just "teach"?

Do the students listen?

How does the staff handle discipline? How do they deal with a scapegoat? A crying child? A fighting child?

Are the teachers consistent in their handling of problems? Are they fair? Evenhanded in their application of ethical principles?

Do the teachers use the students' ideas effectively, giving credit and praise when appropriate and not being insulting or personal even if the response is inappropriate?

Do the professionals attempt to understand (first-hand, if possible) the family life and social context of their students?

Do they know what is going on in the rest of the students' world, for example, public school, groups, recreational interests, and sports?

THE THEORY AND PRACTICE OF A SCHOOL—
WHAT TO LOOK FOR

After observing the school in action, you will still not have a complete picture. There are other dimensions in the school, including the administrative structure, philosophical principles, and the curriculum design. Within the administrative structure you should be able to discover anything from the school's budget to its emergency procedures to where the decision-making power lies and the process by which decisions are made. Taking the administration step by step, you probably will be interested in the following: (1) tuition and other fees (membership requirements?); (2) school calendar and absence policy; (3) cumulative record keeping; (4) the procedures for parental contact; (5) background and experience criteria for the faculty; (6) staff salary and personnel codes of practice for full-time and part-time faculty; (7) class size and teacher-student ratio; (8) graduation and bar/bat mitzvah requirements; (9) other academic requirements and academic standards; (10) the state of the equipment and physical plant; and (11) the quality of the communication among professionals and school committee, faculty, and administration.

These, then, become the basic elements of school administration necessary as enabling bases on which the educational program can be built. It is important that there be some systematic way of determining salary scales, staff benefits, and other administrative necessities. Though individual schools may approach each area differently, the "better" schools will at least have some method of applying each of these basic administrative elements with fairness and equality.

THE PHILOSOPHICAL PRINCIPLES

It is more difficult to determine what the overarching principles of a school are than to discern its administrative structure and functioning. However, one of the two following stances would resolve a portion of these dilemmas for most people. First, if the school has a carefully written document stating its principles and "goals" or even some of its philosophy—a thoughtful, logical statement of basic beliefs, somewhat more particular than "motherhood" and "apple pie"—and it seems willing to "live" by that document when it counts and whenever possible, you have the opportunity to either agree with the statements and affiliate with the school or disagree and withdraw. Even if you disagree, you may still decide to affiliate for many other reasons, including the fact that at least the school and you both know what it is about and you can anticipate and deal with any conflict.

Alternatively, the school may plainly state—also in some kind of articulated form—that it is searching for its credo. As long as the search is an active and intelligent one, you can decide to affiliate or not, based on some real information about the direction and content of the struggle or on some willingness to contribute (or not) to the search process.

CURRICULUM DESIGN

Since most things that happen in a school (or any educational setting, for that matter) are, in truth, part of the curriculum design, this area is perhaps the most important of all. There are, again, certain questions and issues that might help guide your information gathering. First, in terms of the course of study or the subject matter of a school, you should understand the logic of its sequence and progression from year to year, even from unit to unit. The curriculum should exhibit a cohesiveness in two dimensions: cohesiveness from the initial experiences in the school to the final experiences and cohesiveness in the selection and presentation of information, materials, and ideas. The curriculum should therefore be concerned with comprehensiveness and certainly with the presentation of the most important aspects of those experiences and subject matter that match the school's credo or theoretical stances. In other words, while there should be a confluence between the school's "philosophy" and the subject matter it chooses to teach, the selection of that subject matter must also meet the tests of coherence.

The school also should show a commitment to the continuity of Jewish education, from the early years through meaningful educational experiences for adults (staff included), as part of its curriculum design. What is the nature of that commitment? Is education for the very young taken seriously and used as a basis for what is done in later years?

You might also want to ask, what are the provisions for remediation? For attending to children's special needs? For paying attention to the needs of individuals while promoting the whole group's progressive development?

What experiences are planned for group and individual participation? Are the individual's senses aroused to the sights, sounds, tastes, and touches of the Jewish tradition? Are emotions touched and brought to bear on the learning experience? Naturally, not every school could possibly cover all these aspects, but a school staff that has at least considered most of these questions is moving in a positive direction.

In addition, the subject matter chosen and the materials selected should have an accessible logic of their own. Some questions in this regard include: What are the implications of adopting a goal of Hebraic conversational fluency in a program with very limited hours? What is and is not sacrificed for the sake of, say, holiday celebrations? Is there

some attempt to understand the cognitive and moral development of a child in the selection of subjects, materials, and approaches? Where possible, are outside experts brought into the school? And the truly critical questions: Is the teaching well planned and well thought out? Is the information conveyed correct?

In terms of evaluation, are goals clear enough (and articulated) so that everyone is aware of the basis for evaluation (students, staff, administrator, school committee)? Does "objective" evaluation (one person evaluating another's progress or performance) take place regularly? Are people's evaluations based on their own abilities or on some group standard of achievement (the class, the grade, the school, the city, the nation)? Is self-evaluation an ongoing process in the school, particularly for the administrator, staff, and school committee? Is feedback from the school's constituent groups gathered on a regular basis? Is educational change a desired outcome of the ongoing self-evaluation? Is educational change approached rationally and carefully? Is innovation haphazard?

These questions provide a bridge between the administrative and the curricular domains. One other set of questions will bring us full circle and bridge the philosophical and the curricular domains. Is there an organizing principle around which the school is structured? What is eventful in the school? In the life of a student in this school? What are the symbols and the symbolic meanings and experiences (including esthetics) generated by the school? What are the ideals of the school? What (or who) is the school's agenda, and how does it make use of it? In what ways, both substantively and methodologically, does the school act as agent in the lives of its people? In sum, as seen through its philosophy and design, what does the school *do?* What does it *urge?* What does it *create?* What does it *believe?*

Finding the right school is difficult and chancy. No one can be expected to do the kind of evaluative study suggested here even though this is not an exhaustive approach. But if you can ask yourself and the school some of these questions, your search can at least have a direction.

If you're the organized type, the chart below will help you record your observations in the appropriate spaces.

	ATMOSPHERICS	PERSONS
ADMINISTRATIVE STRUCTURE		
PHILOSOPHIC PRINCIPLES		
CURRICULUM DESIGN		

In any event, in determining the "rightness" of an educational program for you, you are ultimately concerned with

WHAT HAPPENS?

WHY DOES IT HAPPEN THE WAY IT DOES?

WHO DOES IT?

DO THEY DO IT WELL?
and
WHO ARE THE OTHERS AND WHAT DO THEY DO?

Finally, you have to ask yourself, Is this one good for us?

CHAPTER SEVENTEEN

IN PRAISE OF JEWISH DAY SCHOOLS

Robert Abramson

In the face of increasing assimilation, we see a growing commitment to day schools by many Jewish families and the community as a whole. More and more Jews seem to choose day-school education for their children, and, paradoxically, many of those considering day schools are the very people who would have found the idea totally alien ten years ago.

From 1962 to 1980, the number of day-school students in America increased from 62,000 to 92,000. These students now constitute one-fourth of the total Jewish school enrollment. In addition, while all types of day schools have been growing, the most dramatic growth has been among non-Orthodox schools. Since its founding in 1964, Solomon Schechter (Conservative) Day Schools have grown to fifty schools with ten thousand students; and there are also six Reform day schools.

What accounts for the increased popularity of day schools among disparate segments of the Jewish community? No one factor can be isolated; rather, a cluster of reasons explain the change.

Within the American Jewish community, there has been a bilateral cultural movement, with parts of the population moving toward greater assimilation and another part toward stronger Jewish identification.

Israel, ethnicity, and spiritual searching have all contributed to this move toward intensified Jewish identity. From this intensification, the situation arises where couples with little formal Jewish knowledge seek greater involvement for themselves and their children. Consider the following scenario:

A Jewish couple in their early thirties have a first child who is approaching school age. For one reason or many, often stimulated by the vicissitudes of Israel's well-being, the parents are concerned with holding on to or developing their Jewish identity. They are third- or fourth-generation Americans, college graduates, totally at home in American life. No longer are accents or even intonations in speech a self-conscious problem, and they know their kids will be firmly a part of American society. If their grandparents saw Americanization as their first priority, these parents are anxious about Jewish continuity. In suburbia, Jewishness does not come with neighborhood identity, and since it is not a part of the turf, the parents know they will have to make decisions.

They might have had a good Jewish education, but it is more than likely that they did not and that they see themselves as Jewish illiterates. (Perhaps this feeling is the one positive outcome of their Jewish education.) They perceive their supplementary Jewish education to have been inadequate, something that failed them, and they want something better for their children. They want an education that will succeed in teaching Hebrew and that will replace Jewish ignorance with Jewish literacy: most simply, they want their children to know more Jewishly than they do.

To such a parent, concerned Jewishly yet freed from the Americanization "hangup," the day school seems a viable option. It eliminates the inevitable problems of "after school" programs, since the day school does not show Jewish education as an extracurricular addition to what children know as "real school." With this advantage, combined with high standards in general education, the day school becomes an alternative that many more Jewish parents are investigating for their children.

There are, of course, other factors that have influenced the growth of day schools. Perhaps the most negative reason is a growing lack of faith in the public schools' academic standards and a concern with social problems created by bussing. The growth of alternative day schools in the country has made the Jewish day school a choice for larger numbers of Jews. Moreover, increased affluence in some segments of the community makes day-school education more possible. Finally, since the melting-pot ideal has given way to the "orchestra" model—with each group in America contributing that which is unique to it, even though the result recently seems more of a social cacophony—there has been an increased emphasis and legitimization of group differences. Indeed, the preservation of ethnic identity is now an American value and makes the choice of day-school education more legitimate.

> We decided to send Phillip to our local day school even though we felt ambivalent about it. We live in a small Southern town, and all our neighbors are non-Jews. We care about getting along with them and were afraid that the day-school experience would isolate Phillip. It's true, it does isolate him somewhat, but he still plays with his friends on the block after school, and Cub Scouts also allows him to mingle more. We're happy with the education he gets at the day school and are satisfied that, despite the costs, for Phillip it was a good choice.
>
> ANNE COHEN

If you've been brought to the point of considering a day school for your child by a constellation of personal and social factors, there are many issues to be seriously considered.

The fact is, choosing a day-school education for your child means additional financial obligations.

Most day schools expect and obtain far more parental involvement than do public schools, both in fund raising as well as in policy making. Indeed, day schools can range in structure from parent controlled to professional dominated, with all kinds of variations.

Day schools are not value-free institutions. If you are practicing Orthodox Jews, you probably have clear criteria in the form of beliefs and practices and will seek out a school in harmony with your convictions. Given the Orthodox movement's long-standing commitment to day schools, chances are that there will be such a school in your community. What is true of Orthodox Jews, of course, could be said of any parents who have worked out a Jewish philosophy of life.

If you have a coherent Jewish philosophy of life, you will seek a school in harmony with that philosophy. If one does not exist, you'll have to decide what compromises you are willing to make. A Conservative couple might have to use an Orthodox school. An Orthodox parent may have to use a community school. You can take some comfort from the fact that school is not the only source of a child's education, particularly in the sphere of beliefs and values.

But if you are one of the majority of Jews without a coherent ideological position, you are likely to approach any day school with more confusion and apprehension. You may know that you want your child to have a good Jewish education, but are not sure of the form that should take. You want Jewish values to be taught but are apprehensive that such an education might be judgmental.

In communities where there is more than one day school, you can carefully investigate the values and ideologies of the schools and choose accordingly. If there is only one day school in the community, you may have to face some difficult decisions. You will have to consider the benefits and drawbacks of the school and determine whether you can live with the price.

Whichever is the case, there are certain questions you will want to ask of any school to be clear on where it stands Jewishly. This is by no means a definitive set of questions, but the answers should reveal the school's ideological position. Keep in mind that feeling comfortable with the values of a school depends more on how accepting the school is of different patterns of Jewish observance than on what specific Jewish rituals or texts are taught.

1. How does the school understand the origins of the Bible (Torah)—as revealed truth, a mixture of human and divine, or an inspired human work?
2. How does the school teach Jewish law *(halakhah)*, and what stance does it take toward observance—indoctrination, invitational, laissez faire?
3. What role does the school assign to Hebrew, and how is it taught?
4. What subjects are emphasized in the Judaica curriculum?
5. How is the division of time between general and Jewish studies determined?

It is important to realize that there are good and bad reasons to choose day-school education, and some honest assessments are in order.

If you choose a day school because you want a good private education for your child, you are probably making the wrong decision. Quite simply, while day schools aspire to the highest academic standards and do indeed achieve them, the day school is far more than a private school. It is an agency of the Jewish people; as such, it has an agenda that goes beyond a good general education. The "plus" in day schools is to be found in Jewish studies and not in the recreational or artistic programs that are the accoutrements of secular private schools. On the

---

It wouldn't have occurred to either Sharon or me not to send Judith to a day school. We both come from traditional homes and our own Jewish values are quite traditional. Moreover, it matters deeply to us that our child be an educated Jew. But what angers both of us is the tradeoffs. Why does the Jewish community, by the very nature of the schools it creates, make us choose between progressive, humanistic education and Jewish education? Why can't we find a day school that cares as much about Judith's *neshamah* (soul) as it does about her math grades?

MARK KLEINSTEIN

other hand, "Make a Jew out of my child" puts an unfair burden on the day school despite its expanded Jewish resources. The day school cannot guarantee future Jewish commitment, nor is it a bulwark against intermarriage. It is unrealistic to feel disillusioned if a day-school graduate grows in some Jewishly disappointing direction. Indeed, it is too early to evaluate the influence of day schools on the child's subsequent Jewish identity. All we know now is that there is some evidence of a positive correlation between the number of hours of Jewish education and later Jewish identity. The best that can be said (and this is a great deal) is that a day-school education is a hedge against Jewish deflation. If, for whatever reason and because of whatever influences, the child, when he or she grows into adulthood, chooses to live a Jewish life, the day school will have provided him or her with the resources of a basic Jewish literacy and practice.

If you have found a school that you are comfortable with Jewishly, there remains the important expectation that the school will provide a quality general education. Many parents who are new to day schools question whether the school, as a result of its double curriculum, allots less time to general studies than do public schools. And if it does, how can it get the same or better academic results? One response to this question is simply to look at the "product." In fact, day-school children consistently score high in standardized tests and do well in their post-elementary education. There are at least three reasons why this is so. First, educational success is determined by the way time is used and not by the time available. Second, day schools usually have selected populations as a result of self-screening and/or admissions policies. Third, you should never make the error of thinking that the only "real" education is general studies. It is true that general studies may be allotted less time in day school than in public school, but teaching and learning take place throughout the day, as much in Judaic studies as in general studies. The

Judaic study program teaches and reinforces many of the intellectual skills needed in the general-studies program. Hebrew as a second language, the study of traditional texts, how to think clearly—all of these are necessary for both pieces of the day-school pie. If you look at both dimensions of the curriculum as supplementing one another and reinforcing one another, the academic achievements of day schools are not so surprising. There is less time spent on certain subjects, but not less time spent on education.

Will you know if a given school offers the quality education you seek? In general, it is helpful to speak both to parents who are currently sending their children to the school and to parents of alumni. Find out about the structure of the school. How are students grouped? What spectrum of student abilities and types can the school handle? Is there one or more class per grade? For the answers to such questions, a lot of discussion will be necessary, as well as a visit to the school. (Consult Chapter Sixteen.)

Above all, in choosing a school, you will be looking for educational quality and stability. Schools are not consumer products, easily bought and discarded. You want an institution where your child will be able to finish as well as start. While no institution is perfect, the school must basically be what you want for your child or you won't be willing to live with problems. In other words, if the school is to work for your child educationally and psychologically, you must commit yourself to it.

GOALS OF DAY SCHOOLS

Many day schools are affiliated with Orthodox, Conservative, Reform, or secularist movements, while others are community schools. Such

labels do not reflect accurately the even greater array of orientations, local conditions, faculty, and institutional leadership. Even though different goals distinguish the various orientations, there are at least three Jewish goals that are common to all schools: producing a learning Jew, developing the student into a *mensch* (untranslatable: closest is "worthwhile person"), and instilling a love for the Jewish people. The substantive content of schools will vary. Some will consider the Talmud the subject matter for the learning Jew, others the Bible, and others Jewish history. Some will see a love for the Jewish people expressed in bringing the students to *mitzvot;* others will see concern for Israel or perhaps *aliyah* (settling in Israel) as the ultimate expression of the love of the Jewish people. Regardless of the orientation, the day school is clearly a superior educational vehicle among the available options with at least the potential to accomplish these and other goals. In its program, there is sufficient time to give the child a grounding in Jewish texts, to develop Jewish skills, and to teach those basic learning and language skills that will make continued Jewish study a possibility and hopefully a great joy.

The real distinction between schools lies in value differences, which should be investigated carefully. What attitudes are taught? What values are stressed? How are they taught? What is open to question? What are considered fundamental values? To what extent must members of the faculty share the same values? How such questions are answered should be of paramount importance to you in choosing a school.

Integration of studies is one goal of some day-school proponents. The question becomes: Is it possible not only to teach Judaic and general studies but to integrate those studies at the same time? Can we develop materials and train staff to make such integration a reality? If the integrity of subject matter becomes an issue as a result, keep in mind that the school need not have a totally integrated curriculum. For educational/psychological purposes, islands of integration can be enough. A final question is whether the student has the opportunity and guidance to integrate the values and knowledge that he or she has learned. This question applies more to adolescents than to younger children, but it is a crucial and not greatly explored dimension of an education that could enable a student to begin developing a Jewish philosophy of life.

Despite any of the problems endemic to day school, it is clear that the day-school movement is the success story of Jewish education. Whether measured by growth, student success, parent satisfaction, or the satisfaction of professionals, the day school is increasingly becoming the educational form with the greatest potential for intensifying Jewish life.

> There is a Jewish day school in every city with a Jewish population of more than six thousand people.

CHAPTER EIGHTEEN

CHOOSING AN AFTERNOON HEBREW SCHOOL

The idea of the afternoon Hebrew school is so attractive. It holds out the promise that we can "have our cake and eat it, too." We can send our children to that really wonderful private school of our dreams for the ultimate educational experience, which will help them become learners for the rest of their lives or help them get into Harvard. Or we can send them to that really good public school for which we pay taxes and where we hope they will participate in the American dream and get to know children from all kinds of backgrounds. Our children would then receive the schooling we want for them and receive in the afternoon Hebrew school a good Jewish education and a social context for getting to know not only other Jewish children but also positive adult Jewish role models after school. In the best of all possible worlds, we would not have to sacrifice anything. We would be able to help our children become fully American Jews whose participation in different subcultures would be authentic to their identities.

This is the dream of the afternoon Hebrew school, which is supported by positive products of the system: adults we know who really did learn Hebrew in Temple Bnai Abraham in Newark in the early 1950s or Boston's Kehillat Israel in the early 1960s or Park Avenue Synagogue in the 1970s. The skills and commitments of these alumni of afternoon Jewish education hold out the hope that if it could work for them, it can work for our children.

As is true of the dream of the Hebrew day school, there is a great discrepancy between our ideal and the reality of the afternoon school. Occasionally, we hear about a really exciting Hebrew school, one where basic education and creative experiences combine to stimulate and support the Jewish interests of students, parents, and faculty. But the norm of Jewish afternoon education is, as we know so well, abysmal. Teachers are insufficiently paid and not treated as professionals. The job is attractive only to college students who want supplementary income but are not well trained as teachers or to "schleppers" who were certified as teachers by the dullest institutions of the American Jewish or Israeli community. The exceptional teacher who is well qualified and committed to teaching children about Judaism is in an intrinsically frustrating position. There is never enough money or status inherent in the job, and what exists is often dispensed grudgingly by parents whose only Jewish educational experiences left them deeply ambivalent or subconsciously hostile. Children go to Hebrew schools after long, full days; they arrive at just the time they need to unwind and nosh. As they walk in the door, they know the difference in seriousness between "real" school and Hebrew school.

While in our dreams we have not compromised anything of their Jewish and general educations by sending them to two schools, the children feel desperately compromised when Hebrew school conflicts with lacrosse games and ballet lessons and Little League. Yet we want our children to be well behaved and "turned on" to Hebrew school in such a state of "nudginess." Miracle of miracles, some actually do sit still and learn something. Elsewhere in this book (see Chapter Twenty-seven) we have spoken of "hidden curricula" and of the need to understand this important concept; we must then ask what our children are actually learning in Hebrew school. The principal may hand us a carefully thought out curriculum, but the bottom line for us still has to be "Curriculum aside, what is my child learning?" What messages are being conveyed? Do children learn that Jewish study can be exciting, that Hebrew can represent a key that can unlock hidden treasures, that the thoughts and feelings of other Jews can challenge their own? Or are they learning skills in passing notes without being caught, in sitting still and looking involved while weaving a fantasy of freedom in their imaginations? Many of us fear the latter scenario and are wary of choosing an afternoon school for our children because of it.

On the other hand,, we know there are some powerfully good reasons to choose an afternoon Hebrew school. As one parent of our acquaintance put it:

"I am well aware of the fact that what my daughter gets in Hebrew school is not what my friend's child gets in Hebrew day school. But I do not want her to get what she might get from the day-school experience. She certainly cannot conjugate a Hebrew verb to save her life, but she is growing into the kind of *mensch* that her father and I want her to be through the psychological sensitivities of her teachers in the private progressive school we send her to. I honestly believe that to be a *mensch* is more important than to know Hebrew, and I am deeply impressed by the skills and priorities of her teachers. I also know that she is receiving a general education of high caliber and is meeting kids from a variety of walks of life. Reading the names of her classmates is wonderful; there is even an Arab child, as well as black, Chinese, and Hispanic children.

"Yes, we have to help her deal with 'us and them' issues when her classmates invite her to birthday parties on Jewish holidays or want her to join them in Christmas celebrations. But learning to deal with these issues is a realistic part of living in the United States.

"I worked hard to find her a good Hebrew school. I am satisfied with our choice of a school that is trying to provide children with positive Jewish experiences. They bake *hallah* and learn to make Jewish things. I want my daughter to know that she is Jewish and that being Jewish is a good thing. And when she is older, I hope that all that backlog of positive experience will add up to her wanting to find out more about her Judaism. Why does everybody feel that educationally they have to 'build Rome in a day'? Why can't we trust enough in the power of our heritage to believe that our kids don't have to learn everything today but will continue to learn all their lives? What is more important, to be able to recite a Bialik poem or to be a decent, Jewish human being?"

How do those of us who believe in the afternoon Hebrew school go about creating the kind of school that will generate positive Jewish experiences for our children?

What can we do to bridge the gap between our dreams and the reality?

Certainly, we must understand that no matter how hard we work, we are fighting against powerful communal forces and norms of our larger society that may ultimately undermine our efforts. We must begin, then, in the obvious first place by talking, talking, talking with other parents and with Jewish professionals. We have to clarify what we want, what we can honestly expect, and what goals are realistic. Do we really want, for example (leaving aside initial, wildly enthusiastic urges), to found a new Jewish school? What is implied in such an ambition? Is it realistic? A nice idea that was discussed briefly in our community was to establish an alternative afternoon program in an existing private school. The scheme was for children to attend an excellent school during the day and go to a supplementary Hebrew school that would meet in the same building at the end of the school day. The underlying notion was to convey to children that Hebrew school extended out of and was related to their "regular" education. The idea failed in some measure because there weren't enough children to carry it off but also because the parents themselves were not committed enough to the idea ultimately to make it work.

Alternatively, we may want to commit ourselves to working with an existing school. Often such a commitment is accompanied by membership in an existing synagogue; after shelling out all that money, we may feel more like asking, "What can they do for us?" rather than, "How can we help them?" Although we may remind ourselves that we will get out of the experience only what we put into it, we must also be careful and sensitive about the ways in which we relate to staff and parents already involved in the school. The faculty members of the

school often care even more about the Jewish education of children in the school than do many parents, and the frustrations with which they normally work defy imagination. More basically, we want to become supportive workers in the school, not the community *kvetch* (complainer). It is important to remind ourselves of the maxim "If you did not bring the beets, do not criticize the borscht." We also have to remember that given the ways in which Hebrew schools are funded, we are in a powerful position and must use that power judiciously. We know, for example, of situations in which parents have gotten teachers fired. Sometimes these teachers deseved to be fired; sometimes they did not. Always such use of power reflects a compromising of professional ethics that undermines the very professionalism that we seek to nurture in teachers.

Working for the betterment of a school can provide us with learning experiences ourselves. Who are our initial allies and friends? Do teachers see us as partners in the process of trying to make things better or as threatening board members? How much time and effort are we prepared to invest? What is realistic? Can we really work in the context of the Hebrew school, or should we go elsewhere in pursuit of quality Jewish education?

Yes, there are a few schools in this country that are able to create learning environments that stimulate children both affectively and cognitively. Unfortunately, there are many, many more that promise us all manner of education for our children and are incapable of fulfilling those promises. And yes, there are children who learn and grow Jewishly in those flawed environments. Given the imperfect world in which we live, generations of Jewish educators have debated priorities of how best to use the few hours a week that children spend in Hebrew school. Some, as represented by the venerable Boston Hebrew College, would argue in favor of pursuit of solid Hebrew language skills. Others, such as our friend quoted above, would argue for more experiential learning. If our friend's suspicions are accurate, and the best an afternoon Hebrew school education can do is provide children with positive feelings about their Jewishness so that the children will *want* to go on to explore their Jewish identities later, how, then, do we encourage our schools to do this? Among the issues to raise in this context are: Does the school provide enough "hands-on" types of projects (baking *hallah*, sewing a *tallit*, doing Israeli folk dancing)? Does the school make use of supplementary nondidactic teaching possibilities—trips, libraries, movies, etc.? Can the school provide contexts for special-project work for children?

We suspect that a school stressing either Jewish skills or experiences is more viable than schools (especially small schools with insufficient staff) that try to be all things to all people.

Finally, in making the conscious choice to sacrifice an academic Jewish education in favor of other important personal values, do we also acknowledge the other responsibilities we simultaneously assume:

to make our family's life together an especially rich one Jewishly?
to encourage our children to join Jewish youth groups?
to enroll our children in Jewish camps?
to make periodic family visits to Israel?
to search out the Jewish people's places in whatever other cities we visit?

The choices are ours. They reflect some of the most basic visions of ourselves living as Jews in this country. They also reveal some of the most fundamental dilemmas of American Jewish education. As we stop visiting schools and sit down to decide where to send our children next semester, our thinking becomes intensely personal. We assess our needs and think about ourselves and our children. Perhaps as we ask ourselves what kind of Jewish person we want our children to become, we should also consider not only what kind of Jewish person we are now but what kind of Jewish person *we* want to become.

A COINCIDENTAL COMPLIMENT

We have discovered that the principals of two Hebrew schools praised in this article are, in fact, father and son: Solomon and Joseph Colodner.

CHAPTER NINETEEN

10 WAYS TO BE A RESPONSIBLE PARENT IN A SCHOOL

1. Support your child's loyalty to school and teachers. Try to convey your confidence in the adults with whom you have entrusted your child. Young children need to know that you believe their teachers will take good care of them. Older children need to know that you support their looking to teachers for leadership. Remember the sweaters that grandmothers knit for the first day of school? Remember the new book bags and pencil boxes? By buying or making such treasures, you convey your enthusiasm about your child's going to school and your belief in the enterprise.

2. What if you do not feel 100 percent enthusiastic about the school your child is attending? Perhaps you are even in the unhappy position of having chosen between two schools on the basis of the lesser of two evils. Having weighed the alternatives and arrived at your decision, try not to burden your child unnecessarily with your ambivalent feelings. At those times, when it is important to share your honest thinking with your child, be sure the information is appropriate to your child's age.

3. While encouraging your child's self-discipline and sense of responsibility, show interest in his or her assignments and projects. Try to be sure that homework is completed on time. Remember, it is not your job to do homework; it is your job to be sure that there is both time and space in which homework can realistically be completed. Obviously, you do not want to become a police officer, but your encouragement may make the difference.

4. Walk the narrow line of not intruding too much but still involving yourself in what your child is studying. Issues that emerge from an older child's classroom discussions can stimulate interesting dinner conversation. ("Well, Dad, how would you vote on capital punishment? But, Mom, what if the person were a Nazi?") On the other hand, who wants their parents to emerge suddenly as authorities on topics with which they are just coming to grips? ("Well, when I wrote that memorandum for Justice Frankfurter after the Nuremberg trial . . .")

5. Visit your child's class and attend school-wide activities but remember that your child experiences your attendance at a school play very differently from your presence in the classroom. Attending a play expresses your support and involvement. Children at varying ages, however, react differently to their parents' presence in their classroom. A young child may love your being there; an older child may be intensely embarrassed. Make sure you prearrange your visit with teacher, school officials, *and* your child. Your attitude should be that you are there to learn. You, your child's teacher, and your child are all partners in the process; you are not sitting in the classroom as inspector or judge.

6. Make sure you understand the regulations of the school. Let school officials know your specific needs and concerns. Try to be as clear and firm as possible in the messages you send to school and be realistic in what you ask of school officials. You may be surprised by their helpfulness if you are effective in the way you make requests. Emergencies do occur and make it necessary occasionally for us to ask people to help in ways that are really difficult. In situations that are not emergencies, think about what you are asking of a staff member when you call the school at 3:25 and ask that a message be delivered before the 3:30 dismissal time. Take a cue from a good executive who may assign difficult tasks but makes sure that the tasks are also do-able.

7. When problems do arise, address your complaints immediately to the appropriate school personnel. In fact, adhere to the school's "chain of command." Bring a problem to the attention of the person most immediately responsible. Thus, the first person to consult about a classroom problem should be the teacher. If the problem cannot be resolved at that level, move up the hierarchy. Do not begin by telephoning the superintendent of schools or the chairperson of the board of education even if these people are your close personal friends. Avoid *kvetching* to other parents or airing your complaints at large group meetings before raising the issues with school officials. Either of these pitfalls can undermine school morale and may earn you a reputation as an unconstructive, complaining parent. Prompt and direct contact with the appropriate school officials is much more likely to bring about the change you want.

8. Listen to teachers' perceptions of your child. Know that each of us behaves differently in different environments. For example, an extroverted child at home may become shy at school or vice versa. The more you learn about your child in different situations, the more complete a picture you will have. Additional insight into your child can only help you in parenting.

9. Yes, you are your child's advocate, but take care not to fall into the psychological trap of identifying so fully with your child that you confuse your own personal agenda with your perceptions of your child and his or her performance at school. Try to stand back and

evaluate what is going on. A low grade on your child's report card need not be a threat to your ego. The high mark that you are earning in parenting will never come to you on a little grade card slip from your child's school.

10. Involve yourself in school activities as a volunteer. Let the school staff, your child, and other parents and children know that you support the values of the school. Help drive not only the car that gets children to school but also a car caravan to take them on an extracurricular visit to a Jewish old-age home, an exploration of the Lower East Side, or a visit to a Jewish museum.

KIDS SAY . . .

Alisa: I have learned that people who yell loud enough almost always get what they want. You know: the squeaky wheel gets the grease? I think that what schools have to begin doing is to give students the confidence to believe in themselves and then to get things changed. When I have confidence and believe in what I'm saying, I'm willing to squeak really loudly, and usually I can get things changed even within the gigantic bureaucracy of my school or the state I live in.

If schools are constantly reinforcing the idea that teachers know everything and are all-powerful, that living within the system is the only way to get through it, and that given these two elements, there's no point trying to change anything because the student doesn't know anything, then kids will never gain that confidence and may never learn to change things they feel are wrong throughout their lives. I mean, it is easier to say, "This system's been around for so long, it's gotta be good," than it is to say, "Holy cow, this system is totally archaic. Why hasn't some change been instigated?" and then to work for change.

Change is healthy. We are the new generation. We have to know how to change things that dissatisfy us. For instance, it is our obligation as Jews and human beings to protest and try to change the treatment of Soviet Jews today. But people tend to forget that it's important to protest the things that are unfair to us as individuals as well. Soviet Jews go through hell and high water protesting what they think is unfair, so shouldn't we be able to walk down to the principal's office to have a friendly chat about things that dissatisfy us in school?

Carol: I definitely feel that young people have the power to change things within the system that they feel are unjust or simply unfair. I have seen school policies changed because the student body spoke out. We have got the power if we just use our own voices.

(Continued)

Heidi: I hate school now, and I'll hate it in college. I hate the system, the competition—the smartest get into the best colleges, etc. I hate it all, but I have no alternative ideas. I don't know why. I just have no ideas yet that sound logical. Most students fall into a middling category. They like some parts of school and dislike others.

Morty: I don't like the system, but I want to succeed in life, so I'm not going to fight it.

Noam: The American educational system is fantastic, the best in the world. It is modern, with few exceptions, and offers a good range of educational opportunities for all ages. Some people think American schools are too competitive, and have tried to organize institutions without competition—like high schools with only pass/fail courses and without mandatory attendance. What they end up with is unattended high schools. The pass/fail atmosphere is inappropriate for the competitive world we live in. You cannot shut yourself off from reality by trying to teach a kid to grow up without competition, because when he finally does grow up, he will not function successfully in the modern world.

CHAPTER TWENTY

INFORMAL EDUCATION: JEWISH PLAY

Some of the most important Jewish education does not happen in Jewish schools but in informal environments—summer camps, youth groups, trips to Israel. Only recently has this fact been taken seriously. Accordingly, the Jewish community has begun to reexamine the role of informal education in the Jewish educational process.

Parents, too, have begun to understand how their child can benefit from participation in a youth group or Jewish summer camp. And let us be clear: while there certainly are some mitigating factors, such participation can have a profound effect on the future Jewish identity of the child.

Much of the content of the programming in youth groups and the better summer camps centers around study about and discussion of Jewish values, Jewish life, and Jewish ritual. (For Zionist groups, the agenda is slightly different, focusing on Israel and Zionism.) Participants experience *Shabbat* together, actually living out what for most of them has been only an artifact studied in school. In addition, they are able to reinforce their Jewish commitment by participating in a variety of experiences in a peer environment, which permits the merger of the social and Jewish content aspects of their lives. The opportunity to experience a full Jewish moment in the company of one's friends can act powerfully on the minds of adolescents.

In addition, kids are exposed to alternative Jewish adult role models who are in constant personal quest regarding their own Jewish lives. As a result, the kids are exposed to a variety of adult responses to questions of Jewish identity.

Generally, these settings provide adolescents with their first opportunity to function socially, independent of their families. Such programs allow parents to begin the separation process that generally culminates in the final separation of college, and let the adolescent know that his or her parents have the kind of respect and confidence that permit such social separation.

There are risks in encouraging your child to join a Jewish youth group or attend a Jewish summer camp. The first lies in the very success of such experiences. Because they will encourage your child to identify positively and deeply as a Jew and to practice a living Judaism, such experiences may, directly or indirectly, be challenging the way you live your Jewish life. Your family may not keep kosher, or you may not celebrate a full *Shabbat*, yet your child will be participating in an experience advocating both.

Be prepared for a story like Jonathan's:

"My parents positively identify as Jews but are certainly not in any way traditionally observant. They are well-educated people who care about quality education and sent me to the best Jewish school that our community had to offer. I learned a lot. I became curious and eager to experience in some real-life way the rituals I read about in a theoretical way in Hebrew high school. I had been part of a youth group because everybody was, but I really leaped at the opportunity when the group offered a *Shabbat*-experience retreat. The experience of that weekend was incredible. I resolved to have more such experiences. And there I was with teachers and group leaders who were showing me that such experiences were not voluntary, like going to a concert, but were my constant obligation according to *halakhah*. As good liberals, my parents were fairly open and understanding about my desire to observe *kashrut*, but I thought my mother would faint when I refused to eat the ice cream because I was not sure about some of the ingredients on the package."

The other risk lies in the fact that in such environments your child's peer group is a Jewish one. For the child who attends a large, integrated urban high school, this probably will not be a problem. But for the child already in a Jewish day school, we have to question the ghetto effect of participation in a youth group or summer camp. Unless the young person has other contact with non-Jews, the gilded ghetto walls slowly being constructed may be impossible to tear down later. And the fact is, we are a minority within a larger culture. The people we live next to, work with, shop with, work politically with, sometimes eat with, are non-Jews. Creating an artificial environment that belies this fact is harmful and unrealistic.

Despite such concerns, however, there can be no doubt of the value of the educational experiences in such programs. Any informal survey of committed Jewish adults will inevitably turn up a significant number whose Jewish identity was profoundly affected by their camp or youth-group experiences. Encouraging your child to become involved—despite the risks—can only be seen as a good decision and an important commitment.

YOUTH GROUPS

Youth groups function on local, regional, and national levels, usually under the aegis of adult, "parent" organizations. What groups are available to teenagers in your community? We have created a directory below of all the national organizations we could find which sponsor youth divisions. We have listed each organization's name and address, followed by a brief description and the names of its groups that are open to teenagers before they are "college age." We strongly encourage you to explore local groups, because of potential variation between individual chapters of any national organization. As you learn more about your community's resources, you may find that teenagers have banded together to create an exciting, indigenous group or club with no national affiliation. *"Kol ha-kavod,"* more power to them! You may also find that your community lacks youth groups or that existing ones need additional support or stimulation. In such cases we hope our directory will prove helpful in contacting national organizations for advice in developing your own resources.

Agudath Israel of America, 5 Beekman St., New York, NY 10038; committed to the perpetuation of Orthodox Judaism; youth groups: Pirchei Agudath Israel, Bnos Agudath Israel, Bachurei Agudath Israel, and Zeirei Agudath Israel

Americans for Progressive Israel, 150 Fifth Ave., New York, NY 10011; a socialist-Zionist organization; youth group: HaShomer HaTzair

B'nai B'rith, 1640 Rhode Island Ave. N.W., Washington, DC 20036; this large fraternal organization sponsors such wide ranging programs as the Anti-Defamation League and campus Hillel foundations; youth group: B'nai B'rith Youth Organization

Federation of Reconstructionist Congregations and Havurot, 432 Park Ave. South, New York, NY 10016; the congregational organization of the Reconstructionist movement; youth group: T'hiyah

HaBaD, Lubavitch Hasidic Organization, 770 Eastern Parkway, Brooklyn, NY 11213; the best organized of all Hasidic groups in its out-reach programs; youth groups: Tzeirei Agudas HaBaD, Pirchei HaBaD, and Bnos HaBaD

Hadassah, the Women's Zionist Organization of America, 65 E. 52nd St., New York, NY 10022; the largest women's Zionist organization in the United States; youth groups: Ha Shachar and its affiliate Young Judea

Jewish Welfare Board, 15 E. 26th St., New York, NY 10010; agency of the Jewish community services Y's and centers; with your local Jewish community center or YM/YWHA, many of which sponsor clubs and special interest groups for teenagers

Labor Zionist Alliance, 575 Sixth Ave., New York, NY 10011; this liberal-oriented, Zionist organization is affiliated with the Mapai party in Israel and sponsors such groups as Pioneer Women and Farband Labor Zionist Order; youth group: Habonim

Mizrachi-HaPoel HaMizrachi—Religious Zionists of America, 200 Park Ave. South, New York, NY 10003; an organization which seeks synthesis between commitment to Orthodox Judaism and labor Zionism; youth groups: Bnei Akiva and Noam

National Council of Young Israel, 3 W. 16th St., New York, NY 10011; the national organization of Young Israel, Orthodox synagogues; youth group: Yisrael Hatzair

Student Struggle for Soviet Jewry, 200 W. 72nd St., New York, NY 10023; this organization of young people seeks to promote activities beneficial to Soviet Jews

Union of American Hebrew Congregations, 838 Fifth Ave., New York, NY 10021; the central congregational organization of the Reform movement; youth group: North American Federation of Temple Youth

Union of Orthodox Jewish Congregations of America, 116 E. 27th St., New York, NY 10016; the central congregational body for many Orthodox synagogues; youth group: National Conference of Synagogue Youth

United Synagogue of America, 155 Fifth Ave., New York, NY 10010; the central congregational and service organization of the Conservative movement; youth groups: United Synagogue Youth and Leadership Training Fellowship

Yugntruf—Youth for Yiddish, 3328 Bainbridge Ave., Bronx, NY 10467; fostering Yiddish language and culture among young people

Zionist Organization of America, 145 E. 32nd St., New York, NY 10016; a Zionist organization which leans to the right of center politically; youth group: Massada

My involvement in a Jewish youth group might be seen as a metaphor for my adolescence. It represented a transition from childhood to adulthood. I joined the group through our temple, intending to have a good time with my friends and please my parents and hoping not to be too bored. I was intellectually challenged to think about real issues which affected me as a Jew. I believe that I experienced these issues more personally than parallel questions which were being raised in my good public school, because the issues were Jewish. In any case, I became increasingly involved and began to attend conventions. The materials which came from the national office were excellent. I met young adults, often themselves college and seminary students, who were prepared to take me and my religious questions seriously. I became a regional and later national officer. As I assumed increasing responsibility within the organization, I became more committed Jewishly and more in need of the social and emotional rewards that I gained through my involvement. When I went to college, my work within the organization had to change, and the involvement became more problematic and less satisfying. I had to grow away from it to mature personally and Jewishly. Eventually I had to redefine myself Jewishly as separate from it. Now I do some advisory work for the national office, but it, of course, is not my central arena of activity anymore. I owe it a great deal and gave it my adolescent best.

ANONYMOUS *Macher*

CHAPTER TWENTY-ONE

JEWISH CAMPING

Marilyn Sladowsky

The environment is total. Every aspect of the facility was intended for your intellectual and emotional growth. Schedules were designed to offer you as many possibilities for learning as time would allow. You are far from home and family pressures in a mountain retreat, living in close proximity with your peers. Your only anxieties have to do with your performance in classes and on the baseball field. Your feelings are deeply aroused in relationships with beautiful young girls and boys who are your best friends and worst enemies. And you know that on a certain day in July or August you will be going home. The stage is set for some of the most intense experiences of your young life. The environment? Jewish summer camp.

No wonder that many of us recall summer camp experiences as the most significant of our young Jewish lives and identities. Also no wonder that many of us, despite ever increasing fees, choose to send our children to summer camp. In the following article Marilyn Sladowsky discusses ways of finding the right camp for your child.

There can be a *good* Jewish camp for every child, no matter what his or her interest, degree of Jewish involvement, or family's income. Every child should experience one summer at a Jewish camp, and every parent should have a summer without the child at home.

When looking for a camp, here are some questions and answers not about specific programs but about health and safety:

Q: How many children in a bunk?
A: Depending on the size of the structure, no more than ten to twelve. Otherwise, unless there is a third counselor, the individual child gets short-changed.

Q: What are the ages of the counselors?
A: At least one counselor in the bunk should be nineteen or over and have completed some college.

Q: How many counselors per bunk?
A: There should be at least one counselor and one junior counselor, someone who has completed high school.

Q: Does the camp have resident nurses?
A: A camp should have at least one and preferably two R.N.'s, depending on the size of the camp.

Q: What about the waterfront?
A: All waterfront personnel should have a W.S.I. (water safety instructor) certificate from the American Red Cross. Back-up staff, such as counselors, should minimally have a senior lifesaving certification.

Q: Is the camp generally well kept? Are proper safety measures maintained?
A: Items that have to be on everyone's checklist include the plumbing, the roofs, the steps and railings. In public buildings, proper numbers of fire escapes and ventilation should be checked. Does *every* building have at least one fire extinguisher? Is all of the electrical wiring done properly? Does the camp have an emergency system, including a good public address system? Are counselors taught elementary lifesaving skills? Do they know what to do in case of an emergency? Does the camp conduct fire drills regularly? Does it have a permit to operate from the local Board of Health? Are playing fields safe, level, and free of glass and nails? Are there proper indoor facilities in case of bad weather?

Q: Are the camp specialists really specialists?
A: Make sure, for example, that if your child is learning woodworking, the person in charge knows how to use the tools properly and instructs your child *before* the activity begins. The same holds true for the use of kilns and radio equipment. Keep in mind, though, it is not necessary to have Marc Chagall as the painting instructor in your child's summer camp.

The food at camp should not necessarily be fancy, but it should be reasonably good, well balanced, nourishing, and attractively served. The kitchen should be clean, and those who work in it should be supervised by a professional. In many states, food workers are required to have physical examinations, including TB tests, and to keep their hair covered while working with food. Check the state health laws.

The program of the camp is also very important. Since the midsixties, the trend has been toward specialty camps. These specialties include the Hebrew language and Jewish culture, various sports, weight loss, camping and hiking, and the arts. In addition, most Jewish movements, whether synagogue oriented or Zionist, run camps or networks of camps. Each camp has its own standards of admission.

With regard to Jewish programming in camps, parents should be very careful to make sure the camp suits not only the child but the family life style or expectations. This is the same issue raised earlier in the article on informal education. Your child's Jewish identity will most certainly be stimulated if you choose to send him or her to a camp with a different Jewish approach from that of your family. However, if your child

spends an intense period of time living and exploring a style of Judaism different from the one he or she currently knows, you can expect some straightforward challenges to your own Jewish life style when your child reappears at the end of the summer.

Another area to consider is that of religious observance. If your family keeps kosher, be careful not to select a camp that says "American Jewish Cuisine" or "Kosher Style." If your family has no Yiddish interest, sending your child to Boiberik can be a disaster.

Our shock when confronted by camp costs notwithstanding, camps are an expense, but not necessarily expensive. Some have a "pay-out" system; others work on a sliding scale according to income; still others have sources of scholarship aid. These must be explored on an individual basis with the camp you are considering. Be sure to include all extras when you consider the cost of a camping experience for your child (clothing, insurance, canteen, special excursions, transportation to and from camp, and the cost of shipping trunks). Any camp that is ACA (American Camping Association) accredited does not permit tipping of the staff.

A word about professionalization: The ACA is the major camping organization. If a camp bears the ACA symbol, it has been through a rigorous inspection in order to become accredited. The ACA also spot checks camps periodically and does a reaccreditation if the camp changes owner, directors, location, or name. The ACA publishes a listing of all its accredited camps, as does the Association of Jewish Sponsored Camps, which includes information on tuition. This is also true of the Jewish Welfare Board. (See listings at the end of this chapter.)

There are also camps for "special" Jewish children. These camps are either solely for the handicapped child or part of a larger camp that integrates these children into its "regular" camp program. The Tikvah program of the Ramah Camps is a good example. Again, the standards for admission of each camp differ greatly (see Chapter Twenty-three).

Day camping is popular—especially in communities where there are large Jewish centers and Y's—and is a good steppingstone to overnight camping. The same questions parents ask about an overnight camp can, for the most part, be asked about a day camp. (By the way, it is very important to make sure the buses or vans used by the day camp to transport children are in the best condition possible. Ask questions about the caliber of drivers as well.)

If your child is hesitant about going to camp, give him or her a gentle push. Find out the names of former campers in your community and let your child call them directly. If you want, arrange a visit to the camp before the summer. Just remember one thing. A camp, no matter how beautiful or picturesque physically, has no real character. A camp only becomes alive when children fill it. The camp will have even less of its real character if you visit it.

Once your child is in camp, be sure to write regularly. Avoid telling your child how much you miss him or her, or all the things that they're missing at home. Do let them know how hot it is and how lucky they are to be in a place where they can swim every day. Try to overlook early letters that talk about homesickness. Most children are homesick at first. More important, recognize the fact that you might be "childsick." Many times it is not a matter of whether or not the child is ready for camp but if the parent is ready to send him or her. Most camps require that campers write home regularly three times a week. One way to ensure getting mail is to send along self-addressed, stamped envelopes or postcards. Letters might be slow in arriving in the beginning simply because most camps start around the Fourth of July weekend and mail is always slow at that time. Remember, no news is not necessarily bad news. This is especially true in camps where kids are always on the go.

If the camp your child is attending has a visiting day, go, or make sure you arrange for someone you know to visit your child. Camp is a very lonely place for a child who has no visitors on that day. Be sure not to bring too much "junk food," and encourage your child to share whatever it is that you bring with his or her bunk mates. Seek out the director, counselors, teachers, specialists, and anyone else who is working with your child. Don't be afraid to ask questions. Be prepared to be introduced to a lot of people that day. Once the official visiting day is over, leave. Camps and campers have to get back in a routine. Don't worry if your child sheds a few tears. Tears usually stop before the dust from your car settles. One of my favorite visiting-day stories happened when a ten-year-old began to cry the bitterest tears I'd ever seen when his parents were ready to leave. Since they were friends of mine, I pushed them into their car and urged them off. Before they were halfway down the road, the tears abruptly stopped, and a glowing smile appeared as the child complacently said, "My mommy would have thought I didn't love her if I didn't cry."

Although in recent years there have been many debates about visiting day at camp, with some people maintaining that a camp that only has one or two visiting days a season and does not permit parents to visit at any other time has something to hide. This is palpable nonsense. Any camp that is involved in educational endeavors has a responsibility to see to it that this endeavor is carried out seriously. A "drop-in" visit not only disrupts the camper but the other youngsters as well. And if a camp "gussies up" for visiting day, what's wrong with that? Everyone likes to put their best foot forward for company, and certainly every child likes to show off for his or her parents.

There is an enormous variety of Jewish camps. They range from Hebrew- or Yiddish-speaking camps to traditional camps, camps that require daily classroom study, to Zionist camps, to work camps. Investigate fully the Jewish component of what ever camp in which you have an interest before you send your child there. Some questions to ask include:

1. What is the *kashrut* observance of the camp? Is it in consonance with your own observance? Is there a *mashgiah* (a *kashrut* supervisor) or someone in charge of verifying that *kashrut* standards are maintained?

2. What is the *Shabbat* observance of the camp?
3. What kinds of formal Jewish educational demands are made on the campers?
4. What kinds of informal Jewish educational experiences does the camp plan?
5. How Jewishly sophisticated and knowledgeable is the staff? Are they appropriate Jewish role models for your child?
6. Is there a good Jewish library accessible to the campers? Is it attractive, appealing, and up-to-date?
7. What are the daily Jewish rituals and experiences that are observed or maintained? Prayer? Hebrew language?
8. What are the Jewish cultural components of the program? Jewish music? Dance? Arts and crafts?

Listed below is a sampling of agencies that sponsor camps or maintain lists of camps that are recommended:

American Camping Association
Brandords Woods, IN

Association of Jewish Sponsored
  Camps
130 E. 59th St.
New York, NY 10017

B'nai Akiva
25 W. 26th St.
New York, NY 10010

B'nai B'rith
1640 Rhode Island Ave., NW
Washington, DC 20036

Cejwin Camps
71 W. 23rd St.
New York, NY 10010

Division of Communal Services
Yeshiva University
186th St. and Amsterdam Ave.
New York, NY 10034

Habonim
575 Ave. of the Americas
New York, NY 10011

Hadassah Zionist Youth Camps
817 Broadway
New York, NY 10003

Jewish Welfare Board
Department of Camping
15 E. 26th St.
New York, NY 10010

National Ramah Commission
3080 Broadway
New York, NY 10027

Union of American Hebrew
  Congregations
835 Fifth Ave.
New York, NY 10021

Other single Jewish camps are:

Brandeis Camp
Brandeis, CA 93064

Massad
426 W. 58th St.
New York, NY 10019

"My summer camp experience was fantastic. I met a whole new group of kids, and the program was great. Since I go to a pretty rigorous private school, and my parents aren't all that into Jewish stuff in their own lives, this was really my first experience with living a Jewish life. It blew away all my stereotypes. Celebrating *Shabbat* in camp with all my friends was fantastic, and I'm really looking forward to going back again next year."

LISA,
age fourteen

"I hate mosquito bites and showers with muddy floors. I never would go to summer camp as a kid. 'You want to get rid of me that badly?' I would ask my parents, and they would let me stay home. My university's Hillel director got me to go to Hillel's summer institute at Starlight, Pennsylvania, for a week between my sophomore and junior years, and it proved to be the most important experience of my Jewish life."

ANONYMOUS

CHAPTER TWENTY-TWO

ISRAEL, A LEARNING LABORATORY

David Zisenwine

A Canadian friend of ours living in Jerusalem was asked in which ulpan *he was studying Hebrew. He replied, "All Israel is my* ulpan." *Every verbal encounter, from the most trivial counting of change by a bus driver to the most erudite lecture of a Hebrew university professor, helped our friend's growing language skills. Beyond vocabulary and grammar, the totality of any individual's experience in Israel can function as a learning laboratory. Where can you begin if you want to provide your child or your family with some of the wide range of potential learning experiences offered by Israel?*

Most young people who visit Israel unaccompanied by their families are adolescents. If you and your teenager are interested in his or her visiting Israel, you should begin by considering the same issues that a good curriculum planner faces. First, you must carefully select your goals. Your goals can be anything from wanting your child to bring home a real understanding of Jewish history (from the biblical period to the modern state) to wanting your child to understand how archeological digs are organized and work, to life in a rural community setting, or to learn to empathize with and appreciate the social problems of people from the four corners of the earth with their special cultural and linguistic differences. Identifying your goals is vital to any program and should be your first priority. This process of goal clarification can be a learning experience in itself and is most fruitfully undertaken as a cooperative venture shared by parents and child. Much will depend on your offspring's level of maturity and ability to function independently.

Once your goal or combination of goals has been established, you must consider what activities can best serve to bring about your objective.

Here are some basic questions to help clarify goals and activities.

1. How much time will be available—a year, a month, or a week?
2. Is this experience to be in conjunction with other Americans of the child's age group or is it solo?
3. Is it a rural (kibbutz) or urban experience, or perhaps some combination of both?

Not making these kinds of distinctions or leaving them to well-intentioned friends or travel agents often leads to serious disappointment. The standard travel-agent whirlwind tour has as its objective bombarding the senses in order to experience as much of the variety of Israel as possible within the allotted time. The goal is to give a sense of the dynamic life of Israel in a kaleidoscopic manner, without much concern for depth or understanding. This kind of program does heighten consciousness, and if it's what you want, you can find it at any travel agent's desk.

If, however, you see this journey in a broader context, it is worthwhile to investigate some of the study programs available and their implicit and explicit objectives. Keep in mind that almost all programs have implicit objectives of exposing the participants to a life style based on a particular ideology. You should be aware that ideology is far more important in Israeli life than in America and more often than not is the underlying principle in organized social life in Israel.

Let's take a look at some of the possibilities you can consider in selecting a program.

KIBBUTZ

One goal might be to present your teenager with the possibility of a vastly different Jewish life style. The most obvious framework is the kibbutz, which offers communal living in Israel in a rural setting. It is important to realize that the kibbutz movement is not monolithic. It is really *four different movements*, each of which has a different ideology expressed in different life styles and activities. Your selection of a kibbutz movement will affect the nature of your child's experience. All too often, Americans hear the word *kibbutz* and assume that if "you've seen one, you've seen them all" and then select any program that is presented. Your first question should be, To which kibbutz movement does this program belong? Here is a brief list of the movements' differences.

1. Ihud HaKibbutzim V'Hakvutzot is the kibbutz arm of the Israel Labor Party. Its youth arm in Israel is Noar Oved, and abroad it is known as Habonim. Its ideology is socialist-Zionist, and Jewish ritual life—for example, *kashrut*, synagogues, and worship—is almost nonexistent. Instead, you will find interesting new ways to deal with Jewish life, with a heavy emphasis on the agricultural and natural aspects of the holidays. The openness to experimentation with tradition can be exciting.
2. Kibbutz HaMeuhad strongly emphasizes socialism coupled with Zionism and Jewishness. It was once part of Ihud but chose to stress socialist doctrine. It is affiliated with Achudat HaAyodah, a part of the labor coalition. Its approach to Jewish life is similar to that of Ihud.
3. Kibbutz HaArtzi emphasizes socialist doctrine and Zionism even more strongly than the other two movements. It is part of the Mapam party and sponsors the Shomer Hatzair youth movement in Israel and abroad.
4. HaKibbutz Hadati represents a combination of religious Orthodoxy with socialism and Zionism. Here you will find Jewish observance in a very different setting from the usual urban one. This movement is affiliated with the religious Zionist party (Mizrachi) and sponsors the B'nai Akiva youth movement in Israel and abroad.

(There is a fifth movement sponsored by Agudat Yisrael, but it has only two kibbutzim, with limited facilities and programs.)

Knowing something about these movements tells you about their programs and activities. Whether your child spends a year or a week in one of these kibbutzim, he or she will experience Jewish life as lived and practiced by that movement. An important point to remember is that by selecting one program, you have closed off for the duration of that experience other options that are available: Beware of making serious generalizations about Jewish life in Israel without recognizing that you are really seeing Jewish life as lived and practiced by X group.

High School

Another possibility is a boarding high school in Israel. Here your child will not only learn to deal with a new culture and environment but will also be involved in developing independence and initiative. There are several of these institutions in Israel offering American high school programs, with tutoring when required. They offer continuation of regular American school work and a peer group of other American children. Of course, you will have to decide whether this environment will best accomplish your goals.

Some of these school programs include the Tochnit Yerushalayim Semester Program, Goodman Academic High School of the ZOA, and High School in Israel at Beit Berl. See the resource listing at the end of this article for addresses and further information.

An interesting program that offers a high school experience in Israel is the Miami Quinmester Program, sponsored by the Jewish Federation of

Miami and open to all high school age young people around the United States. The objective of this program is to take a group of American high school students for an eight-week period during the school year and offer an intensive course in Jewish history with a coordinated tour to the site, institution, or, when possible, the person or group studied. Many high schools now permit this break in the school year and offer full credit for participation. Note that this program is based on the idea of an American peer group living and studying together in Israel; its contacts with Israeli and Jewish life are well organized and preselected.

Torah Study

Many people see Israel as the center of Torah study and religious experience. If this is your approach, then you will want to consider a program that will provide your teenager with serious Torah study and with a peer group and environment that reinforce study with religious activities. The variety of available institutions is large and representative of the *yeshivah* world. Here, too, you are selecting a unique experience for your child and limiting other aspects of Israeli life while he or she is part of that framework. *Yeshivah* life is also not monolithic, and you must ask what the particular program offers and what it represents on the religious spectrum. Contact the following agencies for further information about the nature of programs.

1. B'nai Akiva, 7 Dubnow Street, Tel Aviv
2. Hezkiya Institute—a center for educational activities and seminars for Orthodox youth. Youth & Hechalutz Dept., World Zionist Organization, P.O. Box 92, Jerusalem
3. Gesher—a program for an interchange between religious and non-religious youth WZO, Youth & Hechalutz Dept., P.O. Box 92, Jerusalem
4. Education Dept. of the Jewish Agency, 515 Park Ave., New York, NY 10022

The Reform, Conservative, and Orthodox movements, as well as Young Judea and B'nai B'rith, also offer summer and year-long programs that attempt to encounter and experience Israel from their particular perspectives. Their year courses as well as those of the Hayim Greenberg Institute and the Institute for Training Youth Leaders from abroad (Machon L'Madrichai Chutz) are almost exclusively for young people who have finished high school. Those of the Reform movement and Young Judea have *aliyah* (immigration to Israel) programs and have each established a kibbutz to absorb their course or movement graduates. They see their programs as part of their commitment to *aliyah* and not as a year's experience. These are fairly recent developments in their own ideology, and their two kibbutzim are still young and exciting experiments of these American movements.

Probably the most popular, wide-ranging, and condensed way to see Israel is one of the summer youth tours run by almost all American youth movements. They are all well organized and often serve as the stimulus for a more extended visit and experience in Israel. Any of them offer an initial, exciting taste of Israel but should not be seen as the end of the process of confronting Israel.

A "DREAM CURRICULUM"

While many programs are tailored to the needs of relatively self-sufficient adolescents, what if you really want to expose yourself and your younger children to Israel? The specific resources, from day care to summer camps to educational institutions and organizations for adults, are too numerous to begin to catalogue here. But the idea of an entire family spending an extended period of time living in Israel represents our "dream curriculum." In such a maximalist scheme, the family could live in Israel for an extended period, anywhere from a month to a year. The family could set up house and actually live a day-to-day life in a setting appropriate to its tastes and life style. This type of adventure would allow for prior planning by all family members; such planning might realistically include study of Israel, communities, weather, food, etc., before the trip, as well as serious decision making about how to live for the selected period. Israel would then serve as the curriculum bank and resource center, and the family members would be their own teachers, facilitators, and guides.

Like all good programs, it requires careful planning: a process that in and of itself could be a real education. There is nothing like doing and experiencing, and nothing better than first-hand experience in cooperating with others. Several families have lived in this way in Israel and have reported that it was not only a unique Jewish experience but a unique family experience.

An alternative to this approach might be an exchange program with an Israeli family. Here, too, the personal interaction and planning offer great possibilities. (Your local chapter of the American Friends Field Service might be helpful in planning such an exchange.)

When you're planning an experience of Israel, a key word must be "doing." Programs that stress direct activity, involvement, and commitment offer the greatest possibility for learning. Israel is the real-life laboratory of contemporary Jewish life. To observe it or see it is far too passive; doing Israel in any way, shape, or form is a guarantee of something happening to you—and that's education.

> The Cohen family of Teaneck, New Jersey, spend their summer vacations in Israel and dream of buying an apartment in Jerusalem. "We know it may sound quixotic, but we feel so good when we are in Israel, and we know that our children learn so much being part of the Israeli social fabric. Our love of Israel makes us willing to put up with all the frustrations of daily life in Israel. No, we do not want to leave our families and life commitments in the United States; our summer visits make it possible to have our cake and eat it, too. No, it is certainly not easy but it is rewarding. We think about our friends who own summer homes on Fire Island, and we know that we are not, in many ways, that different from them."

PROGRAMS IN ISRAEL

High Schools

Huleh Valley Regional High School at Kfar Blum

This is a one-year program designed for tenth-graders. Students live with Israeli students at the school and are "adopted" by Israeli families on the kibbutz. For information, contact

America—Israel Secondary School Program
515 Park Ave.
New York, NY 10022

Tochnit Yerushalayim Semester Program

This program for twelfth-graders is located at the Hayim Greenberg College in Jerusalem and is open to students enrolled in day schools. The program runs from January to June. For information, contact

America—Israel Secondary School Program
515 Park Ave.
New York, NY 10022

ORT at Kibbutz Ein Hachoresh

This one-year program is open to tenth- or eleventh-graders. For information, contact

America—Israel Secondary School Program
515 Park Ave.
New York, NY 10022
or
Women's American ORT
1250 Broadway
New York, NY 10001

EIE of the Union of American Hebrew Congregations

This program is open to sixteen- to eighteen-year-olds, in either a six month or a one-year option. For information, contact

International Education Dept.
UAHC
838 Fifth Ave.
New York, NY 10021

NFTY Half-Year Work/Study Program

Students who have completed all requirements for high school graduation in January are offered the opportunity to study at an *ulpan* and take seminars. For information, contact

NFTY Half-Year Program
UAHC Youth Div.

838 Fifth Ave.
New York, NY 10021

Goodman Academic High School of the ZOA

Open to students in the tenth, eleventh, and twelfth grades, this program extends from September to June and is located at the Kfar Silver campus near Ashkelon. For information, contact

Zionist Organization of America
4 E. 34th St.
New York, NY 10016

High School in Israel at Beit Berl

This program, open to high school students in grades 10–12, runs in eight-week sessions in September, November, January, April, and June. For information, contact

High School in Israel
4200 Biscayne Blvd.
Miami, FL 33137

Six-Month Study/Work in Israel

This program has three options, each of which is a six-month commitment: (1) students live in Jerusalem and study at an *ulpan* for two months, then spend the next four months living and working on a kibbutz; (2) students study four months at the Hayim Greenberg School in Jerusalem and also travel throughout the country; (3) students spend six months in study as day-school students. For information, contact

WZO Dept. of Education and Culture
515 Park Ave.
New York, NY 10022

Yeshivah *high school programs for boys or girls*
Many of Israel's *yeshivot* will accommodate American students. Here are a few:

For girls	For boys
Ulpanot Bnei Akiva	Yeshivot Bnei Akiva
Ulpana, Kfar Pines	Netiv Neir,
Amana, Kfar Saba	Jersalem
Segula, Kiryat	Kfar Haroeh
Motzkin	Or Etzion, Shafir
	Tikvat Yaakov,
	Sdeh Yaacov
	Ohel Shlomo,
	Beersheva
	Natanya
	Yeshivat Shaalvim,
	Kibbutz Shaalvim
	Medrashiat Noam,
	Pardes Hannah

For information, contact
> Torah Education Dept., World Zionist Organization
>> 515 Park Ave.
>> New York, NY 10022

Tochnit Yud Gimel for Boys and Girls (separate programs)
For boys or girls who have completed their secular studies at an American school in three and a half years, this program offers five months of intensive study in Jerusalem. For information, contact
> Torah Education Dept., World Zionist Organization
>> 515 Park Ave.
>> New York, NY 10022

Kita Tet
This half-year program for ninth-graders begins in April and ends in August. For information, contact
> Torah Education Dept., World Zionist Organization
>> 515 Park Ave.
>> New York, NY 10022

Tochinit Yud Gimel for Boys and Girls
This program offers two options. Option one offers a study/work program to seniors who have completed their academic work by January. This program takes place at a religious kibbutz. Option two offers a study program for college credit at Bar Ilan University. For information, contact
> Torah Education Dept., World Zionist Organization
>> 515 Park Ave.
>> New York, NY 10022

Israel Summer Happening
This is a summer program for high school kids. For information, contact
> American Zionist Youth Foundation
>> 515 Park Ave.
>> New York, NY 10022

Gesher Summer Seminars in Israel
Open to students between the ages of thirteen and nineteen, this program is designed for teenagers seeking a religious program. For information, contact
> Torah Education Dept., World Zionist Organization
>> 515 Park Ave.
>> New York, NY 10022

Bureaus of Jewish Education Programs
Various bureaus of Jewish Education around the country sponsor summer educational programs in Israel: Atlanta; Atlantic City; Baltimore; Brandeis School, Long Island; Cleveland; Dallas; Denver; Framingham, MA; Houston; Indianapolis; Los Angeles; Milwaukee; New Orleans; Rochester, NY; Syracuse, NY; Temple Israel, Great Neck, NY. To find out about them, contact your local bureau or institution or
> Dept. of Education and Culture
> World Zionist Organization
>> 515 Park Ave.
>> New York, NY 10022

Bar/Bat Mitzvah Pilgrimage
This six-week program of travel, education, and camping is open to boys and girls thirteen to fourteen years of age. For information, contact
> Dept. of Education and Culture
> World Zionist Organization
>> 515 Park Ave.
>> New York, NY 10022

Confirmation Class Study Tour in Israel
This is an individualized six-week program of study, travel, and work. For information, contact
> International Education Dept.
> UAHC
>> 838 Fifth Ave.
>> New York, NY 10021

Weizmann Institute International Summer Science Program
This four-week program is for science-oriented high school seniors. For information, contact
> Science Program
>> 515 Park Ave.
>> New York, NY 10022

The NFTY Israel Academy
This is a six-week tour and work experience. For information, contact
> International Education Dept.
> UAHC
>> 838 Fifth Ave.
>> New York, NY 10021

Karen Kupcinet International Science School Summer Work Program
The Weizmann Institute will accept a limited number of juniors, seniors, and graduate students on a research project. For information, contact

American Committee for Weizmann Institute of Science
515 Park Ave.
New York, NY 10022

The NFTY Mitzvah Corps in Ben Shemen, Israel

This six-week program is focused on work and study in the agricultural village of Ben Shemen. For information, contact

International Education Program
UAHC
838 Fifth Ave.
New York, NY 10021

Adventure in Kibbutz

This six-week program for sixteen- to seventeen-year-olds offers three weeks of work on a kibbutz and three weeks of field trips and travel. For information, contact

American Zionist Youth Foundation
515 Park Ave.
New York, NY 10022

Yedid *on Kibbutz*

Six and a half weeks of kibbutz living and nature study at a center are available in this program for high school juniors. For information, contact

American Zionist Youth Foundation
515 Park Ave.
New York, NY 10022

Israel and Moshav for High School Students

This four- to six-week program consists of touring the land and working on a moshav. For information, contact

Histadrut Tours
630 Third Ave.
New York, NY 10017

Experiment in Kibbutz Living

This is a summer program for students aged fifteen to seventeen. For information, contact

Histadrut Tours
630 Third Ave.
New York, NY 10017
or
Kibbutz Aliya Desk
575 Avenue of the Americas
New York, NY 10011

NFTY Archeological Seminar in Israel

In this program the students live in Ben Shemen Youth Village and work at the excavation dig at Tel Afek. Touring is

included in this six-week program. For information, contact

International Education Dept.
UAHC
838 Fifth Ave.
New York, NY 10021

ZOA-Masada Teenage Tour in Israel

This is a six-week summer program for kids aged fifteen to seventeen. There are both touring and studying components to the program. For information, contact

Zionist Organization of America
Youth Dept.
4 E. 34th St.
New York, NY 10016

Hebrew University Summer Science Seminar

For those who have completed three years of high school, this six-week program offers a combination of touring and study at Hebrew University. For information, contact

American Zionist Youth Foundation
515 Park Ave.
New York, NY 10022

United Synagogue Youth Israel Pilgrimage

USY Pilgrimage is open to fifteen- to eighteen-year-olds and offers a program of extensive touring and participation in traditional Jewish living. For information, contact

USY Israel Pilgrimage
155 Fifth Ave.
New York, NY 10010

National Conference of Synagogue Youth Summer Seminar

NCSY Summer Seminar is open to students fourteen to eighteen years old and combines in Orthodox life-style with travel and study seminars. For information, contact

NCSY Summer Seminar
116 E. 27th St.
New York, NY 10010

Summer Hebrew-language Ulpan *Programs*

Three summer programs—Kfar Galim, Akiva Natanya, and Youth Ulpan—are open to high school students for summer study. For information, contact

Baltimore Hebrew College
5800 Park Heights Ave.
Baltimore, MD 21215

Gratz College
10th St. and Tabor Rd.
Philadelphia, PA 19141

American Zionist Youth Foundation
515 Park Ave.
New York, NY 10022

Colleges and Universities

Hebrew University

Hebrew University offers a variety of programs designed to fit into different university schedules:

1. One-year program—available to sophomores and juniors; includes a university *ulpan* as well as a nine-month academic period; specialization can be arranged in the fields of natural sciences, business administration, or computer science
2. Regular studies program—a course of study for American and Canadian students who have completed at least one year at an accredited institution and want to finish their degree at Hebrew University
3. Special cosponsored programs—the Hebrew University cosponsors special programs with the following institutions: Education Abroad Program of the University of California; the California State University and Colleges; the Office of International Education of the University of Colorado; Program of Study Abroad of

the City University of New York; the Overseas Study Programs of Indiana University; the International Programs Office of the State University of New York; Spertus College (Chicago); Washington University (St. Louis); the University of Rochester; University of San Francisco; and York College of the City University of New York
4. Graduate programs—Hebrew University offers master's degree programs in humanities, social sciences, mathematics, and natural sciences for students with BA or BS degrees; in addition, special doctoral programs can be arranged in a variety of fields

For information, contact

Office of Academic Affairs of the American Friends of Hebrew University
11 E. 69th St.
New York, NY 10021

Student Affairs Committee
American Friends of Hebrew University
1506 McGregor Ave.
Montreal H3G 1B9, Canada

Tel Aviv University

Tel Aviv University also sponsors a plethora of programs designed to fit many needs:

1. college semester for midyear high school graduates—available to high school graduates who are given the opportunity to earn nine to twelve college credits during the semester
2. freshman year program—designed for students who are considering enrolling at Tel Aviv University or who plan to continue studies elsewhere
3. *mechina*—a year of preparatory courses leading to enrollment on a regular college program
4. *ulpan*—intensive Hebrew program mandatory for people participating in the Overseas Student Program
5. summer session—four-week program available to English-speaking students who have completed a year of college study
6. archeology program—three six-week summer sessions open to students who have completed at least one year of college
7. one-year program—open to sophomores, juniors, or seniors who wish to study for a year abroad at Tel Aviv University

8. semester program—same as one-year program but shorter
9. graduate regular studies—Tel Aviv University offers a variety of programs leading to graduate degrees
   For information, contact
   Office of Academic Affairs
   American Friends of Tel Aviv University
   342 Madison Ave.
   Suite 1426
   New York, NY 10017

Bar Ilan University

Bar Ilan University is the religious university in Israel. It offers a year-long academic program for freshmen, sophomores, or juniors. The semester begins in October, and an *ulpan* is offered in July. Qualified male students may combine traditional yeshivah studies in the mornings with the university's college programs in the afternoon. For information, contact
   Office of Academic Affairs
   Bar Ilan University
   641 Lexington Ave.
   New York, NY 10022

Haifa University

Haifa University offers a variety of programs to fit the needs of different students:

1. semester program—undergraduate program that grants sixteen credits and is available in either the fall or spring semester
2. one-year program—open to all undergraduates; grants thirty-two credits to academically qualified students
3. winter work-study program—eight-week program from January to March. Students are placed in moshavim, kibbutzim, or development towns or various social-welfare institutions and conduct research projects based on their experiences
4. kibbutz university semester—participants spend ten weeks working on a kibbutz while studying Hebrew and doing research, which is then presented as a paper
5. challenge program—permits students with a strong background in Hebrew to attend regular university courses offered in Hebrew
6. graduate regular studies—overseas students can enroll in graduate studies programs in maritime history, marine archeology, and coastal geography
   For information, contact
   American Friends of Haifa University
   60 E. 42nd St.
   Suite 1656
   New York, NY 10017

Colleges for Women

Gold College

Orthodox institution for women who will spend a minimum of one year in intensive Jewish study. Special *mechina* program is available for students with limited program. Stern College for Women cosponsors a credit-transfer program. For information, contact
   Torah Education Dept.
   World Zionist Organization
   515 Park Ave.
   New York, NY 10022

For Women Students with Good Jewish Background

The following institutions are designed for women students with good Jewish backgrounds who want to pursue their Jewish studies in an Orthodox atmosphere: Michlala, Machon Sara Schenirer (Beis Yaakov), Midrasha, Bruriah, Bet Midrash L'Nashim. For information on any of these schools, contact
   Torah Education Dept.
   World Zionist Organization
   515 Park Ave.
   New York, NY 10022

For Women Students with Limited Jewish Background

Several Israeli institutions for women sponsor programs designed for the student with little Jewish background. Among them: Neve Yerushalayim, Machon Bruriah, Or Sameach, Diaspora Yeshiva, Bet Midrash L'Nashim. For information on any of these schools, contact
   Torah Education Dept.
   World Zionist Organization
   515 Park Ave.
   New York, NY 10022

Kibbutz Maaleh Hachamishah

Kibbutz Maaleh Hachamishah sponsors a one-year program for students who wish to combine an academic program with work on a kibbutz. Students enroll in courses at Hebrew Union College–

Jewish Institute of Religion while working at the kibbutz. Open to students who have completed one year of college course work. For information, contact
HUC–JIR
UAHC Youth Div.
838 Fifth Ave.
New York, NY 10021

Teachers Institute Seminar of the Jewish Theological Seminary
This is an eight-week program of intensive study designed for graduate students working toward their master's degree. For information, contact
Ms. Sylvia Ettenberg
Jewish Theological Seminary
3080 Broadway
New York, NY 10027

Hornstein Program of Brandeis University
This four-week program is geared to students who are enrolled in graduate programs to prepare for professional careers as Jewish communal workers. For information, contact
Dr. Bernard Reisman
Brandeis University
Waltham, MA 02154

Colleges for Men

For Men Students with Good Jewish Background
Several Israel institutions offer programs designed for graduates of yeshivah high schools. These are Midrasha, Yeshivat Kerem b'Yavneh, Yeshivat Hakotel, Yeshivat Shaalvim, Yeshivat Merkaz Harav Kook, Yeshivat Kol Torah, Yeshivat Har Etzion, Machon HaRaShal, Beit Medrash LeTorah, Dvar Yerushalayim, Yeshivah Chafetz Chaim, Itri, Torah Or, Porat Yosef, Yeshivat Torat Israel, Yeshivat Or Samayeh, Yeshivat Kiryat Arba, Jerusalem College of Technology, Yeshivat Hamivtar, Yeshivat Aish HaTorah. For information on any of these schools, contact
Torah Education Dept.
World Zionist Organization
515 Park Ave.
New York, NY 10022

For Men Students with Limited Jewish Background
The following Israeli institutions have designed programs expressly to suit the needs of men who have a limited Jewish background: Dvar Yerushalayim, Shappel Center, Or Sameach, Diaspora Yeshiva, Aish Hatorah, Yeshivat Hamivtar.

For information on any of these schools, contact
Torah Education Dept.
World Zionist Organization
515 Park Ave.
New York, NY 10022

Bet Midrash LeTorah
This Orthodox institution is designed for students who have graduated from *yeshivah* high schools. Yeshiva University cosponsors a one-year program. For information, contact
Torah Education Dept.
World Zionist Organization
515 Park Ave.
New York, NY 10022

Hebrew-Language Programs
Israel-America Ulpan at Ulpan Akiva-Hachoff Hayarok
This is an eight-week program open to adults who want to pursue serious language study combined with a tour visit to Israel. For information, contact
Dept. of Education and Culture
World Zionist Organization
515 Park Ave.
New York, NY 10022

USY Autumn Ulpan at Kibbutz Ein Tzurim
Open to recent high school graduates and college students, this program combines kibbutz life with weekend seminars and tours. The program is a five-month program—from September to February. For information, contact
USY Autumn Ulpan
155 Fifth Ave.
New York, NY 10010

Summer Programs
Israel Summer Institute
This is a six-week institute for college students and young adults. For information, contact
American Zionist Youth Foundation
515 Park Ave.
New York, NY 10022

Yavneh Israel Summer Tour
This seven-week tour is for traditional college students. For information, contact
Yavneh
156 Fifth Ave.
New York, NY 10010

Kibbutz and Vacation in Israel
This is a four- to six-week program for college students. For information, contact
Histadrut Foundation for Educational Travel
630 Third Ave.
New York, NY 10017

Summer in Moshav
This seven-week program for college students is designed to permit participants to live on a moshav, study at an *ulpan,* and tour. For information, contact
Youth Dept.
Zionist Organization of America
4 E. 34th St.
New York, NY 10016

Student Summer Tour
This is a six-week program that combines four weeks of kibbutz work with two weeks of touring. For information, contact
American Zionist Youth Foundation
515 Park Ave.
New York, NY 10022

NFTY College Academy
This program consists of a six-week tour of the land. For information, contact
International Education Dept.
UAHC

838 Fifth Ave.
New York, NY 10021

Family Experiment in Kibbutz Life
This summer program for families with children (youngest child must be four years old) involves work on a kibbutz plus an eight-day tour. For information, contact
KX Histadrut Tours
630 Third Ave.
New York, NY 10017

NFTY Kibbutz Summer
This is a seven-week program for college-age students. For information, contact
International Youth Dept.
UAHC
838 Fifth Ave.
New York, NY 10021

Medical Work Summer Program
For students who have completed two years of medical school this program offers an opportunity to spend the summer months in supervised work at Shaare Zedek Hospital. Touring is included. For information, contact
American Zionist Youth Foundation
515 Park Ave.
New York, NY 10022

Summer Seminars for Jewish Center and Camp Workers
In-service training is included in this four-week program. For information, contact
Jewish Welfare Board
15 E. 26th St.
New York, NY 10010

Summer Seminars for Rabbis and Educators
This is a four-week program of workshops and seminars. For information, contact
Torah Education Dept.
World Zionist Organization
515 Park Ave.
New York, NY 10022

College Summer Program
This six-week program for students eighteen to twenty-two years old is designed to allow them to immerse themselves in Israel's culture, land, and history. For information, contact
American Zionist Youth Foundation
515 Park Ave.
New York, NY 10022

Summer Ulpan on a Kibbutz
This nine-week summer *ulpan* for singles or married couples includes working on a kibbutz and studying Hebrew. For information, contact
Kibbutz Aliyah Desk
575 Ave. of the Americas
New York, NY 10011

Other Year-Long (or Longer) Programs

The Institute for Jewish Youth Leaders from Abroad
This is a leadership development program for youth who have been recommended by their Jewish organizations or movements. For information, contact
Long-Term Programs
American Zionist Youth Foundation
515 Park Ave.
New York, NY 10022

Bnai Akiva Program
Bnai Akiva sponsors a year-long program for members. For information, contact
Bnei Akiva
200 Park Ave. South
New York, NY 10010

Habonim Program
Habonim sponsors a year-long program with a three-month kibbutz stay. For information, contact
Habonim
200 Park Ave. South
New York, NY 10010

Hashomer Hatzair Program
Hashomer Hatzair sponsors a program for its members that includes touring. For information, contact
Hashomer Hatzair
150 Fifth Ave.
New York, NY 10010

Noar Mizrachi Program
This is a one-year program featuring work in an Israeli development town. For information, contact
Noar Mizrachi
200 Park Ave. South
New York, NY 10010

Young Judea Program
This year-long program includes kibbutz work. For information, contact
Young Judea
817 Broadway
New York, NY 10007

For Social Workers Only
There is a two-year program of social work in Israel's development towns. For information, contact
Long-Term Programs
American Zionist Youth Foundation
515 Park Ave.
New York, NY 10022

For Chemists Only
There is a one-year program for chemists that includes study at an *ulpan* and then nine months of work at the Technion. For information, contact
Long-Term Programs
American Zionist Youth Foundation
515 Park Ave.
New York, NY 10022

Pardes Institute
This is a two-year program for adults who want to engage in serious Jewish study without denominational commitments. For information, contact
Long-Term Programs
American Zionist Youth Foundation
515 Park Ave.
New York, NY 10022

Six-Month Programs

Project Etgar
Open to eighteen- to twenty-five-year-olds, this program combines travel, Hebrew-language study, and kibbutz work. For information, contact
Kibbutz Aliyah Desk
575 Avenue of the Americas
New York, NY 10011

Mate Yehudah
This is a six-month service learning program for people eighteen to thirty-two years old. For information, contact
Long-Term Programs
American Zionist Youth Foundation
515 Park Ave.
New York, NY 10022

Project Development Town
This six-month volunteer program is for nineteen- to thirty-year-olds. For information, contact
Long-Term Programs
American Zionist Youth Foundation
515 Park Ave.
New York, NY 10022

Seminars

Reform Educators Seminar
This five-week tour features seminars, Hebrew-language study, and lectures. For information, contact
UAHC Dept. of Education
838 Fifth Ave.
New York, NY 10021

Seminars for World Jewish Service
This is a six-week program of seminars and discussions. For information, contact
Office of Academic Affairs
American Friends of Hebrew University
11 E. 69th St.
New York, NY 10021

Middle East Studies Institute for American Educators
This one-month program earns six graduate credits. For information, contact
National Committee for Middle East Studies in Secondary Education
9 E. 40th St., 5th fl.
New York, NY 10016

ZOA-Masada Leadership Training Course
This is a six-week program of work and study. For information, contact
Youth Dept.
Zionist Organization of America
4 E. 34th St.
New York, NY 10016

Hebrew Educators Seminar
Three-week programs are sponsored by the Board of Jewish Education of various cities:
Board of Jewish Education
4650 N. Port Washington Rd.
Milwaukee, WI 53212

Bureau of Jewish Education
2030 S. Taylor Rd.
Cleveland, OH 44118

Jewish Educators Assembly
155 Fifth Ave.
New York, NY 10010

Herzl Institute Study Tour
This is a four-week tour with lectures on Israeli society. For information, contact
Program Coordinator
Herzl Institute
515 Park Ave.
New York, NY 10022

CHAPTER TWENTY-THREE

EDUCATING THE SPECIAL CHILD

Gila Fogel

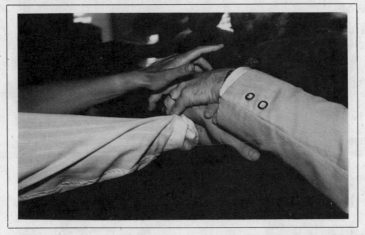

From the time Michelle was old enough to question her birth defects we have always answered, "You were born this way. God made you." And the answer was sufficient. But recently she asked, "Why did God make me with no feet and two fingers?"

"We don't always know why God does things, Michelle."

"Well, I wish I was like everyone else. Anyway, God is not like this. How would He like it."

HELEN FEATHERSTONE,

A DIFFERENCE IN THE FAMILY (New York: Basic Books, 1980)

In her excellent new book Ms. Featherstone has shared some of the very private agonies with which special children and their families must live. In so doing she has given us all hope that we are not alone in our struggles, and even managed to provide us with some helpful resources and references. The monumental difficulties experienced by parents of disabled children know no denominational bounds, but as Jews we are distinctive in two ways. First, as parents we want to raise Jewish children, and that leads us to seek Jewish educational experiences for our children. Second, as Jews and as members of the Jewish community we are obligated to be responsive to the needs of our fellow Jews. We take seriously such biblical injunctions as Ahavat Yisrael, to love the People Israel and "all Israel is responsible one for another" and we understand responding to the special needs of these children and their parents as basic among our commitments. The Jewish community logically needs to begin with the children and their families and parents as it tries to respond. As parents we ask ourselves where to begin. Ms. Featherstone provides a model in the help she describes deriving from a parent support group. We have found that almost any kind of reaching out is a step in the right direction, although we each have our own atrocity stories of attempts to reach out which were rebuffed and we cannot overemphasize the need for sensitivity. In the article which follows below, we find an illustrative survey of Jewish educational opportunities which do exist. The survey does not begin to tell us what we already know, of what ought to exist in every community or within easy access to us. Our hope is that the descriptions will prove helpful and stimulate further development of programs responsive to individual needs.

Jewish parents of "special children" are in a uniquely difficult position. The Jewish community has never seen the education of any special group as a priority, and the Jewish resources that exist for the special child reflect this lack of priority.

> One of the most poignant moments of my life as a volunteer teacher was hearing a little girl who was "mentally retarded" say the *Shema*. I had taught her the prayer over several months, using lots of games to drill the words. Then one day she covered her eyes with her arm and put her head down on the table as though she were going to sleep and said the *Shema*. I am glad her eyes were covered, for I do not believe she would have understood the tears in my eyes.

The goal of Jewish education for special or disabled children is to provide all children with the opportunity to become an integral part of the Jewish community. Too often, children with special needs identify themselves only as part of a handicap group: retarded, learning disabled, etc. Instead, through special Jewish education programs, they can be offered an identity shared with the nonhandicapped. This identity is part of their birthright as Jews.

The term *special* or *disabled child* includes children with a wide range of needs. In this chapter the term *special child* includes the trainable mentally retarded, the educable mentally retarded, the emotionally disturbed, and the learning disabled. Obviously, no chapter can deal fully with the needs of even one, let alone all, of these groups. As a result, what appears below is a list and description of a number of special education programs that can be found within the Jewish community. These programs have been chosen as representative of the various genres of programs that exist and as models that can be adapted to meet the needs of different populations.

Keep in mind that:

1. The field is a new one and many programs come and go. It is therefore important to be aware of the age of each program.
2. Information has been included about the number of children and staff involved so that you can evaluate the scope of each program.
3. Evaluating educational materials is impossible, since formal curricula and Judaica materials are almost nonexistent. Teachers in each setting usually produce their own materials or adapt regular materials and create their own games, worksheets, etc. The development of books and materials emerges as the greatest need of the field.
4. The trend in special education today is to place children into the least restrictive setting possible and to provide opportunities for interaction with "normal" peers. Therefore, the extent of integration of the children into "normal" settings is noted in describing the various programs.
5. Finally, the unique aspects of each program have been pointed out to present ideas of what can be done.

Maimonides Institute
34–01 Mott Ave.
Far Rockaway, NY 11691
Senior Vice President: Rabbi Nahum Shulman
Date Established: Far Rockaway Residence, 1964
Monticello Residence, 1967

Maimonides was initially established as a day school for mentally handicapped children in 1959. It has now grown into a network of three day schools, two centers, summer programs, community religious instruction programs, and vocational training programs. Children between five and fifteen are generally sent to the Far Rockaway campus, and those between fifteen and twenty-one usually go to the Monticello center. Children must be referred by the Department of Social Services (New York State). Those accepted are multihandicapped children. Their handicaps include retardation, brain damage, and emotional disturbances. Non-Jewish children are accepted; however, the orientation of the school is toward traditional Judaism.

The centers are 90 percent funded by the Department of Social Services. The Maimonides Institute is a religious and charitable organization that provides the remaining funds. These are used for the religious components of the program, for construction, and for deficits incurred when governmental funding is insufficient.

The goal of the program is to try wherever possible to provide children with the skills necessary to function in the community. The curriculum includes self-help skills, communication skills, health and safety, social skills, work skills, and motor skills as well as functional academics. The staff/child ratio is one to one, and the staff includes: teachers, therapists, child-care workers, aides, psychologists, social workers, and medical and nursing personnel.

There is a full-time coordinator of religious activities. Children who can benefit from religious academic work and whose families request it are given instruction in small groups or on a one-to-one basis. Teachers make their own games and materials for the most part. Hershel Stiskin developed a series of holiday activity books for use in the Maimonides schools. (See "Jewish Educational Materials" at the end of this chapter.) Holidays and *Shabbat* are celebrated through school observances, assemblies, and festive meals. There is a special *Shabbat* counselor whose role is to provide a *Shabbat* atmosphere for the children. A daily children's *minyan* is conducted. The children can attend the Maimonides Synagogue together with members of the community at large who attend services there.

The Maimonides Institute also sponsors six religious education classes in three different settings for children with learning disabilities. Local synagogues provide the space; Maimonides enrolls and screens the children, provides the teacher, establishes the curriculum, and assumes the financial responsibility for these classes.

A Special Day School

Jewish Center for Special Education (JCSE)
1377 42nd St.
Brooklyn, NY 11219
Director: Rabbi Aharon Fried, Ph.D.
Date Established: Fall 1976

JCSE was established to meet the needs of learning-disabled Orthodox and Hasidic boys. Although it is a separate school, JCSE shares the facilities of the Munkacs Yeshivah. Dr. Fried is the principal of both schools JCSE has two divisions: separate classes and a resource room. There are two special classes, one for ages three to six, and the second for ages seven to ten, and although there is some mainstreaming when possible, the children spend most of their day in separate classrooms. The resource room is for children ages seven to eleven who spend most of their time in regular classes but come to the resource room for tutoring or training in specific skills. The resource room is also used as an enrichment room, which helps to eliminate the stigma of "special" and to avoid the problem of bad peer relationships. As of November 1977, there were forty children in the program. Eighteen were in the special classes, and the rest were served by the resource room. The staff includes two speech therapists as well as seven teachers.

The children in the program are taught primarily in Yiddish, with some English as well. The curriculum emphasizes "limudei kodesh" (Judaica). What is unique about this program is that the learning disabilities are remediated through the use of Jewish materials rather than secular ones. For example, matching, counting, and visual discrimination skills are practiced with such materials as matching pictures of Torahs rather than sleds, or counting Hanukah candles and not balls. This fits in with the experience and needs of these youngsters. The children are introduced to reading Hebrew first, and only later do they learn English (as in most such *yeshivot*). Prereading skills are taught with Hebrew in mind. For example, the visual-discrimination exercises go from right to left.

> We took our mother, who is a stroke victim, to a Jewish music festival. She has worked very hard in a rehabilitation program, but she does make little, involuntary sounds now and then, and with her walker she is identifiably a stroke victim. We were enjoying the music, and suddenly a matronly woman sitting in front of us turned around and said, "Can't you keep your mother quiet?" After I recovered from my own (and my mother's) pain and anger, I began to think that such responses in public places are daily experienced by parents and children who have special needs. And we encourage them to come out of the closet.

Obviously, such a program requires an emphasis on curriculum and materials development. The staff at JOSE has been at work creating such materials. A group of parents has formed a company known as Educational Enterprises that has published these materials. Many of these will be useful for all types of special Jewish education programs. Some of the materials already developed include: *alephbet* puzzles, slides, stickers, dominoes, coloring books, and tapes. Some work has been done on teaching "Parshat Hashavuah" (Torah portion of the week). In addition, work is progressing on a Hebrew reading program that will begin with prereading skills. Also planned is a Jewish social studies curriculum. Positive behavior modification and reward systems are a part of the learning system. Children in the resource room have "contracts" that clearly spell out what is to be done and what the reward will be.

JOSE has several other components as well. There is a Sunday recreational program and a special summer program. Wednesday-night tutorials are held for children in all *yeshivot* who need help with secular subjects. The center provides diagnostic services for the community. Many families prefer to have their children tested in a *yeshivah* setting rather than in a clinic or hospital. The staff accepts speaking engagements for the purpose of aiding the formation of other programs and providing information about learning disabilities. Dr. Fried serves as a consultant to the Prospect Park Yeshivah, which has begun a similar program for girls.

In addition, there is a teacher internship program that trains young women for work with learning disabled children in the *yeshivot*. Parents are closely involved in the school. There are monthly workshops attended by parents and staff in which professionals present information that can be of use to parents.

The program is geared to fill a gap in the Orthodox and Hasidic communities. Many such children would be forced out of the *yeshivot* and into public and secular schools. Boys are accepted from all over. The screening process includes educational and psychological evaluation as well as informal evaluation. As a measure of the need this school fills, there is a waiting list, although all publicity has been word of mouth.

A Special Class Within a Day School

Ramaz
22 E. 82nd St.
New York, NY 10028
Coordinator: Dr. Constance Skor
Date Established: Spring 1976

The Ramaz program is designed for children already enrolled in the school who are identified as having specific learning disabilities. Before the start of this program, children who began to have difficulties in learning were forced to leave the day school to get the type of education they needed. This program enables the children to remain in the *yeshivah* setting; its primary goal is to return the children to the mainstream as quickly as possible.

There is one class for grades 1–3, which serves up to ten children. Two full-time teachers are employed, one for general studies and the other for Judaica. The services of the school psychologist are available. The program is financed from a fund for curriculum development and innovative projects. The parents pay regular tuition.

One of the major goals for the children is to eliminate the impact of bad peer relationships. The children spend a great deal of time within their regular classes. They are mainstreamed in all specialty areas—music, art, science, etc.—and they participate in plays and special programs. Other children are often invited in for various projects and visits. This movement in and out fits in with the overall style of the school. Children in the special class and their families are involved, as are all Ramaz families, in informal programs sponsored by Kehilat Jeshurun, the adjoining synagogue.

The Judaic curriculum is modified for individual children. Whereas the rest of the school follows a teaching system of *Ivrit B'Ivrit* (Hebrew subjects taught in Hebrew), in the special class the system is *Ivrit B'Anglit* (Hebrew translated into English). Less time is spent on Judaica than in the rest of the school. Often, learning to read Hebrew must be delayed. The curriculum stresses affective learning. Most of the materials used are teacher-made games, books, worksheets, etc. Children who are ready to return fully to the mainstream receive intensive help in Hebrew language.

A Synagogue Sunday School Class

Temple Solel
5100 Sheridan St.
Hollywood, FL 33021
Teacher: Mrs. Rose-Edith Grosswald
Date Established: Fall 1975

Temple Solel, a Reform synagogue, sponsors one class for twelve children with learning disabilities who range in age from eight to thirteen. In addition to the teacher, who has background in both special education and Judaica, there is a high school student who volunteers as an aide.

The class meets on Sunday mornings for a two-and-a-half-hour session. The children are integrated into the rest of the school only during assemblies.

The major goal of the program is to provide a positive and warm Jewish experience, avoiding the frustration students would experience in regular Hebrew classes. The curriculum includes individualized Hebrew reading and Judaica (holidays, Israel, history, personalities, etc.). Games, cooking, music, and art are utilized as teaching aids.

During the first two years of the program, Mrs. Grosswald developed and utilized a method of teaching she calls "Stim-You-Learn." This program is based on the concept of learning stations, and the children rotate through the stations during each lesson. The stations have activities that focus on each of the following learning channels: visual, auditory, and tactile. A fourth station, the "teacher station," consists of varied learning experiences that require the presence of the teacher. The curriculum deals with Hebrew reading and writing and briefly covers the holidays.

A Community-wide Religious School Program

Board of Jewish Education
5800 Park Heights Ave.
Baltimore, MD 21215
Program Director: Dr. Shmuel Litov
Date Established: 1967

The Baltimore community-wide program has a total of thirteen classes that serve children with different needs, including the trainable mentally retarded, the educable mentally retarded, the emotionally disturbed, and the learning disabled. The goal of the program is to make Jewish education available to all. Indeed, the range of available classes is an attempt to do this and is uncommon in Jewish communities. Eighty youngsters are currently enrolled. No class has more than ten young-sters. Most of the teachers are qualified both Judaically and in terms of special-education preparation. They are paid on the same scale as Baltimore Hebrew school teachers. Most classes have an aide in addition to the teacher.

Classes meet once or twice a week. The curriculum includes: Hebrew, prayers, holidays, Bible, personalities, and history. The children are prepared for bar and bat mitzvah. A whole range of options exists and can be adapted to suit the needs of each child. Dr. Litov has developed some unpublished curriculum guides for his teachers that deal with the holidays in an integrative approach, including customs, language, and history. He has also published a prayer book that can be used with nonreaders. (See "Jewish Educational Materials" below.)

The uniqueness of the program lies in the fact that it is decentralized. Most community-wide programs sponsor classes that meet in a single "neutral" building such as the Jewish Community Center so that all groups can participate. In the case of the Baltimore community, the classes are spread among eight different synagogues. This decentralization is the source of the strengths and also some of the problems of this program. Because they attend classes as part of a synagogue school, the youngsters identify with that congregation, its rabbi, principal, and other students. In addition, it is more difficult and somewhat more costly to administer such a program. The children participate in assemblies, and individual children can be integrated into regular classes.

An Integrated Summer Camp Program

Tikvah Program
Camp Ramah
3080 Broadway
New York, NY 10027
Director: Herbert Greenberg (Ramah in Palmer, MA)
        Ellie Bach (Ramah in Wisconsin)
Date Established: 1970 (Palmer program)
              1973 (Wisconsin program)

The Ramah camps are educational camps run by the Conservative movement. The Tikvah program, co-sponsored by the National Ramah Commission and the United Synagogue Commission on Jewish Education, is designed to meet the needs of learning disabled teenagers within the normal camp setting.

The Palmer Tikvah program has grown to include thirty-five youngsters, while the Wisconsin program can serve up to fifteen. Because of its larger size, the Palmer program accepts children with a broader range of handicaps, including the educable mentally retarded and the behaviorally disordered. The screening process includes evaluating medical, educational, and psychological reports as well as a personal interview with the child and the parents.

There are two counselors for each bunk of six youngsters as well as an educational director, group leaders, and resource personnel. The staff must meet the Hebrew knowledge and study requirements for employ-ment at Camp Ramah in addition to interest and background in special education.

The program stresses integration and individualization. The Tikvah bunks are situated in buildings that are shared by regular Ramah bunks (common bathroom, porch, etc.), which increases the amount of contact between campers. Tikvah campers participate, to the extent possible, in activities such as evening programs, religious services, trips, and skill activities with their peers. Alternative activities and programs are pro-vided to meet individual needs of Tikvah campers.

All Ramah campers spend a portion of the day in formal classes. Classes for Tikvah campers are held in a variety of settings, such as small groups, peer tutoring, and the regular Ramah classes. Over the years, a variety of courses have been offered. These include such topics as Hebrew, *Shabbat*, Bible, Jewish life cycle, holidays, Israel, and the Holocaust. The teachers have developed their own curricula and mate-rials, often using a multisensory approach. *The Shabbat Kit* by Herbert and Barbara Greenberg has been used. (See "Jewish Educational Mate-rials" below.)

Unlike school programs, Jewish education in camp is not limited to the classroom setting. Learning experiences and Jewish experiences take place constantly throughout the whole camp community, since Ramah seeks to provide a total Jewish environment. The Tikvah youngsters are accepted as part of this community. The benefits are not all one-sided by any means. Sensitizing children to respect individual differences and living Jewish value concepts such as *mitzvot bein adam l'chavero* and *tikun olam* (obligations between people and improving the world) are goals in

general Jewish education that are enhanced by contact with the Tikvah program.

There are many other components of the Tikvah program. A job program, through which campers work in various areas in camp, is intended to help children learn skills and to learn how to deal with the responsibility of having a job. Group meetings are held on a regular basis and are designed to provide a forum for dealing with social and individual problems. An extensive peer tutoring program provides an opportunity for youngsters in the regular program to help the exceptional camper gain proficiency in academic, social, and recreational skills. These programs all provide further opportunities for integration in camp.

The Palmer program includes a three-day conference for parents. This provides a forum for parent education, for discussion of common needs, and for learning what each child has accomplished in order to enhance carryover after the summer.

A Teacher Training Program

Project Educaid
Jewish Parents United
980 E. 19th St.
Brooklyn, NY 11230
Director: Rabbi Burton Jaffa
Date Established: 1975

Project Educaid is a federally funded program for regular classroom teachers in *yeshivot* of the Boro Park community of Brooklyn, New York. The project was established because teachers and administrative staff in the *yeshivot* generally are untrained in recognizing and dealing with learning-disabled children in the classroom. Forty teachers participate each year, and each receives a stipend.

The teachers attend a weekly course in special education. In addition, each teacher works with a special-education instructor in remediating the difficulties of specific students in their classrooms. The teachers select those students on whom they wish to focus. The work is then used as a model for developing diagnostic skills and developing prescriptive programs of remediation. The program also includes the administrators of the *yeshivot* so that there will be support for teachers as they begin to make changes in the curriculum.

Parents must come to understand that giving their children with special needs a Jewish education is important. Many parents are often hesitant about sending children to yet another school program in which they anticipate failure. They feel that there will be too much pressure or that their children will be placed in one more situation in which they will feel different and isolated. A Jewish education program should be viewed as a source of positive experiences and as an opportunity to develop the sense of identity spoken of earlier. Instead of being hesitant to seek Jewish education for their youngsters, parents of children with special needs should be insisting on it. The Jewish community must respond. It must assume a goal of making all youngsters a part of the Jewish community. The number of programs must be expanded so that more children can be served. A variety of programs for children with different handicaps should be available. Informal as well as formal education programs are needed. We must see Jewish education as a lifelong process and begin to develop programs for people of all ages and of all needs.

In the beginning I do not think that anyone, least of all his parents, believed that our son, who has cerebral palsy, would be able to participate in a bar mitzvah ceremony. But he wanted it badly; I am not sure exactly why. Imagine what it meant to his grandparents and sister and us to be in the synagogue and hear him recite the blessings at being called up to the Torah. Can you imagine where we had come from to be able to arrive at that moment? When my husband and I said the *"she-heheyanu"* prayer for having been kept in life and being brought to that moment, we meant it passionately. I think the event of the bar mitzvah was also important for the members of the congregation and the rabbi. When we broached the subject of bar mitzvah, there had been some resistance and fear voiced, but afterward everyone was proud. I guess in our synagogue the first is always the hardest.

GENERAL REFERENCES

BLANK, CATHERINE A. *Teaching the Retarded.* Englewood Cliffs, NJ: Prentice-Hall, 1974.

HAMMILL, DONALD D., AND BARTEL, NETTIE R. *Teaching Children with Learning and Behavior Problems.* Boston: Allyn & Bacon, 1975.

HEWETT, FRANK M. *The Emotionally Disturbed Child in the Classroom.* Boston: Allyn & Bacon, 1970.

JOHNSON, DORIS J., AND MYKLEBUST, HELMER R. *Learning Disabilities: Educational Principles and Practices.* New York: Grune & Stratton, 1967.

LERNER, JANET. *Children with Learning Disabilities.* Boston: Houghton Mifflin Co. 1976.

MAGER, ROBERT F. *Preparing Instructional Objectives.* Belmont, CA: Fearon Publishers, 1962.

ROBINSON, H. B., AND ROBINSON, NANCY M. *The Mentally Retarded Child.* New York: McGraw-Hill, 1965.

JEWISH SPECIAL EDUCATION REFERENCES

ALTERNATIVES IN RELIGIOUS EDUCATION. 1110 Holly Oak Circle, San Jose, CA 95120. (Plan to publish a column on children with special needs in future issues.)

AMERICAN ASSOCIATION FOR JEWISH EDUCATION. *Bibliography of Jewish Special Education Materials.* 1969.

GREENBERG, BARBARA. *Bibliography of Resources in Jewish Special Education.* New York: United Synagogue Commission on Jewish Education, 1973.

ROSENFELD, HILLEL, AND HALPERN, NAOMI. *Implementation of a Diagnostic and Remedial Program at a Hebrew Day School.* New York: National Society for Hebrew Day Schools, Torah Umesorah, 1976.

SCHWARTZ, ELLIOT S. *A Manual for Organizing Classes for Jewish Special Children.* New York: United Synagogue Commission on Jewish Education, 1975.

STISKIN, HERSHEL M. *A Survey of Jewish Religious Programs for the Handicapped.* New York: American Association for Jewish Education, 1968.

TORAH UMESORAH. Listing of Orthodox Schools and Programs for Special Children. New York, 1976.

Some Materials Adaptable for use with Special Needs Children

Educational Enterprises
5317 15th Ave.
Brooklyn, NY 11219

Catalogue of materials available. Includes *alephbet* slides, stickers, guides for Bible study, and coloring books

Our Prayerbook by Martin Syden, 1958
Union of American Hebrew Congregations
838 Fifth Ave.
New York, NY 10021

Prayerbook by Shmuel Lister and Barbara Freilich, 1976
Board of Jewish Education
5800 Park Heights Ave.
Baltimore, MD 21215

The Shabbat Kit by Barbara and Herbert Greenberg
United Synagogue Book Service
155 Fifth Ave.
New York, NY 10019

Special Reader Activity Books (Maimonides Institute Education Series)
Holiday Series by Hershel M. Stiskin, 1965
Jewish Education Committee Press
426 W. 58th St.
New York, NY 10019

Stim-You-Learn by Ross-Edith Grosswald, 1977
For information write:
Rose-Edith Grosswald
571 N.E. 177th St.
North Miami Beach, FL 33162

ORGANIZATIONS

Jewish Education for Exceptional Persons (JEEP)
American Association for Jewish Education
114 Fifth Ave.
New York, NY 10011
  A recently formed professional organization which aims to serve as a clearing-
  house for programs and materials across the country

Jewish Parents United
980 E. 19th St.
Brooklyn, NY 11230

Parents for Torah for all Children (P'TACH)
980 E. 19th St.
Brooklyn, NY 11230

Shalaym
United Synagogue Commission on Jewish Education
218 E. 70th St.
New York, NY 10021
  Three organizations working toward establishing programs and education of
  parents

SOME MATERIALS ADAPTABLE FOR USE WITH SPECIAL NEEDS CHILDREN

Czigler Publishing
331 Beardsley Rd.
Dayton, OH 45426

Materials such as tear/press letters and large Hebrew letters

Ktav Publishing House
120 E. Broadway
New York, NY 10002

Games and materials such as magnetic letters, blocks

Holiday Ditto Pak by Barbara Glassman
  Alternatives in Religious Education
  3945 South Oneida
  Denver, CO 80237

Let's Learn about Jewish Symbols
  Union of American Hebrew Congregations
  538 Fifth Ave.
  New York, NY 10021

Our Synagogue
  Behrman House
  1261 Broadway
  New York, NY 10001

Reading Hebrew by Lillian Adler, revised 1974
  Behrman House
  1261 Broadway
  New York, NY 10001

Programmed text, useful for individuals

Sader Ukrah and *Sader Ullemad*   (Tel Aviv: Yavneh)
   Available from:
   Lazar   Workbooks stressing concepts and begin-
   156 Fifth Ave.   ning reading, can be used as games
   New York, NY 10010

Sefer Tmunot by Zehava Blackman
   Bricklin Press   Simple drawings that can be adapted
   323 N. 13th St.
   Philadelphia, PA 19107

Torah Toys
P.O. Box 5416
Beverly Hills, CA 90210

CHAPTER TWENTY-FOUR

JEWISH BOOKS FOR CHILDREN

Books can serve as vehicles of communication between children of all ages. Sitting with a young child and reading a book together provides not only an opportunity for sharing the book but also a framework for talking about all manner of things, most of which the book's author never intended. Giving a book to an older child and talking about problems and issues raised by the book can enrich the dialogue between you.

When you want the adult/child dialogue around a book to be distinctly Jewish, where do you begin? First, there are some points about evaluating children's literature that you should keep in mind when looking for a "good" book. Realize that authors and illustrators of children's books know that their works are generally bought by adults. Therefore, they struggle to make their books appealing to both adults and children; they would like both readers to be amused or touched, and so they work to make their material appealing on a variety of levels. The success of authors and illustrators in this difficult task varies. As you browse through an assortment of books, try to clarify for whom you are making your selection. Ideally, a book should appeal to both you and the child; otherwise, sharing will be difficult. If your concern is really the child, be sure that the book is "age appropriate," and be prepared to sacrifice a measure (although not all) of your enjoyment. A good example of concern with age appropriateness is illustrated by Marilyn Hirsh's *Where is Yonkela?* The book is beloved by two-and-a-half-year-olds and provides valuable pre-reading practice in scanning. Although adults enjoy the colorful illustrations, it is difficult to imagine an adult who would be intrigued by the plot.

When you spot a favorite author's newest book, look carefully. Remember that authors are not necessarily consistent in their work, and one superb book does not guarantee equal quality in the author's next. Also, realize that the same author may have worked with a different illustrator, which can mean a wide discrepancy in style between books. It also means that you have to be careful not to be misled by pictures. A good example of this problem can be seen in Isaac Bashevis Singer's wonderful *midrash, Why Noah Chose the Dove.* The illustrations by Eric Carle are beautiful, but if you only glanced at the pictures without reading the words, you would think the book appropriate for a much younger child than is demanded by the rather sophisticated and complex vocabulary of the narrative. The moral of the story is that whenever possible, you should read the book yourself before buying it to share with a child. Obviously, this is not always possible; for example, the wonderful novel *A Boy of Old Prague* is simply too long to read while standing on one foot in a book store. In such cases, trustworthy recommendations and intuition become essential.

Where can you go to find good Jewish children's books? Unfortunately, we do not yet know a single store that specializes in stocking a truly thorough range of Jewish children's books. That places you in a difficult position. You can consult the *Jewish Book Annual*, published yearly by the Jewish Book Council (15 E. 26th St., New York, NY 10010), or the glossy, semiannual *Judaica Book News* available from Book News (303 W. 10th St., New York, NY 10014), and see an increasing number of juvenile book offerings. The problem is that you will not find them all in one place on one shelf. This dilemma commits you to a life of browsing. The quality of collections in Jewish book stores varies from store to store. The collection at the Israel Book Store in Brookline, Massachusetts, is better than many; but none is "complete." Large general book stores and even discount paperback or remainder book stores may surprise you with a hidden treasure. Your odds of finding something good may increase in a book store that is devoted exclusively to children's literature (e.g., Eeyore's at 2252 Broadway, New York, NY 10023).

You may be surprised to find a book you were looking for in a synagogue gift shop. Try Jewish libraries, including synagogue libraries. There may be books to borrow, or you may be able to use the library's copy as a way of deciding whether you want to order a particular book through a book store or directly from the publisher. Our general advice is to keep browsing; when you find something you like, buy it immediately. You may not find it again, and you are better off keeping the book until you find the right recipient than risking not finding it when you need it.

The dilemma of seeing what appear to be lots of good books listed in the *Jewish Book Annual* and then not being able to find them on a store shelf points to a basic eccentricity of publishing Jewish books for children. Some books are published by large companies with wide distributions. Others are published by small companies, which distribute books to only a few stores or schools. The quality of the book is not reflected in the size and distribution of the publisher.

Another route is to order books through Jewish book clubs. (For a listing of clubs see item 2 under "Choosing a Bar/Bat Mitzvah Gift" in Chapter Thirteen.) The advantage and disadvantage of these clubs is that their listings are pre-selected. Your task in working with a Jewish book club is to get to know the tastes of the person or persons doing the selecting. Your trust of their judgment will determine the usefulness of membership in the club. The further removed you are from a book store which stocks Jewish children's books, the more useful a club may be to you. Ordering by mail does limit your ability to browse, and you might do well to clarify in advance the circumstances under which you can return books.

Sometimes your task is limited to the search; you buy the book, gift wrap it, give it to the child, and are done with the process. Other times, finding the book is only the beginning of the process of sharing it with the child.

Over the years, we develop patterns for sharing books with children. We sit with the child on our lap and ask her to turn the pages. We give the teenager a book with the offer to talk about it with him later. Nothing beats these simple and warm modes of sharing, yet sometimes we want a change of pace. For such moments, here are some of our favorite creative alternatives for sharing books with children to enhance your personal repertoire. Of course, you will need to adapt these to individual needs and ages.

Bruno Bettelheim in *The Uses of Enchantment* suggests that we tell, rather than read, fairy tales in order to leave the "pictures" to the child's imagination—which will not be limited by an artist's vision. This idea is especially appropriate with some Jewish stories, for example, biblical stories, *midrashim* (interpretive stories), Hasidic tales, even tales of the wise men of Chelm. You can experiment with a variety of ways of telling stories. Try asking children to listen to a story with their eyes closed. Ask a child to describe or draw a picture of how a character in the story (Moses, Aaron, Abraham, Sarah, Isaac, or Rebecca) looked. "With your eyes closed, what colors did you see in the coat of many colors?" Try (with your eyes opened) to stop in the middle of your narrative and ask, "What do you think happened next?"

How committed are you to reading the words? Try asking a child who is not yet a skillful reader to tell you the story by reading the pictures in a new book before you read the words.

With an older child, especially a child who is studying Hebrew, try "learning" with the child. Be sure that the level of material you are studying together is neither too difficult nor too easy. Try, for example, to do a line-by-line reading of a small section of *Humash* (Bible), questioning and explaining and trying to understand as you go along. Or try this traditional study with the new Jewish Publication Society Torah translation or poem.

Older children also enjoy role playing, play reading, choral reading of poetry, reading dialogue out loud, and reading poetry dramatically. The whole range of dramatic play and reading is open to you on a rainy afternoon or snowy evening. Play reading can be expanded into film production with the help of home-movie equipment. Also, consider joining with other families to show a rented movie or video tape of a Jewish story your children have been reading. (See *The Jewish Catalogs* for sources of films.)

Do not feel limited by what you perceive as the intended content of a book. Use it as you will. For example, the book can be seen as a resource for reading-readiness work. Some fine reading-readiness activities include asking a child to find the big letter "C" or "Q" or whatever on the page, scanning a page to find a small, hidden object (such as the mouse in his hole in *Joseph Had a Little Overcoat*), identifying colors or shapes on a page. A slightly older child can (especially with an anthology or collection of several stories like *Fuzzy Top* or *Mitzi*) be told that a desired story is on a particular page number and then asked to turn to that page.

Books need not necessarily be read; they also can be sung, like, for example, the lovely *On Prepachick,* which was illustrated by Gabriel Lisowski.

Writing your own books, including the sequencing of a family activity (the day we made *hamantaschen,* put them in baskets with other food, and delivered them to our friends), can prove rewarding. Jean Piaget, the great theoretician of child development, has taught us that such "sequencing" or structuring of events in their correct order is the foundation on which children build a sense of history. Also, try typing out the saga that a "preliterate" child has dictated to you. Children enjoy illustrating their own stories. The problem with self-made books is that in order for them to be enjoyed, they have to be designed at the proper time in a child's life. A calligraphy project for a twelve- or thirteen-year-old runs the risk of frustrated tears because, at about that age, young people become concerned with producing a polished and professional-looking finished product, which often is beyond their skills.

Given that books do not necessarily have to come from the book store, consider "reading" an old family photograph album. The child does not need to be able to recognize a single person in the album. Those of us who are fortunate enough to have access to such collections of photographs know that children of all ages can become fascinated by stories about ladies in long dresses and men on horses who look out at us from distant and lost worlds.

Hand puppets, finger puppets, and felt story boards are the stock-in-trade of "professional" storytellers. Creating puppets for a very special story—like Megillat Esther on Purim—suggests uses outside the home. We know of a woman who lived on the North Shore of Boston and developed a coterie of young friends who each year worked with her to increase and refine their collection of Purim puppets. This informal Purim puppet theater would then perform for local synagogue groups.

Commercial educational supply companies produce felt story boards with illustrations of classic fairy tales. With dexterity and small pieces of brightly colored felt you can cut out your own "story book" characters. (Lacking great artistic skill, you can use simple illustrations printed in the story book you are working with as your model for felt. Your felt cutout characters will adhere naturally to a larger piece of felt. You can even buy felt backed with adhesive that you can attach to a piece of cardboard.) Thus, you can create an almost free-standing felt background on which a child can manipulate the story characters made out of contrasting felt. You can also volunteer to take such a felt-board creation into your child's class or Hebrew school where the teacher will appreciate the home support and reinforcement you are giving.

The range of creative ways of sharing a book with a child is limitless, as is the advantage of occasionally varying your approach. Yet nothing can surpass the enthusiasm generated by people simply reading a good book together.

What follows is an annotated listing of books that we believe merit your perusal. Because of the eccentricities of book distribution and our own taste, the list simply cannot be complete. It is our hope that you will add to it and share your recommendations with all of us who seek quality children's literature in the Jewish community. As you read through the titles, you will notice a bias toward books devoted to nostalgic rather than present-day themes. The bias is not necessarily ours; rather, it reflects current publishing. (Myra and David Sadker in an article entitled "Jewish Americans in Children's Books," which appeared in *Now Upon a Time*, suggest that this bias is symptomatic of our collective self-image and desire to maintain a "low profile.") You will also notice, as you read through our bibliography, that we have resisted being too specific in identifying age appropriateness. Such distinctions are often artificial, given variations between children. We also have found it not unusual for literature earmarked for adolescents to appeal to readers who are in the middle years of childhood and for adolescents to devour "adult" fiction.

BIBLIOGRAPHY

My Little Dictionary/Hebrew-English Picture Dictionary, published by the Center for Educational Technology of the Rothschild Foundation, Israel. The illustrations of this dictionary are colorful and appealing. Some five hundred vocabulary words are grouped according to categories such as zoo animals, carpentry tools, Jewish holidays, and months of the Hebrew calendar. Despite the fact that the volume has appeared fairly recently, it unfortunately contains no information about the author, illustrator, or year of publication.

ADLER, DAVID. *The Children of Chelm*, illustrated by Arthur Friedman. New York: Bonim Books, 1979. Mr. Adler nicely presents Chelm stories in English.

_____. *The House on the Roof*, illustrated by Marilyn Hirsh. New York: Bonim Books, 1976. Here we find a graphic retelling of the old joke about the judge who orders the removal of a *sukkah* within ten days. A very young child could enjoy (and hopefully identify with) the pictures of children in the *sukkah*, although, ideally, the reader should be old enough to understand the humor.

ARONIN, BEN. *The Secret of the Sabbath Fish*, with pictures by Shay Riegger. Philadelphia: Jewish Publication Society, 1978. The author uses a mythlike tale about the origin of gefilte fish as a vehicle for telling the history of the Jewish people. The line drawings, which are simple and direct, may unfortunately convey the impression that the book is appropriate for a younger child than could actually understand the more complicated words and concepts of the story. Parents of preschoolers will probably find themselves paraphrasing parts of the text.

BLAU, JUDITH HOPE. *The Bagel Baker of Mulliner Lane*. New York: McGraw-Hill, 1974 & 1976. Ms. Blau recounts the adventures of her own grandfather who was a bagel baker. The book is weak in Jewish content except for the fact that Grandpa Izzy bakes bagels for both Hanukah and Christmas. Despite our resistance to the Christmas and Hanukah parallel, the book could be useful in its legitimization of preparation for the two holidays. It is easy to imagine sharing the volume with public-school first graders.

BRODIE, DEBORAH. *Stories My Grandfather Should Have Told Me*. New York: Hebrew Publishing Company, 1976. Ms. Brodie provides older children with an anthology of collected short stories taken from works that have been very popular for a long time.

CASHMAN, GREER FAY. *Jewish Days and Holidays*, illustrated by Alona Frankel. New York: SBS Publishing, Inc., 1979. This beautifully illustrated volume explains each important holiday and celebration of the liturgical year. Information is consistently accurate and clearly presented. Parents might use the pictures and descriptions of an upcoming holiday as a part of preparing a child for *yom tov*. The illustrations are charming enough to make the book a potential gift for an adult just learning about Judaism.

COHEN, BARBARA. *The Carp in the Bathtub*, illustrated by Joan Halpern. New York: Dell Publishing, 1972. With wonderful wit, Ms. Cohen describes how two children just before Passover befriend a fish. Ms. Halpern's sophisticated line drawings equal the high quality of the text. School-age children (and children of all ages) who are themselves preparing for Passover will appreciate this book. The risk is that they may become vegetarians.

EISENBERG, PHYLLIS ROSE. *A Mitzvah Is Something Special*. New York: Harper and Row, 1978. Here we see a realistic portrayal of the relationship between a contemporary grandmother and granddaughter. The caricature drawings support a sense of realism but might be frightening to a very young child.

FRIEDMAN, MARCUS, AUDREY AND RAYMOND A. ZWERIN. *But This Night Is Different*, illustrated by Judith Gwyn Brown New York: Union of American Hebrew Congregations, 1980. The clear text and illustrations make this book a good vehicle for talking about the Seder with young children.

GOLDBERG, LEA. *Room for Rent*, pictures by Avner Katz. Los Angeles: Ward Ritchie Press, 1972. With this book, English-speaking children have an opportunity to encounter the work of a great modern Hebrew poet. "Room for Rent" is a narrative poem that lends itself to being chanted and remembered.

GRAY, BETTYANNE. *Manya's Story*. Minneapolis: Lerner Publications Company, 1978. Manya's American-born daughter recounts her mother's sojourn through pogroms and suffering, from Ukrainian *shtetl* to South Philadelphia. The use of old photographs helps convey a sense of the book as an authentic family document.

GREENE, LAURA. *I Am an Orthodox Jew,* illustrated by Lisa C. Wesson. New York: Holt, Rinehart and Winston, 1979. The object of this book is to explain Orthodox Jewish practices through a week in the life of a young boy. It is to the author's credit that difficulties regarding the role of women in Orthodoxy are not glossed over. We wish that the volume were rather called "I Am a Traditional Jew," which would broaden the spectrum of children who might identify with Aaron and his sister Rachel. Despite the fact that the story is more didactic and less literary in its priorities, we can imagine a day-school student using the book to explain himself or herself to a non-Jewish playmate.

HIRSH, MARILYN. *Potato Pancakes All Around.* New York and London: Bonim Books, 1978. Ms. Hirsh provides a nostalgic story of Hanukah around the turn of the century and nicely includes a recipe for potato pancakes and some information about the holiday.

———. *The Rabbi and the Twenty-nine Witches.* New York: Scholastic Book Services, 1976. School-age children will enjoy finding out how an eastern European village rid itself of witches. A younger child might find the witches nightmarish.

———. *The Tower of Babel.* New York: Holiday House, 1981. Ms. Hirsh's version of the biblical story would be lovely to share with a five-year-old on the *Shabbat* afternoon of the reading of that Torah portion.

———. *Where Is Yonkela?* New York: Crown Publishers, Inc., 1969. Very young young children are fascinated by the search for the missing Yonkela, which is presented in colorful folk pictures. A parent could use the hidden clues in the illustrations as an exercise in prereading "scanning" and identification. The book was obviously well thought out by Ms. Hirsh, and the pictures charm children of all ages.

HURWITZ, JOHANA. *Once I Was a Plum Tree,* illustrated by Ingrid Fetz. New York: William Morrow and Company, 1980. Mature children, especially girls, will appreciate this story of an assimilated American Jewish girl's encounters with her heritage through her neighbors who are refugees from Nazi Germany.

ISH-KISHOR, SHULAMITH. *A Boy of Old Prague,* illustrated by Ben Shahn. New York: Pantheon Books, 1963, reissued recently in paperback by Scholastic Books. Ms. Ish-Kishor presents older children with a sophisticated and stimulating story. The plot deals with the conflicts and prejudices experienced by a non-Jewish servant boy in a Jewish household in medieval Prague. The problems raised by the story should engender interesting conversations among older readers.

LISOWSKI, GABRIEL. *How Tevye Became a Milkman.* New York: Holt, Rinehart and Winston, 1976. What is important about this simple retelling of a classic Sholom Aleichem story is Mr. Lisowski's drawings, which are magnificent.

MEE, CHARLES L., JR. *Moses, Moses,* with pictures by Ken Munowitz. New York: Harper and Row, 1977. A very young child (and parents and grandparents) will be charmed by Mr. Munowitz's illustrations. Our only problem with this account of Moses in the bulrushes is Mr. Mee's explanation of Moses' name.

NEUSNER, JACOB. *Learn Mishnah,* 1978; *Learn Talmud,* 1979; and *Meet Our Sages,* 1980. New York: Behrman House, Inc. Each of these three volumes is designed to introduce a young person to a different variety of rabbinic text. The books are appropriate for classroom use or individual study by mature young people. The series reflects the *Ahavat Yisrael* (the love of the Jewish People) of Dr. Neusner, a great and sophisticated scholar who did not disdain investing time and effort in creating these intelligent presentations of classical texts for our children.

RICHMAN, CAROL. *The Lekachmacher Family.* Seattle: Madrona Publishers, Inc., 1976. In simple and straightforward terms, Ms. Richman describes the journey of her family from czarist Russia to the United States. Her illustrations are cute and unpretentious; Ms. Richman is providing us with a map of time and space. A prerequisite for the child reader would be some sense of history and geography.

ROSE, ANNE. *The Triumphs of Fuzzy Fogtop,* pictures by Tomie de Paola. New York: Dial Press, 1979. Ms. Rose merged a number of Chelm-style, humorous folk stories into the person of Fuzzy Fogtop. Despite its weakness in Jewish content, we were so amused by Fuzzy's adventures that we hardly noticed the anachronism of stores in nineteenth-century Pinsk being labeled "barber," "tailor," and "bakery."

SHULEVITZ, URI. *The Treasure.* New York: Farrar, Straus & Giroux, 1978. Mr. Shulevitz retells the classic tale of the man who journeys far and wide in pursuit of a treasure, only to find it at home. The book is distinguished by Mr. Shulevitz's subtle and colorful illustrations.

SINGER, ISAAC BASHEVIS. *The Fools of Chelm,* with pictures by Uri Shulevitz. New York: Farrar, Straus & Giroux, 1973. Here we have another fine rendition of Chelm stories; this time accompanied by Mr. Shulevitz's beautiful illustrations.

————. *The Power of Light,* illustrated by Irene Lieblich. New York: Farrar, Straus & Giroux, 1980. Since the publication of *Zlateh the Goat and Other Stories* (by Harper and Row in 1966), it is hard to think of a more prolific writer of fiction for children than Mr. Singer. In *The Power of Light,* Mr. Singer provides sophisticated younger readers (and, really, children of all ages) with another collection of stories; this time, the beautifully wrought tales all relate to Hanukah and some are set in contemporary times.

————. *A Tale of Three Wishes,* pictures by Irene Lieblich. New York: Farrar, Straus & Giroux, 1975. Mr. Singer spins a fine tale around a folk belief that late at night on a holiday the sky opens for a moment and wishes are granted. Ms. Lieblich's pictures are beautiful.

————. *When Shlemiel Went to Warsaw & Other Stories,* with pictures by Margot Zemach. New York: Farrar, Straus & Giroux, 1968. Here we have more Chelm stories "for children of all ages." For children of very young ages, an adult using this volume would do well to read and then tell a story rather than to read the story directly from book to listeners.

————. *Why Noah Chose the Dove,* translated by Elizabeth Shub with pictures by Eric Carle. New York: Farrar, Straus & Giroux, 1973. The text is Mr. Singer's *midrash,* really a commentary on the biblical narrative, and contains an answer to the question posed in the book's title. Mr. Carle's pictures are dramatic and at times genuinely powerful.

SOBOL, HARRIET. *Grandpa: A Young Man Grown Old.* New York: Coward, McCann & Geoghegan, 1980. Ms. Sobol combines elements of oral history and family album in ways that may prove inspirational in your own attempts to preserve and communicate familial recollections.

STADTLER, BEA. *The Adventures of Gluckel of Hamelin.* New York: United Synagogue Youth, 1973. Ms. Stadtler has given readers in the middle years of childhood a biography of the great woman memoirist of late seventeenth-century and early eighteenth-century Germany.

————. *The Holocaust: A History of Courage and Resistance.* New York: Behrman House, 1974. This history is appropriate for more mature children. See Chapter Thirty-two below.

TABACK, SIMMS. *Joseph Had a Little Overcoat.* New York: Random House, 1977. Mr. Taback has translated an eastern European folk song into a witty and sophisticated book for young children and adults. His illustrations are great, and the search for small objects in pictures provides opportunities for scanning and other reading-readiness activities. The "Jewish connection" of the tale is subtle.

TAYLOR, SYDNEY. *All-Of-A-Kind Family Downtown*, illustrated by Beth and Joe Krush. Chicago: Follett Publishing Company, 1972. Here we have another installment in the adventures of a Jewish family "downtown" in Manhattan around the turn of the century. What makes these stories special is their literary merit; plots are interesting and well written. We know a fifth-grade girl who knows by heart the names of every friend and member of the family.

————. *Danny Loves a Holiday*, illustrated by Gail Owens. New York: Dutton, 1980. Danny, our hero, is a boy of about six who looks and acts like many children we know. He does not live in a quaint eastern European *shtetl*. Rather, he might live next door. He loves celebrating holidays, one of each constituting a chapter of the book. What saves the book from being limited to a vehicle for conveying information about the holidays is Ms. Taylor's wit, but it is unfortunately flawed by inaccuracies that an adult reader should correct. (For example, we say the blessing *before* cutting *hallah;* we stand rather than sit while the *shofar* is sounded.)

VINEBERG, ETHEL. *Grandmother Came from Dworitz*, illustrated by Rita Briansky. Plattsburg, NY: Tundra Books, 1969 (first published in the United States in 1978). Ms. Vineberg listened to her mother's stories of her family's journey from Lechovitch and Dworitz to Canada in the period 1820–1909. She wrote down the stories for her children and grandchildren; this book is the record of her family and its journey. Older children will be best equipped to appreciate the significance of this historical document. The illustrations are beautifully graceful and appropriate to the text.

WEILERSTEIN, SADIE ROSE. *The Best of K'tonton*, with new illustrations by Marilyn Hirsh. Philadelphia: Jewish Publication Society, 1980. Since K'tonton first appeared in 1930, children have been fascinated by his adventures. This attractive new compilation presents adults with the dilemma of missing some of their favorite illustrations. Because over the years different artists illustrated *K'tonton,* the publisher sought to unify the fiftieth anniversary collection under the brush and pen of Ms. Hirsh. Purists may still be able to turn up earlier and more expansive volumes of *K'tonton,* while young readers will appreciate his narrow escapes regardless of edition.

ZEMACH, MARGOT. *It Could Always Be Worse*. New York: Scholastic Book Services, 1976. Ms. Zemach retells the Yiddish folk tale of what happens when you take a goat into an already overcrowded house. The details of her colorful drawings are fun. Marilyn Hirsh has also created a rendition of this folk tale. Interestingly, Ann McGovern wrote and Simms Taback illustrated a volume that traces the same motif, devoid of any Jewish association (*Too Much Noise*. New York: Scholastic Book Services, 1967).

————. *Self-Portrait*. New York: A. W. Publishers, 1978. Ms. Zemach wrote her autobiography, which she illustrated as she has many children's books. The autobiography is really for adults or mature children who would like to get to know the person behind the books. It could be used as a resource when talking with younger children about the people who write and illustrate books.

Collections of the Work of Children

Children of the World Paint Jerusalem. New York: Bantam Books, 1978. This "art book" permits children to see how other children envision (sometimes in their wildest fantasies) Jerusalem. While their pictures might be used to trigger the fantasies of children who have never lived in Israel, children who know the city themselves find the representations familiar and/or interesting.

I Never Saw Another Butterfly. New York: Schocken Books, 1978. These drawings and poems by children from Terezin Concentration Camp permit older readers to reach beyond the safe perimeters of their imaginations to encounter another world.

My Shalom/My Peace. Tel Aviv: Sabra Books, 1975. Through this collection of paintings and poems by Jewish and Arab children living in Israel, we have the opportunity of learning some of the effects of war. American children have the opportunity to gain insight into the lives of others in very different circumstances.

L'ENGLE, MADELEINE. *Ladders of Angels—Scenes from the Bible Illustrated by Children of the World.* New York: Seabury Press, 1979, cloth; New York: Penguin Books, 1980, paperback. These biblical illustrations can serve as *midrashim,* as commentaries to the text, and could be used to stimulate children to create their own interpretations.

Adolescents, and Their Literature

Despite the best efforts of publishers and authors to reach adolescent readers, a recent (and informal) survey of some of our local synagogue librarians suggested that teenagers tend to borrow adult fiction. Some of the "old" favorites that were most frequently being borrowed from libraries included:

FRANK, ANNE. *The Diary of a Young Girl.* New York: Doubleday, 1952.

KEMELMAN, HARRY. *Monday the Rabbi Took Off.* New York: G. P. Putnam's Sons, 1972; and the rest of the series of which this is only one entry.

POTOK, CHAIM. *The Chosen.* New York: Simon and Schuster, 1967; and Dr. Potok's later books: *The Promise, My Name Is Asher Lev,* and *In the Beginning.*

ROTH, PHILIP. *Goodbye, Columbus.* New York: Bantam Books, 1959.

URIS, LEON. *Exodus.* New York: Doubleday, 1958.

WIESEL, ELIE. *The Jews of Silence: A Personal Report on Soviet Jewry.* New York: Holt, Rinehart and Winston, 1966.

————. *Night.* New York: Hill and Wang, 1960.

Besides this listing, other bibliographies or listings of children's literature that may prove helpful to you include:

Resources

Book List for the Jewish Child, which contains evaluations and annotations of Jewish children's books published through June 1971. This booklet is available from The Jewish Book Council, 15 E. 26th St., New York, NY 10010.

Encyclopaedia Judaica, "Children's Literature," pp. 427–459, vol. 5. Jerusalem: Keter Publishing House, Ltd., 1971. This article represents a careful historical survey rather than a current bibliography but provides interesting information about "classics" of Jewish children's literature.

"Jewish Americans in Children's Books," an article by Myra and David Sadker in *Now Upon a Time,* New York: Harper & Row, 1977, contains careful analysis of a number of books, essentially for older children.

Jewish Book Annual, published by the Jewish Welfare Board's Jewish Book Council, 15 E. 26th St., New York, NY 10010, under "bibliographies of new books," contains a section entitled "Jewish Juvenile Books." This section is an annotated bibliography of all books published in English in the United States for children in a given year and is often compiled by Ms. Marcia Posner.

The Jewish Catalog, eds. Strassfeld, Sharon, and Strassfeld, Michael, and Siegel, Richard, Philadelphia: Jewish Publication Society, 1973, contains an article by Liz Koltun entitled "Creating a Jewish Library/Children's Books," pp. 242–247. The books listed are generally for older children. Also contained within the general section "Creating a Jewish Library," p. 240, is a listing of general bibliographies which are available for use within the adult Jewish community.

Judaica Book News is a glossy, semiannual periodical that also contains advertisements of recent books. It is our experience that the *Judaica Book News* along with the *Jewish Book Annual* is heavily relied on by librarians in popular, nonacademic Jewish libraries.

"New Books for Jewish Children: A Review," by Rita Frischer, appearing in *Moment* (magazine), November 1979, pp. 43–51, is an excellent guide to some current titles. As is true of any of these listings, the author's taste is reflected. Analysis is careful, but the listings are fewer than those in the *Jewish Book Annual*.

"Our Shelves Runneth Over," by Rita Frischer, *Moment*, vol. 5, no. 10, November 1980, pp. 34–40. Here we have Ms. Frischer's update of both new titles and fluctuations in Jewish publishing. We hope that these two articles represent an ongoing commitment on the part of *Moment* to keep its readers informed about developments in Jewish juvenile literature.

"Plays of Jewish Interest: A Preliminary Catalogue," edited by Edward Cohen, lists and describes over two hundred plays. Future supplements to the catalogue are planned and will be available from the National Foundation for Jewish Culture, 122 E. 42nd St., Suite 1512, New York, NY 10168.

CHAPTER TWENTY-FIVE

THINGS TO MAKE FOR (AND SOMETIMES WITH) CHILDREN

The best gifts we can give are those that come truly from ourselves. By logical extension, that often means gifts that we somehow make ourselves. What follows here are ideas of gifts to make, gifts that either can be personalized for a specific, young recipient or because of Jewish content are not commercially available. We hope the list will stimulate your imagination and that you will enjoy expanding on our ideas. Further inspiration for gifts you can make for (and sometimes with) children may be gleaned from general crafts books and homemaking magazines and can be adapted to your specific, Jewish needs. You may also want to consult *The Work of Our Hands* by Mae Rockland (New York: Schocken, 1974) and *Jewish Holiday Crafts* by Joyce Becker (New York: Bonim Books, 1977).

GIFTS TO MAKE FOR YOUNGER CHILDREN

Hebrew Letters
Hebrew letters can be cut out of felt, calico, gingham, or other cheerful fabrics and stuffed with polyester fiber filling. The letters comprising the child's name can be hung from a mobile, whose basic structure is formed by an inexpensive embroidery hoop covered with thick yarn. Hang the letters on yarn cut in varying lengths from the hoop. Letters can also be attached to one another to spell out the child's name in a straight line. Loop elastic at each end, and the line of letters can be strung across a crib for the infant to "bat" against. Gail Riemer of Cambridge, Massachusetts, suggests attaching letters to one another with velcro; the child can then have fun pulling them apart. Letters can be appliquéd onto a quilt and fashioned into a wall hanging. Model Hebrew alphabets are available at the end of *The Work of Our Hands*. Simply increase the size of the letters on graph paper.

Also see *Hebrew Calligraphy/A Step-by-Step Guide* by Jay Greenspan, published by Schocken Books in 1979. Pursuing creative visions of Hebrew alphabets for your adaptations, you will want to check *The Book of Letters* by Lawrence Kushner, published by Harper and Row; *The Alphabet of Creation* by Ben Shahn, published by Schocken Books; *A Book of Hebrew Letters* by Mark Podwal, published by the Jewish Publication Society; and the "Alphabet, Hebrew" article in volume 2 of the *Encyclopaedia Judaica*.

Baby Blankets

The possibilities are limitless. Create great messages with appliqué. For example, imagine a Hebrew alphabet quilt where each square is a different Hebrew letter. If you're a skillful knitter or crocheter, consider rendering the Jewish symbols and letters in your usual knit or crocheted baby blanket.

Wall Hangings

Wall hangings can be made with a wide range of techniques. If you're intimidated by batik, experiment with crayon. Try crayoning a design on cotton. Iron the design into the fabric, using a paper towel to absorb excess wax. Or spread the cloth over a Salton hot tray and crayon directly onto the warm fabric. The heat produced by the tray will melt the wax and make the colors seem to flow onto the fabric. Cover the hot tray with a sheet of tinfoil to insulate it before placing the cloth on the tray. Glue felt to felt or collage-type "found objects" to felt to create artistic wall hangings without sewing.

Wooden Alphabet Blocks

Occasionally, it is possible to find Hebrew wooden alphabet blocks. If you see them, buy all you can for many possible uses. Seymour Epstein suggests that you glue them together to spell out the child's name and any message you want to convey. Then drill a narrow hole through the center of your vertical pile and thread through the electrical cord of a premade lamp assembly. You will have made the base for a child's lamp. You can also glue the blocks together to create a picture or mirror frame, spelling out the child's name or an important message. If you make a wooden tray frame that can surround the blocks when they are laid out flat, you've got a puzzle.

Messages intended for framing and wall hanging

Your choice of medium and your style of execution will depend largely on your artistic and calligraphic skills. It is not uncommon to use passages from old amulets intended to protect an infant from all manner of harm. Such texts can be found in the *Second Jewish Catalog* under "Birth." Also refer to "Amulets" in the *Encyclopaedia Judaica*, volume 2. We have recently seem some beautifully rendered in colorful script and in paper cutouts.

Hebrew letter play and recognition

We learn from Maria Montessori of the benefits to the child of tracing letters in varieties of media and textures. Try cutting out Hebrew letters in fine-grain sandpaper and gluing them to cardboard or construction paper. Create letters by gluing a variety of objects to cardboard—macaroni, string, beans, Styrofoam packing chips, beads. Assemble letter patterns and packets of materials as kits for children to assemble as their own craft projects.

Door or Name Plates

Cut out a rectangle in a material that accepts glue and can be hung later on the child's door as a name plate or as a *baruch ha'ba* welcome sign. Write your message in white glue and then liberally sprinkle on glitter. This name plate project can involve a two- or three-year-old who will be happy to help pour on glitter.

Other door or name-plate designs may become too complicated for help from young children. Writing messages in ceramic clay can be fun; be sure to punch holes in the clay, which will allow it to be screwed to the wall later. Ceramic clay, which can be painted or glazed, also lends itself to *mezuzah* case making. Create a matched set of *mezuzah* case and name plate or welcome sign for the door of a child's room. Signs can also be rendered in needlepoint or embroidery. Colorful signs can be made simply by cutting out letters from interesting materials and gluing them onto wood or cardboard. Use batik and crayon-fabric techniques, then mount the fabric over wooden frame stretchers.

Placemats, Plates, and Mugs

These can be fun projects for children. Schools sometimes will supply children with placemat or plastic plate-making materials. (The plates are obtainable for $3.95 from Small Fry Originals, Plastics Manufacturing Co., 2700 S. Westmoreland, Dallas, TX 75224. Mugs are available from Kiddie Kreations, 906 N. Woodward Ave., Royal Oak, MI 48067— although Kiddie Kreations only deals in larger orders.) The child can draw a design—perhaps for Rosh Hashanah or Hanukah or Pesah. The plate, placemat, or cup is then mailed back to the supply company, which returns the finished, laminated, and dishwasher-safe product. Children and parents alike appreciate and enjoy the keepsake.

An adaptation of this school project was developed by Lawrence Kushner, himself a skilled calligrapher, who discovered that the plain plastic plates are sometimes available commercially, sometimes in department stores, toy stores, or bookstores. He bought a plate and proceeded to apply his considerable skill to designing a special *Shabbat* plate, decorated with candlesticks, *hallah*, and appropriate biblical verses as a gift for a newborn baby. He also made special plates for his own children, using their Hebrew names. Unlike the plates, placemats can also be created independent of the manufacturing companies. At the simplest level, you can create your own lamination by covering both sides of the placemat you have designed with clear contact paper.

Greeting Cards

Suggestions for creative cards abound in Jewish crafts books. The neat thing about making these cards yourself is that the range extends from your own sophisticated designs to the potato-printing skills of a toddler-helper. Remember that Xerox and photo-offset greatly expand the possibilities of reproducing sophisticated designs. Obviously, what is true of

New Year's cards also applies to invitations, announcements, and birthday, anniversary, and holiday greetings.

Sukkah decorations

Self-hardening clays and dough with high salt content can be shellacked to preserve a design. You could make *sukkah* decorations using cookie cutters of Jewish symbols produced by Ktav Publishers (751 Varick St., New York, NY 10013). You might also decide to glue your clay or dough design to a neatly cut piece of wood, creating a wall hanging.

Doll house equipment

Young and not so young children love the fantasy worlds that they can create within the rooms of doll houses. We hope occasionally that our children will want their doll house people to "make Shabbos" or prepare for a *Yom Tov* or even build a *sukkah*. Glazing or shellacking clay for *hallah* loaves or pretend candles and candlesticks is one way to begin. A scrap of cloth can be hemmed and decorated in crayon to produce a *Shabbat* tablecloth.

Kippah crocheting

Kippot for special occasions are wonderful gifts. For further details, see the *First Jewish Catalog*, Siegel, Strassfeld, and Strassfeld (Philadelphia: Jewish Publication Society, 1973).

A wall hanging with pockets

Sew pockets onto a square or rectangular piece of material. Then cut out and attach felt (or other fabric) identification labels for the outside of each pocket. Place within each pocket a small version of the object named on the outside. For example, a small ball should be found within the pocket labeled *kadoor* (ball in Hebrew); inside a pocket labeled *aleph*, the child should find a small Hebrew letter *aleph*, perhaps made of gingham stuffed with polyester fiber. The object of the game is to associate the name or letter and the object.

Cookie baking and cake decorating

These can be fun activities to share with children and can produce delicious gifts. Try using cookie cutters or free-form creations of Jewish symbols or letters in cookie dough. With a cake decorating tube, write *Yom Huledet Samayach*, which means happy birthday in Hebrew.

Shalah manot

The preparation of *shalah manot* food gifts for delivery on Purim should be a fun family activity. It can include baking *hamantaschen* and designing baskets or containers to hold the gifts, which are, by tradition, composed minimally of two kinds of food. Recipes for *hamantaschen* abound; see any Jewish cookbook. This activity is especially important to share with children, for it involves them in a basic kind of Jewish gift giving.

Lotto games

Remember how to play lotto? Each player holds his or her own master card, which has pictures of six different objects. The leader of the game has a deck of cards on which each of the objects is individually printed. The leader turns over cards from his or her deck, and the players try to find each object on their master cards. The winner is the one who covers all squares first. Two-, three-, four-, and five-year-olds generally love lotto.

Commercially made lotto sets of Jewish symbols will probably not be any better made than those you make yourself. The simplest plan is to draw the six object master cards and run them off on ditto or mimeograph paper. Remember that you will have to vary the objects so that different players will have different master cards. Take several out of your pile of ditto or mimeograph sheets and cut them up to produce the deck of individual cards. A variation on this theme is to draw or cut out pictures of Jewish objects, have them color copied, and then laminated.

Clothing with a child's name on it

Names can be embroidered or appliquéd onto clothing. Jewish book stores also sometimes carry iron-on Hebrew letters produced by Hebrew Iron Ons, P.O. Box 2072, Teaneck, NJ 07666, or Ktav Publishers, 75 Varick St., New York, NY 10013. T-shirt stores that will "iron on" letters of your choice open the doors to the most incredible possibilities of messages or biblical passages for your child.

Scrapbooks and photo albums

Children love to find themselves and people they know in pictures. They also love to tell you the story of what is happening in the picture. Assembling a scrapbook or photo album of Jewish interest can be fun; for example, "There are the pictures of when we made *hallah*"; "There's David delivering *shalah manot*," etc.

Puppets

Puppets can range from the simplest finger puppets to the most elaborate hand puppets and complicated marionettes. Directions for varieties of puppet designs are widely available, but the ideal occasion for puppetry is Purim, when you will be able, with a king, a Queen Esther, a kindly, courtly uncle, and a cruel villain, to tell the story of Purim.

A Shabbat surprise box

Cover a box and lid with attractive contact paper. You may want the contents of the box to include objects of Jewish interest or small gifts and fun surprises of a *Shabbat*-appropriate nature. We know of someone who over the years made a collection of small toys that were kept in a *Shabbat* box and played with only on *Shabbat*. A variation on the *Shabbat* surprise box theme is the touch-and-feel box or bag. Such a box should have a cloth cover with a slit or draw-string opening. The object of the game is for the child to stick his or her hand in the box or bag and without looking—only by touch and feel—identify the objects.

Noah's Ark

What a marvelous gift for that *Shabbat* in the fall when the story of Noah and the flood is read! Potential media out of which to construct animals and ark include stuffed fabric or balsam wood. Consult pattern books in fabric stores or hobby shops for "professional" designs. A shortcut might be to buy a double set of commercially made zoo animals so that they can enter the ark two by two. Consider coordinating such a gift with one of the many *midrashic* story-book retellings of the tale.

For example, see *Why Noah Chose the Dove* by Isaac Bashevis Singer, illustrated by Eric Carle, published by Doubleday in 1974, or consider *Noah's Ark*, illustrated by Peter Spier, who based his vision on an old Dutch Christian poetic version of the story (published by Doubleday in 1977). Also see *The Story of Noah's Ark* by Tony Palazzo (Garden City, NY: Garden City Books, 1955). Think carefully about whether, for the specific child you have in mind, a story book will enhance his or her fantasy play or will limit imagination to the pictures in the book.

Dioramas

These small worlds are best made out of shoe boxes. Cut out one side. Create the imaginary world of your choosing and, if desired, replace the lid to provide a "ceiling" or "sky." The scene or stage set is thus visible from the shoe box's side that you have cut out. Four-, five-, and six-year-olds especially love to create these miniature worlds. For a child of that age, a shoe box filled with the materials he or she will need for a miniature *sukkah* is a great gift at *sukkot*.

Lego

These building blocks offer the possibility of writing out Hebrew letters and words, or building models of Jewish interest like the *mishkan*, the Temple, or a structure the child might recognize, like a *sukkah* or his/her family's synagogue.

Sewn cloth books

On each page attach an object of Jewish interest or significance. Experiment with varying textures of objects that you are attaching to the fabric pages.

Patchwork quilts

You can tell a story in patchwork or present a scene from the Jewish past (the trees, the *shul*, the men with beards and long black coats, the women with kerchiefs and long skirts, the snow, the wagon driver) or depict important events in the recipient's life or tell the story of Noah and the ark with an animal in each square of the quilt, or . . . (See the *Second Jewish Catalog* or *Work of Our Hands* for more patchwork ideas.)

Prayer books and Haggadot

Children of varying ages enjoy using their very own prayer books and Passover *Haggadot*. Check commercially published ones for children. How would you adapt such a prayer book or Haggadah for a specific child you have in mind? Consider loose-leaf binding and perhaps pictures that would stimulate your child into interesting discussions during a Seder. A prebound book with blank pages offers space for both you and the child to write or draw significant prayers that the child might use to supplement a traditional prayer book during services. Material could vary from serious to funny—contours of Hebrew letters, simple mental puzzles, or evocative poems—depending on the child's age and interests. Just as content may vary, so, too, may form. Consider the wide range of possibilities in bookbinding; see *How To Make Your Own Books* by Harvey Weiss (New York: Thomas Y. Crowell, $7.95).

Hallah covers

With embroidery, batik, or crayon, you can make *hallah* covers yourself or personally assemble kits for older children. In fact, some *hallah* cover and *Shabbat* tablecloth embroidery kits are distributed commercially through Jewish book stores and synagogue gift shops.

Collages of Jewish symbols

Collages can truly be works of art. Hunting for and assembling materials can be a rainy-day activity for a home-bound child.

Jewish calendars

Such calendars can list all the months of the Jewish liturgical year or the days of the week as they are counted in Hebrew. Reference to commercially produced calendars might provide you with helpful models. (See Chapter Thirteen for references to some specific commercial calendars.) Ideas for illustrations are limitless, the results can only be better than the ones you receive from your kosher butcher and your Jewish undertaker. Remember to include not only Jewish holidays but also days important to the child or recipient of the gift—his/her birthday, for example.

Coin collecting

Returning travelers often bring back coins of modern-day Israel, which children enjoy identifying and classifying. Children may also be excited to see museum collections of ancient coins and books of photographs—for example, of the Bar Kokhba coins of *Massada* by Yigael Yadin (New York: Random House). More sophisticated Jewish coin collecting resources are available through such specialists as the Israel Numismatic Society of Illinois, Highland Park, Illinois; Coins and Medals Dept., Government of Israel, New York; Gal Ed, The Israeli Commemorative Society, New York; Israel Coin Distribution Co., New York; and Holy Land Judaica, Toronto, Canada.

Stamp collecting

Israeli stamps also can prove an educationally exciting venture. Consult the following publications:

"Concentration Camp and Ghetto Mail," Judaica Historical Philatelic Society, P.O. Box 484, Cooper Station, New York, NY 10003.

LINDENBAUM, ARIEH. *Great Jews in Stamps.* Amis Publishing Co., 38 W. 32nd St., New York, NY 10001.

MATEK, ORD. *The Bible through Stamps.* Ktav, 75 Varick St., New York, NY 10003

RICHTER, JOHN HENRY. *Judaica on Postage Stamps.* Irvin Girer, 27436 Aberdeen St., Southfield, MI 48076.

WEITZ, EMIL. *A Glimpse into Jewish History through Philately.* Israel Coin Distributors Corp., 327 Park Ave. South, New York, NY 10010.

Recipe books

A collection of recipes, perhaps of Jewish holiday foods or favorite foods made by favorite relatives and friends, will be treasured for years to come. The food at our friends Alan Lehmann and Joanne Schindler's wedding was cooked by Joanne's mother's friends, who were members of the sisterhood of the synagogue. As a special gift to the bride and groom, the women created a cookbook of the recipes for all the dishes served at the wedding.

Book Plates

Older children and adults often enjoy identifying their books with book plates. Consider designing a sample book plate, perhaps exercising your calligraphic skills and including an appropriate biblical passage (e.g., *zeh hashAar laShem*—this is the gateway to God) and the owner's name in Hebrew. The sample can then be copied, either by Xerox or photocopy, and applied with glue or mucilage.

Utensil holders

Make utensil holders for your child's desk using contact paper over different-size cans. Then print the Hebrew words for the objects on the front of the cans.

Ritual objects

Making your own ritual objects out of clay or ceramic clay can be fun for both adult and child. Consider a *menorah* for Hanukah, candlesticks for *Shabbat*, or a Seder plate. Making a *Shabbat kiddush* cup is more tricky, because the glaze will have to seal the clay in order for the cup to hold liquid. Jewish crafts books offer many suggestions for making *kiddush* cups. Creating a kit for an older child by collecting the necessary material and instructions could help make a rainy day pass quickly.

PART FOUR
ISSUES

We often encounter hard questions we wish would go away but never do. Our toddler asks, "Why?" and we have no answer. As children ask more complicated questions we begin to think that they are voicing curiosities and doubts and confusions which dwell silently within us. Sometimes an answer is easy, really at our fingertips; often we must grope and grow within ourselves. In the next seven chapters we find some ways of responding Jewishly to such difficult questions as those about sibling rivalry, Hanukah and Christmas, sex, God, death, the Holocaust, and money.

How do we react as we witness cut-throat competition between our children? How do we behave as we shop in a department store during December?

How do we respond to our children's questions about sexual ethics? Can we afford simply to avoid talking about sexuality?

What can we say when our child innocently asks, "Do you believe in God? Well, what does God look like?" The history of Jewish thought demonstrates how difficult it is for us to talk about God.

How do we begin to talk with our children about the Holocaust? How strange it is for those of us who are the children of survivors to realize that our children and grandchildren could conceivably grow up without ever having met anyone who experienced the Holocaust first-hand.

When death occurs in a family, how can we help children mourn? Are there Jewish ways of talking with children about death?

Money may be the best kept secret in any family. How can we help children learn the value of a dollar without prizing it too greatly?

We hope that the chapters which follow will prove helpful when the inevitable questions are raised.

CHAPTER TWENTY-SIX

SIBLING RIVALRY

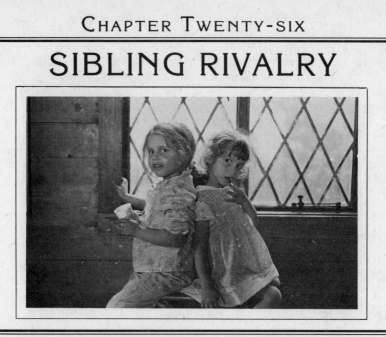

Now the man knew his wife Eve, and she conceived and bore Cain, saying, "I have bought/acquired a man with the help of the Lord." She then bore his brother Abel. Abel became a keeper of sheep, and Cain became a tiller of the soil. In the course of time, Cain brought an offering to the Lord from the fruit of the soil; and Abel, for his part, brought the choicest of the firstlings of his flock. The Lord paid heed to Abel and his offering, but to Cain and his offering He paid no heed. Cain was much distressed and his face fell. And the Lord said to Cain,

"Why are you distressed,
And why is your face fallen?
Surely if you do right,
There is uplift.
But if you do not do right
Sin is the demon at the door,
Whose urge is toward you,
Yet you can be his master."

And Cain said to his brother Abel . . . and when they were in the field, Cain set upon his brother Abel and killed him. The Lord said to Cain,. "Where is your brother Abel?" And he said, "I do not know. Am I my brother's keeper?"

GENESIS 4:1–9

This passage initiates the turbulent family history that characterizes the book of Genesis. We are struck by many things in the passage. First, there is the ambiguity of Eve's comment on the birth of Cain: "I have bought/acquired a man with the help of the Lord." If "the man" she is talking about is Cain, we are puzzled and say to ourselves, "Yes, of course you acquire a man through the birth of a male child." But what if the man she refers to is not Cain but Adam, who has estranged himself in his anger at her over the expulsion from the Garden? This explanation makes more sense. Eve uses her pregnancy and the birth of her child as a lure to win back her husband. How sad it is for the child whose birth is greeted only with triumph that the ruse worked. We ask ourselves, "With such a reason for giving birth, with so sad a reception, what is the future of this parent-child relationship?"

Once when Rabbi Mordechai was in the great town of Minsk explaining the Torah to a crowd of people who were hostile to his way, they jeered at him, saying, "What you say does not at all explain the verse."

"Do you really think that I was trying to explain the verse in the book?" he asked them. "That does not need explanation. I want to explain the verse that is within me."

Cain and Abel chose vocations in opposition to each other. Cain brings an offering to God, and as the text carefully tells us, Abel brings an even better offering. The text continues: "The Lord paid heed to Abel and his offering, but to Cain and his offering He paid no heed." Thus we learn that God, the parent figure, rejects not only the gift but the gift giver himself. We can think up ways to comfort ourselves, denying that God is a cruel or rejecting parent in this scene. The *midrash* (commentary) tells us that there was a meanness in Cain that prevented him from bringing God the best that he had. But, ultimately, we feel a sense of pain for Cain, whose rejection by God is so very complete. Even God's subsequent words to Cain are harsh and barbed. The stage is set by the rejection, which fuels an already explosive sibling rivalry. Cain kills Abel, and even here, instead of exploding in rage, God plays a kind of cat-and-mouse game that is in itself another form of stubborn rejection. Ironically, had God lashed out in real rage, it would have indicated the passion of His bond to Cain. Divine anger would have been an acknowledgment of God's feeling of betrayal at Cain's murdering his brother. Instead, God strips Cain of his humanity by toying with him about the murder ("Where is your brother Abel?"), and Cain, of course, plays right into the scene by denying any knowledge of Abel's whereabouts.

A MODERN MIDRASH

When Buber and Rosenzweig translated the Bible from Hebrew into German, they decided to translate the word *mikra* not as it is usually translated—"Scripture"—but as Calling Out. Thus, they sought to convey a sense of the text calling out to us and of the demand that we stand in relationship to that call. As we read Torah *Shabbat* morning, many of us seek to hear the message, both spoken and unspoken. We recall a mystical view of Torah that maintains, "Some people believe that Torah is black words written on white parchment. In truth, God wrote many Torahs before He was satisfied that the Torah that we know was the right one for us. He even wrote a Torah of white fire on black as well as black fire on white."

We seek to perceive both the words of the Torah that are written and the words that are unwritten, the spaces between the words. Sometimes we participate in Torah discussions. We create our own *midrashim* (our own understandings). Sometimes our *midrashim* stand the test of time, and sometimes they do not. No matter; the same portion of the Torah will be read again next year, and we will build on last year's insights. Sometimes, as we look self-consciously at our *midrashim*, we realize that our interpretations tell us more about ourselves than about the biblical text. We struggle to understand and to stand in relationship. Throughout this volume, we find people using examples and insights gleaned from their readings of biblical texts. Certainly, the Torah, concerned as it is with issues of sibling rivalry, of parenting, of leading and following, provides a fertile source from which to talk about ways in which we are raising our children. We are all in the process of creating *midrashim* in our own lives. It is a process and experience that we recommend. For further ideas about how to begin Torah discussion, we recommend the book *God Wrestling* by Arthur Waskow (New York: Schocken, 1978).

We who are parents are haunted by Cain. We know what it means to love a child unequivocally, with no reservations. Acknowledging our children's faults, we realize that the intensity of our love is not diminished. We also know that we relate to our different children differently. The quantity of our love is, we earnestly hope, not different. But inevitably the quality must be.

On a superficial level, one of our children may look like our favorite grandparent, and we melt every time we notice the resemblance. Or another child may have all those qualities we most yearned for in ourselves, whether it be quiet self-assurance, swaggering extroverted-ness, or deep intuition and self-awareness. Such knowledge may some-times cause us painful moments of self-questioning. Are we being overly generous to Rachel, because she is so self-confident, when Judith really needs our time and efforts more? Do we, without realizing it, convey our subtle feelings of admiration for one child in ways that are not healthy for either that child or for our other children?

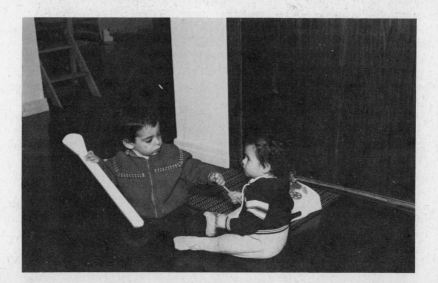

> Privacy, I think, is of utmost importance. I used to share a room with my brother until I was about eleven. As each of the older kids went to college, we got rooms of our own. Since my brother is only sixteen months older than I, we had been together since we were little. Until I moved upstairs, I had no idea what privacy was all about. Now that we have had privacy for quite some time, I find it difficult to even share a room with him for the night, when necessary.
>
> NOAM,
> eleventh grader

There is, I am sure, no parent with more than one child who has not either secretly or openly thought about such questions.

We know we must be vigilant, although not about apportioning things out in quantifiably equal measures to all our children, for ultimately such equality is impossible. We have to be vigilant in striving to give each child what he or she needs from us. One child may need private time alone with a parent. Another child may rebuff the suggestion of such private time as an infringement on play or homework. It is useless to give to one child what the other child needed all along, and we only breed potential Cain and Abel scenarios when we try to do so.

Can we diffuse totally the existence of sibling rivalry? Of course not. The child who witnesses the addition of another baby to the family will always feel displaced by the new offspring, as, indeed, he or she was. Certainly, for most of us, the amount of time and energy we lavish on our first-born cannot possibly be duplicated for our second child, nor can it even be continued for our first-born once there is a second. When the second child becomes an entity to be dealt with in the household, almost inevitably the first child wonders if the parents have enough love to go around. The key is to try to let the child know that love has no limits, that regardless of the "amount" of love we lavish on one person, we have more love left to give to others, including our spouses, our own parents and siblings, and our friends. Such a sense of balance helps our children grow to see themselves in perspective in the family. (A woman in my grandfather's town was asked how she managed to raise twelve children by herself. She replied: "It's really very easy. When I had one child, that child took up all my time, all of my energy every minute of every day. So I thought to myself, How could eleven more take up any more time?")

But despite all our good intentions, there will inevitably be those times when we hear loud thumps followed by piercing wails emanating from the direction of the playroom. This, minus all philosophizing, is sibling rivalry with a vengeance. What do we do?

One school of thought tells us to leave our children alone, for they will work out their own differences in the ways that are peculiar to children. Another school of thought (our own irrational one) tells us to enter the room dramatically and scream impartially at both combatants, thereby showing no favoritism to either side and also, not incidentally, permitting ourselves to remain emotionally uninvolved with the entire enterprise. A third school of thought would have us hear both sides of the fight and serve as litigator over the *issue*, thereby diffusing the emotional intensity into purely practical disagreement (i.e., "It's not that Sam hates his brother; it's just that they both wanted to play with the pick-up-sticks"). Yet another school tells us that our own intuition is the best guide for how to handle each situation. (This is the "what feels right to you" school of thought.)

We know, however, without resorting to soliciting expert advice that each child is different, and each child's relationship to his or her sibling is different. No one can say categorically that any one method is best. For siblings who do have basic love and trust and who only occasionally erupt into violence, the "they'll work it out" method may indeed be right. For the older child who absolutely hates the younger child, a reassessment of how you, the parent, are relating to each child individually and both together may be in order. Intuition will be the guide for many situations, but parents also have to leave themselves open to hearing the still small voice either of our child in pain or of our own bad patterns that we are letting our children work out for us. Do we fight weekly with our own siblings or our spouses' siblings and thereby establish unconscious patterns for our children to follow? Do we invariably take the side of the younger or weaker child, leaving the other child seething with resentment? Do we have trouble allowing ourselves to hear that one of our children is truly brutalizing or tormenting another?

As we read the book of Genesis, we are confronted by models of sibling struggles that are transmitted from one generation to the next, of patterns of parental favoritism that descend through families like curses. Genesis teaches us about the depths of rage that the very existence of siblings can engender. Our task as parents is to defuse that rage so that the love that cohabits with hatred can emerge and flower.

Your little brother may want to talk about comic books right after you've just broke up with your girl friend of eight months. Hitting him won't solve anything. Unless you let him know, he has no way of guessing how you feel, just as you may have had no idea that your mother had a very hard day working when you asked her if she would take you to an amusement park and she yelled at you. So talk to each other.

STUART,
eleventh grader

Biblical parents also failed. Generations later, the rabbis (Shab. 10b) warned against favoring one child over another and used Joseph as an example, "because of two sela weight of silk [that went into the coat of many colors] which Jacob gave to Joseph in excess of his other sons, the brothers became jealous of him and the mantle resulted in our forebears' exile in Egypt." Think how dearly the aged Jacob loved his youngest son Benjamin once Joseph was gone. Reading the biblical account, we feel the beauty and sadness of that love, and yet we cannot help but wonder about the feelings of Jacob's remaining sons.

The Bible says, "For God heard the voice of the lad." And Rabbi Mendel commented on this verse, saying, "Nothing in the preceding verses indicates that Ishmael cried out. It was a soundless cry and God heard it."

CHAPTER TWENTY-SEVEN

HANUKAH AND CHRISTMAS: LIVING IN TWO CULTURES

"We don't have Christmas, do we, Tatie?" asked our four-year-old. "No, my dear," replied the father. "We don't have Christmas, but we do have Tu b'Shevat (Jewish Arbor Day)." The father was trying to make light of that common move of Jewish parents: the attempt to substitute something positive (Hanukah) for Christmas. The dilemma of Jewish parents confronted by Christmas is in many ways what both this book and the present uses of Hanukah are about.

Much of this book reflects modes of living within two cultures, of evolving a viable and meaningful Jewish life style within the United States. Were our lives sheltered from the larger American society, there would be no need to consider such issues as Hanukah and Christmas, Jews and other religions, interdating, or choosing a Jewish baby name that "works" in English as well as Hebrew or Yiddish. But it is very clear that we live in more than one culture. There are ways, as Will Herberg and others have pointed out, that we are marginal and critical in American society. On the other hand, we acknowledge that we are part of that society, too, and that there are aspects of American life we value and appreciate. Our feelings at Christmas reflect our dual identity. Of course, twinkling Christmas tree lights are attractive to us, as, at a deeper level, is the Christian spirit of giving. We drive past beautiful Christmas displays, we are awed by the beauty, yet we do not get out of the car. We are only passing by. Christmas is not ours.

Ironically, as our children go to school, we tend to respond to their attraction to Christmas by trying to substitute Hanukah. Hanukah celebrates not only the miracle of the oil lasting eight days in the newly rededicated Temple but also records the struggle of the Maccabees against the oppressive reign of ancient Syria. Scholars point out that the Maccabees were fighting against the hellenizing influences of the Syrians, who had conquered the land of Israel. While the Maccabees were battling such political and religious oppression as the Syrian control of the Temple in Jerusalem and the Syrian systems of taxation, they were also fighting Hellenization, which came along with the Syrians and attracted their own people. The military struggle against Syria helped inhibit Jews from giving their children Greek names or patronizing Greek-style baths. Elie Wiesel pointed up the problem well when he asked: What is the difference between Purim and Hanukah? On Purim, the Jews were threatened with physical extermination at the hands of Haman. They responded spiritually by praying and fasting. On Hanukah, Jews were threatened by spiritual extermination as represented by the attractiveness of Greek culture; and the Jews responded physically by fighting. How ironic that, confronted by another attractive and alien culture in America, we respond by celebrating a holiday that began in the throes of a very similar dilemma.

We are confronted by Christmas, but are we necessarily threatened by Christmas? How we answer that question determines a great deal of how we will behave around the last few weeks in December. And it should also be pointed out that regardless of our own feelings, the age of our children will also greatly influence us.

It has been pointed out by Merle Feld and others that by saying to a child, "We do not have Christmas, but we do have Hanukah," we are suggesting a Jewish lack. We are saying, "No, my poor child, we lack Christmas; but we do indeed have something, albeit lesser, to substitute." The problem begins when we weigh the relative religious importance of Christmas and Hanukah. Christmas and Easter are Christianity's most basic celebrations. Hanukah is a lovely, not tremendously important Jewish holiday. If you choose to secularize Christmas and see it as an extravagant and materialistic American national holiday, then you are in more trouble. Some Jews would like to celebrate Christmas devoid of religious meaning. ("Stockings by the fireplace, filled by Santa, are charming and have no religious meaning." (The problem with this position is that is supports a variety of American materialism that most of us wish to combat. The truth is, there is no way in which a Jew can be anything more than a sympathetic guest at a Christmas celebration, but what does that say about Hanukah?

In the best of all possible worlds, we would like to disassociate Hanukah and Christmas. In fact, we know that children find it helpful in conversations at school about "what-you-got-for-Christmas" to be able to chime in with what they got for Hanukah. Early childhood and elementary school teachers' resource books often have sections on the holidays; these books will list Halloween, Thanksgiving, Christmas, and Hanukah. The juxtaposition reflects not only how far we have moved in liberal American society but also how religiously unaware the designers of such books are.

A great deal is determined by a child's age. We have a sixteen-year-old friend who is a student in a local Jewish day school. Each year the young man helps his next-door neighbors trim their Christmas tree. Our friend's reactions are mature and knowledgeable and are very different from those of a four-year-old who is just learning about similarities and differences among people and innocently needs to clarify that all people do not celebrate Christmas.

Perhaps our fears are unfounded. Because a child is enchanted by Santa does not mean he or she will be less a Jew, or does it? A friend reported overhearing her daughter tucking in her dolls. The child lives in an intensely Jewish atmosphere and attends a "good" Jewish school. Our friend reported feeling discomfort as she heard the child tell her dolls, " 'Twas the night before Christmas." Our friend said, "It was not that I was afraid that Shifra would go out and celebrate Christmas. It was that I was saddened; I wanted her fantasy life to revolve around Jewish symbols. I felt that a lot of what we do is work to make Jewish symbols attractive, and I resolved to make Shifra a terrific costume for Purim!"

Gershom Scholem, a great Jewish scholar and thinker, in his memoir *Between Berlin and Jerusalem* (New York: Schocken Books, 1980) described the last Christmas he celebrated with his family. Using the excuse that they were only doing it for the Christian maids in their household, his family orchestrated elaborate Christmas celebrations complete with tree and presents. As a boy in Berlin, Scholem became fascinated with Zionism. That fateful Christmas, Scholem found a picture of Theodor Herzl under his family Christmas tree. Scholem's mother explained that she had thought the picture would be an appropriate gift for him, since the young man was so interested in Zionism. Scholem could no longer tolerate the inconsistency and avoided future family Christmas celebrations.

Do such celebrations make a difference? We have to share in the conclusion illustrated by the following rabbinic story:

For days and days, the sage sat at the Gates of Rome. Finally, a friend approached him and asked, "Do you really believe that your sitting here will change Rome?" The sage replied: "I do not believe that my sitting here will change Rome, but by sitting here I know that Rome will not change me." Perhaps our rejection of Christmas celebrations and our observances of Hanukah will not matter or change things for our children, but at least we (and they) will know where we stand.

Given that we are, in fact, going to observe Hanukah, where can we go for help in enriching our experience of the holiday? Some resources include:

BECKER, JOYCE. *Jewish Holiday Crafts*. New York and London: Bonim Books, 1977.

Encyclopaedia Judaica. Jerusalem: Keter Books, 1973, vol. 6.

GASTER, THEODORE. *Festivals of the Jewish Year*. New York: William Morrow and Co., 1953.

GOODMAN, PHILIP. *Hannukah Anthology*. Philadelphia: Jewish Publication Society, 1976.

"Hannukah for Grown-Ups," *Menorah* (journal). December 1979, Project on Jewish Institutions, Public Resource Center, 1747 Connecticut Ave., N.W., Washington, DC 20009.

HIRSH, MARILYN. *Potato Pancakes All Around*. New York and London: Bonim Books, 1978.

"Latkes and Hamantashen." Phonograph record by Jackie Cytrynbaum and Fran Avni. Lemonstone Records, P.O. Box 607, Cote St. Luc, Montreal, P.Q. H4V 2Z2, Canada, 1980.

ROCKLAND, MAE SHAFTER. *The Hannukah Book*. New York: Schocken Books, 1976.

SIEGEL, RICHARD, STRASSFELD, MICHAEL, AND STRASSFELD, SHARON, eds. *The Jewish Catalog*. Philadelphia: Jewish Publication Society, 1973.

Our family has always made a point of hosting at least one festive Hanukah party each year. These parties began as a way for our four-year-old to share the songs she had learned with her school friends who did not celebrate Hanukah at home. The first time we hosted a Hanukah party we were transformed by the experience of watching the *menorah* light reflected in twelve pairs of shining eyes. Hushed silence filled our living room as each child took turns lighting candles on the many *menorahs* we had provided. The children were round-eyed with the wonder and sensuousness of the flickering lights. Quiet singing, louder singing, some dancing, *dreidel* spinning, a Hanukah-present hunt, and a taste of cake decorated with a *menorah* completed the party.

As the kids have gotten older, we've added different pieces to the party, and as the parents have gotten older, we, too, want our share of the fun. Last year, we initiated a Hanukah "talent" party. As their ticket of admission, everyone who came had to perform, and the resulting evening of card tricks, singing duets, ballet improvisation, poetry recital, and dramatic renditions was exhilaratingly fun. The kids say they want to do the same at their party this year. We keep evolving new ways to celebrate, which are fun, joyful, and not competitive with Christmas.

Today is Hanukah, and tonight we plan to take our whole family downtown to join with other Jews in lighting an enormous *menorah* in front of the electric company. Our lighting that *menorah* represents an attempt to say something about our belief in alternative energy sources and to protest the electric company's plan to bill state residents for the repair of the crippled Three Mile Island nuclear power plant. Telling you about this particular segment of our Hanukah celebration does not reflect an effort to convert you to our beliefs about energy and ecology; it does represent our desire to encourage you to use Jewish symbols in new ways and to integrate environmental and social concerns into your Jewish ritual life. Sometimes we have failed in our attempts and orchestrated moments that were at best corny or trivial. Often, though, we have found our efforts enriching to ourselves, to the very old rituals to which we bring new dimensions of societal concern, and to the larger world that witnesses and participates in such moments.

A resource for exploring such socially conscious, new Jewish rituals is *Menorah*, edited by Arthur Waskow, a journal published through the Public Resource Center, 1747 Connecticut Ave., N.W., Washington, DC 20009. Arthur is happy to discuss ideas for future projects as well as eager to publicize in *Menorah* good ideas that worked.

Theology and ideology aside, how does a little Jewish kid feel at Christmas time in his nice, progressive school? A lot depends on how the school handles the holiday season, and what individual teachers emphasize. But what's so wrong with saying to a little kid, "Yeah, they have Santa Claus, but their holiday is only for one day, and our holiday is for eight days"? It makes the kid feel a little better defended against his attraction to something that he knows is closed off to him. At the same time, you know that neither you nor the kid will necessarily fixate on that kind of chauvinism all the rest of the kid's life. Maybe he just needs it for this year.

CHAPTER TWENTY-EIGHT

TALKING WITH OUR CHILDREN ABOUT SEX

Estelle and Eugene B. Borowitz

Until recently, Jewish parents did not feel compelled to teach their children about sex. Mostly, the Jewish tradition sought to cultivate a modesty and decency in adults that, as centuries passed, often transformed euphemism into careful avoidance. With the teaching of modern psychology that mental health is related to sexuality, the old Jewish affirmation of life brought many of us to see the nurturing of positive sexual values as a basic parental responsibility.

Some attitudes are widely accepted among parents today. For example, since repression and furtiveness are generally harmful, going to the other extreme and making a point of absolute revelation likewise is seen as harmful. If we are to be fully human, we must retain a measure of modesty and a respect for personal privacy. So, too, proper communication begins by sensing what information is genuinely desired, knowing or acquiring that information and conveying it, being careful not to tell the child more than he or she wants to know. This sense of appropriateness reflects the true art of communication, as every parent, teacher, or friend knows.

In sex as in every other important matter that helps a person grow, the nonverbal sets the context of what can be effectively said and heard. In the earliest days and weeks of life (some insist even prenatally) highly significant communication goes on through holding, touching, kissing, cooing, playing, dressing, bathing, and all the other acts that make up the normal repertoire of parenting. Sexuality may not be directly genital at this stage, but the attitudes toward body, sensation, and human relationship that are established in these early stages of life will determine how children will learn what we will later try to teach them directly.

Parents are extraordinarily influential in the model they set for their child. Who we are in relation to our own sexuality, the values we embody, the attitudes we convey, the standards by which we live, will all be far more powerful in fixing the child's attitude to sex than almost anything we or anyone else later tries to "teach." And our words will be evaluated by them, largely unconsciously, in terms of what in fact they have known us to be truly like. Being an example on so deep a level puts a severe strain on modern adults. Instead of being able to rely on rules, as previous generations did, we must become the instrument of our own teaching. Worse, despite our supposed freedom and greater experience, we often do not truly know who we are or what we actually believe in as we pass through the stages of young adulthood and become parents. Our times do not help, for they buffet us with doubts about our values. Amid our insecurities, how can we set a proper example for our children? All the more reason, then, to see the process of getting to know ourselves and our beliefs better as the first step in any effective education of our children.

As the children move from the preverbal to the verbal stage, it becomes increasingly important for us to pay attention to the sort of relationship we are creating with them. All the years ahead (not excluding the difficult years of adolescence, young adulthood, and the more mature phases that follow) will rest on the framework we create for being together. Do we relate to our children in ways that allow or even encourage them to be able to ask us serious questions? Or are we responding to them in ways that quietly teach them that in important areas it is best not to ask us? Can we help them to be so at ease with us as to be able to say what may not come easily despite all the good will and knowledge we have attained? Or have we, perhaps without knowing it, built patterns of not hearing or of irritating one another so that any effort to speak with intimacy is a success if it avoids disaster? Our difficulties are compounded by our desire to guide rather than to impose in an uncongenial fashion. Children quickly learn to think for themselves, and they will find many diverse instructors awaiting them in our society. We need to convey our respect for their ability to make responsible decisions for themselves even as we seek to give them the Jewish values through which their personal freedom will find its proper fulfillment.

If it seems that we have thus far avoided the questions that trouble parents ("Where did I come from? Why are boys different from girls?"), it is because we do not believe that sex in Judaism can be considered apart from love, from personhood, from the ideal of holiness. To turn sex education into basic biology is to debase it from a Jewish point of view. Biological data are important, but only as a means. The end is a loving human being whose sexuality is expressed with another in a way that makes them both holier—that is, closer to God—than they were before. If such sexuality is too high an ideal, then we suggest that settling for the current notion that efficient functioning is everything is precisely what demeans humankind in our time. Any sex education that does not try to teach one how to be a loving human being creates a new trauma in the name of eliminating an old one.

Values and information inevitably accompany one another in all discussions of sexuality. It can be helpful to consider the relative balance between the two in various stages of a child's maturation. The infant or young child, from preverbal times to prepuberty, is more likely to be interested in information than in hearing about values. As the search for individuality takes over (i.e., for adolescents, young adults, and those adult children who may still want-to talk with us about sex) concern for values will be more important than need for information. But we must add that we have met adults whose information about sexuality was far more faulty than they realized and whose ability to live as loving Jews involved their learning some important data.

One happy result of our changing sexual ethos has been the production of new materials to teach children about sex. There are even picture books that do not require reading ability yet provide children with the information they seek.

See, for example, *Making Babies* by Sara Bonnett Stein with photography by Doris Pinney, published by Walker and Company of New York in 1974, or *How Babies Are Made* by Andrew C. Andry and Steven Schepp, with illustrations by Blake Hampton, published by Time-Life Books in New York, 1968. Such books might have been banned as pornography a few years ago. Today, looking at their wholesome, natural pictures, we can easily see how they teach positive attitudes toward sexuality while not hiding things that young children are curious about. As parents, we owe it to ourselves to explore the many kinds of materials available, not the least for the insights we may receive into what our children may be asking and how we might respond.

The communication of values is a far more difficult task. We do not know very much about how values can be directly taught or what the best way is to communicate them so that people will see their virtue and accept them as their own. Worse, there is very little agreement in America today as to just what constitutes proper sexual values. The widest variety of views may be found, from people who believe that "anything goes" between consenting adults to those who insist that we return to something like the prudish standards by which the Victorians purported to live. There is less diversity in the Jewish community insofar as we take our heritage seriously. Even so, there is no clear agreement over how much Orthodoxy can accommodate itself to new understandings of sexuality or to what limits liberal Jews might reasonably go in making their consciences rather than traditional law their guide in sexual behavior. Since even the selection of books to give data to children necessarily involves attitudes, we believe it is essential to gain a clear sense of our own understanding of a proper Jewish approach to sexuality. A talk with your rabbi, the study of some materials on this topic, or discussion with other members of the community who are similarly concerned, or perhaps with a professional resource person can be helpful. One unfortunate remnant of the old Jewish reticence about sexuality is that we are often afraid to ask for help in this area. In our experience, if someone only has the courage to ask an initial question, he or she will discover that many of us are eager to learn and that there are many resource people in the community willing to help.

The traditional Jewish attitude toward sexuality can be summarized this way: God created human beings as male and female; therefore, sexuality is good. God commanded that people marry and procreate; therefore, sexual intercourse in marriage is a sacred duty. While procreation is the major purpose of marital relations, it is not the only one. The joy of sex is a recognized goal for husband and wife, and though the male has some priority in a traditional Jewish marriage, he may not withhold intercourse from his wife but must gain her consent for its proper performance. Despite all that, sexuality is not seen as a major part of a life of Jewish piety. To give sexuality much attention suggests a low level of spirituality. Genital sexual activities other than marital intercourse are considered sinful. While there are many nuances and some variations of opinion, the contrast with the contemporary situation should be clear. Those who steadfastly maintain these traditional Jewish attitudes are well advised to find a like-minded community of Jews so that their children may be raised among others of similar standards and not be exposed to values that their parents find objectionable.

Numerically, the overwhelming bulk of American Jews seem convinced that classical Jewish attitudes and practices need to be modified, perhaps drastically, in the light of modern views of sexuality. At its best, this seems to be the personalist view, which is reflected above in our comment that sexual information devoid of concern for the loving person involved demeans sex and dehumanizes the person. The mature self is substantially a sexual creature, but neither essentially nor centrally so. There is far more to life than sexual activity, but rich sexuality will be a substantial part of a healthy person's life. That should not be understood in simple genital terms. While genital expression is the climax of a rich sexuality, the abilities to relate to others, to do so in various forms of love, and to share intimacy with some people are all parts of mature sexual self-expression.

By this standard, the older Jewish attitudes appear repressive. Considering the broad range of human personality and the variety of situations in which modern people find themselves, the old rules appear too restrictive, though the modern permissiveness clearly tends to a paganism in which the sanctity of personality gets lost. Personalistic sex thinks

more of play and enjoyment than Jewish teaching has; it is, for example, concerned with women's sexuality in ways that were hardly spoken of in classical, Jewish literature. It can tolerate the notion that two consenting unmarried adults who responsibly find that they cannot now marry but love one another deeply can ethically have sexual relations with one another. That opinion is already a matter of controversy in our community, though widely practiced, particularly among young adults. To extend the personalist view further into areas of Jewish sexual practice necessarily raises more controversy.

Perhaps it will help to list some of the problems that Jews taking a non-Orthodox approach to sexuality must now confront. Should masturbation be accepted as a natural part of sexual maturation, and when it is not compulsive, should it *not* be considered a matter of religious concern? What limits should operate as to the mingling of sexes, sexual enticement, flirtatiousness, and petty promiscuities? Are there forms of sex play that are appropriate to unmarried adults or others that are inappropriate for consenting spouses? With whom and under what circumstances is sexual intercourse right? What should be our community's attitude toward homosexuality or bisexuality? Is Jewish marriage still to be founded on the notion of fidelity, and is adultery still to be considered a major sin?

In contrast to these serious, perplexing questions, the problems of explaining specific *Jewish* attitudes toward sex appear almost minor; that is, as Jews, we are obligated to inform our children what Judaism has taught about the rite of circumcision and the practice of *mikvah* (the ritual bath), which is so closely associated with menstruation and childbirth.

This agenda—the need to explain these issues to our children—is so weighty as to seem unbearable. Yet Jews are parents today, and good ones, as they have been in the past. While we are not satisfied to repeat the mistakes of the past, there is comfort in knowing that Jews are not called on to be perfect, only to do what they can and then try to be a little better than that. Every Jew should recognize what an extraordinary range of resources is available in our community to help with these matters. No ethnic or religious group has a higher proportion of its members who are experts in the fields of human guidance and personal development. We urge you not to try to carry by yourself all the burdens of being a parent in this difficult time. All of us have problems, and for all of them we can get some help—if not definitive solutions. The information problems about physical makeup and differences are the easiest ones to handle. If your physician cannot help you, ask for a reference to someone who can, or contact your local Jewish Family Service. Printed material abounds. The most difficult problems are philosophical and spiritual. Let your rabbi know that these are matters of concern to you, and find those other families in your congregation with whom you can meet and discuss these issues.

The majority of real problems in this area are emotional and psychological. For example, children's problems of extreme shyness, poor body image, and profound embarrassment, on the one hand, or flaunting, exhibitionistic, and inappropriate experimentation, on the other, need expert attention. In this realm, our professional resources are unparalleled. For your children's sake, for your own sake, don't let the years go by before finding an adequate therapist. Ask your physician, Jewish Family Service, or rabbi for suggestions. It is not too much to say that when children have problems with their sexuality, almost certainly the parents will need to be involved in treatment, separately or with them. This often takes enormous courage to recognize but is well worth acknowledging. In becoming truer to ourselves and our beliefs, we not only serve our families better as models and guides, but also we become more the Jews we were created to be.

When Rabbi Shmelke had returned from his first trip to visit the *magid* of Mezritch, he was asked about his experiences. He replied: "Up until then I mortified my body so that it might endure the soul. But now I have seen and learned that the soul can endure the body and does not have to separate from it."

It is because of this that the Torah teaches us, "And I will set My abiding Presence among you and My soul shall not abhor you." For the soul must not abhor the body.

CHAPTER TWENTY-NINE

TALKING WITH OUR CHILDREN ABOUT MONEY

The Jew and his money. We are haunted by the stereotype. The medieval Jew as middle man, banker, money changer; he worked with money, not his hands or back, performing valuable services for the local prince and the peasant alike. Both elements of society owed him money and hated him. That he represented a small segment of the total Jewish population made no difference. All Jews were seen as Shylock. Today, we rightfully label the stereotype anti-Semitic and reject it. We realize that for most American families, Jewish and non-Jewish, rich, poor, and middle class alike, money represents a significant concern. Can we cull from our Jewish knowledge and history a series of insights that will help us deal with issues of money with our children?

The Ba'al Shem Tov, the great eighteenth-century Hasidic master, taught that we should only trust in God Almighty and that therefore people should not save money. His recommendation and his own practice was to give any money that remained at the end of each day to the poor. Contrast this absolute commitment to "God will provide" with contemporary estate planning and trust funds. Yet what Jewish parent does not want to set aside some money for his or her child's future benefit? Perhaps a college education fund? (After all, even the Talmud states that one of a parent's responsibilities to children is to help them have a profession or trade.)

How was money handled in your family when you were growing up? Were your family's investments or income a deep, dark secret? We all know of families in which children are never told anything about parents' incomes both because the parents want to buttress their own power to distribute or deny money and because parents are afraid that children will confide financial secrets to greedy relatives or to strangers. Some parents don't trust their children. ("If my daughter knew what I made this year, she would spend it twice over at Bloomingdale's.") Others don't trust their relatives and business partners. ("If my cousin knew I could afford it, I'd be supporting his mother-in-law.")

Often what is at stake is not money but some other difficulty in family dynamics; money simply becomes the metaphor through which the difficulties find expression.

"I want you to know the value of money." Do you remember when your parents recited those words to you? Have you heard yourself speaking the same words to your children? The problem is that you *really* want your child to know the value of money. You want the child to understand that money represents effort ("I worked hard for that money!") and that money should be budgeted wisely. The loophole or catch in spending money wisely is the degree to which one person's extravagance is another's economy. Arguments over ways in which money is spent often reflect conflicts of values or tastes. ("I would not mind it so much if he would buy Beethoven, but why must he own every record Kiss ever put out?") There are conflicts that simply have to be worked through. Chaim Ginot, a great child psychologist, observed a mother shopping in a department store with her daugther who wanted something the mother was unprepared to buy, and commented appreciatively on the following tactic:

> The mother did not simply tell her child "No" nor did she denigrate the child's desire or taste ("Why do you want that dumb thing? It's no good anyway"). Instead the mother sympathized with her daughter's desire ("I know you really want it"). At the same time she carefully explained why she could not produce the money to buy the object. Thus, the mother could let her child feel that she, the mother, understood and identified with the child's legitimate feelings while at the same time helping the child come to grips with the reality that her mother would not spend money on the desired object.

Wanting our children to know the true value of money also means that we do not want them to value money too much. We do not want them to make money into an *avodah zara* (an idol to be worshipped and served). "No one made more personal sacrifices than my husband did for his company; even with his heart condition, after the doctor told him to slow down, he would . . .") Also, we do not want our children to value money so greatly that they find it difficult to spend money appropriately or give money away to *tzedakah*. ("Do you know how much women's coats cost nowadays? I just cannot bring myself to replace this old *shmateh*.")

But how do we teach children the value of money? First of all, because there are no easy or automatically "right" answers, it can be useful to raise the issue when talking with other parents. What ideas or insights have they found helpful? To date, we have observed two basic models. In one model, children work for money, which they receive through allowances. Often allowances follow a pattern: for young children the allowance represents a reward for successfully fulfilling some expectations. ("Make your own bed.") As the child enters the middle years, expectations become jobs. ("Carry out the garbage," or, "I'll pay you five bucks to clean the basement.") Eventually, in or near the high school years, the allowance income is supplemented by jobs in the world outside the family. (Baby-sitting is classic. The most creative alternative we have heard is Aaron Polak's business. For a fee he will clean and kasher your oven and stove.) The other extreme is seen in

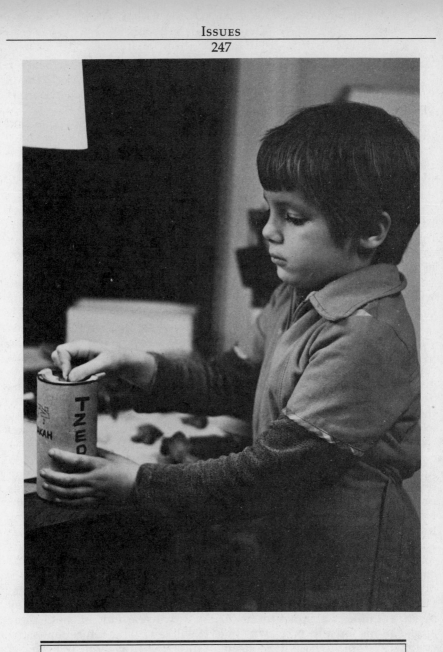

If you have anything, you have *tsoris* (troubles). And if you have nothing, you have more *tsoris*.

MRS. MARIE TOFFLER
(Jan. 3, 1862–Mar. 14, 1951)

families that simply give children money. ("If I need something, I buy it. My parents have never hassled me or felt I abused the privilege. When I earn money, it goes back into the family, but my father wants me to open a savings account in my name.")

Intrinsic to each of these models is a problem, which centers around the role in which the model places the parent. Thus, in the allowance scenario, the parent, who is the source of money, becomes the employer. In the model in which money is simply supplied the child, the parent becomes the benefactor-philanthropist. Are you comfortable with either identity?

It is easy to imagine abuses of either role: the employer can sometimes be stingy, and the benefactor can become capricious. More important is to consider the messages or hidden curricula that either model conveys to the child. Will your child understand more about money by earning it? At what age is this learning most valuable? Should it best happen in your home environment or on a newspaper delivery route? Perhaps you will mix these models, deciding that at some ages (e.g., infancy) earning money or giving allowances is preposterous and at other ages it is appropriate. Some parents argue that allowances that supply a limited amount of money over a short term (like a week) help the child learn to budget his or her expenses. The catch here is that allowances must realistically keep up with the escalating cost of living. It does no good to give a child fifty cents per week when chewing gum costs thirty cents. So much also depends on the individual personalities of children and their degrees of independence within the family structure. A child, for example, who never enters a store without a parent hardly needs pocket money.

We want our children not only to learn how to comparison shop and to know the cost of things but, more importantly, to learn the value of things. To truly understand the value of money and to put it in its proper perspective in this consumer society, children must also learn how to give money away. We want our children to learn to give money to *tzedakah*. Jean Piaget, the great Swiss scientist and thinker who has taught us so much about how children develop cognition, has helped us to understand two important concepts. First, he has shown us that children's thinking inevitably moves from the concrete to the abstract; in other words, that young children first understand objects around them tactilely, kinesthetically. Only over the years, as they mature, do they begin to think in abstract terms. Thus, a five-year-old can hold three apples in his lap and take away one. It will take time before that same child will be able to hold the concept of three-take-away-one in his mind and do arithmetic. This understanding of children's proclivity for the concrete helps us understand their attraction to material objects and lends insight into the terrible vulnerability young children have to television ads for toys. It is right and appropriate that young children are attracted to the concrete, the physical, the material. Our problem is how to balance this legitimate involvement with the physical world with other values so that it is not translated into the most negative aspects of materialism.

Second, Piaget has helped us understand some of the advantages of exposing children to real, live experiences at appropriate ages rather than simply talking theoretically, philosophically, or abstractly to them about ideas. Remember when your American mother told you to eat because there were starving children in Europe? You had no concept of those starving children; you knew about the food in front of you that you could only suggest she send them. In considering ways of teaching and learning about *tzedakah*, explore ways of exposing children to the potential recipients of *tzedakah*. Consider taking children to visit a community home for the aged or an impoverished Jewish library. Obviously, you will have to ecise care in planning your visits: you want the experience to be positive for the child. A problem with those school projects that sell candy or cookies and donate the proceeds to a Jewish charity is that children become so involved in their selling campaigns and the subsequent competitions for the most sales that the underlying purpose is forgotten. Hebrew school teachers have spent years collecting for Jewish National Fund (JNF) Forests. Originally, the idea was a great one. Today, however, this small change donation to JNF frequently may be the child's only contact with *tzedakah*.

How do we help our children understand their own responsibility to respond to Jewish needs by giving *tzedakah*? One important answer is to make giving a habit for your child. There is no doubt that this is one of the reasons the custom arose to give *tzedakah* before lighting *Shabbat* candles. One of the advantages of this custom is that it establishes a pattern, a habit of giving. We know of families who take very seriously traditional Jewish moments of giving: before Purim, before Pesah. Thus, the Jews of the alternative *minyan* housed in the Germantown Jewish Center, the West Philadelphia *minyan*, the West Side *minyan* in New York, the New York *havurah*, the Washington *fabrengen*, and the Boston *havurah* have worked hard over the years before Passover to collect leavened, non-Pesah food and give it to emergency food distribution centers in their cities. We know of someone who for years personally delivered packages of matzah and other Passover supplies to poor Jews in Chicago. Accompanying this *baal tzedakah* on his rounds in Chicago slums was itself a learning experience recalled years later by a Jew who was an adolescent at the time. Another *baal tzedakah*, Danny Siegel, collects money here in America to donate directly to projects and people in Israel when he goes there each summer. (See *The Third Jewish Catalog* article on *tzedakah*; see also Chapter Ten, where Shoshana Silberman describes ways in which her family contributes money each evening of the counting of the *omer*.)

Creative possibilities that adapt some traditional mode or metaphor of holiday or *Shabbat* observance are limitless. We hope we have stimulated your thinking about specific opportunities within your community. Another variety of giving is suggested by what happens to the money that relatives give your child or give you for your child. Sometimes the relative really earmarks the funds: "I want you should take this money and go out and buy my *bubbelah* a doll." Or, "This money is to go into a certificate of deposit." But for nonearmarked funds, do you make ad hoc decisions or do you have a standard policy? What power does the child have over the money? A child who gives a portion of bar or bat mitzvah gift money to *tzedakah* must have been educated in one way or another toward doing so for the preceding twelve or thirteen years.

Our dream is that a child will grow and become a *shayneh yid*, a person who can put material needs and desires within perspective and who can properly order priorities. In other words, we want to raise a person who can distinguish what is important. Rabbinic sages fifteen hundred years ago observed that if you want to know what a person is really like, you should see him with his glass (when he drinks), with his purse (when he spends money), and with his anger. Our goal is that with their purses our children will be *menschen*, doing justice to their brothers and sisters who need their help and doing justice to themselves as human beings.

DANNY SIEGEL'S 1980 TZEDAKAH REPORT

According to Hasidic teaching, each of us has one mitzvah, one commandment, that we fulfill with such intensity that it comes to characterize us. The mitzvah of welcoming guests was so enthusiastically practiced by the Biblical figure Abraham that it came to characterize him. It is tantalizing to ask, "Nu, so what is my mitzvah?" Sometimes it is easier to identify a friend's particular mitzvah, and that is the case with our friend Danny Siegel, an American Jewish poet, whose mitzvah appears to be tzedakah. Danny is a baal tzedakah, a master of the art of giving, who helps others fulfill their obligations through his 'Tzedakah Report', an excerpt of which follows.

To my *tzedakah-hevrah* of friends and relatives and to other interested individuals, once again I say *Shalom* and *Yashir Koah!* The summer's work is now over, and this report will clearly show how our work in Israel has expanded—more people contribute, more read the *tzedakah* reports, and a greater number and wider range of recipients have been reached. This year, as your *shaliah*-messenger, you allowed me to distribute $12,720, a substantial sum, even with disheartening inflation. In the past, as you may recall, we have distributed $955, $1,667, $2,903, $6,396, and $9,102, bringing our total contributions over the past six years to $33,770.

As is customary with this report, I will begin with the details of this summer's distribution of money.

Four Major Projects: Places that
Absolutely Must Be Visited in Israel

A. Ma'on LaTinok: Hadassah Levi's home for infants with Down's syndrome continues to provide warmth and hope for almost forty children. A visit here can become, by far, the most powerful experience of any trip to Israel—she, fighting for the dignity of the retarded; they, living the lives of children free of cares, as is the right of all children. Hadassah bought a new floor in one of the rooms—the neighbors had been complaining of the noise the infants were making rocking their cribs! Hadassah needs supplies of infants' clothes, which I hope our *tzedakah-hevrah* will help supply. Eventually, she hopes to found a kibbutz for retarded people somewhere in

(Continued through page 261)

Israel (Hadassah Levi, Ma'on LaTinok, 4 Ma'alay HaTzofim St., Ramat Gan, 03-721-565).—$2,000.

B. Yad LaKashish (Life Line for the Old): Mrs. Myriam Mendilow's array of workshops for the elderly and disabled of Jerusalem functions at full strength despite the ever-growing economic hardships. The Meals-on-Wheels program and afternoon activities (such as the choir) also continue. They hope to open a bakery and café in the near future, a lovely addition to the work she has carried on for nearly twenty years. One point I have forgotten to mention: this is *not* an old-age home. No one lives at Life Line. Everyone comes from his or her own home to work at the bookbindery, needlecrafts, metal shop, and other workshops. They—these elders of Jerusalem—are part of society: I see them frequently in the streets, shopping, on their way to meetings, wherever people as people are supposed to be going (Yad LaKashish, 12 Shivtei Yisrael St., Jerusalem, 287-829. Tax-exempt contributions may be sent to American Friends of Life Line for the Old in Israel, 1 State St. Plaza, New York, NY 10004, Phyllis Hertzberg, Chairperson).—$652

C. Yad Sara: Uri Lupoliansky, the director, is an angel. His manner is unassuming and his devotion is intense. He supervises three hundred volunteers in twenty centers around Israel, lending medical supplies at no cost to people who (for bureaucratic or economic reasons) cannot get the wheelchairs or oxygen or vaporizers or walkers or crutches they need. Our *hevrah* contributed $350 toward part of an expensive emergency alarm system Yad Sara is setting up in people's homes, with a central receiver and printout at Yad Sara and Magen David Adom. We also gave $80 for a large sign in English, so passersby will take notice (Yad Sara, 49 Nevi'im Street [around the corner from Bikkur Cholim Hospital], 244-242; Uri's home: 813-777).—$430

D. Yad Ezra: Reb Osher Freund's extensive network of projects expands each year—Passover, more than $115,000 in food distributed to more than 5,000 families; 250 families receiving free food each week; hundreds more buying food at discounts; clothing at discounts; dental clinic; x-ray clinic and other medical services; day-care center; free-loan society; birthday parties for mental patients in the institutions; lending of dishes and kitchen facilities for *simkha* catering—the list is very long. Our contribution was given specifically for the sewing-machine workshop (Yad Ezra, 15 HaRav Sorotzkin St., Jerusalem, 526-133. Shmuel Katz will arrange visits and tours. His home phone is 817-767. You may also contact Yehoshua Lendner, Ron Hotel, Zion Square, Jerusalem, 223-471).—$400

Scholarship for a Couple to Continue Our Work in Israel During the Year

During the past year, Beth Huppin, a close friend of mine, spent the year in Israel introducing a variety of people to our *tzedakah* work. For the coming year, Gordy and Sharon Fuller will be there to take individuals and groups to these places and will serve as our *shelihim*-messengers for other *tzedakah-mitzvot* that arise. They are our matchmakers, bringing our people together. They will be based, of course, in Yerushalayim and welcome calls and letters. Please try to convince your synagogue, AJC, Hadassah, Women's League, or federation tours—any tours at all—to avail themselves of this service we are offering. We left $2,000, which was matched by another $2,000 from someone in Israel. We have possibilities of additional, limited funding for the scholarship and would welcome any supplementary contributions toward this part of our work. We anticipate a total budget of $6,500–$7,500 for the year.—$2,000

Individual and Specific Contributions— The Guts of the Matter

Following our pattern of seeking out situations of immediate need, we arranged through a number of friends to provide a variety of goods, services, and educational materials for people who have direct contact with families who need these things. For example, money toward purchase of a washing machine; materials for a household budgeting class; books and games for children; scholarship money for a kindergarten student for next year. ($14! Fourteen dollars is all that was needed for that one.) And teeth. One young lady was having serious dental work done when budget cuts brought about an immediate halt in the treatments. For $120, the work could be finished, without long-term delays and serious consequences.—$774

Soviet Jews in Israel

Avital Shcharansky, a woman of presence, gentle, soft-spoken, genteel. Beth arranged for both of us to meet her. In her apartment are posters of Anatoly Shcharansky, posters we have seen everywhere, except that there, in her home, it is her husband, not just a cause or a bunch of slogans. We gave her $500 to use as she would determine best for her personal contacts with Soviet Jews in Israel and in the Soviet Union.

Beth also introduced me to another Soviet Jewish activist in Israel, to whom we gave $250 to assist her in organizing activities and maintaining contacts with her family and other refuseniks still unable to leave.—$750

People on the Personal Lookout for Tzedakah-Mitzvot to Perform

We gave four contributions ($150, $150, $250, and $300) to individuals to use at their discretion as their contacts bring *tzedakah* situations to their attention during the year.

Three of these four wish to remain anonymous, but the fourth, Si Levine, is available when you come to Israel to take you around: 23 Horkania St., #8, Jerusalem, 666-864. He informed me that each of five or six first-class hotels in Jerusalem (the Plaza and Hilton among them) provide a once-a-week buffet, with entertainment, for groups of twenty elderly Jews. He says it is done with great dignity and style. Just one more variation on the *mitzvah!*—$850

For the Handicapped: Services and Materials

A. Micha-Jerusalem: My friend Toby Wolinsky continues to do fine work at this school for preschool deaf and hearing-impaired children. We gave $200 to Micha for books and materials and $350 to Toby for whatever she felt was necessary for her work (Micha, Director, Brenda Eichler, Akiva St., Jerusalem, 232-031. Toby, Lincoln St. 12b, 227-502).—$550

B. Akim: Curt Arnson's branch of Akim (which is the national organization for retarded people in Israel) is the center for multiply handicapped children. He does wonders and fights tooth and nail to achieve his goals with the children. Our contribution helped him continue his summer programming throughout

August (Akim, 4 Ben Shimon St., Jerusalem, 232-633).—$400

C. Magen-The Irene Gaster Hostel for Retarded Adults: nearly twenty adults are now living at the home, and a few more come in during the day for substantial, creative programs. Lewis Warsaw, an American who has made *aliyah*, is supervising the program. Our contribution was used for sports equipment and summer activities (Magen, Mrs. Eva Michaelis, Honorary Chairperson, Lloyd George St. 4a, Jerusalem, 665-945).—$200

D. Alumim School for Retarded Children: My friend Lorraine Lemberger informed me that there were fifty-five children involved in the summer program. Our contribution was used toward summer activities and other needs Lorraine may find. She gave me a good example of inflationary costs: the rental of a bus for a day trip has skyrocketed in the recent past (Lorraine Lemberger, 51 Shachal St., Jerusalem, 662-284).—$300

E. Ilan: Ilan is the national organization for the handicapped. Rachel Gur-on's workshop for people with cerebral palsy, located next door to Life Line for the Old, is functioning well. Our contribution was also used for summer activities, specifically toward a day trip to Kibbutz Tzor'ah—for everyone to see what a kibbutz is like (Ilan, 16 Shivtei Yisrael St., Jerusalem, 286-555).—$100

F. The Central Library for the Visually Handicapped: Uri Cohen, the director, supervises the preparation of Braille books and tapes for the entire country. Our contribution will be used to add to the library of books and tapes (Central Library for the Visually Handicapped, 4 HaHistadrut St., Netanya, 053-25321 or 32422).—$125

Interest-Free Loans

1. Our fund supplied $300 in free loans this year ($200 and $100) directly to two individuals.—$300

2. Gomel L'Ish Chessed: Dr. David Weiss, Jew *extraordinaire*, continues to work with this free-loan society (nineteen years without a default). He is chairman of the Department of Immunology at Hadassah Hospital, a Torah scholar, and one whose sense of Judaism and Judaism's profound insights into the nature and ways of human beings is a great joy to

discover. Our contribution went into his fund (Dr. David Weiss, 20a Radak St., Jerusalem, 669-363 or 428-726).—$300

3. Free-loan society in East Talpiot: Miriam Itchkovitch, an older Russian woman, works with immigrants and the elderly (and nearly everyone else in that part of town). She has set up contacts with over three hundred old people, seventy-eight of whom are all alone, with thirty-two Meals-on-Wheels delivered every day. She organizes volunteers, clinics, block committees, and homemakers (much like Project Ezra, Dorot, and Hatzilu in New York), to allow these elderly people a dignified life-style. Not a single one of them has had to move into an old-age home. She wanted to start a free-loan society. Beth had $300 available, and we added another $200 (Miriam Itchkovitch, 12 Alfasi St., Jerusalem, 630-350).—$200

4. Another $900 was available from free loans from last year's work, which was turned over to another person as a free loan.—$900

Additional People and Projects—New and Old

1. Isha L'Isha: This is a refuge for battered women in Jerusalem. Two such centers already exist, one in Haifa and the other in Herzliya. The women involved in establishing this center are (unfortunately) filling a great need in Israel—a place for battered women to go until reasonable solutions can be reached in the individual domestic situation (Isha L'Isha, Dvora Barka'i, 22 Koray HaDorot St., Jerusalem, 662-705, or Joan Hooper, 32 Shimoni St., Jerusalem).—$300

2. The Rabbanit Bracha Kapach: Every conceivable *mitzvah*—help with families, help for Pesah (1,300 families this year, amost $12,000 worth of food), outings for mothers, camping for children, family problem-solving, and a warehouse of clothes for distribution. To send clothes: packages of up to twenty-two pounds, labeled "Used Clothes." She also takes used wedding dresses and lends them to brides who cannot afford to buy their own. Send them the same way (The Rabbanit Kapach, 12 Lod St., Jerusalem, 249-296).—$439

3. The Daniel Kuttler Charity Fund: Daniel and Charlotte Kuttler continue their work lending out wed-

ding dresses, along with a number of other individually oriented *mitzvot*. If you send dresses to the Kuttlers, they must have long sleeves and a high neck. Bridesmaid's dresses are also of use to them. Beth's sister and cousin in Spokane organized a Wedding-Dress Tea, complete with dresses, dress-contributors, tea, cake, explanations of the program *(hakhnassat kallah)*, and packaging materials. One item they sent, a corsage of silk flowers, arrived just in time for one bride. The Kuttlers say she soared with joy when she saw the corsage (Daniel and Charlotte Kuttler, 7 Keren HaYesod St., Jerusalem, 233-991).—$100

4. Americans and Canadians in Israel (AACI) Jerusalem Scholarship Fund: Mr. and Mrs. Bargteil informed me that their program assisted 224 junior and senior high school students last year (textbooks, school supplies, field trips, etc.)—scholarships for relatives of people who have died in Israeli wars or terrorist attacks. They hope to reach 300 students this year. It has been our good fortune, through our *tzedakah* work, that we have encouraged others to contribute sums totaling $20,600 (beyond our own small contributions) to this fund. The supervisors of this project are careful to take individual interest in each student's progress (contributions from the United States may be sent to: P.E.F. Israel Endowment Funds, Inc., 511 Fifth Ave., New York, NY 10017. In Israel: Meyer and Hannah Bargteil, 4 Ben Tabbai St., Jerusalem, 664-278).—$100

5. Committee for Families of the Fallen Paratroopers: The central committee of 15 paratroopers oversees this group that reaches about 120 wives and 300 children of paratroopers who have died since the 1956 Sinai campaign. Everything from summer camping and field trips to bar mitzvah presents, legal assistance—even plumbers and contacts for car repairs are supplied, through personal contact (Arele Marmarosh, HaNassi HaRishon St. 13, Rehovot, 054-75912, or Motka Weissbord, Sh. Ben Tzion St. 34, Rehovot, 054-58341).—$250

6. Zahavi: Dr. Eliezer Jaffe explained to me that Zahavi, the Israeli grassroots organization for families with four or more children, continues to fight legal battles as well as provide immediate services to large families. Most amazing was a visit I made to a

development town for a book ceremony. Piles of books were distributed to carefully selected children for school use—dictionaries, atlases, Jewish books of all kinds—to keep. Half of our contribution went to the book project, half to the general Zahavi fund (Dr. Jaffe, 37 Azza Rd., Jerusalem, 661-908 or 637-450).—$200

7. Keren Pe'ulat Ya'akov Maimon: As with the three previously mentioned contributions, this group is also working to give Israeli children a decent chance to integrate into society. Maimon, who died three years ago, had reached thousands—teaching English and a battery of other subjects to immigrants, students, and anyone else who needed his personal touch—through a corps of volunteers he personally supervised. Now his followers have concentrated on Mevaseret Yerushalayim, an absorption center, and Ma'oz Tzion, a tough neighborhood, where the volunteers continue their work with enthusiasm and great energy (Dr. Kurt Meyerowitz, Keren Kayemet LeYisrael St. 21, Jerusalem, 639-970).—$250

8. Keren Nesi Yisrael—The President's Fund: President Navon is personally involved in many *tzedakah* projects, large ones, and also those of a personalized, individual nature. Both he and Mrs. Navon have established a reputation for *tzedakah* work, and I felt it important that we share in his work. It is critical for Jews to know that all Jews, whether presidents or truck drivers, should be actively involved in this *mitzvah* (Ruth Shaul, Mishkan HaNassi, Jerusalem, 668-231).—$100

9. Alyn: Through a friend, I found a woman working in the summer program for crippled children—a volunteer—who brought games and arts and crafts materials with her from the States. She was well aware of ways to stretch our dollars, buying materials at discount prices, knowing exactly what and how much to purchase, etc. We added to her supplies and allowed her greater leeway in her programming for the summer (Naomi Vogel, c/o Winter, 11 Bartenura St., Jerusalem, 669-663, or Brenda Hirsch, Alyn, Olsvenger and Shemaryahu Levin Sts., Jerusalem, 412-251).—$200

10. Matav-Homemakers: This is a service, similar to that in the States, where people come into the home to assist others with household work during periods

of illness and other stress situations. Budget cuts have taken away payments for Matavi workers to continue their work if their clients go into the hospital. We gave our contribution specifically to continue that hospital service for some specific clients Mrs. Rivka Jaffe knew of through her work (same address as Dr. Eliezer Jaffe, no. 6 above).—$150

11. Gemillut Chessed Fund: A general *tzedakah* fund supervised by Dr. Pesach Schindler, director of the United Synagogue in Israel, set up to take care of needs that would arise within his purview during the year. Dr. Schindler also informs me that they are setting up a small Holocaust lending library at the Conservative Center, particularly periodicals with articles on the subject (Dr. Pesach Schindler, 2 Agron St., Jerusalem, 226-386).—$200

Miscellaneous: Trees, a Little
Cloak-and-Dagger Work, and Flowers

1. To one USYer to encourage him and others in his USY group to avail themselves of *tzedakah* opportunities in Israel.—$10

2. To one person on this report for expenses to investigate matters concerning a large grant for the blind in Israel. We are not certain if this will succeed, but the investment in time and effort, and the few dollars, is well worth it if somehow we can free some thousands for the blind.—$25

3. Flowers: A sum of $10 to a USYer (he and others added more) to make the rounds in some hospital on a Friday afternoon, giving out flowers and wishing the patients a good Shabbos. The rest was used by a friend and myself near the end of my trip for a similar visit to Hadassah Hospital on Mt. Scopus.—$35

4. Trees: Six gum trees in the Jerusalem Peace Forest, adding to the already breathtaking view. One tree was planted for each year of our work—in honor of us. One certificate was given to Rabbi Ron Hoffberg of Cranford, New Jersey, for his assistance in making preparations for the work this summer and another to Bea Dickstein for her help with the bookkeeping and mailing. The others—well, I am keeping them here for myself.

   Now JNF can count 150,000,006 trees to its credit! It was a beautiful morning: most of the money had already been distributed, and gazing at Yerusha-layim in the distance, I thought, *Next year the* tzeda-kah-hevrah *should come and plant for themselves.*—$30

Some Summary Comments from Your Shaliah-*Messenger*

Over and over again, and yet again, I am dazzled by "our people": the old ones we know from past years and the new ones. They hammer at the hearts of all who meet them. The economy moans, the Exodus from Israel grows, distress and unease are common feelings in the streets, yet there are all those good people. They take money (even the smallest sums) and create monuments of hope and meaning, markers reminding us of the grandeur of the human being. Even in our failures.

Last year, and for two years before that, we paid a music teacher to give a chance to an emotionally disturbed child. Now she has been moved to another institution out of Jerusalem, and the lessons have ended. Still, the remaining money from the salary will be used for music lessons for a promising child.

The stories multiply: more people give, including a half-dozen Jewish schools, bigger and smaller contributions ($3.17 from a child's *pushka*, a check for $1,000 after a program I gave); more receive, too. But the principles are the same—people must make *tzedakah* a daily issue in their lives, and they must aggressively seek out the good people. The principles apply to the big money— UJA, federations, Hadassah, JNF—as well as to us. Indeed, articles about our work have been used by some of these organizations. We complement each other, though our scales of operation are vastly different. Our goals are the same: to educate Jews to take joy in turning money into *mitzvot*.

I, personally, have gone beyond my bounds of time and energy. While I will continue to function as a resource person and lecturer on *tzedakah*, I cannot maintain the pace and extent of the work demanded. You must make use of Beth and Gordy and Sharon and become yourselves resource centers for *tzedakah* work. I will, of course, continue to manage funds throughout the year; to cover mailing and phone expenses (now at 5 to 6 percent), to supplement Gordy and Sharon's scholarship, and for other occasions that arise.

What is my main disappointment? Let me express it clearly, with a touch of anger and bitterness. It is this: that the major institutions of the North American Jewish community—the Bureaus of Jewish Education, the national organizations such as the CCAR, Women's League, and Hadassah—have not seen fit to call upon any of us—Beth, myself, and others—for our particular expertise in these matters, nor have they done the simplest of things: picked up the phone and asked to have their tours go through our places and meet our people. There, it is said!

I must limit my correspondence, must hope that others who read this report will fill in the gaps, must hope (against my better judgment in these matters) that sufficient numbers of Jews will become missionary about our work and will pass the ideas on to others: to teachers, to businessmen and women, to children, to the many administrators and supervisors who hold so much power in their hands.

I did one teachers' seminar last year—in Providence, Rhode Island. I would hope this year to do many more and that Beth will do the same, and you, yourselves.

A technical note: after November 1, please use this address for letters to me: 1600 S. Eads St., 712N, Arlington, VA 22202.

Again, as always, a great, warm heartfelt *Yashir Koah* to all of you. Being your *shaliah* for six years has been the greatest blessing of my life!

CHAPTER THIRTY

TALKING WITH OUR CHILDREN ABOUT GOD

Hershel Matt

Now that many of us have become less uncomfortable in talking with our children about sex and have even brought ourselves to discuss issues surrounding death and dying, one subject remains taboo: God. And there are a host of reasons for our deep and widespread reluctance to broach the subject.

Some of us defend ourselves by saying, "In Judaism, belief in God has not been stressed; behavior is what's important." At the same time, others claim that if we teach our children the beliefs of their own tradition, they'll be confused and troubled by the different, perhaps contradictory beliefs they encounter from children of different religious backgrounds. Still others say that religious concepts are too profound and too abstract for immature minds. Children are not ready for such things; there'll be time enough for that later on; why bother them now? And finally, we sometimes question whether we have a right to indoctrinate our children at all; shouldn't they be allowed to grow up and then arrive at their own religious conclusions, make their own faith decisions—unbiased, unprejudiced, "unprogrammed"?

The truth is that often we try to avoid engaging in God talk with our children because of our feelings of inadequacy about our own Jewish backgrounds and knowledge. We refrain from bringing up the subject of God and hope our children will, too. When they do ask religious questions, we try to change the subject or stall. When they confront us directly and insistently, having become puzzled or troubled or intrigued or excited by some religious issue that has come to their attention, we find ourselves saying, "Let's go down to the library and take out some books on the subject," or, "Guess it's time to enroll our children in religious school," or, "Let's ask the Rabbi; he or she should be able to provide the answer." Now, these are all good things to do, but what a shame to have to depend on others and delegate to them what we could do ourselves. In any case, the influence of our own teaching and example, including that which comes through our neglect and silence, is likely to be at least as significant as the influence of others.

As for the other issues we raise, each deserves serious consideration.

Certainly, it is true that mere verbal profession of belief, not accompanied by deeds, is faithlessness; it is also true that a nonbelieving Jew is still a Jew. But sincere faith in God is and always has been of central importance in traditional Judaism; and while religious doctrines are often abstract, they need not necessarily be remote. Children can display a keen interest in religious subjects; they are full of questions about God and prayer and miracles and creation. They often demonstrate, in childish form, a deep awareness of the mysteries of religion and a striking grasp of its profundities. It may be that some concepts cannot be grasped as well at one age as another; experts on children's intellectual and moral development differ on what is appropriate at which stage. But even given the individual difference of all children, what they cannot understand of what they are taught now, they will come to understand later. Almost any religious issue, when formulated in simple terms, can be accessible to most children at some stage of their development. And it is important to make such issues accessible, if only because the children are less likely to be confused if they *do* know what their parents' tradition teaches. To the degree that they can verbalize their family's beliefs, they are helped to know what *they* believe, who they are, and where they stand.

But what about the issue of free choice? Here we come face to face with what is indeed a paradox. Religious faith, by definition, *is* a matter of free choice and personal decision by a mature person. But faith decisions are often shaped and influenced by training, environment, and atmosphere in which a person has been reared and by the models to whom she or he has been exposed. Since our children's religious faith will inevitably be influenced by circumstances, relationships, and "significant others" of their childhood years, we parents certainly have the right—even the obligation—to seek consciously to influence our children's faith along the lines of what we ourselves affirm to be true.

Silence on such important issues can only give our children the message we want to avoid. Even when we have our own doubts about God, we have to see that not teaching anything does the children an injustice. Those people who believe children should never be taught anything that they'll later have to unlearn or that they'll discover upon growing up is not true often feel that the disillusionment and resentment children will feel toward both their parents and their religious tradition will be psychologically, morally, and religiously harmful. Granted, we should not teach our children anything—and surely anything about God—that we deem to be false. It is important, however, crucially important, to remind ourselves and help our children understand—to the extent and at the pace they are able to—that there are various dimensions of truth; that language has multiple levels of meaning; that words are multivocal. Even in prose, to some extent, and all the more so in poetry, the expressions we employ are often metaphorical, symbolic, figurative. In religious discourse, this is particularly true. The tradition, for example, sometimes speaks of the Lord, Ancient of Days, sitting upon His heavenly throne, high and exalted, observing all who are on earth beneath, writing in His book the fate of each of us. Yet a Jew who recites these words and affirms them to be true need not be claiming that God has a body and a beard or is a man; or that His throne is of gold or ivory or some other material; or that the book is of a certain size or that its pages are of paper or of parchment; or that He and His throne and His book are a certain number of miles "up there" and could be located, reached, touched, or photographed if we traveled long enough in the right direction with the right equipment. The validity of one's religious affirmation does not depend on the literal truth of the words in which the affirmation is couched. It may well be that a child, having been taught those graphic and boldly anthropomorphic words, may, as a child, take them literally and, upon maturing, may come to no longer take them literally. She or he need not, however, consider them false and unlearn them. The words can still be accepted as true, but true in a different sense. (Many adults I know have grappled with and worked through their own religious questions by means of a renewed awareness of such nonliteral truth.)

I believe that doubt itself has a fruitful role to play in the life of faith and in our efforts to nurture faith in our children. Our doubt can help keep us from being glib, insensitive, and self-righteous in professing our faith. When openly shared with our children, doubt can help us rear them to be alert to such moral and spiritual perils. (We and they will never boast that "we're religious and 'those people' aren't.") Furthermore, doubt can serve as a humbling reminder that, being human, we can never attain a full understanding of God's thoughts and ways. ("*We* don't understand, but then we're not God.") Doubt can thus even deepen our sense of wonder at the mysterious paradox of God's transcendence and presence. ("Yes, darling, it's hard to understand how God can be 'out there' and yet so near to us; I, too, don't understand exactly what that means.")

Our concern to be honest with ourselves and with our children can, if we summon up the courage and temporarily suspend our own disbelief, be directed into a shared religious search into the various possible meanings of the traditional formulations of Jewish faith. ("Now what might this passage mean? What could that story be trying to tell us? Let's read it over again and think about it some more.") In order to maintain our self-respect, of course, we will want to keep ourselves from being *childish*, but in order to grow in spiritual insight, it may be helpful to be *childlike*, at least for a while. (For those who find themselves unable to make such a distinction and find that trying to be childlike is childish, we offer another possible approach in the last section of this chapter.)

What are some of the ways in which our tradition has been accustomed to speak of God? What are some of the word pictures by which it has sought to portray Him?

Judaism frequently speaks of God as the Creator, who called the universe into being. When our child asks us, in challenge or in wonderment, "But who created God?" or, "How old is He?" we can respond, in explanation but also in shared wonderment, "God is the only one who wasn't created, who had no beginning but was always there; there was a time when there was no world or anything, only God." And then we can proceed, on various occasions and in various connections, to spell

out on a child's level and in a child's language some of the many implications of creation; that it didn't "just happen," but that God planned the universe and arranged it to function in orderly patterns; that theoretically He could interrupt its workings, since the Creator is not bound by the "laws" of His Creation but that He prefers to maintain its regularities; that not only did He create it in the beginning, He renews each day the work of Creation, in accordance with His plan for the advancement of His purpose; that God's Creation is good; that *Shabbat* is the climax of Creation, constituting the goal and purpose of it all. And if at times our child asks a question about Creation for which we have no answer ("Why did God create earthquakes, floods, and hurricanes?"), we can acknowledge our shared ignorance and then add, "Even if we do not know the answer, God does; and maybe someday we, too, will know."

Not only did God create the universe in all its vastness and variety, but He also created human beings, multitudes of us, yet every single one He created in His image, including you and me. How rich is this concept of Creation-in-the-image—richness that can be shared at every stage of our child's growth. We can point to the capacity of every normal human being to think, reason, learn, remember, and imagine; to be aware of self and others; to communicate with others; to know right from wrong and choose between them; to be responsible for choices made; to regret, repent, and change; to be aware of God and pray to Him. There are also many implications of the doctrine of Creation-in-the-image for the worth of every human being. Each human being is unique and infinitely precious, to be loved, to be held in awe as a symbol of God. No one is to be abused, degraded, disdained, treated as a thing, used merely as a means to our own advancement. Once again, our children will raise problems: "image and likeness" may make God too anthropomorphic, even corporeal ("How tall or strong is He? What does He look like?"); substituting "spirit" may make him too ethereal or too pantheistic ("If He's everywhere, He's in everything, so He can be hit or burned or even flushed down the toilet!"); if all that God created is good, what about the imperfections ("Why are some children born blind or deaf or deformed or mentally retarded or dead; why are some people cruel and evil?"). But, once again, we can be honest enough to share our children's ignorance and bewilderment before Creation's seeming imperfections and try to let them know that our faith can encompass our doubt.

The Torah tradition also speaks of God as Lord and Master, as our King. What are some of the implications of these titles that we might include in our God talk with our children?

If God truly is our Lord, He is our only Lord, which means that He is our absolute and final authority in all things. He is also the Source of right and wrong; His will determines and His command constitutes what *is* right and wrong. There are other authorities in our life, to be sure—parents, teachers, governments—but their authority has limits. God's has none. His commandments govern all areas of our life and supersede any conflicting demands of all these lesser authorities. To Him alone we owe utter loyalty and absolute obedience. Which means, of course—and we must readily admit this to our children—that even governments and parents can be wrong and that when children feel sure that in a given case the parent or the government *is* wrong, it is God and not the government or parent that should be obeyed! (It is also true that the less mature the child, the more responsible the parent is for making the decision and controlling the behavior!)

If God is truly King, He is also ultimate Judge. Again, there are other judges in our life who call us to account and, within limits, have this right. But it is to the Judge of all earth alone that we are ultimately accountable. Furthermore, He is the only one who really knows, fully and accurately, all our intentions, all our deeds, and also the exact degree of our freedom and the exact measure, therefore, of our responsibility. Because He is not only all-knowing but incorruptible as well, subject to no bias and no bribe, His judgment is always just payment in accordance with our just deserts.

For there *is* payment; there *are* consequences of our deeds, and it is God who is the ultimate source of such "reward and punishment." For the most part, it appears, God works indirectly, allowing the consequences of our actions to come about through the operation of various "laws"—physical, psychological, social, moral, historical. (When we neglect or mistreat our bodies, when we let our minds atrophy, when we become habituated to pernicious patterns of behavior, when we mistreat other people, we usually reap the consequences.) With the eyes of faith, however, these "laws" are seen to be the vehicles of God's justice. Not that we can always discern the workings of God's justice; at times—let us admit it readily to and with our children—there seems to be great disparity between what people deserve and what they receive ("They get away with murder!"); the workings of God's justice are discernible only at times and only in part, yet often enough and in sufficient measure for us to be able to reassure our children and ourselves and reaffirm our trust that our King and Judge is indeed the King of justice.

There is, of course, a danger in talking this way with our children. We may dwell so much on God's role as King and Lawgiver and Judge that the picture may become too awesome, too threatening, too frightening, too guilt producing—to the point of being religiously overwhelming, morally incapacitating, psychologically damaging. Fortunately, however—thanks to God—He has other titles, qualities, faces, and these others may be the ones we'll decide to stress.

God is the Source of all our blessings. Some of them have already been alluded to: the "distant" blessings inherent in the wondrous workings of His vast Creation, the moral blessings of instruction and guidance inherent in His commandments and our capacity to know them and obey them. But there are a host of more immediate, personal blessings: of food and clothing; of health and healing; of growth of body, mind, and character; of warmth; of family and friends; of sex and love and marriage; of beauty that we find in nature and of beauty that we ourselves create. All these and countless other blessings are tokens of God's love.

For above all else, God loves us—like a father, mother, husband or wife, our dearest friend, and even more than they. He knows our weaknesses and limitations and makes allowances for them; not only that, He gives us strength. When we are depressed and "down," He raises us up and comforts us. When we are ignorant, He instructs us. When we feel lost or lonely, He befriends us. When we feel rejected. He accepts us— even if in our own eyes we are unacceptable. When we feel defeated, overburdened, unable to function or accomplish, convinced we can't do it or go it alone, He reminds us that we're not alone.

Not always, of course—perhaps not often—do we pause to take note of these many manifestations and offers of God's love. But that is because we so seldom engage in prayer, in the acknowledgment that we stand in His presence. Most Jewish parents do not attend synagogue services regularly; when we do attend, we seldom find the experience to be a worshipful one. Even when it is inspiring, we may not take the time or make the effort to engage in prayer outside the synagogue, in our home and with our family. We thus manage to shut off our children and ourselves from God's ever-available presence. Instead of developing, deepening, and refining our religious sensitivity, we allow it to languish and to atrophy. If we can make the effort to pray together with our children, using words of traditional Jewish prayer, occasionally supplementing them with words of prayer from other sources, and at times just engaging in informal God talk, we may well become strengthened in our conviction that God hears our prayer and cherishes it and that He responds as well.

We might find that our prayers of praise are not only an acknowledgment of His blessing but a means of deepening our awareness of the myriad instances and multiple dimensions of His blessing. We might find that our prayers of confession serve not only to make acknowledgment of sins committed but serve as well to cleanse us and remove the burden of our accumulated guilt and to disclose new resources of strength to keep from sinning more. We might find that our prayers of petition for whatever we consider our genuine need are indeed answered, but that God answers in a variety of ways: sometimes by giving us what we ask for; sometimes by correcting our sense of values and our evaluation of our needs so that we come to see that what we began by asking for is actually against our own best interests or is unnecessary for us and is against the well-being of our fellows; sometimes by helping us see that what we asked for depends not only on God but on us as well—and then by strengthening our will to perform that which it is within us to do; sometimes by enabling and ennobling us to accept what is not to be changed, thus making our will coincide with His. But always He responds. Always, therefore, we can be confident and hopeful when we turn to Him.

It is the Lord who is our ultimate hope. Upon Him we can always depend. In Him we put our absolute trust. There are others, of course, upon whom we depend and in whom we trust—for one thing or another, at one time or another, to one degree or another. But all of them—parent, child, spouse, leader, or friend—may someday fail:

through forgetfulness or neglect, bankruptcy of one sort of another, desertion, or death. God alone is completely dependable, utterly trust-worthy.

But once again our children may interrupt such pious talk and challenge us by saying: "If God is so dependable, then why do the righteous sometimes suffer and the wicked go free? How long does it take for God to right what's wrong? Meanwhile, the victims die!" What they are saying, even if they don't yet know the term, is that this world remains unredeemed.

Here we can begin to talk with our children about the coming of the

Messiah: when God *will* right all wrongs; will restore Israel's glory and the People Israel to its land; will vindicate all just struggles and all unjust sufferings and defeats; will disclose to us the full meaning of our lives; and will vanquish death forever. How and when this all will be brought about, we do not know and should not pretend to know. (Childlike formulations need not be insisted on; they also need not be rejected and certainly should not be ridiculed.) *That* it will occur, however, in God's own time and way, we can stoutly affirm, for to believe in the Creator, God and King, who is wise, powerful, and just, and to believe in the God who loves us is to be sure that the divine promise of redemption will be fulfilled.

One further aspect of redemption should be included in our God talk with our children, however abstract it may seem at first: redemption not only as something that will occur at the end of history but redemption also as a dimension of life here-and-now. This word picture may prove useful: picture an overarching, curved line, stretching above the horizontal line that represents the course of history from beginning to end; picture an infinite number of tiny windows in that arch, a different window facing each of us at each moment of our lives: whenever you or I look inward-upward, turning to God, the window of that particular moment opens up, enabling us to catch a glimpse of how that moment is seen from His perspective; the true meaning of that moment is revealed; eternity for a moment has entered time; we are redeemed. ("Now everything looks different!")

But how do we know all this to be true? Our children put this challenge to us at one age or another ("How do you *know* that there's really a God? Some of my friends say there isn't!"), and we, of course, ask this question of ourselves. This question actually represents several different questions.

One question is: can all or any of these God affirmations be proved? The answer to that question is, of course, "No." We can cite indications of orderliness and purposefulness in nature; we can point to the presence of a moral and spiritual dimension in every human being and of some form of religious belief and practice in every known society; we can argue that without acceptance of some ultimate power, life would be meaningless and unlivable. All these may constitute evidence for the validity of our religious affirmation, but there is contrary evidence as well: chaotic aspects of nature, barbaric aspects of human behavior; and, in any case, evidence is not the same as proof. We cannot prove, logically or empirically, that God knows or cares about us or promises to redeem us—or even that He exists. Basic religious affirmations, by definition, can never be proved. (Of course, they cannot be disproved, either.)

On what basis, then, do we know our belief to be true? On the basis of our Jewish tradition—let us say—the tradition received by us from believing parents and grandparents, whose faith-tradition goes back, in turn, more than three thousand years to our ancestors in the time of Moses. Those were the Jews who were led forth from Egyptian bondage, heard God speak to them as they stood at Sinai, received Torah and commandments there, and became the Covenant People Israel. We are their descendants and their heirs; we accept as true what they, on the basis of their own experience, perceived to be true and handed down to us.

This moving answer is a powerful claim on which to base the validity of our belief. But a perceptive mind—and our children's minds are, at times, at least as perceptive as our own—may well press on and ask: "How do we know that what our ancestors heard at Sinai was not an illusion? How do we know that what the Israelites thought to be the voice of God, speaking from within the cloud, was not an imaginary voice, or else the voice of Moses, who either pretended to be God or sincerely but mistakenly believed that he had heard God speak the words that he was now conveying to the people? The Israelites at Sinai were sure that it was God who had spoken to them, and Jews throughout the centuries have been sure, but how can *we* be sure?"

We can have no external proof. But our ancestors, even those who stood at Sinai, had none either. All depends on whether we can individually, existentially, affirm that it was God who brought them—and us along with them—forth from bondage; that it was God who spoke to them—and to us along with them—at Sinai; that it is He who continues to speak through the Torah book and tradition, telling us enough about Himself and about ourselves that we can live the holy life of the chosen, Covenant People Israel.

If we *can* acknowledge that in some sense God did choose our People Israel, redeeming us from bondage and giving us the Torah, does that mean that we must tell our children and ourselves that He cares about other peoples less, that we are more precious in His eyes than they? In our God talk with our children, how shall we deal with this concept of the "chosen people"?

There are a number of aspects of traditional teaching about Israel's chosenness that can relieve some of the moral concerns that trouble sensitive persons, children and adults alike. For one thing, that Israel was chosen to receive the Torah was not due to our own worthiness or righteousness. Scripture makes this clear (even though we cannot deny that there are *midrashic* passages that state or imply otherwise). Furthermore, the chosenness certainly does not entail lesser demands, lower standards, or greater leniency in judgment; on the contrary, it entails greater obligation. We are obligated to live on such a high moral and spiritual level that we will serve as God's witness people, "a kingdom of priests and a holy nation." (Not that we always do!) And the actual, historical experience of this "chosen people" has frequently, almost regularly, entailed a greater measure of enmity, persecution, and suffering than that of other peoples. (Indeed, sometimes what troubles us and our children about our chosenness is not a feeling of embarrassment but of bitterness and resentment. Who asked to be chosen? Who *wants* to be chosen? Why did *we* have to be chosen?)

Nevertheless, it would not be honest or worthy to deny that in the eyes of the tradition there *are* overtones of privilege, favor, and blessing inherent in belonging to the People Israel. For one thing, the Torah, for the sake of which we came into existence and remain alive, is far too precious for us to deny or minimize the distinction it confers on us. What is also true, however—as we should remind ourselves and our children and non-Jewish friends—is that in the eyes of our tradition, every single human being is equally precious in God's eyes because every single human being is equally created in God's image; that the "pious among the nations," who faithfully keep the commandments that are binding upon non-Jews (the so-called "seven commandments of the children of Noah"), have their share in the world to come and therefore have no reason to become Jewish; that those non-Jews who nevertheless desire to convert to Judaism and take upon themselves the additional obligations of a Jew are always welcome, since Israel's chosenness is not in any sense "racial" or closed; and that, in any case, Christians (and Moslems as well), by virtue of their worship of the same one God as Israel worships and their acceptance of Israel's sacred Scriptures, in a genuine sense share in God's Covenant with Israel.

Many of the issues discussed thus far are not entirely new; they may well have been faced by previous generations of Jewish parents in talking with their children about God. One problem, however, is new—or at least its urgency and intensity are new: the problem of sexist language when referring to God. ("Why is God 'He' and not also 'She'?") Most men, and at least some women, are not yet troubled by this problem. The question has either not yet occurred to them or has been casually dismissed as of no consequence. To a growing number of women, however, and to at least some men—and to a host of children of the "new generation"—this type of sexism is becoming a real problem. And they are not likely to be satisfied with the cold and glib grammatical answer: "Most languages have no convenient way of referring to living beings as other than male *or* female." True, they may admit, but beside the point: if God must be spoken of and spoken to as either male or female, why in Judaism should it always be as male? The religiohistorical explanation—the Judaism sought to guard against pagan notions of fertility goddesses and actual fertility rites and sexual orgies—is equally unacceptable. Indeed, such an "explanation" itself reflects a male sexist bias. Why should one assume that masculine locutions and male imagery are inherently less sexual than their counterparts? Similarly, the explanation that such divine qualities as strength, authority, knowledge, and justice are most "naturally" associated with masculinity is exactly what is meant by sexism!

But what can even the most sensitive parents *do* in the face of the tradition's consistently masculine language in referring to God? Not much, perhaps, but something. In God talk with our children, we can point to the crucial passage in Genesis that "God created humans ("adam") in His image . . . male and female He created them," which, though employing the usual masculine verbs and prepositions, clearly affirms nevertheless the equal likeness to God of man and woman and thus clearly implies the sexlessness (or bisexuality?) and genderlessness of God. We can also point to the few biblical references to divine roles or qualities specifically identified as feminine ("As a man is comforted by

his mother, so shall I comfort you") and to the widely accepted deriva-
tion of the Hebrew word for compassion *(rahamim)* from the word for
womb *(rehem)*, keeping in mind that God is often called the Compassionate One. We can point further to the feminine word for God's near
presence *(shekhinah)*, so common in Talmudic writings and so prominent
in *kabbalah*. (The *kabbalah* even makes so bold as to speak of male and
female aspects of God's "inner life.") Furthermore, we can try the experiment, in our informal prayer conversations with our children and
even in our formal prayer, of referring to God as "She," and then sometimes parenthetically add: "Of course, God is not really male *or* female."

Which brings us to a problem that for some parents is the key problem
in their whole religious outlook and the greatest single obstacle in talking with their children about God, a problem far greater than the problem of God's sexuality—the problem of God's personality. Throughout
the centuries-old tradition, with near unanimity and consistency (except
at times by philosophers), God has been spoken of in personal terms—
as, indeed, we ourselves have been speaking of Him throughout this
chapter. Yet how can God be a person? Presumably, He doesn't have a
body; but what is a bodiless person? Where does a bodiless person live?
How does a bodiless person function? How can a modern person *not* be
troubled by the notion of a personal God? (Actually, premoderns, too,
were evidently troubled: medieval thinkers, Talmudic sages, and even
some of the biblical writers reflect, in various ways, their problems with
this notion of a personal God.)

Perhaps we can never believe that God "is a person"; perhaps it was
never intended that we should. But surely if God "is not a person" like
us human persons, He must be not less personal but more personal than
we. Can we imagine God to be less knowing, less concerned about right
and wrong, less sensitive and caring, less filled with righteous indigna-
tion, less disappointed and hurt, less planful and hopeful than we, who
are created in His image, know ourselves to be? Granted, He is not
subject to the weaknesses and defects of our human personality, but is
He inferior to us in our virtues and our strengths? If we find ourselves
unable to say that God "is a person," can we not at least say that he is
the living God who personally affects us, personally relates to us, and is
personally available to us?

But what of those of us who find ourselves unable to go that far? What
if, after appropriate reading, talking with some approachable believers,
reexamining and reflecting on our religious situation, even attempting
to pray, we still feel dishonest in talking about a living God at all? Is
there anything further that we can do?

For one thing, we can make sure not to try, by pressure, argument, or
ridicule, to disabuse our children of their "childish notions." After all,
they may be open to dimensions of truth and worlds of meaning that
are, at least for the present, closed to us. Second, in talking with our
children on religious matters, we can substitute other words and images
for the traditional ones, "translating" the language of tradition into what
we find to be more acceptable language—but still seeking to retain the
dimension of the ultimate, the transcendent, and the mysterious. We

can express joy and gratitude for our blessings but also—without mentioning a personal, living God—our wonderment that these blessings have "somehow" been given to us, beyond our own doing or our own desert. We can express contrition at what we have done wrong or failed to do right toward both our fellow human beings and whatever "powers that be," and express our resolve to change and then—without so much as mentioning a personal living God—express wonderment at the cleansing and unburdening that comes from our confession and at the resources that are somehow made available for changing our ways.

We can acknowledge our need for help and our dependency on powers that are somehow there. We can express our joy and gratitude for being members of the age-old, worldwide Jewish people, heirs to the Torah tradition. We can express our wonderment that somehow, against all odds, we have survived. We can express our confidences—even when confronted, as Jews or as human beings, by trouble, suffering, defeat, sickness, or death—that life is somehow still worth living, and—without alluding to a living, personal God—we can affirm, in the face of life's impenetrable mysteries, that beyond the mystery there is meaning and that someday the meaning will be revealed.

The Berditschever *rebbe* overheard a young man mumbling his prayers. He called him into his presence on the plea of asking a question. When the youth stood before him, the rabbi began to mumble his words, and the young man could not understand him. He said this to the rabbi, who remarked: "Is it not exactly in this manner that you have prayed to God?"

"Yes," answered the youth. "I was in a hurry and therefore did not recite distinctly. Yet it is my hope that God understood me as a father always understands the mumblings of his little child."

This explanation pleased the rabbi and he made use of it on numerous occasions.

CHAPTER THIRTY-ONE

TALKING WITH OUR CHILDREN ABOUT DEATH

Earl Grollman

Parents and teachers are convinced by mental hygienists that they should be honest in discussing the biological process of birth. But when it comes to life's end, they fall strangely silent.

Of course, it's not really strange. In other eras, death was an integral part of life. The extended Jewish family lived in close proximity to one another. Old people (and younger people, too) died at home surrounded by friends and family. Inhabitants of rural areas were closer to nature where they were regularly confronted with death in plants and animals. Jewish beliefs that could once offer total—or near total—solace have been noticeably shaken. The word *dead* has become the new four-letter word.

Children's feelings and perceptions are overlooked in our death-denying, death-defying culture. A recent study has demonstrated that 44 percent of children were not even told of the death of a significant close relative. The parents were struggling with their own grief and could not believe that children would understand the tragic situation.

Not only parents but rabbis, too, may heighten the feeling of the child's isolation. They comfort the adult mourners but pay scant attention to the "little ones." Too many rabbis hide behind a variety of masks in order to avoid genuine person-to-person encounters.

The easiest and most obvious is the mask of theological language. To the young child, the clergy spew out such words as *immortality* and *resurrection* (*techiyat hametim*) when such abstruse concepts are difficult for many adults and religious leaders.

Then there is the mask of ritualized action where rabbis rightfully participate in external, age-hallowed traditions but wrongfully neglect interpersonal relations. The child may participate in the *shiva minyan* but is not encouraged to say anything, least of all talk about his or her anxieties. The most significant of inner spiritual questions are neglected in the midst of our ceremonies. If only rabbis, parents, and teachers could simply say, "Tell me how you really feel. I care."

After a death in the family a child returns to religious school. By silence, the teacher indicates that nothing significant has occurred, as if the youngster's life is unchanged. A hand around the shoulders of a child or a warm handshake and an expression of sympathy might dispel the charade of denial.

But can children really understand death?

A child growing up today is all too aware of the reality of death—perhaps more than adults realize. Even at a very young age, the child is confronted with that process when life no longer exists.

A pet is killed. A funeral procession passes by. A grandfather dies. A leader is assassinated. Television brings us pictures of death in living color. Bible stories are replete with descriptions of the deaths of matriarchs and patriarchs.

The child encounters death in many forms. Silence only deprives him or her of the opportunity to share grief.

But if the parent and teacher are confused, then how can they help the child?

Adults do not understand the complete meaning of death. Theologians continue to wrestle with this thorny question. No mortal has ever pierced the veil of its great mystery. Yet we have the inescapable responsibility to share with the child the fragments of our experience and knowledge.

While insight is a gift, we must first place ourselves in a position to receive it. We must prepare ourselves for it by being quiet and learning to listen to our children. We must sit down and watch them while they work and play, observe them in action, and hear the tone and timbre of their voices. Children should be encouraged to tell us how they feel about death, what they think, what they know, where they need to go. We should try to answer the questions in the spirit in which they are asked.

Do not teach children as if we have the final answers that they must accept. We show our maturity when we respond, "Are you surprised that I do not know everything about death? Don't be. We can still talk about it. You can learn something from me. I can learn something from you. We can help each other."

Can children understand the meaning of death?

The terms *dead* and *die* are common in young people's vocabulary, but these words conjure up different meanings.

Psychologist Maria Nagy, studying Hungarian children in the late 1940s, discovered three phases in the child's awareness of mortality. She learned that the child from age three to five may deny death as a regular and final process. To the child, death is like sleep; you are dead, then you are alive again. Or it is like taking a journey; you are gone, then you come back again. The child may experience many times each day some real aspects of what he or she considers "death"—for example, when a parent goes to work.

Between five and nine, children appear to be able to accept the idea that a person has died, but may not understand death as something that will happen to everyone and to themselves. Around the ages of nine and ten, the child recognizes death as an inevitable experience that will even occur to him or her.

Of course, these are all rough approximations with many variations, but they may prove valuable when children ask questions. Nagy's investigation also demonstrates three recurring questions in the child's mind: "What is death?" "What makes people die?" "What happens to people when they die: where do they go?"

Dr. Robert Kastenbaum of the University of Massachusetts states that adolescents and even adults have childlike views of death. They "know" that death is inevitable and final, but most of their daily attitudes and actions are more consistent with the conviction that personal death is an unfounded rumor.

Should we share religious convictions with the child?

Of course! Judaism is more than a creed; it is a way of life. And death is a reality of life. How a Jew handles death indicates much about the way he views his religious life.

In suggesting religious interpretations, a most important consideration is honesty. Many parents affirm an unyielding conviction about dying and death to their children, while they themselves have gnawing doubts and fears. *When someone else's* loved one dies, they say that she will live eternally. When death strikes their own loved one, they may mourn a person irretrievably dead. They spin out a theology of heavenly happiness for *others*. When it strikes them, a hopeless finality fills their heart. The time has come when all must admit that in contemplating the complete mystery of death, we *finite* people have only conjectures, not omniscience. God alone is infinite.

Is there a general agreement among Jews over the ritual and theology of Judaism?

As there are diverse ways in which Jews throughout the ages have viewed life, so there are different approaches by which Jews practice the rites of death.

There are those who believe in a fixed authority from supernatural revelation. Others recognize the principle of development in Jewish life and would affirm the right of the person to follow the dictates of individual conscience and preference. Your rabbi can give specific information concerning ritual and theology for both adults and children.

Are there not special and unique customs that delineate Jewish ceremonies of death?

Over the centuries, the rabbis have evolved patterns of practices for

the rites of death. Shock and grief are structured by solemn procedures. Teaching about death and dying has recently become popular at all levels of Jewish education.

The wise parent and teacher will not wait until the death of a loved one to discuss the Jewish ceremonies and philosophies of death. In recognizing the value of historical continuity and tradition, information and discussions could evolve as to how one is labeled a mourner (Hebrew: *avel*); the tearing of the mourner's clothes *(keriah)*; the first seven days of intensive mourning *(shiva)*; the meal of consolation *(seudat havra'ah)*; the thirty days of mourning *(shloshim)*; and the anniversary of death (the *yahrzeit*).

Explain the prayers of the funeral, that is, *El molai rahamim* ("God full of compassion") and the *kaddish*; as well as the purpose of the eulogy *(hesped)*. Children are more relaxed and less disturbed if they understand what they will someday encounter. All the emotional reactions that children are likely to express—sorrow and loneliness, anger and rejection, denial and guilt—are considerably lessened when they know what is occurring and that adults are not trying to hide the unspeakable from them.

Death is sad, but sadness is an integral part of the life cycle. The funeral is an important occasion in the life of the family. Children should have the same privilege as other members of their household to express their love and devotion. To deprive them of a sense of belonging could well shake their future mental health.

As to concepts of an afterlife, it is important for both adults and children to understand that Judaism has no dogmatic creed. During the course of the centuries, *many* ideas have been presented. The scholar George F. Moore enumerated the diverse speculations of death in Jewish literature and stated, "Any attempt to systematize the Jewish notions of the hereafter imposes upon them an order and consistency which does not exist in them." However, in spite of the various beliefs throughout its circuitous history, there are central and unifying patterns: the inevitability of death, the deathlessness of the human spirit, as well as a belief by many in a continued existence after death, in recompense, immortality, resurrection and the soul's transmigration *(gilgul neshamah)*. Always remember that concepts must be translated into the language and comprehension of the child. It is neither necessary nor possible for a child to accept the totality of the adults' religious philosophy.

Suffering and death should not be explained as the result of sin and divine punishment. Children experience enough guilt without the added measure of God's supposed chastisement. (See Chapter Thirty.)

Are "fairy tales" a helpful explanation of the enigma of death?

The question arises constantly of what we should tell a child when death occurs. Should we avoid acknowledgment that the person has died? Should we suggest that a grandfather became ill and had to go away to a hospital where he could recuperate and become cured, hoping that the memory will gradually fade away and the child will come to accept the absence as normal?

Such evasions indicate your own uncertainty about the child's capacity to deal with existing situations. These avoidances encourage the child to "forget about things" and do not prepare him or her to deal with life's realities. We should never cover up with a fiction what we will someday repudiate. There is no greater need than that for trust and truth.

How about "Mother has gone on a long journey" instead of the harsh words "Mother has died"?

The statement "Your mother has gone away for a long journey for a very long time" is meant to provide solace and ease the strain of the mother's disappearance. But the child might interpret this explanation to mean that his mother has abandoned and deserted him without saying "good-bye." Far from being comforted and cherishing the memory of the deceased, the child may react with anger and resentment.

The child could also develop the delusion that someday the mother will return, or the child may unconsciously assume, "Mommy didn't really care about me, so she stayed away." And if the mother only went away on a long journey, why is everyone crying?

Or "God took Daddy when he was so young, because your father was so good that He wanted your father for Himself."

Do you really believe that there is a relationship between longevity and goodness? Reread the Book of Job. The righteous may surely die young, but they can also live unto a ripe old age.

One little girl replied, "Don't Mommy and I need Daddy more than God does?" The child developed a deep resentment against a God who capriciously robbed her of her father, and became upset with the thought "But God loves me, too; maybe I'll be the next one He will take away."

Is death like sleeping?

It is only natural to draw the parallel. Our Scriptures speak about "*sleeping* with the fathers." In the *Iliad*, Homer alludes to sleep (*hypnos*) and death (*thanatos*) as twin brothers, and there are some prayers that entwine the ideas of sleep and death. Be careful, however, to explain the difference between *sleep* and *death*: otherwise, you run the risk of causing a pathological dread of bedtime. There are children who toss about in fear of going to "sleep forever," never to wake up again. Some children actually struggle with all their might to remain awake, fearful that they might go off into the deceased's type of "sleep."

Understandably, it is easier to respond with fiction and half truths that will make the adult appear to know all the answers. But the secure person has no need to profess infinite knowledge. It is far healthier for children to share the joint quest for additional wisdom than to have their immediate curiosity appeased with fantasy in the guise of fact.

How should the facts of death be explained to the child?

The answers can be expressed in two words: *naturally* and *lovingly*.

You might initiate the conversation by talking about the flowers growing in the spring and summer only to be followed by their fading away in the fall and winter seasons. This is the sequence of life. For all living things there is a time to grow, to flourish, and then to die.

Explanations should be presented without lurid, gruesome, or terrifying description. Proceed slowly and simply, step by step, with patience and gentleness. Fears will be lessened when the discussion is initially focused not upon the morbidity of death but upon the beauty of life.

Should the child be discouraged from crying?

Only the insensitive parent could say of a child who had encountered tragedy and remained dispassionate, "The child is taking it so well. He never cries."

Children should be allowed to express their grief. It is natural. They loved him. They miss him. To say, "Be brave!" sounds as if you are minimizing the loss.

Don't be afraid to cause tears. They are like a safety valve. So often parents deliberately try to steer the child's conversation away from the deceased, apprehensive of the tears that might start to flow. They do not understand that expressing grief through crying is normal and helpful.

Tears are the tender tribute of yearning affection for those who have died but can never be forgotten. The worst thing possible is for the child to repress them. The child who stoically keeps his grief bottled up inside may later find a release in an outlet that affects his inner self more seriously. Remember, "Abraham came to mourn for Sarah and to *weep* for her" (Gen. 23:2).

OTHER RESPONSES TO DEATH

For the child, death may bring a variety of reactions:

Denial

"I don't believe it. It is just a dream. Daddy will come back. He will! He will!"

The child may seem unaffected, because he is trying to defend himself against the death by pretending that it has not really happened. We may even feel that the child's apparent unconcern is heartless. Or we may be relieved and feel, "Isn't it lucky! I am sure he misses his father, but he does not seem to be really bothered by it." Usually, the lack of response signifies that the child has found the loss too great to accept and goes on pretending secretly that the person is still alive.

Bodily Distress

"I have a tightness in my throat!" "I can't breathe." "I have no appetite at all." "I have no strength." "I am exhausted." "I can't do my homework." "I can't sleep." "I had a nightmare." Here anxiety is expressed in physical and emotional symptoms.

Hostile Reactions to the Deceased

"How could Daddy do this to me?" "Didn't he care enough for me to stay alive?" "Why did he leave me?" The child feels abandoned, deserted, and angry.

Hostile Reactions to Others

"It's the doctor's fault. He gave him the wrong medicine." Or, "Mother didn't take proper care of him. That's why he died." Or the rabbi, the surrogate of God, becomes the killer of the loved one. "The rabbi (God) has taken him away."

The resentment is projected outward in order to relieve guilt by making someone else responsible for the death.

Replacement

"Uncle David, do you love me, really love me?" The child makes a fast play for the affection of others—teacher or friend—as a substitute for the parent who has died.

Assumption of Mannerisms of Deceased

"Do I look like my father?" The child attempts to take on the characteristic traits of the father by walking and talking like him. The boy may even try to become the head of the family and the mate of the mother.

Idealization

"How dare you say anything against Daddy! He was perfect." In the attempt to fight off his own unhappy thoughts, the child becomes obsessed with the father's good qualities. The falsification is out of keeping with the father's real life and character.

Anxiety

"I feel like Daddy when he died. I have a pain in my chest." The child becomes preoccupied with the physical symptoms that terminated the life of the father. He transfers the symptoms to himself in a process of identification.

Panic

"Who will take care of me now?" "Suppose something happens to Mommy?" "Daddy used to bring home money for food and toys. Who will get these things for us?"

This state of confusion and shock needs the parent's supportive love: "My health is fine. I will take care of you. There is enough money for food and toys."

Guilt

Children are very likely to feel guilt, since in their experience bad things happen to them because they are naughty. The desertion of the parent "must" be a retribution for their wrongdoing. Therefore, they search their minds for the "bad deed" that caused it.

Many young children harbor fantasies that they are responsible for the death in the family. They may believe in a primitive magic—that is, if one wishes someone harm, the wish will bring results. The boy says to his sister: "I wish you were dead." Then when the sibling dies a year later, the lad is terror-stricken by his own power. Or the child may fear that he made his mother work too hard. He can still recall her saying, "You're such a messy kid. Picking up after you will be the death of me yet!" This is why it is so necessary to help the child express his or her own fantasies and fears.

These are some of the reactions of adults as well as children. Some may never appear. Some come at the time of crisis. Others may be delayed, since so often the child represses emotions and tries to appear calm in the face of tragedy. That is why it is essential that we give vital support for the terrible pain of separation.

SOME GUIDELINES

1. *Do not* avoid the subject of death. Clifton Fadiman writes in an afterword to Louisa M. Alcott's *Little Men:* "The most moving episode has to do with John Brooke's death and funeral. As I read it, I found myself wondering why most books for children these days are afraid to mention death."

2. *Do not* discourage the emotions of grief. Anger, tears, guilt, despair, and protest are natural reactions to family disorganization. Never be so closed to human feelings that you do not accept the emotional reactions of those young people who hurt.

3. *Do not* close the door to doubt, questioning, and differences of opinion. Respect the other's unique personality, for in the long run it is he or she who must arrive at an individual understanding of the questions of life and death.

4. *Do not* tell a child what he or she will later need to unlearn. Avoid "fairy tales," half truths, circumlocutions. Honesty is the *only* policy.

5. *Do not* legislate your own theological convictions. Avoid abstractions. Thoughts must be translated into language that is comprehensible to the child.

6. *Do* spend time listening to the needs of the child. The dedicated adult is an astute listener to the spoken word and a perceptive follower of nonverbal communication.

7. *Do* refer to other supportive people. There are times when even the best-informed and well-intentioned parent is simply inadequate. Seeking further help from a guidance counselor or psychologist/psychiatrist is not an admission of weakness but a demonstration of your own security and ego strength.

8. *Do* remember that the process of adjustment to death is longer than the funeral. The depth of depression may occur many months after death. Grief may be expressed in the child by poor grades, lack of attention, daydreaming, and hostility.

9. *Do* be human. It is not wrong to express your *own* emotions of grief, to shed a tear, to touch a person in pain. Just remember the words of Thornton Wilder: "There is a land of the living and a land of the dead and the bridge is *love*—the only survival, the only meaning."

10. *Do* consider death-education courses in the religious-school curriculum. Children are already confronted with the fact of death in word and song as well as in the natural world of plants, animals, and friends. Death education begins when life begins. And always understand that the real challenge is not just how to explain death to children but how to make peace with it yourself.

CHAPTER THIRTY-TWO

TALKING WITH OUR CHILDREN ABOUT THE HOLOCAUST

Bella Savran and Eva Fogelman

"Mommy, somebody in school said that they should have killed all the Jews. Why did they say that?" Someday your child may come home with this question. Perhaps he or she already has, and you found yourself without a ready response. As Jewish parents, we would like to be able to answer such questions in a reassuring and responsible way, but often we don't know where to begin.

In confronting the enormous task of talking with our children about the Holocaust, the first thing we must realize is that there is no single "answer." The essential messages we must convey to our children are:

They have a right to ask questions.
We share their concern and confusion about the Holocaust.
The issues are important enough to warrant ongoing discussion.

Once we have made a commitment to discuss the Holocaust with our children, we must each find our own way to do it. Above and beyond our individual differences, as Jews, we all share the goals of guiding our children toward a positive Jewish identity and a positive self-image. This chapter is written with the hope that it will help people feel less anxious about the process of teaching than they feel about the Holocaust itself.

CAN'T WE LET THE SCHOOLS DO IT?

Most of us would agree that education about values and personal identity is too important to be left entirely to teachers and institutions. Learning is done in many different settings, each serving a particular purpose. The sudden discovery of anti-Semitism, even as part of past history, can raise such fears in a child as "Can it happen to me here?" Parents are in the best position to help their children express these feelings and to provide the necessary reassurance to continue to trust in the world and in other people. Even when we can't supply much factual information, we can always say, "I know it's really scary. I also think about it some-times and hope it will never happen again." If we are moved to tears as we mourn the collective losses of our people, we can share that with our children, too.

Since many public schools in America have not yet begun to teach about the Holocaust, input from us as parents is crucial. We should suggest that information about the Holocaust be included in history courses, and we might even serve as consultants for curriculum de-velopment. When units on the Holocaust are taught, children may react at home to what they have learned in school or request our participation in homework assignments. We should try to respond to these requests fully and openly.

BUT I'VE NEVER EVEN THOUGHT ABOUT IT!

According to a recent survey, neither have most other parents. Before we can teach our children the facts about the Holocaust, we have to explore our own feelings about it. It takes a conscious effort to focus on the Holocaust and the events that led up to it. People tend to repress events and feelings that are too painful to remember. It is no wonder we avoid the memories of Jews being gassed, burned, and buried alive. Even children of Holocaust survivors who have heard their parents describe their wartime experiences over and over again have difficulty remembering precisely what happened because it is so at odds with their present-day reality. The real horrors of the Holocaust were far worse than most nightmares.

Another survey, taken in a class on the Holocaust at a major univer-sity, revealed that prior to the course few students could name even one concentration camp. They were unfamiliar with even the most public symbols of the Holocaust: Yom ha-Sho'ah (Holocaust Memorial Day) and Yad VaShem (a memorial museum and institute on the Holocaust in Jerusalem). Even more surprising was that after the course was over, most students were unable to retain hard facts about dates and places. We should attribute this inability not to the students' lack of intelligence but to their need to repress the reality of the war against the Jews.

Once we do allow ourselves to "remember," the feelings are often very unpleasant. We are filled with shock and terror, disgust and helplessness. Our sleep may be disturbed by nightmares. We are flooded with rage at the Nazis and a deep sense of betrayal and mistrust in our own American democracy and the American Jewish community for not having done more to save the Jews. Moreover, we feel guilt about not having done something ourselves to stop the annihilation and about not doing more to fight oppression today. Sometimes we experience so much shame and fear about simply being Jewish that we cannot react to these events with any true emotion, only with numbness and indifference.

In light of these reactions, it is understandable that we don't want to face the Holocaust alone. For this reason, we suggest organizing classes, study groups, or less formal discussion sessions with friends or professionals. In this way people can realize that others have similar feelings, that they are not alone. Families themselves can serve as support groups and can learn together. What is needed is some degree of knowledge about what happened and, even more important, reflection on implications for today.

There are a number of excellent study guides that can be obtained through local Jewish schools, libraries, and organizations. We particularly recommend the guide by Bea Stadtler in *The Second Jewish Catalog* (by Strassfeld and Strassfeld, Jewish Publication Society, 1976). In addition there are two other books of history that would serve as excellent starting points for families who want to study together or on their own. These are *Hitler's War Against the Jews* by David Altshuler (New York: Behrman House, 1978), a young reader's version of Lucy Davidowicz's famous work *The War Against the Jews* (Philadelphia: Jewish Publication Society, 1975), and Milton Meltzer's *Never to Forget*, available for $1.25 from the Anti-Defamation League (823 UN Plaza, New York, NY 10017).

The Holocaust raises unanswered, often unanswerable questions for Jews, regardless of their belief and practice. It is too much to expect complete clarity and consistency about such questions. As with all difficult subjects, the process of teaching implies the need for ongoing learning and struggling with issues.

I JUST WANT MY KIDS TO BE NORMAL, HAPPY AMERICANS

Like all good parents, we want the best for our children. In our interviews with other parents, many expressed the fear that telling their children about Jewish persecution would be damaging to their personal and Jewish group identity. They wanted to know why they should inflict nightmares on their children and possibly instill in them mistrust of friends. Wouldn't it be better to teach only the positive aspects of Judaism like Hanukah and Passover and faith in mankind and the goodness of God?

While this is an understandable attitude, we as parents have a responsibility to be honest with our children. Experts agree that parents only hurt their children by denying them preparation for the painful realities of life. Although we are proud and happy about being Jewish and certainly want to convey that to our children, we must also teach them the unfortunate realities of Jewish history. The Holocaust did not happen in some far-off century or some ancient civilization. It happened only forty years ago! We must not allow that event to become just another date in history.

On the other hand, there is no point in alarming our children or encouraging obsessions with evil and horror. We should take into account the child's capacity to absorb different material at different levels of maturity. In the pages that follow, we will offer suggestions on what we consider some appropriate ways to present the Holocaust.

QUESTIONS CHILDREN ASK

The Holocaust poses some of the most difficult questions of our time. Although the specific ways of responding should be tailored to each situation, we would like to outline some general ways we have found helpful in dealing with these questions. You may find yourself agreeing with some of our responses but strongly disagreeing with others. We cannot emphasize enough that because these issues are so difficult, the ways they are handled will be diverse, complex, and often contradictory. Beyond objective learning, we have each to find our own answers and our own beliefs.

WHY DID IT HAPPEN?

Even fairly young children can be taught that there is discrimination in the world, that some people think they are better than those different from themselves. We should explain that because the Jews have had beliefs and customs different from those of many of their neighbors, they have been discriminated against throughout history. There are good overviews of anti-Semitism in the *Encyclopaedia Judaica* (vol. 3, pp. 87–159) and Jean-Paul Sartre's *Anti-Semite and Jew*. We should try to place the Holocaust in a historical perspective; Jewish history did not begin with the Holocaust and certainly did not end with it.

We should then explain that for four hundred years Europeans had been hating Jews for being different and conveniently blamed Jews for their problems. After losing World War I, Germany was in a state of hardship. There were many dead and wounded, and there were food shortages. Rather than face their own mistakes, Hitler and his followers found it easier to encourage the German people to feel better about themselves and instead blame the Jews for Germany's military defeat and economic problems. He devised a plan to kill all the Jews in the world. Although there had been similar plans made before in our history, such as at the time of the Purim story, this time, which was not so long ago and not so far away, many Jews were killed before Hitler could be stopped. There were some good Germans who defied Hitler and his army and saved Jews, but most Germans supported him either by actively carrying out his plans or by allowing others to do so because they did not want to risk their own lives.

WHY DIDN'T THE JEWS FIGHT BACK?

First of all, we have to consider who these people were. One and a half million of the six million Jews slaughtered were infants or children. Many others were old and infirm, as the Nazis tended to designate the weakest people to be killed first. Yet even among the stronger Jews there was little sense of military organization. Jews had been living for hundreds of years with no land of their own under laws that discriminated against them and often prohibited them from any but the most primitive means of self-defense. And the Germans moved in on the Jews in a gradual way. At first (1933–1938), Jewish property was seized by the government, and Jews had to pay special taxes; they had to carry identity cards all the time indicating they were Jewish, and they were even restricted as to what they could name their children; all Jewish males had to be named Israel and all Jewish females Sarah. These measures were humiliating, but most Jews responded by feeling they were temporary and could be endured rather than assuming that they should pick up their entire family and move to another country. Even the next escalation of persecution (1938–1941) was considered by most Jews to be a terrible but temporary situation. Jews were denied such freedoms as the freedom to go to school, to work, or to public places like theaters and beaches. In 1939, Germany invaded Poland. It was following that invasion that worst persecutions began. It was then that Jews were forced to live in ghettos, limited, very crowded areas, and from there it was much easier to round them up for concentration camps or other forms of mass murder. When German soldiers invaded people's homes, Jews had no weapons for resistance. Those who could hide or escape did so. Those who could and did fight back were publicly executed before their own families and townspeople. In addition, an individual decision to resist often led to bitter reprisals against family and friends.

Also, many Jews were deceived by the German propaganda that they were just being transported to work camps. Once they were in the camps, inhuman conditions gradually stripped them of their strength and dignity, leaving them too weak or too frightened to fight back. They were given so little food that some adult men and women came to weigh

forty pounds. Disease was rampant. The Nazis even abused people's bodies for "medical experiments."

It is important to keep in mind, however, that with courage, luck, and the will to live, several hundred thousand did survive. There were many acts of resistance. A good way to begin teaching about resistance is to read—with your children—Bea Stadtler's *The Holocaust: A History of Courage and Resistance* (New York: Behrman House, 1974)—fifth grade and up. Some formed Jewish fighting groups (Partisans), while others joined the Russian army. There were organized rebellions in many places, the most famous being the Warsaw ghetto (April 1943). It is important to note that even in the ghettos and concentration camps, people continued to live in a remarkably human and caring way. As one survivor's child poignantly remarks: "Knowing that people had the will to live was very important to me. We found love-letters that my grandmother wrote to a man she fell in love with in a concentration camp, and that was so real. They communicated, and in my mind I thought, 'How can people communicate beyond depression?' I had read books and seen cattle cars in movies, but till then I didn't know the life force. My older brother even learned to walk in camp. Can you imagine that?"

WHY DIDN'T ANYONE HELP THEM?

For a long time the German officials cleverly deceived the world about what they were really doing. Even when reports did leak out, the horrors described seemed too inhuman to be believed. When a Czechoslovakian woman came home from work one day and told her family that she had seen people being burned alive in the neighboring village, they thought she was crazy. The Nazis had a model concentration camp, Theresienstadt, where the Red Cross made on-site visits and reported to the rest of the world that conditions weren't so bad for the Jews. When the American people finally began to learn the gruesome details, they felt helpless to stop the process. Despite pressure from various Jewish groups, the American government did not take even the most rudimentary steps to halt or slow down the extermination of the Jews; the government considered the bombing of the railroad tracks that led people to the gas chamber a very low priority. (For more information on this subject, see *While Six Million Died* by Arthur Morse ([New York: Random House, 1969]).

Religious Jews will naturally have different ideas from those of non-religious Jews. However we try to understand this dilemma, Auschwitz continuously forces us to question our belief in God.

WASN'T THE HOLOCAUST JUST LIKE OTHER OPPRESSIONS?

No, it was worse than other oppressions and must be remembered as it really was, not lumped together with events that were far less drastic. The Holocaust was the first time in history that a government set up a systematic mechanism to obliterate completely a people and their memory from the face of the earth. It was not a few random individuals being attacked in a pogrom. It was not like religious persecutions in the past where people could save their lives by converting. It wasn't like the situation of the American Indians where the white settlers robbed them of their land but were not pledged to wipe out the entire race.

However, we must remember that other nations have suffered great losses as well. In World War I, the Armenian nation was almost totally destroyed by the Turks. The Nazis murdered nearly all the gypsies and exterminated five million non-Jewish civilians in the concentration camps and by other brutal methods.

CAN IT HAPPEN HERE?

Life for the Jews in America has become very comfortable. The freedom we have today in no way resembles what the Jews experienced in Europe for centuries before World War II, even in "enlightened" Germany. Yet despite this good situation, we must not try to deny or ignore incidents of discrimination and oppression against the Jews both today and in the past. Here we make a distinction between responses to a younger child and an older child. A younger child needs more reassurance that America is a safe place; an older child should be taught to recognize that while America is relatively safe, similar feelings of safety and complacency were widespread among German Jews prior to the rise of Hitler. This should be done not to encourage any sort of "paranoia," rather to place the issue of Jewish security in a realistic perspective. Although the Holocaust might not happen again exactly as it did, the frightening truth is that there are many ways in which Jews can be discriminated against and abandoned even by present-day America.

OTHER QUESTIONS THAT MAY COME UP

Were children treated better than adults? What do you feel toward the Nazis and Germans today? Did Jews hurt other Jews? Can I trust my Christian friends? Do you think maybe we should convert? Any of these questions warrant an ongoing dialogue in the process of helping our children develop a positive Jewish identity.

HOW TO COMMUNICATE ABOUT THE HOLOCAUST

Each individual and family is unique. Some children learn easily by direct discussion, whereas others prefer reading, seeing pictures, or hearing stories. We need to determine what each of our children is ready for, cognitively and emotionally, at various stages of his or her development. Usually, it is best to begin by telling about the Holocaust in a general way and add more details gradually as the child gets older. We don't want to shock our children into awareness. It is helpful to use analogies from the child's own life experience in explaining what happened, such as the fact that children will pick on those who are different from themselves even though it is mean and cruel.

We should also communicate in the style that comes most naturally to us. Some of us may prefer to use books or various activities as a way of broaching the subject, whereas others prefer just to tell about it in their own words, especially if they are the children of survivors or personally know people who were in the war.

We may find that our children appear indifferent or even antagonistic to discussions of the Holocaust. They would much rather go out and play or tell you what went on in school. They don't want to be different from their friends. We needn't take this as a signal to avoid the subject altogether. It is only natural that they would rather not hear about such a frightening and unpleasant subject. We should try to understand their response and acknowledge the validity of their feelings; it doesn't mean they are selfish and uncaring. It simply may not have been a good time to bring it up, or they may have been in the wrong mood to listen. Therefore, it is important to bring it up again at a time when they may be more receptive to it, when they are not preoccupied with other things.

On the other hand, sometimes our children are more interested in pursuing the subject than we are. One father we know was distressed because his daughter wanted to focus on the Holocaust in her bat mitzvah speech, which he considered an inappropriate setting. Families sometimes have to decide together how they will deal with the story of the destruction of European Jewry in public activities.

Above all, we should be attuned to our children's feelings and reactions to what we try to teach them. Sometimes they will react only in disguised ways; sometimes they won't react until weeks or even months later. By providing an atmosphere of open discussion and direct encouragement, we can help our children express and cope with whatever may arise. Children do appreciate it when we make it possible for them to share fears and fantasies about the Holocaust.

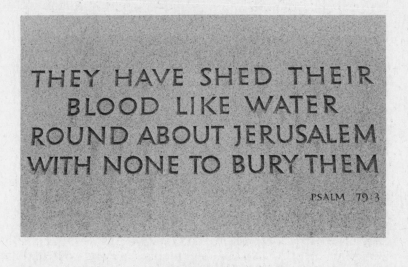

THEY HAVE SHED THEIR
BLOOD LIKE WATER
ROUND ABOUT JERUSALEM
WITH NONE TO BURY THEM

PSALM 79:3

PASSOVER

The Passover Seder is a natural occasion for remembering the oppression as well as the liberation of the Jewish people. The Haggadah, the traditional vehicle for discussion, describes four types of children and wisely tells us to respond to each child according to his or her nature. At different times, we are all like each of the children.

The first child, the inquisitive child, asks complex questions that we must attempt to answer completely. Though he may challenge us to address issues we have not yet fully considered, he is easier to teach, because he initiates discussion and gives us cues about what he is ready to hear. The second is the defiant child, whose lack of interest is often discouraging. Here we depart from the traditional response of scolding the child. Instead, we must approach his reactions with a great deal of patience and find subtle ways of engaging his attention. Then there is the one who asks simple questions and needs honest, direct answers that are not too complex or disturbing. Last is the child who is too young or too naive to even know what to ask. Responding to this situation, we introduce the issues to him gently and in such a way as to increase his own natural curiosity.

Aside from spontaneous discussion, there are a number of ways to introduce Holocaust themes into the Passover Seder. Jews throughout the world have added the following prayer to their Passover service:

> On this night of the Seder we remember with reverence and love the six million of our people of the European exile who perished at the hand of a tyrant more wicked than the Pharaoh who enslaved our fathers in Egypt. Come, said he to his minions, let us cut them off from being a people, that the name of Israel may be remembered no more. And they slew the blameless and the pure, men, women, and little ones with vapors of poison and burned them with fire. But we abstain from dwelling on the deeds of the evil ones lest we defame the image of God in which man was created.
>
> Now, the remnants of our people who were left in the ghettos and camps of annihilation rose up against the wicked ones for the sanctification of the Name, and slew many of them before they died. On the first day of Passover, the remnants of the Ghetto of Warsaw rose up against the adversary, even as in the days of Judah the Maccabee. They were lovely and pleasant in their lives, and in their death they were not divided, and they brought redemption to the name of Israel through all the world.
>
> And from the depth of their affliction the martyrs lifted their voices in a song of faith in the coming of the Messiah, when justice and brotherhood will reign among men: *"Ani ma'amin b'emunah sh'lemah b'viat ha-mashiach, v'af al pi sh'yitmahmayah im kol ze ani ma'amin."* ("I believe with perfect faith in the coming of the Messiah, and though he tarry, nevertheless I believe.") (From Emil Fackenheim, *God's Presence in History* [New York: New York University Press, 1970], pp. 96–97.)

CONCRETE SUGGESTIONS FOR ACTIVITIES

Children start carrying within themselves images of things they have seen, heard, or experienced from early on in life. The combination of a special school program with lighting candles at home and attending a memorial service can leave a lasting impression. The images we create often convey messages more powerful than words or endless explanations. Along these lines we would like to share some of our suggestions and encourage you to develop your own activities according to your family style, the ages of your children, and the lessons you want to face this year.

Yom ha-Sho'ah (Nisan 27) is a day of remembering man's inhumanity to man. It is a day for memorial symbols in our homes. Some people might want to light special *Yahrzeit* (memorial) candles. Others may want to begin the day with a special prayer, to make a long-distance call to a fellow Jew in Russia, or to contribute to organizations that work from the freedom of Soviet Jews and the punishment of Nazis. (We think especially of Simon Wiesenthal and Beate Klarsfeld, 196 Avenue de Versailles, Paris, 75016, France.) This, of course, does not preclude doing these things on other days, but a special effort should be made to incorporate them into Yom ha-Sho'ah as a way of joining together with the Jewish people. Many families attend a yearly memorial service or a special program devoted to the Holocaust. If there are few Jewish families in town, they can gather together to commemorate this day with reading or viewing a relevant film.

A more ambitious effort would be to gather a group of people (preferably families with older teenagers) to reenact *Nightwords, A Midrash on the Holocaust* by David Roskies (available from B'nai B'rith, 1640 Rhode Island Ave., N.W., Washington, DC 20036). It begins with participants lining up in a row as they enter the room and relinquishing their shoes to the ushers. Then the storyteller narrates, "In the beginning there was the Holocaust . . . We must therefore begin again . . . from then on nothing could be the same," and proceeds through a very powerful dramatic reading in which all those present take part.

CONNECT WITH YOUR OWN ROOTS

Have you ever stopped to think about whether you personally had a relative who was a victim of the Nazis? Perhaps your grandmother had a cousin whom she has long forgotten. As the majority of the Jews in the United States came from eastern Europe, it is very likely that there are relatives who were left behind, never mourned or remembered by the living. Tracing your family roots can be a way to find out. (See Chapter Thirty-four.)

TRAVEL

Families who can afford to take trips abroad should make a special effort to go to eastern Europe or to Israel. We often meet Jews who are so conflicted about their Jewish identity that although they have been to western Europe many times, they have never been to eastern Europe or to Israel. Many Jews living in America thus cut themselves off from their roots by avoiding the places from which many of their ancestors came. For those who wish to revive the connection with their own roots, there is no more powerful way than by visiting the primary locations of recent Jewish history.

With older children, you might consider a visit to Dachau Concentration Camp in Germany or Auschwitz in Poland or the Anne Frank house in Amsterdam. In Israel, if you want to visit sites related to the Holocaust, there are Yad VaShem in Jerusalem, Kibbutz Lochamei Hagetaot in the North, and Kibbutz Tel Itzhak near Tel Aviv. The former kibbutz was founded by ghetto resistance fighters and has a good museum; the latter accommodates people for a week at a time to study the Holocaust. Lectures are given by professors and survivors from the kibbutz who share personal accounts. You can write to them directly for further information.

THE ARTS

Movies are a good medium for communicating about the Holocaust. However, parents must judge the appropriateness of films for each child. Consult the Jewish Media Project of the Jewish Welfare Board (15 E. 26th St., New York, NY 10010) or local teachers, critics, and film lists. Ideally, you should preview a movie yourself before recommending it to your children. Don't take your ten-year-old to see *Night and Fog;* she has plenty of time to learn about the atrocities. At times, we depend on movies to say what is difficult for us to say in our own words. Prepare yourself and your children for viewing by talking with them before and after the film.

People often express themselves best in artistic forms. A parent may suggest a family mural of the Holocaust, or perhaps a few families could gather together to do group murals, in which each family could share their imagery with others. Thoughts and feelings about the Holocaust can also be expressed in sculpture, drawing, music, dance, drama, or creative writing. All these might be utilized according to the particular interests of your children.

THE LEGACY OF THE HOLOCAUST

No Jew today can live as though Auschwitz never happened. But conveying the legacy of the Holocaust must be preceded by, or combined with, some account of the positive aspects of being Jewish and the richness of Jewish history and culture. It is much more difficult to convey these positive aspects in isolation. We need the support of a larger community to provide our children with the gratifications inherent in belonging to a nation and a people.

The Holocaust exemplifies both the utter depths to which human nature can sink and the ability of people to retain courage and a belief in the sanctity of life even in the most inhuman situations. What is truly remarkable is not only that people were able to save themselves but that they constantly tried to help each other at the risk of their own lives.

We have a moral responsibility to tell the tales of the Holocaust for those six million who did not escape. As Elie Wiesel has said:

> The Nazis were not satisfied with mere murder. Before murdering Jews they were trying to reduce them to numbers. After murdering them, they were dumping their corpses into nameless ditches or making them into soap. They were making as sure as possible to wipe out every trace of memory.

Millions would be as though they had never been . . . ("A Plea for the Dead," *Legends of Our Time* [New York: Holt, Rinehart, and Winston], 1968, pp. 174–197.)

Emil Fackenheim in *God's Presence in History* teaches us that after Auschwitz there is an eleventh commandment:

A Jew may not respond to Hitler's attempt to destroy Judaism by himself cooperating in its destruction. In ancient times the unthinkable Jewish sin was idolatry. Today, it is to respond to Hitler by doing his work.

He adds:

We can no longer fall back on the beliefs of yesterday that man is good, progress real, and brotherhood inevitable. Yet neither can (we), on account of Auschwitz, despair of human brotherhood and cease to hope and work for it. (Emil Fackenheim, *God's Presence in History*, [New York: New York University Press, 1970], pp. 90–91.)

BIBLIOGRAPHY

An excellent annotated bibliography on the Holocaust appears in *Horizons*, spring, 1977, vol. 4, no. 1.

BERKOWITZ, ELIEZER. *Faith after the Holocaust.* New York: Ktav, 1973.

DAVIDOWICZ, LUCY. *The War Against the Jews.* Philadelphia: Jewish Publication Society, 1975.

FACKENHEIM, EMIL. *God's Presence in History.* New York: Harper & Row, 1972.

GREENBERG, IRVING, AND, GREENBERG, BLU. "Telling Your Children About the Holocaust."*Jewish Living*, March/April, 1979.

HILBERG, RAOUL. *The Destruction of European Jewry.* New York: Quadrangle, 1967.

LEVIN, NORA. *The Holocaust: The Destruction of European Jewry, 1933–1945.* New York: Schocken Books, 1973.

MORSE, ARTHUR.*While Six Million Died.* New York: Random House, 1969.

ORBACH, WILLIAM. "Post Holocaust Jewish Theology." *Reconstructionist*, vol. XLIII, January, 1978.

ROSKIES, DAVID. *Nightwords.* Washington, D.C.: B'nai B'rith, 1973.

STADTLER, BEA. *The Holocaust: A History of Courage and Resistance.* New York: Behrman House, 1974.

———. "Teaching the Holocaust to Children." *The Second Jewish Catalog.*, ed. Strassfeld and Strassfeld. Philadelphia: Jewish Publications Society, 1976.

WIESEL, ELIE. *Night.* New York: Farrar, Straus, 1959.

CHAPTER THIRTY-THREE

WHEN WORDS FAIL: CHILD ABUSE

In the preceding chapters we explored ways of talking with our children about subjects that make many of us feel tongue-tied. We have asked ourselves how to respond when our children raise questions about sex, God, death, the Holocaust, and money. Hard as each of these subjects is for us we cling to the hope that we can put our thoughts and feelings into words and share them with our children. Now we must turn our attention to an area which betokens the failure of words: child abuse, the acting out of pain and anger which were not channeled into some manner of parent-child dialogue.

No, you say, Jews do not abuse children; yet improved reporting methods indicate otherwise.

In 1974, the U.S. government passed a law that attempted to define child abuse and created a national center for its prevention. A side effect of this law was that teachers, child-care workers, and health-care professionals were made legally responsible for reporting incidents of child abuse. Because more and more cases of child abuse were being reported, we learned that child abuse is not limited to lower-income or underprivileged elements of our population. It crosses socioeconomic and ethnic lines and can be found in the homes of affluent Jewish suburbanities as well as in inner-city welfare hotels.

What constitutes child abuse? Experts disagree. There are some who would maintain that even a *patch* (slap) is abusive; others would argue that the real issue is one of parental loss of control. We know that, in fact, abuse can take many forms, from outright physical violence to psychological abuse to pathological failures in nurturing that result in nutritional deficiencies.

In other words, experts and parents are not sure where to draw the line beyond which behavior becomes abusive. It is easy to identify gross injury to a child. For many of us, the distinctions are more subtle and therefore more difficult. Are we all child abusers? Who abuses their children? Some experts see child abuse as a continuum. They will say that it is normal for us to become angry with our children, yet that anger may be seen on a scale with a small percentage of us becoming so furious that we do violence to our children. Other experts understand child abuse pathologically and see abusive behaviors as "off the continuum," as different from the normal angers and stresses of child rearing.

Regardless of how you see child abuse, increased reporting of incidents to the police enable us to know much more about the syndrome. We know, for example, that most adults who abuse children were themselves abused in childhood. The pain of child abuse is self-perpetuating. Children never cease to love their parents. Severely battered children will continue to protect their parents by maintaining that the abuse was their own fault. The self-image of these children has been so injured that they see themselves as worthless. From such a terrible lack of confidence, they grow up and become parents who seek love from their children that they did not receive themselves. Frustrated by the inadequacies of their lives, by the inevitable difficulties of child-rearing, they perpetuate the terrible patterns with which they were raised. We all must work to stop the pattern.

Because you have felt anger toward your child, because you fantasized "putting that kid through the wall," does not mean that you abuse your children. It means that you are normal and feel anger. On the other hand, if there are moments when you feel your self-control slipping, when you suspect that you might act out your fantasies, then it is time to seek help from counselors, professionals, or parent-support groups in which you can discover that you are not alone in your frustrations in parenting.

Where can you go for help? Cities and states vary in the resources available to you. Within the Jewish community, you might turn to an understanding rabbi who can refer you to more experienced professionals. The Jewish Family Service in some areas has established groups to

help and support parents. Cities and states have also established child-abuse-prevention hot lines and eight hundred numbers that are answered twenty-four hours a day. Wherever you turn, the hardest and most important step is the first step, the first reaching out.

What are your options if you as a responsible and concerned adult think you know a child who is being abused? Realize that anything you do is an "intervention." Your problem is to weigh the pros and cons of the intervention you might make. To what degree are you prepared, despite legal assurances of anonymity, to take responsibility for your actions? What are the foreseeable consequences of your plan? Often, it can be useful to get the advice of someone who works professionally with abusive parents. Such a professional may be able to help you think through which alternative is in the best interests of the child. Your resources include your local child-abuse hotline number, a national clearing house called National Committee for Prevention of Child Abuse, 332 S. Michigan Dr. Chicago, IL 60601, (312) 663-3520, and Jewish Family Services. For specific names and numbers in your locale, try calling your state or city welfare office. Children's hospitals and pediatricians have generally been working in this area and should be able to give referral information.

A PLEA FOR HONEST FEEDBACK

Of all areas of life, the ways in which we raise our children are most vulnerable and easily threatened. Recently, we were unwilling witnesses while a dear friend proceeded to express profound favoritism of one son over another. We watched as the eyes of the less favored child became more and more pained. We felt we could say nothing, for we sensed our friend's vulnerability. To say anything risked hurting her and endangering our relationship. Later, we realized that by saying nothing, we were behaving very "normally" and without courage. Most of us have learned over the years not to say anything, that "feedback" about the ways in which we and others raise our children is taboo. Our plea here is for honest, caring, concerned, supportive "feedback." None of us wants to be the recipient of unsolicited, judgmental pronouncements or the chatter of *yentas* and busybodies. But there are times when all of us can use the help, the insight of real friends who see our interactions with our children from a different perspective. "And you should love your neighbor as yourself."

Chapter Thirty-four

PLANTING THE SEEDS TO GROW JEWISH ROOTS

Arthur Kurzweil

When a Jewish child is born, he or she becomes, quite literally, the product of Jewish history. The child is suddenly one more link on a Jewish chain that has been forged over generations to create the history of our people. Had any one piece of that chain not existed, that child would not have been born into our tradition. A mathematical example illustrates this best:

How many ancestors do you have in the last ten generations? Take a guess. Each of us, in only ten generations, has 2,046 direct ancestors. We have two parents, four grandparents, eight great-grandparents, and so on. Add the last ten generations together and each of us has 2,046 ancestors. Let's imagine for a moment that *one* of your ancestors in the last ten generations did not grow up to get married and have children. Any *one* of them. The result would be that you simply would not be here.

This is not only an argument for marriage and children; it is also an illustration to make real the idea that each of us is a link on a chain called Jewish Tradition. When your own child is born, he or she becomes the newest link.

But how do we teach our children to understand this notion? How can we help to show them that they come from a family that is part of a tradition that continues to move forward with history?

Since the triumphs of Alex Haley, genealogy has often been thought of as a fad. In Jewish tradition, however, this is not so. Genealogy has been a vital part of our tradition from the very first chapters of the Bible, which contain the famous "begats." Our Jewish names are genealogical, containing both our first names along with the first names of our parents (Reuven ben Moshe v'Sarah). Our gravestones indicate our genealogy by including our Jewish names. Much of our liturgy focuses on this concern, with frequent use of phrases like "from generation to generation" illustrating our concern and respect for a vision of Jewish tradition linked together through family history and genealogy.

We all want to believe that our children have a deep love for their family history, a profound sense of their connection to that history, and a desire to continue it. We all want to believe that after our children have grown up, they will keep in touch with relatives, visit and write to their grandparents, appreciate family traditions, and feel a great warmth and connection to the tradition out of which they have come. We want them to be the kind of people who will speak lovingly about their grandparents and who will talk about their family history with a sense of its richness. How can we ensure that this will happen?

Simply put, we cannot. Not every child will want to know about his or her family history. Not every child will care about ancestors and ancestors' histories. One child will seem to be naturally interested in old family stories; another will squirm in his or her seat at the very thought of it. You probably know this from your own experience. You may absolutely love family reunions, for example, but you may have a brother or sister who wouldn't be caught dead at one of those gatherings.

In trying to inspire a child to cultivate an interest in family history, we encounter two problems. The first is simply wondering what to do to inspire the child, but the second problem, that of the frustration of not knowing whether or not you are succeeding, is more subtle and needs some exploration.

Inspiring a child to be interested in family history and to appreciate the sense of "connectedness" to Jewish tradition is a process of *planting*

When our children look back upon their childhood, we all secretly hope they'll forget the times of pain, turmoil, and friction and remember instead the warmth, closeness, and sharing moments of the family life. We want our children to identify with their family, to feel a bond not only with us and their siblings but with Aunt Sylvia, whom they see only once a year, on Pesah. Also, we want our children to know and care about their family's heritage. We want them to know who their grandparents and great-grandparents are and where they came from. If we are named Finkelstein, we want our children to be able to say, "We Finkelsteins came from Mezritch in Poland. My great-grandfather was a carpenter who was known for his acts of charity. There was a story told about him that once he . . ."

This is what we want for our children. How can we achieve it?

When I was a child, my mother began a custom that we continue to this day. We take walks. Long walks. Sometimes for miles at a stretch. And while we walk, we talk. My mother is an indefatigable gatherer of family tales. She has a marvelous memory and can conjure up family tales—ones she heard from her mother or ones she personally knows about—on demand. She tells them not as heavy-handed learning devices, but so that I will get to know some of the same people she, too, never met. She tells of exploits that are alternately funny, wise, cruel, illegal, unethical, and beautiful. We talk about our family, and I have now a sense of who and what we have been, what our family history has been, what some of our inherited traits are, and how it is that some aspects of who we are reoccur from generation to generation.

I look forward eagerly to taking those same walks with my children. I know many of the stories by now, and my mother has promised to give me some of the family photo albums for my children. In addition, I take my own family photographs and movies on every conceivable occasion. I've even made tapes of my children singing songs, reciting *berakhot*, and telling stories. All of this I hope to leave to my grandchildren.

The question of how we can give our children a commitment to and close identification with their own family is another issue. (See Chapter Ten.) Recently, we were visiting the home of a friend and were served

(Continued)

taygelekh and tea. For the uninitiated, *taygelekh* are pieces of dough covered in a honey sauce and rolled in nuts. I refused the *taygelekh,* and when pushed to try them, I explained that my family had always had a *minhag*—a tradition—not to eat nuts on Rosh Hashanah lest the new year not be a "smooth" one and also because the Hebrew numerical equivalent of the word *egoz* (nut) is virtually identical with the numerical equivalent for *het* (sin). We began to talk about *minhag* and discovered that each of us had a whole host of family customs that we grew up with. Some of them we continue to practice; others we have allowed to lapse. Passing on these family *minhagim* is important in letting children know that families have histories, that for ten generations in their family the groom's gift to the bride has been a pair of candlesticks and the bride's gift to the groom has been a *tallit.*

In addition to passing on what is already there, we can be thinking about creating our own family *minhagim.* Our family sings and dances at the end of *havdalah* (the ceremony that marks the end of *Shabbat*). We then kiss each other and wish each other a week of peace. The custom began un-selfconsciously when my husband and I used to sway together with our first child in our arms. Swaying turned into jumping when she was just beginning to learn to walk. And jumping turned into the dancing that continues now, years later. What we have is a family *minhag,* a treasured time that I recently overheard my eldest child explaining to her friend. "Well, in *our* family, we've always danced a lot after *havdalah.*" "Always" can have such a very short historical past for a child, yet once the child perceives it as an "always," it becomes integrated into his or her life and into the family's life as a very special time of family celebration and closeness.

seeds, and this process of seed planting implies *patience.* Ninety-nine times out of a hundred we will not see the results of our efforts for years and years. It is not like teaching our children a skill. When we teach our child how to recite *Kiddush,* we can see results immediately, but cultivating an interest in family history is just that: a cultivation! It is not just a cute coincidence that we can use words such as "planting seeds" and "cultivation" when talking about family "trees." The real truth is, all we can do is make an investment now and hope that our efforts will flower in the future. Here are some suggestions:

PHOTOGRAPHS

Just about every family has old family photographs. One day, sit down with your photographs and with your children *and* with your children's grandparents (or great aunts and uncles) and *label them!* You will go through the old box of family photographs and suddenly discover that you have no idea who some people are. And the sad probability is, if you don't know now, you probably never *will* know. Don't let that happen to all the photos. Go through your collection and write on the back the names of the people, where the photo was taken, and when. You might even want to have your child—the one who has just learned how to write—do the labeling. It will be an activity that will probably not be forgotten. For technical advice on the preservation of old pictures see *Shoots/A Guide to Your Family's Photographic Heritage* by Thomas Davies (Danbury: NH: Addison House, 1977).

Don't overwhelm your children by telling a million stories about each photo. Perhaps you can just focus your storytelling on the photos of the person your child was named after. But the whole process will be meaningful—we hope.

Also, consider displaying old photographs in your home. Frame a few and hang them up. Make them a part of your home decorations. If your children see a few family photos every day as they grow up, they will be familiar with the people in the pictures. And that's what we want to happen. More seeds.

TELLING STORIES

As I was growing up, my father told me a few stories about my family's history that will be with me for the rest of my life. True, he is a master storyteller, and true, I have always been especially receptive to family stories, but had he not bothered to tell me the stories, they probably would have been gone forever.

The stories were not long, detailed, fascinating yarns. Let me tell you one of them: My father's mother (my grandmother, who died when I was five, and whom, therefore, I *do* remember) was in the dairy business in Poland before she came to America. She bought milk from farmers outside of town and brought it back into the town, selling some as milk and making the rest into butter to sell. To bring the large jugs of milk from the farms to the town, my grandmother carried one jug as far as she could and then went back for the next. After bringing all the jugs to the first stopping point, she then began again, until all the milk was home.

That's the story. Not very detailed, not very exciting. But as I grew up, I had a sharp, intuitive understanding of who my grandmother was and how she had worked, and the story captured my imagination. Because of it, my grandmother is that much closer to me. I am sure my father had no idea that the story made the impression on me that it did, but one thing is certain: I will tell that story to my children.

Don't overdo it. But think about family stories you know and tell them to your children. Have your children's grandparents do the same. The smallest event told to a child can stick. The few family stories my father told me had a greater impact than all the children's books I ever read.

VISITING THE CEMETERY

I find it upsetting to hear that a child was left home from a funeral. Why? Certainly we could debate the issue of when to talk to children about death, but this has little to do with whether an older child can attend a funeral. The child may not even care to ask about "death" at that time. But going to the cemetery allows the child to read the gravestones (that's what they are there for—to be read) and to begin to sense in a vivid way that people came before us. The interesting thing about cemeteries is that even the most assimilated families use Jewish cemeteries and have Jewish symbols on their gravestones. A lot can be learned about our tradition by examining the stones.

A funeral is also a place to see relatives. Certainly, there are happier times to see family than at funerals, but the reality is that often it is at these events that people see each other and renew their familial ties. Funerals (and other life-cycle events) are the best places to get across the subtle message that we are part of a family, that we come out of a family, and that the tie is a very important part of who each of us is.

Also, in regard to cemeteries, you ought to consider taking your children to the cemetery when (if) you visit certain graves once a year.

Again, among the most important memories I have are those of visiting my grandparents' graves. I was with my parents, and they were visiting the graves of my father's parents. It showed me what being connected meant.

DON'T PUSH COUSINS ON THEM

I am convinced that the worst thing to do is to push cousins on your children. How many times do we parents force our children to spend endless hours with cousins with whom they have little in common. Certainly, if an organic friendship seems to be developing, it is wonderful. But there is no reason why cousins—even first cousins—have to be childhood friends. Gone are the days when your best friend was your first cousin.

Don't be alarmed. I am convinced that this does not mean that your children will never know or care about their cousins. As they get older, friendships may develop. Relationships will undoubtedly occur. If your child in New York has a first cousin or second cousin in L.A., chances are good that when they get older, they will look each other up when visiting each other's cities. In the meantime, bring cousins together on occasion and hope that they get to know each other more than a little—and that the experience is positive.

DO SOME HOLOCAUST RESEARCH

For four consecutive semesters when I taught a course on Jewish family history and genealogy at a university in New York, I asked the students

on the first day of the class whether any of the people in their families had been murdered during the Holocaust. Usually, most of them said, "No." On the last day of the semester, each student was again asked this question; as a result of their research, not only did every student say, "Yes," they could even tell me some vivid details about their relatives' lives and fates.

Six million Jews were murdered during the Holocaust, and each of those Jews came from a family. Your family and my family. I would suggest that you do a little bit of Holocaust research. Talk to relatives, and get names and stories from older members of your family. You can even attempt to do more in-depth family-history research. (See *From Generation to Generation: How to Trace Your Jewish Genealogy and Personal History*, by A. Kurzweil [New York: William Morrow, 1980].)

Once you know the names of some of your family members who were murdered (you may even have some photographs or additional information), you might want to consider creating your own personal Yom ha-Sho'ah ceremony, using the family information you have gathered. Yom ha-Sho'ah, the Holocaust Memorial Day, which occurs on Nisan 27 in the Jewish calendar, can include for your family a reading of the names of the people in your family who were murdered. What we are trying to do is teach ourselves and our children that Jewish history did not happen to other people—it happened to us, our family, and that by making the connections between the general historical events and the people in our families who were a part of it, we are helping to forge the link between the past and the future.

FAMILY HISTORY IN GENERAL

What we just discussed regarding the Holocaust can also be said about other events in recent Jewish history. Irving Howe wrote a book some seven hundred pages long called *World of Our Fathers* that discusses Jewish migration to America. While this is a fascinating and valuable book, there are other ways of pointing out to children that their grandparents and great-grandparents were Jewish immigrants. For example, you might send for a copy of the steamship passenger lists of the immigrants' ships on which your grandparents arrived. I have copies from the National Archives of each of the passenger lists of the ships that brought my family to America. They mention the names of my ancestors and various bits of information about them. These passenger lists illustrate Jewish immigration of the world of *my* fathers (and mothers!) better than any book could. Why? Because they are personal by being specifically about my family. Jewish immigration to America can be a broad, general, abstract subject, or it can talk directly to you.

FAMILY REUNIONS, FAMILY CIRCLES, AND COUSINS' CLUBS

Many Jewish families have family circles or cousins' clubs. For decades, these organizations have been important and rewarding for family members. But (to put it bluntly) such get-togethers are usually boring for children, who cannot understand why the meeting is being held. I strongly suggest *not* "shlepping" your children to these meetings *unless* there is something there for them to do. Children grow up with more loathing for these groups than I care to think about. Why didn't you hate the meetings when you were a child? Because when you were a child, you may have known your cousins. They may have been your friends. It's a different world today, and to throw your children into an adult meeting with a few cousins they've never met is to ensure that they'll have, at best, ambivalent feelings about their extended family.

If you do not have a cousins' club or family circle, you may want to consider organizing a family reunion. (It might be as a *result* of your genealogy research, i.e., you may have a nice, big family tree to print up and hand out, or you might get a family reunion together in order to *get* some genealogical information.)

In any event, family reunions can be profoundly important happenings, and even if they won't ensure family devotion forever, they may still plant a seed.

USE FAMILY HEIRLOOMS; DON'T HIDE THEM AWAY

Judaism is a way of life that attempts to transform everyday things into special things. We are a religion of "sanctification," making the events in our lives holy. When it comes to objects we use, we can treat them either as everyday items, or we can elevate them, not so much as to make them idols but enough to make them give *us* more meaning.

When your son becomes a bar mitzvah, will he begin to use the *tefillin* that you give him, all shining and new, or will he use the *tefillin* that may have been his grandfather's or great-grandfather's? The same applies to candlesticks, *siddurim, hallah* covers, Seder plates, Hanukah *menorahs*, and so on. Let your children be aware that the Hanukah *menorah* that they are using is the one that their grandparents used. Tell your children that when they get older, the *menorah* will become theirs to use and to pass on once again. Try to use as many Jewish ritual objects as you can find that have been used by a past generation!

CREATE FUTURE HEIRLOOMS

If you do not have a family heirloom to give to your children, create one. Don't give your child the fanciest, most unusual *kiddush* cup you can find. Rather, get a simple one and have it engraved! The engraving might say, "In memory of . . ." (the person the child was named after) or might even be a short genealogy listing the child's direct ancestors during the past few generations. Suddenly, a possibly ignored ritual object acquires great significance and helps to tie that bond between your child and the future through the past.

KNOW WHERE YOUR FAMILIES CAME FROM

Sooner or later, every child asks, "Where did I come from?" When that happens to me, rather than struggle for the right sex-education philosophy, I plan to answer, "You came from a small town in southeast Poland called Dobromil."

Find out where your family comes from and tell your children. You can tell them by mentioning it to them, or you can get a photograph or two of the town and frame it and hang it in your home. You needn't find a picture so detailed or so rich that it will overwhelm your child with a sense of family history or Jewish history; the very act, however, will be one more way to let the child know that he or she has a past. Your child may never develop a further interest in the subject, but if she or he does, wouldn't it be a shame if the information were lost forever because you never bothered to keep track of it or ask your own parents and grandparents about it.

Don't hit your children over the head with family history; just make it accessible and available. It's the least you can do.

Of course, someday you might want to plan a trip to "the old country" to see what the places where your ancestors came from looked like. You might not find too much—perhaps just a little town with a building that used to be a synagogue, a few remnants of a Jewish cemetery, and perhaps a few remaining Jews. But a trip to eastern Europe—or wherever your family was from in recent generations—can be a deeply moving and unforgettable experience. This would be best left until your children are old enough to appreciate it and remember it, but there *are*

places in "the old country" that can teach us about the history of our families.

I come from a family of two children—myself and my brother. I have a deep interest in family history and family tradition; my brother does not. What made one of us one way and the other another way? I don't know. There are no guarantees that any of the above will work to ensure that your children will sense their connectedness to Jewish family tradition and Jewish tradition. But I believe that although we cannot be sure that our family "trees" will grow, we can do our best by planting the right seeds.

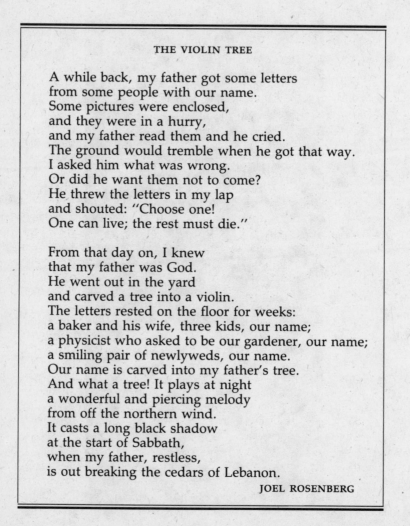

THE VIOLIN TREE

A while back, my father got some letters
from some people with our name.
Some pictures were enclosed,
and they were in a hurry,
and my father read them and he cried.
The ground would tremble when he got that way.
I asked him what was wrong.
Or did he want them not to come?
He threw the letters in my lap
and shouted: "Choose one!
One can live; the rest must die."

From that day on, I knew
that my father was God.
He went out in the yard
and carved a tree into a violin.
The letters rested on the floor for weeks:
a baker and his wife, three kids, our name;
a physicist who asked to be our gardener, our name;
a smiling pair of newlyweds, our name.
Our name is carved into my father's tree.
And what a tree! It plays at night
a wonderful and piercing melody
from off the northern wind.
It casts a long black shadow
at the start of Sabbath,
when my father, restless,
is out breaking the cedars of Lebanon.

JOEL ROSENBERG

CHAPTER THIRTY-FIVE

ETHICAL WILLS

Fiscally responsible parents, aware of the "uncertainty of life and the certainty of death," hasten to their attorney's offices and write wills. These wills are designed to maximize the financial and legal protection of spouses and children (their survivors) and to whatever extent possible avoid inheritance tax. While estate planning is difficult to face but also important for the future financial well-being of your survivors, we wonder if you have ever considered writing another kind of will, one that has a long tradition in Jewish history—an ethical will.

The ethical will first appears in our history in the Bible. Remember Jacob's final instructions to his sons (Gen. 49) or David's advice to his son Solomon (1 Kings 2:1–12): "I am going the way of all the earth. Be strong and act like a man. Keep the charge of the Lord your God, walking in His ways and following His laws, commandments, rules and admonitions as taught by Moses so that you may succeed in whatever you undertake and wherever you go . . ." Talmudic literature abounds with examples of passages that quote the deathbed instruction given by great sages to their students. One way in which authors of medieval Hebrew literature sought to apply their beliefs and theologies to everyday life was to utilize the form of the ethical will, often beginning, "My child . . ." These documents sometimes authentically came from parents seeking to leave instructions to their children and their descendants as to how they should live their lives. In other cases, the documents reflect instructions for ethical conduct for which the author chose to assume the "will" genre.

By the thirteenth century, ethical wills were not only a popular literary genre but also a well-established practice within certain families. Consider the family of Asher ben Yehiel, father of the author of the *Turim*, a famous code of Jewish law. That family moved from Germany to Spain during the Middle Ages. We still have extant a set of "rules" written by Rabbi Asher for his family, along with a will addressed to the sons of R. Jacob, the son of R. Asher. Scholars also believe it probable that R. Judah, Jacob's brother, also wrote an ethical will, which has been handed down as an anonymous work.

Another example is Avraham Horowitz, who, in the sixteenth century, wrote an ethical will that came to be called the "Yesh Nohalin." His son Jacob wrote a will in the form of additions and emendations to his father's work. The grandson, Shabbetai Sheftel Horowitz, the author of *Shefa Tal*, carried on the work of composing ethical wills.

A touching example of an ethical will from a simple man of the Middle Ages comes to us from Eleazar the Levite, who lived in Mayence in the Rhineland in the fourteenth century and wrote to his sons and daughters:

> These are the things which my sons and daughters shall do at my request. They shall go to the house of Prayer morning and evening. . . . Their business must be conducted honestly in their dealings with both Jews and non-Jews. They must be gentle in their manners and prompt to accede to every request. . . . If they can by any means contrive it, my sons and daughters should live in communities and not isolated from other Jews so that their sons and daughters may learn the ways of Judaism. I earnestly beg my children to be tolerant to all, as I was throughout my life. . . . (Regarding my burial) wash me clean, comb my hair, trim my nails as I did in my lifetime so that I may go clean to my eternal rest. . . . Put me at the right hand of my father, and if the space is narrow, I am sure he loves me well enough to make room for me at his side.

Obviously documents that are handed down from one generation to another within a family are in and of themselves amazing. They convey the sense of very old family traditions and history. Even more recent documents within a family, perhaps as recent as letters from grandparents, can serve important functions in transmitting a family's values and ideals, aspirations and heritage. Searching out old letters, which were not originally intended as ethical wills, can bring rewarding insights.

Writing an ethical will can help you know your own values as well as give of yourself to your children. Sharing those wills with others can also enrich relationships: imagine both parents in a marriage privately writing ethical wills for their children and then sharing the documents, discovering similarities and differences.

Where would you begin? Jack Riemer, writing about ethical wills for the National Jewish Resource Center, suggests: Ask yourself: If you had time to write just one last letter, what would you say? Would you talk about success or failure? Would you chastise, forgive or ask forgiveness, rebuke or instruct? Think of your letter as a document which your child(ren) may re-read often after your death, seeking comfort or renewal or inspiration or challenge. It is your last opportunity to focus on those important values, most integrally a part of you, which you want to convey to your descendants. This is your opportunity. Take pen in hand and begin "Dear _____"

For further information about the history of ethical wills and for specific examples in English translation, see *Hebrew Ethical Wills* by Israel Abrahams (Philadelphia: Jewish Publication Society, paperback) and in Hebrew by H. H. Ben-Sasson, *Hagut ve-Hanhagah* (1959). For ways of discussing ethical wills in group settings, see "Guides to Ethical Wills/

Guides to Personal Growth," by Jack Riemer, published and distributed by the National Jewish Resource Center, 250 W. 57th St., New York, NY 10019.

THE WILL OF RACHEL DAVIDSON

I know that I am now growing old, and though I expect to yet live many years, I want to put my wishes in writing so that there will be no confusion when my time does come.

When I die, I want my funeral to be simple, inexpensive, and in accordance with Jewish law as interpreted by our Rabbi Cohen. All the orthodox customs of the Old Country need not be followed, but the Rabbi should be present, and I want my family to sit shiva.

I have little in the way of possessions that I care about. My candlesticks, the challah cover Aunt Sara made, my sketchbook and Bible, along with the Hanukah menorah I have always loved, should go to Pauline, in the hopes that she will pass them on to her own daughter some day. Max, I would like you to keep both your wimpel, which I have been keeping for you, and the one which was made for Karl.

I know that we will always be a strong family, and that you will continue to support and care for each other. The past years have been a struggle for us, holding on to the old, and exploring this new land. We are proud to have become Americans, to participate in all this country offers, yet we must not loose our own heritage. I hope that you, my daughter Pauline, will continue to be a member of the San Francisco Jewish community, both through the synagogue and the Women's Benevolent Society. Brother Max, though it is hard for you, do the best you can to support Pauline in all these things. I know well you will not practice your Judaism according to my views, but remain Jews and live as Jews to the best of your ability.

Rachel Davidson

ETHICAL WILL

So shall it come to pass in the day when I bequeath unto you the possessions which the Creator has preciously bestowed on me, I will hand on to you the honesty of purpose by which God has enabled me to possess this store, for with my staff I crossed over to gain my daily bread and its drink offering, and lo! the Lord has blessed me thus far. Faithfulness has introduced me into places where my kinsmen could not admit me, and has dowered me with more than my fathers had to leave unto me. It has given me authority over men greater and better than I, and I have prospered myself and have been a source of profit to others. Therefore take heed therein, even toward one whose good the Law does not enjoin us to seek. Stand by your words, let not a legal contract or witnessed deed be more binding than your verbal promise, whether publicly or privately given. Disdain reservations and subterfuges, tricks, sharp practices, and evasions. Woe to him that builds his house thereon! For if one getteth riches and not by right, "in the midst of his days he shall leave them and at his end he shall be a fool." Live in sincerity, integrity, innocency! Touch not that which is not yours, be it a small matter or great. Taste not that which is not clearly and decisively your own. Flee from doubtful possessions, treat them as the property of others. Remember that the tasting of the doubtful leads to indifference as to the certain; the little to the great, the inadvertent to the designed, till one becomes a hardened cheat, liar, thief, and bandit, from whom men turn hastily away. "The buyer from him will not rejoice, nor the seller mourn." He shall be ashamed in his life and confounded in his death. All this have I seen and laid it to my heart. "He that conceives chaff shall bring forth stubble," but "he that sows according to righteousness shall reap according to mercy." Let your moral life be your pride of lineage, and your loyalty to truth your sufficient wealth, for there is no pedigree noble as virtue, no heritage equal to honor.

Maimonides (attributed)
From Hebrew Ethical Wills
by Israel Abrahams

PART FIVE
LETTING GO

CHAPTER THIRTY-SIX

ADOLESCENTS: LETTING GO

"More than the calf needs to suck," according to a Talmudic teaching, "the cow needs to nurse." The rabbis continued, "So, too, more than a student needs a teacher, a teacher needs students." All of us who have nurtured and taught children know the truth of these statements, for we know how deeply rooted is our love and need of our children. We do not want to lose our children. We watch them grow, and we see that as they move from one developmental stage to another, the nature of the parent-child relationship changes. Some might even say that the former relationship is sacrificed on the altar of the new relationship. Despite all the positive things in a child's new-found maturity, many of us find ourselves saying, "I want to put a brick on that kid's head." On the other hand, there is also: "I have to cherish these moments, she'll never be that age again." It is no accident that movie-camera advertising is so often directed toward parents, encouraging us to "capture the moment"—as if we could.

We used to live in Somerville, Massachusetts, where a number of the wooden frame houses had been converted into two-family duplex apartments. We observed in those days that the first-floor apartment was often occupied by a middle-income Italian family and that the second-floor apartment would be given to a child of the family upon the child's marriage. Thus, children and grandchildren did not move away; they simply moved upstairs in houses their parents generally owned. Many of us who dread the thought of our children leaving us find the image of these two-family houses not unattractive, yet realistically we know that this pattern is not commonly practiced in the contemporary Jewish community.

What we must learn is how to let our children go while helping them at a later date to come back. We acknowledge that reaching out is not a onesided activity. We not only want to help pave the way for our children to come back to us, but we also want to have the courage and flexibility to go to our children. Thus, we recall how Joseph went into Egypt and was separated from his father Jacob, who thought his son dead. We want to be able, like Jacob, to summon the strength to be able to go to those places where our children are and be reunited with them.

How can we begin to structure possibilities within our own environments to avoid estrangement later? As always there are no easy answers, and each family is unique; but we share here the thoughts of some who struggle with these questions.

What should you do when your child comes home from school with a "significant other"? How do you repond when it begins to dawn on you that the young couple plans to share the same bed? (Give them fresh linen?) Alternately, what do you do when you realize that although they are "serious" about one another, they decidedly do not want to share either the same bed or the same bedroom?

We recommend *Changing Bodies, Changing Lives* by Ruth Bell and other co-authors of *Our Bodies, Ourselves* together with members of the Teen-book Project (New York: Random House, 1980). The book is helpful not only for its direct information but also for its reflection of our society.

Our friend Mel Silberman, a psychologist who teaches in the Department of Psycho-Educational Processes at Temple University, is himself the father of three children and has one dog, one guinea pig, and countless tropical fish. Mel Silberman believes that in early adolescence, it is important to give kids some freedom before they ask for it. If you give kids some freedom before they ask, you retain a measure of control. If you hold on tight and only give freedom when it is wrested from you by the child, then you have lost control. In that latter situation, it is the child who has made the decision that now is the time for some loosening up, and it is the child who gains control in such a conflict. By choosing the time and the place for giving freedom, you retain a measure of parental prerogative or power. The problem is that just at that time when parents feel most threatened and want most to hold on tight is when they should let go, as an investment in the future.

A friend tells us the following instructive story: "The summer I was seventeen years old, I attended what was for me a truly inspirational Jewish summer camp. Through that experience, I became much more traditionally observant than my family, and I also became a much more religiously believing Jew. I was terribly open and eager to share my experiences; of course, I was dreadfully naive. That fall, I talked with a young uncle of mine about my newly discovered religious understandings and insights. I had felt close to my uncle until he began to respond

to my confidences. He teased me and later attacked me for my retrogressive and archaic thinking. He tried to persuade me to return to my family's level and style of Jewish observance. I still remember the cold feeling inside me as he talked on and on. It was then that I realized how vulnerable I really was. I became much more closed. I was careful in whom I confided. My uncle, had he reacted differently and somehow (even though not agreeing with me) been more sympathetic or made me feel that he was on my side, would have fulfilled an important function in our family's life. He might have served as a bridge person, connecting me to my parents, who were much older and didn't understand. Instead, I have never said anything real to my uncle since then."

But sympathy and empathy are not always the solution. Consider the dilemma of the children of some friends of ours. Said one child of that

The son of friends is an excellent skier who owns very fine ski equipment. The kid recently, for good psychological reasons, decided not to ski anymore. Our friends, the boy's parents, explained to us that his skiing had satisfied a constellation of needs and that his rejection of a sport in which he was excelling also bespoke of maturation, really of growing up. Yet they did not necessarily see the rejection of skiing as permanent but possibly a phase. That left our friends with a funny dilemma: what to do with the expensive ski equipment in the garage? The mother, who, truth to tell, would save anything, argued that by hanging on to the skis for her son she could provide him with a kind of security, that he would know an important part of his life remained waiting for him at home, and that he could return to that part of himself when he was ready.

We were struck by the dilemma because it reminded us of a traditional rationale for Jewish observance and made us wonder at the roles we assume as our children move in different directions. Are we, in our steadfast commitments, providing them with a safe home to return to, or might we be more supportive or empathetic were we to reach out and try to share in their new life-styles? For example, should we attend a Saturday-morning meeting with our adolescent of people interested in Zen? While the mother of the skier was fighting to keep the skis, the father was maintaining that selling them was right and that to keep them around might only make them into painful symbolic reminders of a rejected past. Interestingly, in that situation, the boy really removed himself from the decision by going away to college.

Perhaps he was not yet ready to make a decision himself and could avoid the issues his parents raised with each other by going off to school. Yet, for those of us left holding the skis (or the hard-earned, carefully wrought patterns of Jewish observance), the questions are real. We remember how clear the imperatives were when our children were small, and we grope for the courage to continue to grow while holding on to what, for us at least, is deeply meaningful and satisfying.

family, "My parents have always been on my side. They are ultimately understanding. They are, in fact, so automatically liberal and understanding they made adolescent rebellion impossible. During the 1960s, no matter what causes my siblings and I allied ourselves with, our parents understood and supported us. It was suffocating. We couldn't find our own voices."

Are there no answers? Generally, professionals (like Chaim Ginott in *Understanding Adolescents* and Thomas Gordon in *Parent Effectiveness Training*) who write about ways of raising children maintain the importance of clearly stating what you want and don't want. In other words, they advise against "sending mixed messages." They also advocate keeping open channels for communicating. They tend to encourage parents to respect and handle with care their children's evolving egos.

Some parents find it helpful to read about ways in which adolescents think and feel. We recommend the following: Erik Erikson's "Identity and the Life Cycle" and *Childhood and Society;* David Elkind's chapter 3 in *The Child's Reality: Three Developmental Themes* (NJ: Lawrence Erlbaum Associates, 1978); and Lawrence Kohlberg and Carol Gilligan's article "The Adolescent as Philosopher: the Discovery of the Self in a Postconventional World" in the overall excellent issue devoted to adolescence of *Daedalus, Journal of the American Academy of Arts and Science,* Fall 1971. *Twelve to Sixteen,* edited by J. Kagan and R. Coles, was first published as that issue of *Daedalus* magazine and then reissued in book form by W. W. Norton. Other good, although psychoanalytic, essays include *Adolescence* by Peter Blos and *Youth: Identity and Crisis* by Erik Erikson, also published by Norton. These books do not give direct advice on how to deal with adolescent children but provide insights into how they think and feel.

Those of us who worry about our children's growing up and away from us often talk about adolescents' needs for positive role models. Our model comes from the traditional blessings that Jews recite after eating a meal. Among the blessings to God are: "You open your hand and satisfy every living thing with favor." Usually, "you open your hand" is understood to imply generosity; we might say, for example, that a philanthropist is open-handed. We are indebted to Zalman Schachter, who has suggested a reinterpretation. How do you give or feed or nurture with an open hand? Remember feeding young children? We imagine our hands are closed, holding on to something, perhaps the food itself or the feeding spoon or the squirming baby. Any time we imagine holding, in our mind's eye we see our hands closing. And so we suggest a model for ourselves of nurturing not only with generosity but with an open hand, of holding close while letting go.

It is told of Rabbi Bunam that he once said, "On a Sabbath, when my room is full of people, it is difficult for me to 'say Torah.' For each person requires his own Torah, and each needs to find his own perfection. And so what I give to all I withhold from each."

But Abraham
foresaw, as well, the need for discipline,
and so, devised a harrowing initiation
to teach the kids what they were up against.
A child would be bound up like a ram,
and watch his father raise a sharpened knife
to slaughter him . . . but back away, at length,
release him live, and sacrifice a ram instead.
The father then embraced the child,
welcomed him anew to life, and told him:

"Death is everywhere, my child. Today,
you learned to feel its presence.
You will have it with you everywhere you go,
and you will see the cities of the world
where people worship death, revere him as a 'god.'
Today, I placed before you life and death,
and just as I have chosen here to let you live,
so may you choose life. And don't forget
that death is your advisor, not your 'god.' "

And on the day that Abraham escorted Isaac
through this ritual, on a mountain, at high noon,
they sat a long while afterward and talked.
The father told the boy about his own childhood,
and talked about the idols in Haran.
Involuntarily, he raised his hand for emphasis,
above his head, as if to smash them once again,
but caught himself, embarrassed—for he realized
suddenly that he still held the knife above his son.

JOEL ROSENBERG
excerpted from "God of Abraham, God of Isaac"

KIDS SAY . . .

Heidi: My parents have a habit of asking me to do things at the worst times. I'm just as busy as they are sometimes. I usually do what they say only to avoid any fights.

Morty: I usually put up an argument. Otherwise, I simply do it despite myself. I realize that they're my parents, and I've got to go out of my way sometimes. It's hard, though.

Noam: My initial response to an unwanted request from my parents is usually negative. However, I often rethink the request and conclude that fulfilling it wouldn't be so terrible. Let's face it—*most* requests that parents make are trivial and not major to us but usually more important to them than we realize. It's just that kids are so ready to condemn things without thinking them through.

Stuart: My parents' asking me to do some work for them usually does not create too much friction. I may not want to do the job right away, which makes waves, but if left alone, I would get it done. The real problem occurs when my parents expect me to go and seek out the work that has to be done without their telling me anything. If they would just tell me in plain English what to do, I would do it.

Carol: When my parents ask me to take out the garbage or just do a small task, I do it. If it (the decision involved) is taking a certain course at school, we discuss it; they say what they want to say and I say what I want to say. The best way for parents and children to work out differences constructively is through communication, by talking, doing, showing or any other way to get the point across. Communication is the key to working out many problems.

Rona: The only major problems I have with my family have to do with independence, in terms of school, curfew, etc. I think most of these problems will be worked out when I move out of the house.

When you do move out of the house, it will be a lot easier for your parents to accept your growing up, and it will be easier for them to let go and grant you the independence you want. The trouble is that until that time there's not much you can do except work on communication so that your parents at least know

(Continued to page 328)

where you stand, and take a lot of what you may feel is unfair flak. They're your parents, and you're stuck with them for a while, so just try to make it as pleasant as you can for now and wait for time to help work things out.

Stuart: I think that parents should gradually reduce their control over their kids; if we make sure not to take advantage of the new freedom, things will be OK. However, much of the responsibility of growing up rests on us.

Carol: I think by the time people reach high school, *they* should realize that *they* are growing up and should begin to take on responsibility that goes with growing up. Don't ever leave your parents out. They are the ones who can and want to help you grow up; they have some important and worthwhile things to say about it. Just listen. If you do feel that your parents are being unfair and not exercising good judgment, try talking to them.

Rona: I have had my share of problems with my parents, trying to prove to them that I am not a baby anymore. I think that parents and children should talk things out. It is very important for both parents and children to make compromises until they reach some sort of arrangement.

Stuart: The fact that my parents still think I'm their "little boy" is always brought home to me.

Alisa: When I do things my parents are against my doing, they'll be on my case for weeks, about everything, not just that particular incident, because it's hard for people to separate issues. I've found that the more I consider my parents' feelings, the more they consider mine.

A communication gap may just be a result of your being a very different person from your parent(s). It may not come to the surface when you are opposing each other as much as when you are trying to work together.

Stuart: Communication is the biggest problem, closely followed by a real gap between my parents and me when we try to work together, whether it be cleaning up outside or fixing a broken lamp.

If you find that you are having trouble enjoying being with your parents, maybe the best thing to do is not spend so much time with them. The justification for this is that if you are really trying to enjoy and communicate with your parents and it's hard, a little bit at a time may be easier. And trying to think of things you all like doing, not waiting for your parents to suggest something, is another way of ensuring that the time you spend together will be more enjoyable.

Nat: The major problem I've encountered is that a lot of times my parents can't understand my actions or my thinking. The only way to solve this problem is to talk to them in a language they understand and in terms they themselves can relate to. My parents often need explanations, but in the end they understand.

David: Too many parents think that kids have power, but they don't. I was at a Youth Commission meeting. We were discussing the drinking age. There is presently a bill circulating to raise the age from eighteen to twenty-one. Many students voiced their opinions at the meeting against raising the age, yet the commission voted to endorse this bill.

Nat: The only way to let parents know you are growing up is through your actions. Deeds speak louder than words more often than not, and parents can see you mature by the way you act. All a kid can do is be himself. Parents have good judgment.

Missy: I think everyone should listen more carefully and bend a little at times that they might not want to. Then they'll learn tolerance (for one another).

And whatever problems you have, try to understand that you are probably having them because your parents are having trouble deciding how *they* feel. You once *were* their baby, and getting used to having someone changing as drastically as many young people do once they enter adolescence can be trying.

Heidi: The only idea I have is that young people should learn to fight for what they want. We should be treated fairly. If other people treat us like animals, we'll act like animals. Something must be done to make people realize that kids have good ideas, too. We can change the world if we want to, but someone's got to give us a chance.

David: Parents should talk out with the kid any major decision to be made that concerns the kid. Minor decisions (e.g., taking out the garbage) are not worth arguing over.

Heidi: I'm trying my best to get through life without having to run into problems with my parents. I can honestly say that it's not easy, and I'm having trouble, but things will work out.

Stuart: If I want help with a problem or a decision, I'll come looking for it. It may not be in the form of a direct request for help but a strong hint or a hopeless look on my face. But if I'm in my room alone, I really don't want any help, and I may resent someone trying to give it.

When all else fails, two things remain for us: chicken soup and prayer, and one has more cholesterol than the other.

Have you ever noticed that some parents are especially effective in dealing with their eight-, nine-, ten-year-old children and appear inept in relating to these same children when they reach adolescence? Remember the awkwardness of a friend who seemed totally hassled by her newborn baby but appeared transformed into a model of patience when that same baby started to talk? Esther Ticktin, comments: "It is really interesting to ask yourself, for what age child do I experience myself as being the best parent? What age child do I feel that I understand best and can be most effective working with? When you pinpoint an age, think of yourself at that age. How did your parents deal with you at that age? Was it an especially good period for you? Were your parents better equipped to deal with you at that age than at other periods?"

PRIVACY

Missy: I value privacy. It seems to me that all young people should have some place meant only for them—I know I need it. An understanding should be met so adults know "This is my place, especially for getting away, so please don't intrude."

Most of the people who responded to the questionnaire were firm in their beliefs that young people should be able to have a place to themselves. "A place that's 100 percent me" and "a place where I can sit and think alone" are phrases that neatly sum up the importance of a private place to a young person. When one is becoming an increasingly self-sufficient adolescent, it becomes more and more important to be able to be alone—in a sense, to practice independence—to think for, and be with, oneself, alone. The value of such a space may not become apparent until one has found it.

CHAPTER THIRTY-SEVEN

BETWEEN YOU AND YOUR ADOLESCENT

Before our children become teenagers, a part of us truly believes that everything will be all right. We are, in our heart of hearts, quite convinced that given how open, understanding, warm, generous, and sensitive we are as parents, adolescent rebellion will represent a brief, passing phase, the prelude to our children's emergence into exactly the kind of adulthood we want for them.

One sign in *our* growing up is our increasing ability to face, understand, and integrate into our lives discordant information. It is more likely than not that our children's rebellions will not be brief, and it is more likely than not that we, as their parents and the objects of their rebellion, will not breeze confidently through. It is quite possible that we may find the ways our children grow into adolescence and even adulthood dismaying, threatening, and painful.

How do we live with the pain? How do we learn to separate ourselves from our children so that we can say to ourselves, "Ultimately, my child will have to live with the person she has become. I can take neither all the credit nor all the blame for who she is. I have to work hard at maintaining some relationship despite the disappointment I feel in her. I have also to 'de-invest' myself in her identity and move on in my own life." In the end, we all do the very best that we can for our children, and we live with the results. We may not have been the most liberal, psychologically aware, developmentally sophisticated parents, but we give the most that is within us.

When it comes to dealing with specific adolescent problems, we have to present one underlying principle. It is best to try to work through—early—in your own mind how you feel about any issue (whether it is drugs or premarital sex). This helps you to be clear all along about your position, without necessarily being heavy-handed. Thus, you can be prepared to be flexible when you should be. What you don't want to be are parents who say, "Even though I strongly don't believe in premarital sex, I let Danny sleep with Rachel in our home because I know it's a stage he's working through, and he needs to explore his own sexual identity." You don't want to say this for three very good reasons. First, because you *do* care a lot about the issue, and a person, to be respected, has to be true to his or her own principles. Second, because you will *not* be able to eliminate all your children's rebellions by giving in to them; in fact, your children *need* to rebel in order to grow and need you to give them the *rishut* (the permission) to rebel in ways that are healthy. Third, because there is a "*kishke* (gut) price" to be paid when you try to swallow what won't go down, and your system will ultimately force you to pay that price somewhere—whether in ulcers or in hidden resentments that get channeled in other destructive ways.

On the other hand, it is important to avoid the whole game of power struggle. While you may not be able to compromise on the issue of premarital sex, you want to be flexible when you can. Some parents may be genuinely able to say to their teenager, "I don't approve of smoking marijuana. That is why I have never done it. But if you need to do it and can do it in ways that do not endanger you physically or emotionally, then I am prepared to be flexible in this area." Our teenagers certainly need us to be able to stretch ourselves in some areas of conflict, and we ourselves need to know that we are not always cast as "the heavy," that we have made what feel to us like honest attempts to meet our children at least halfway.

Below are a list of some of the more common areas of conflict between parents and their adolescents. The advice below is offered *very* tentatively, since every parent-child relationship is different and since we respond differently to a seventeen-year-old than to a fourteen-year-old.

SCHOOL WORK

Frequently, conflict gets expressed through school—teenagers' performance, their friends, their dress. Parents often have a stronger sense than their children about the importance of good high school grades for admission to top-notch colleges.

Children have more difficulty sacrificing now for rewards later (in other words, delaying gratification). Moreover, the whole area of responsibility comes into play. The high school experience becomes, for most teenagers, the first arena where they function independent of their parents. For example, teachers begin to relate to their students in a significantly more adult fashion; teenagers respond by wanting to separate their parents out of this world that has become so emphatically their own.

But what do you do when your child is doing poorly in high school and you're convinced that she or he could do better and are infuriated by the fact that she or he won't? Or what do you do when your child is an overachiever who is crushed by an A— and uninterested in extracurricular or social activities?

For the underachiever, there are two questions to ask. Is your child not doing well because she or he is testing our independence, trying to discover how far you can be pushed? Or is the child, for some external reason, unable to do better in that particular setting? If your child is bored, defeated, or socially maladjusted *in that particular* school, you will have to intervene to work out alternative programs or possibilities. Or you will have to find a new school setting that will be more supportive of your child.

But what if you know your child is "simply rebelling" and you have already said to your children: "Your performance in school is your responsibility. If you choose to do consistently poor work, there will be consequences. Some of those consequences are . . . But ultimately you are growing up, and I can't serve as your policeman to verify that you did your Hebrew assignment. If you choose to do poorly, you will have to live with that choice yourself." Then, if you are honest about it, you have to live with that statement. How far that child will let matters go will have to be up to the child. You may want to praise the child for academic success without condemning him or her for failure. But if you are consistent, you will want to praise in ways that clearly indicate that you think the success was *his or her* success and not your success.

When a child is focusing on an overachievement as a way of avoiding conflict with his parents from whom he is afraid to separate or avoiding contact with his peer group, from whom he fears rejection, or as a way of letting some unbiased outside factor (the grade) indicate approval of who he is because he is too frightened to find out for himself, then you have to become involved in nurturing ego strength. You will want to gently (not threateningly) encourage the child to recognize that outside interests are healthy and important. Tasks or activities that take him outside the home/school environment, tasks at which the teenager is likely to succeed, are good ways to begin. If the child is truly a hermit and cannot be motivated to move outside himself, then the behavior may indicate deeper problems for which the help of a good counselor or therapist is desirable.

APPEARANCE

Since there is nothing so visible to parents as the actual physical appearance of their child, adolescents delight in appearing regularly in dirty, sloppy, outlandish, or sexually provocative attire. The bottom line becomes how far you can stretch yourself in letting them work through their psychosexual and independence needs. After that comes the question we always have to ask: When does behavior become not merely adolescent rebellion but outside the boundaries of "normal"? A teenager who refuses to shower—ever—is not merely acting out; he is crying out, for professional help. An adolescent who insists on wearing torn jeans and her father's shirt together with too much makeup to a family reunion may be testing your reactions. Then setting clear limits may well be the answer. "Yes, you can wear torn jeans and a T-shirt—to the movies with your friends. When you enter our world, however, you will have to conform to the way we dress in that world. In 'gray' areas, we'll negotiate with you."

DRINKING/DRUGS

Most responsible schools sponsor educational programs dealing with drug and alcohol abuse for twelve-year-olds. Most children emerge from these sessions in one of two ways: they assume the most conservative posture on the subject, or they think the lectures were a lot of "bull" and are eager to experiment.

Either position can pose problems for a parent. We know of one couple who have to arrange for their fourteen-year-old son to sleep at a friend's house whenever they have a party for their pot-smoking friends, because the boy is vehemently opposed to the use of marijuana.

On the other hand, we have friends who spent every Saturday night for two months straight gritting their teeth as their sixteen-year-old son reeled in the door drunk from a party.

What to do?

In the first case, if what you are doing is not in excess (i.e., if *you* are not reeling in drunk every weekend), you will probably try to steer clear of disapproving, teetotaling children and enjoy yourself when they're not around. In the case of the child who is a "user," you have to distinguish between one who experiments and one who abuses. So long as you feel sure that your child is not unduly abusing or endangering his or her physical or psychological health by the need to experiment, you can

afford to be tolerant. But at the point that your daughter is not only experimenting with drinking but is driving at the same time, you must set a very firm limit. You will be happy to pick her up from her party or to pay for a cab home. You will not permit her to be driven by people who have been drinking, nor will you allow her to drive herself. Again, as in the other cases, the habitually drunk or drugged teenager is giving a clear message of "Help!" to which parents must respond.

SEX

Here is the other area (besides drugs) that is most frightening to parents. What if you are afraid that your fourteen-year-old daughter is sleeping with her boy friend, or what if you are afraid that your sixteen-year-old son is sleeping with *his* boy friend?

Let's separate out the two areas of heterosexual and homosexual activity and acknowledge that it is not at all uncommon for adolescents to have a homosexual experience. They are exploring the totality of their own sexuality, testing their limits, your limits, their own moral stances on the subject. Giving them room for *healthy* experimentation may be just what they need. Consistent homosexual involvement, however, may have long-range implications that you and your child will need to confront, probably with the aid of professionals.

In the case of your reaction to heterosexual activity, you have to take into account several factors: the age of your child, the attitude you have previously conveyed, and the child's partner. What may feel wrong for a fourteen-year-old may be within the bounds of acceptability for a nine-teen-year-old. You may not, short of physical force, be able to stop your fourteen-year-old. But you can let him or her know that you profoundly disapprove and hope to be taken seriously. (Certainly, an inquiry into methods of birth control is appropriate, if you are fairly certain that your disapproval is not affecting the situation.)

What about when your freshman in college wants to bring his girl friend home and expects to stay in the same room with her? If you've been consistent all along in conveying a sense of disapproval of pre-marital sex, you are entirely within your bounds to say, "Yes, you are growing up and entitled to make adult decisions. But you may not violate the values of my home. And I have expressed my attitudes. I do not approve of premarital sex at your age and cannot allow you to stay with your girl friend in my home."

Above all, try to be open to letting your children talk to you about their feelings about sexual experimentation (even though it may well be the last thing they'd want to talk to their parents about). Your own position has to be clearly articulated and acted upon, but if you can do so without sounding harshly judgmental, you may well have succeeded in leaving a door open for later communication.

MONEY

This is a tricky one. Money equals power, independence, status, success in our own worlds; why should it mean something different to an adolescent? What about the child who is truly trying to be mature enough to earn his own "spending money." Does he then have the right to spend the money as he wants? We know of a teenager who worked all summer in a factory to earn $1,500, all of which he spent on a stereo system. His parents were appalled; and, as his mother later explained, "*We* couldn't afford a $1,500 stereo system. That's because we have more responsibilities than Carl does. In a very real way, since *we* pay for food and shelter—the necessities—and since we have always made it clear that we will pay for college, then that means all the money Carl earns *has* to be spent—if it is going to be spent at all—on what feels to us like luxuries. And that's a tough pill to swallow." Maybe, though, the problem here is that if Carl is going to have control over large sums of money, then some of his own personal necessities *ought* to become his expenses. Certainly, that is one way to handle the problem—to delineate areas of responsibility (although this can lead to other areas of conflict, as in the case of the sixteen-year-old who took upon herself the responsibility of buying her own clothes and then bought the most outrageous clothes she could find!).

Money, above all, to an adolescent means trust and independence. The child who saves $1,000 toward a summer trip to Israel is making a much larger statement to her parents than "Look how well I save." Parents have to become adept at letting their children learn how to have money, how to earn money, how to save money, and how to spend money. Most importantly, however, they have to teach their children what money is and is not—how it can represent bad things and be used to play out power struggles or how it can be used for growth and happiness.

PEER GROUP

There is almost nothing more important to the adolescent than his peer group. It is the peer group that judges the appearance, intelligence, and social acceptability of your adolescent. Since the peer group represents the "outside world," it is not particularly surprising that the approval of that group is highly valued by an adolescent, who may be suspicious of the uncritical love of his parents.

Sometimes the adolescent will "fall in" with a peer group that is unacceptable, for a variety of reasons, to the parents. The parents then have to make a serious judgment as to just how unacceptable the peer group is. Is the child running around with an older crowd that is "too fast"? Or is the crowd made up of non-Jews when the parents have a vested interest in having their child associate with Jews?

The question becomes, How much is the child acting out? Knowing

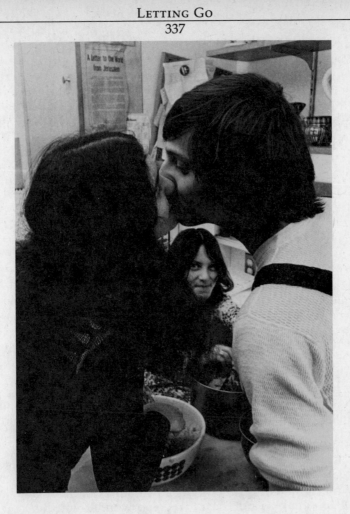

this, what is the limit of behavior with which you can live? You are certainly within your rights to prohibit your child from certain activities with his or her peer group. If the members of the group are going away for a weekend at Malibu or the Jersey shore, and you are seriously alarmed by the prospect, you are certainly within your rights to tell your child that he or she may not go along. Before you "lay down the law," you might do well to examine your own motives carefully and to discuss your feelings with other parents, your friends, and your child.

In addition, it has to be said that you are within your rights as a parent to try to wean your child away from certain friends and into other circles. Such "weaning" can take the form of encouraging your child to join a local youth group, sending your teenager to a Jewish overnight camp or to a summer program in Israel. If your child is open to these suggestions, she or he will come into contact with a different and, to you, more acceptable peer group, after which you can only hope that the graft will "take."

What about the child who cannot, for one reason or another, make good connections with a peer group and is left isolated and lonely? Obviously, if the child is seriously maladjusted, frightened, or out of touch, you have to seek professional help. But what about the child who is shy, quiet, a little withdrawn, but truly desirous of making friends? For such children, interest or hobby groups can be a good answer. Again, the youth group at your local synagogue or Jewish community center or Jewish summer programs can be important. The shy child who is "into" photography, swimming, dancing, pottery, or stamp collecting can be encouraged to develop these interests (together with other young people) at school or at a local community center. The impersonal hobby then provides the excuse the adolescent needs to move beyond the hobby and into the accessible peer group.

RELIGIOUS/ETHICAL VALUES

What about the child who acts out his rebellion in an "impeccable" way. You've always demonstrated your care and concern for your Jewish life. How about the kid who goes off to summer camp and comes back Orthodox? This kid wants you to kosher your kitchen, or worse yet, if your kitchen is already kosher, he doesn't trust you and makes that very clear. This adolescent refuses to drive over to visit grandparents on Saturdays anymore. He wears a noticeably large *kippah;* or she stops wearing pants and sleeveless dresses.

On the other hand, there is the teenager who rebels by abandoning totally his or her religious upbringing. You walk by McDonald's one day, and there, casually eating a hamburger with his friends, is your little Dovidel.

The other side of adolescent rebellion is the ethical-religious issues with which teenagers are struggling during this time. You may find yourself in the midst of furious debate about political or moral issues about which you may not even care. You wonder whether you've inadvertently harbored a fascist in your midst and speculate wildly on why you always found Nietzsche so incomprehensible when the mere mention of his name now sends your stock soaring with this hysterical sixteen-year-old confronting you.

Part of the developing intellectuality of adolescents is the need to sort out basic ethical, moral, and religious questions. One of the ways they do this is to talk about the basic ethics and beliefs of religion. Such inquiry is important: it will form the underpinning for their future belief systems. But it can be hard on the parent who has to endure their searches and experiments.

When the experiments impinge directly on you, as in "No, I'm sorry, Mom; you'll have to throw out all the dishes, kosher the kitchen, and start over again, or I won't eat here anymore," you can discuss in what ways you are prepared to be accommodating and in what ways you aren't, and try to arrive at some mutually acceptable compromise. If you find your child in an enormous *kippah* personally embarrassing, you'll have to either swallow your feelings or risk getting back that great no-win comment: "Oh, I get it, Dad. *Some* Judaism that doesn't *look* too Jewish is fine, but the real thing—that other people can see—is embarrassing!"

More importantly, despite your own needs for acceptance from your peers and from your children, your adolescents need you more. They have to know that you understand and support them in their needs to explore, find out who they are, and separate from you. They care *a lot* about feeling that love and support from you, and insofar as you are able, it is important that you give it.

"Now the Lord said unto Abram (who would later be called Abraham): 'Get you out of your country, and from your family, and from your father's house, to the land which I will show you. And I will make of you a great nation. . . .' " (Gen. 12:1–2). Thus begins the journey of Abraham, the father of the Jewish People. Abraham's journey, and by collective extension our journey, began only as he left his father's house. What a symbol for the young person who needs to travel to independent adulthood by separating himself from his father's house!

Midrash aggadah pushed the image further, suggesting a stronger rejection on the part of Abraham of his father's values. It tells us that Abraham's father was a maker of idols, and one day the boy sneaked into his father's workshop, smashed the idols, and left the ax in the hands of a largest idol. And we think we deal with rebellious adolescents? It behooves us to recall that we are "*bnai* Abraham," the children of Abraham, who had to leave his father's house to found a great nation.

CHAPTER THIRTY-EIGHT

FREEDOM, LIMITS, AND DISCIPLINE

As parents, we often struggle with decisions that fall under the umbrella of discipline or of limit setting. Our son hops out of bed twenty times before falling asleep, and we feel intense anger. Our daughter seeks our consent to attend a Friday-evening birthday dance. *Bubbeh* comes to town and we find ourselves forcing our daughter to apologize for saying something that in another context we would have found perfectly acceptable. Our little boy cries for a *treif* hotdog at a baseball game.

Each situation asks us to decide where to draw the line. At what point do we stop and say "no further?"

Some of us seek help from popular books of psychological advice in parenting. We read, for example, Rudolf Dreikurs, Bernice Grunwald, and Floy Pepper's *Maintaining Sanity in the Classroom;* Haim Ginott's *Between Parent and Child;* William Glasser's "A New Look at Discipline"; Thomas Gordon's *Parent Effectiveness Training;* or Melvin Silberman and Susan Wheelan's *How to Discipline Without Feeling Guilty.* The particular methods or approaches to parenting that attract us give us insight into our own personalities. Some of us are attracted to more permissive approaches; others study basic techniques of behavior modification. We learn new vocabularies. We talk about freedom and limits, about defining boundaries, about logical consequences. Whatever method we choose, we take it into ourselves and use it as a kind of *kavvanah,* an intention around which we orient our thoughts and actions. At deep psychological levels, we try to make the method our very own. And for some of us the process works. The formula, the approach for responding to given situations, becomes such an intimate part of ourselves that we use it unconsciously, without thinking. Others of us have sought a technique to help us at a critical time, and when that period passed, our involvement with the method lessened.

Are there areas in which our Jewish attitudes and the values of humanistic psychology (as expressed in parenting books) come into conflict? Yes, and each of us is endowed with great skill at rationalizing differences away. Yet conflicts may indeed emerge in the following areas:

To the extent that Jewish family life is *halakhic* (that is, standing in relationship to Jewish law), it must have limits and boundaries. No matter how permissive you perceive your style of parenting to be, lighting candles as the sun sets Friday or eliminating milk at meat meals reflects a structure, a definition of boundaries. Thus, absolute permissiveness is in conflict with *halakhah*.

"*Derekh-eretz*," polite respect for other people, especially for people older than yourself, is a traditional value that can readily conflict with free expression of feelings. "I am really angry at you, Zeideh; I hate you, and I wish you would go home," may be seen as therapeutic and honest expressions for the child or as gross transgressions of *derekh-eretz*. As the embarrassed parent who wants your child to be nice to your father-in-law and at the same time sympathizes with your child's feelings, what do you do?

Shalom bayit, the concept of a peaceful household, demands sacrifices on the part of individuals. The pursuit of *shalom bayit* may require the stifling of individual desires. To maintain *shalom bayit* you may need to sacrifice what *you* want for the welfare of the family. As a parent and as a family, how do you deal with "deviance," with a child who legitimately would rather go out for track than participate in family dinners?

Humanistic psychology generally sees the self as the ultimate source of knowledge, while Judaism classically has invested ultimate authority and knowledge in God and in the Torah. By the same token, psychology's primary priority is personal growth and development, while generations of Jews have seen themselves basically committed to God, Torah, and the People Israel. How hard is it for you to sacrifice your own personal or professional development for the needs of a family member? How do you deal with potential feelings of resentment as you drive the car pool to Hebrew school rather than finish that task that you have been putting off?

Here are three responses to our awareness of the conflict between traditional Jewish values and those psychological approaches many of us use for help:

First, we can do what many of us do, anyway: that is, to integrate and adapt. We borrow techniques. We make use of what works for us and ignore conflict areas. Thus, we can find ourselves, for example, using Gordon's conflict resolution structure as we say, "David, I feel angry when I see you putting the *hometzdik* (not permissible on Passover) dog food into the refrigerator which I just finished cleaning for Passover." In fact, what we are doing enriches the integration of our Jewish life style and contemporary techniques of growth and health. Ironically, given the high representation of Jews in the helping professions, we often find ourselves learning psychological techniques from Jews. We are optimistic about this *shiddukh*, this marriage of psychology and Judaism that is being consummated in our concern to raise our children in the most enlightened way we can. We look forward to new visions of American Jewish child rearing.

Second, we can stretch our Jewish spiritual imaginations in an innovative direction suggested by Arthur Waskow, who asked, "What if we were to experiment, by taking a Jewish value (like giving honor to your parents or *shalom bayit*) and using it psychotherapeutically, developing it as a technique or approach within ourselves?" How might such an attempt affect the ways in which we perceive and resolve conflict in our families? Any attempt would require significant inner effort and creativity.

Third, we learn from both psychology and Jewish spirituality that inner exploration should not be done in isolation; that each of us needs the listening ear of another. Our awareness of the helpfulness of companionship leads us to recommend that parents concerned with issues of freedom and limits, setting boundaries, maintaining discipline, conflict resolution, and the like join together to "brainstorm" for the sake of their own lives and those of their children.

The father of eight who now has three grandchildren talked about knowing the right way of doing things with children. "Each generation seems to have the right answers which make sense at the time. For example, I remember when, about thirty-four years ago, we heard about schedules for infant feedings. It made sense. We really worked hard at it for the benefit of our oldest son. The idea that we fed an older daughter when she cried seemed stupid. Now my daughter tells me about the logic of feeding on demand. It sounds so right that I don't understand why we believed in the schedules we made our children live by. Our mothers breast-fed us, and they thought that they were doing the right thing. We gave our babies nice, sterilized bottles, and now my daughters think it's insane not to breast-feed. Is there a right or wrong answer, or do people just do what they believe is right at the time? Maybe what I am saying about feeding babies also applies to theories of raising children that are popular at different times—about being permissive or disciplined or using parent effectiveness training or transactional analysis or assertiveness training for parents or behavior modification or Dreikurs's logical consequence or Ginott or . . ."

Sometimes we need the help of professionals. Occasionally, when we can, we are fortunate enough to have friends who can provide helpful insights into our childraising strategies without intruding too much and without provoking in us hostility when they say things we don't want to hear.

CHAPTER THIRTY-NINE

KIDS ON KIDS: TEENAGERS TALK ABOUT THEMSELVES

Alisa Israel

Struggling with issues of raising Jewish children, we have been excited to find other parents with whom to shmooze, to explore our thoughts and feelings. After our inital joy at discovering other adults with whom to "compare notes," we realized that it would be insufficient if we were just to talk with one another. We needed to listen to our children, lest they become objects of our own projections. We must be challenged to grow in response to our children's thinking which at times is very different from our own. At home the process of parent-child dialogue can be natural; in book-form we resorted to soliciting the help of a friend, Alisa Israel, who was then in high school. Alisa designed a questionnaire which she sent to teenagers she knew in many parts of the United States. The teenagers she contacted included:

Noam: *an eleventh grader from New York*
Carol: *an eleventh grader from North Carolina*
David: *an eleventh grader from Massachusetts*
Nat: *an eleventh grader from Massachusetts*
Karen: *a ninth grader from Minnesota*
Stuart: *an eleventh grader from Connecticut*
Morton: *an eleventh grader from New York*
Heidi: *an eleventh grader from New Jersey*
Missy: *a tenth grader from Connecticut*
Rona: *an eleventh grader from Connecticut*

Their replies are interspersed throughout this book.

We were impressed by the teenagers' eagerness to respond to Alisa's questionnaire, and we believe it important to hear what they have to say. We decided to integrate their responses into the text of this book rather than to isolate them together in one chapter. The teenagers' comments are intended to act as stimuli, foils, diversions, disagreements, and validations of issues we are discussing.

What follows here is Alisa's questionnaire. How would you and your children respond? Alisa herself had some reactions which can be found after the questionnaire.

THE QUESTIONNAIRE

This is a questionnaire like any other in that you should answer the questions that you can and that apply to you. Skip the rest. Try to be as thoughtful, honest, and informative as possible.

You may notice that we've not put any lines between questions for your answers. When there are lines, there is a tendency to use them as a guide to how much one should or shouldn't write. We don't want that to happen. Grab some paper and be sure to number your answers so that we'll know to which question they apply. If you want to give short answers, that's OK. On the other hand, it's great to express yourself! Write for as long as you like.

And try to enjoy yourself, too!

1. Tell us about yourself—a quick autobiographical sketch—and then what you do and what you're like now.
2. What kinds of problems do you have getting along with your family that you think other people might have as well? What do you think that you (and others) can do to solve them?
3. If you haven't already said, how many brothers and/or sisters do you have? Are you the youngest? Oldest? In the middle? What kind of problems do you have that are unique to being in that place?
4. Is privacy important to you? How do you feel that a young person should ensure his/her privacy? (The basics—what if you share a room with a sibling? How do you make sure that parents don't come barging in at every minute? Deeper things—what do you do if you want to be left to make decisions on your own? How do you lead your own life without parents hanging over you all the time?)
5. Have you ever had problems trying to make your parents realize that you are growing (grown) up? In general, what do you think parents and children should do (or not do) to get through these kinds of problems more easily?
6. When your parents ask you to do something that you don't want to do (anything from taking out the garbage to taking a certain course at school), what happens? What do you think SHOULD happen? In general, what is the best way for parents and children to work out differences constructively?
7. Dear Hortense: There are so many things that I want to do with my life, that I feel that I should do. For instance, I want to go see an R-rated movie, and I want to spend some time alone with my boy friend, and I want to drop my terrible Bulgarian history course at school. But I'm afraid of my parents. They're sure to punish me by grounding me, spanking me, not letting me watch my shows on TV, or just making me feel incredibly guilty about whatever I want to do that they consider wrong. What should I do?

   You are Hortense. What should this distressed young lady do?
8. What kind of relationships do you have with relatives outside

your immediate family (grandparents, aunts, uncles, cousins)? How do you think that these relationships affect your life as a whole and/or your day-to-day life?

9. At this point, in this country, Y.P. (young people) are sent through a pretty standard system that takes them to adulthood. They go to preschool, then to grammar school, high school, and college, with extracurriculars thrown in for good measure. How do you feel about this system? If you think it could use changes in any way, talk about them.

10. Do you think that in general young people have the power to change things within the system that they feel are unjust or simply unfair?

11. If you believe that Y.P. do have the power to change things, what is the best way to facilitate these changes? If you don't believe it, what is the best way to change the system in order to accommodate this possibility in the future?

12. What has your Jewish life been like at home?

13. In what ways do you think that being brought up Jewishly makes Jewish young people different from non-Jewish Y.P., if any?

14. Do you think that it is right for parents to impose their Judaism on their child? Do you think that the child should resent it if they do?

15. What do you think Jewish Y.P. should do if they are on a different level of observance from their parents?

16. What do you think Jewish Y.P. should do if their parents don't believe in interdating and they just met this terrific non-Jew they want to go out with?

17. What is the extent of your Judaism? How does it get acted out in your day-to-day life? Is it self-motivated or parentally enforced?

18. If you haven't already, how would you like to develop your own sense of Jewish identity? If you have, how do you do it?

19. What are the things that you feel your parents have done wrong in educating you Jewishly? How would you educate your children Jewishly?

20. What would your ideal Jewish parent be like?

21. What kind of school do you go to for your Jewish education? What do you feel are the benefits and problems with that type of Jewish schooling?

22. What do you think that Jewish Y.P. should do if they hate the Jewish education they're getting? Do the reasons they hate it make any difference? (Poor teaching; don't have time; don't believe in God?)

23. What do you think the most important aspects of Judaism are to teach to Y.P. (Talmud? Zionism? History? Language? Art? Music? Ethics? All? Other?)

24. Talk about your favorite Jewish-school teacher. What made him/her so terrific?

25. If you were creating an ideal Jewish learning atmosphere/school, what would it be like?

26. What Jewish institutions do you make use of (synagogue, USY,

YMHA, Hebrew school, camp)? What are the problems and benefits connected with them? What is the best way to solve the problems and/or make sure that the benefits continue?

27. There are many different ways of celebrating the coming of age of a Jewish person. If you had a coming-of-age ceremony (e.g., bar/bat mitzvah), what was it like? What kind of preparations did you make? Your family? Were you happy with it? Why?

28. If you were to invent a brand-new coming-of-age ceremony, what would it be like? Would it be different for males and females? How old would a person be?

29. What do you think should be done if parents want to have a ceremony different from the one their child envisioned? Or vice versa?

30. What do you think that a coming-of-age ceremony represents to Jewish Y.P. today? To their family? To the community?

I asked several young people to fill out a questionnaire as a way of clarifying— for me and for them—some of their human, family, and Jewish values. This questionnaire was by no means statistically correct, nor did it give us an accurate sense of what all Jewish young people in this country feel about how they are educated or raised. But it did give us, and hopefully you, some idea of the scope of feelings that need to be considered in providing a satisfying, complete Jewish education and in raising children to be educated, concerned Jews and compassionate human beings.

There's no need to remind you that the kids who write here are not professionals; the advice they have to offer comes from experience and from instinct. A psychologist might tell you that their advice is very wrong (although we hope not). It is only advice: to consider, to modify for your own special situation, or just to think about and be able to realize why it's not suitable for you. In any case, we hope it is helpful, and we hope that you enjoy it.

In what follows, I am speaking to adolescents with the hope that adults will be listening. Below are some of the issues I believe we need to address:

FAMILIES

It's possible to take for granted that all young people have problems with their families. Any group of people who spend so much time together, or who have as much at stake as a family does is bound to have problems, even if they are only of the magnitude of who uses the bathroom first in the morning. Most of us, at least occasionally, have more substantial problems. It's not unusual for adolescents to begin to have problems with their families when they hit their teens. We're changing, we're seeing the world, let alone our families, in a different way, and it's bound to cause conflicts, especially because our parents are probably not sure just where we stand, for we probably aren't, either.

The specific problems we young people have may fall into far more general categories. The problem of communication is often a contributing factor to the other troubles we have with our parents. Although we know that the best way for parents and kids to work out differences constructively is through communication, communicating when you feel hostile, angry, and frustrated can be impossible.

Independence is another issue that tries relationships between parents and children. Our parents may try to hold us back because they are used to seeing us as children; now that we are young adults, they don't know which parts of us are adult enough for freedom and which parts aren't yet ready. They may hang on longer than we want them to and impose restrictive rules that we feel are unfair, but they probably do this only because they aren't used to our independent feelings.

The issue of privacy becomes important to us, one we wish parents would understand. A kid growing up in the complex and often confusing or hostile world treasures a space all to him/herself.

Interdating is a central issue to the Jewish community and to some of us as individuals as well. Most of the people who responded to the questionnaire were very opposed to interdating (which should make those who constantly predict the demise of the Jewish people through interdating feel a little better), and even those who were not as vehemently opposed were against intermarrying.

Finally, we discussed school and Jewish education.

It would probably be very hard to summarize the way young people feel about their education, since there are so many different schools with so many different teachers and so many factors that determine whether or not they get anything out of school. A math or Jewish history teacher in eighth grade may make all the difference as to whether or not we like math or Jewish history for the rest of our school career just as an innovative architect who designs our school building in a pleasing way can make us feel good when we first get to school in the morning. Similarly, our group of friends can affect the way we value school.

Basically, however, we care about being Jewish and are struggling to work out our own ideals and relationships with our families. This latter issue is one of the most important ones for us as teenagers.

The ideal Jewish parent:

is a kind, understanding person. The best parent must be a good person

has a strong Jewish identity and is proud of being a Jew. Should be able to instill this in his or her child

is active in the synagogue *along with* children. A Jewish family should stick together in being Jewish

understands why it is important to teach the traditional Jewish customs to his or her children

knows how to educate his or her children about these traditions

gives children the opportunity to learn about the Jewish religion

is consistent about the customs that are observed so as not to confuse or anger his or her children

gives children a good Jewish background

grounds family life in Judaism, but lets children make their own decisions

is fair, honest, and respectful of children

recognizes the importance of physical and emotional privacy of children

celebrates *Shabbat*

recognizes the importance of family

teaches and guides children in Judaism

lives a Jewish life she or he loves and loves sharing with children

is someone who may not exist!

CHAPTER FORTY

INTERDATING

Richard Israel

How can you definitely prevent your children from intermarrying? The answer is simple. Live in the year 1200. Short of that, there is little certainty. Shakespeare's Shylock described a fine intermarriage prevention plan: "I will buy with you, sell with you, talk with you, and walk with you . . . But I will not eat with you, drink with you, nor pray with you." Even that didn't work. His daughter ran away and married a non-Jew.

Intermarriage is one of the higher prices we pay for living in an open society. Since most of us would not want to live in the closed hostile world of the past, the only significant thing the Jewish community can do to prevent intermarriage is to create the most interesting, creative, and appealing Jewish community we can. We must compete in a pluralistic world. After that, we take our chances.

We train our children to be independent, self-directed people in ways that many other ethnic groups do not. When they are small, we let them sleep over at friends' houses. When they are older, we send them away to summer camp. When they are grown, we try to find the money to pay for their tuition at residential colleges.

We encourage them in these directions, not because we want them to break away from us, but rather because we want them to be able to cope with our very complicated world. We innoculate them with increasingly larger doses of that world so that ultimately they will have the wisdom and stamina to adapt. We think it useful to widen their horizons. But, one of the things that a wide horizon brings is a world of values that may not be shared by the home.

I have met Jewish adults who were born and raised in New York City whose Jewish homes were identical with their *yeshivah*-oriented worlds. Their entire lives had been spent within very restricted geographical locations in equally restricted neighborhoods, and within a very few institutions. The English they knew was heavily Yiddishized.

Families who raise such children are less anxious to have their children cope with the wide world than they are to have them live in the world of Torah. If their children steam-press neckties for a living but know Torah and perform *mitzvot*, then that is a sufficient, and even a noble, vision. I want more than that for my children. I want both Torah and the world. As a result, I have to take some very large risks.

One of the biggest risks I take is that my children will interdate. And I know that an exceedingly high percentage of people who interdate will intermarry. The highest rate of intermarriage belongs to those whose parents approve of interdating. Even if you don't approve of their interdating, your children may intermarry anyway—although for this category the statistics are lower. But even one child in one family is a very high percentage for that family. The only way you can be certain that there will be no intermarriage is to be certain that there will be no interdating.

Interdating is bad for the Jews. It is bad for the Jewish family. It is bad for the Jewish community. If I had my "druthers," I would prohibit it.

The fact is, however, that I will never have those "druthers." Few of us have the power to tell our adolescents what they may or may not do and make it "stick" when they are not within the confines of our home. They live in too many places that are beyond our reach. It makes no sense to prohibit things we can't enforce. A child who wants to date a non-Jew will find one. If we prohibit the relationship, we take the chance of driving it out of our sight without driving it out of existence. When that happens, we may buy a little temporary peace, but we also create a situation in which one of the most critical issues of the family can no longer be discussed at home honestly.

Alternatively, we may try to make the necessary uneasy adjustments to the present in the hope that our child's interdating is but a temporary fancy that will not result in an intermarriage.

I used to believe that if you provided your children with a good Jewish education, a warmly Jewish home, a circle of nice Jewish friends, and took them to the synagogue regularly, that nothing could go wrong. It isn't so. There are strategies, including the ones just mentioned, that will help minimize the likelihood that you will be confronted with these difficult choices. They will not, however, guarantee a thing. Here are a few:

Provide your pre-adolescent and adolescent children with as many
Jewish social settings as you can.

Send them to Jewish schools, especially day schools, and particularly
in the teenage years.

Try to live in Jewish neighborhoods.

Be sure your children have extended experiences in Israel, either as
individuals or together with your family. (But recognize that Herzl,
Weizmann, and Ben-Gurion all had children who intermarried.)

Plainly and explicitly discourage them from interdating, but be careful
not to turn interdating into the issue which they use to work out
their adolescent rebellions. You don't want to encourage them to
continue interdating someone they would be content to drop just so
you won't have the satisfaction of "winning."

Hedge your bets. Have lots of children.

If these don't work, you might consider the following:

You want your children to go to a college with a Hillel Foundation (see
College Guide for Jewish Youth, B'nai B'rith Hillel Foundations, 1640
Rhode Island Ave., Washington, DC 20036). Even if they have no
desire to affiliate, its mere presence indicates a sizable Jewish
population, and a set of available Jewish options.

Rent an anti-Semite. They work wonders in keeping a Jewish community together.

Recite Psalms. This course is recommended if your only alternative is
to wait for a miracle.

If *nothing* works:

Remember that more than one fine member of the Jewish community
has come in through conversion.

Finally, just as you have no right to take full credit for the good things
your children do or become, you should not take full blame for the
bad things. There is a point beyond which no human being can
assume responsibility for another, even in the relationship between
parent and children. You may have intended to be a superparent,
but since there are no agencies or institutions authorized to give out
superparent licenses, you have to accept yourself for what you are,
someone who tried to be the best parent you could. And ultimately
that is good enough.

KIDS SAY . . .

Morty: Think twice about interdating. Somewhere there will be just as nice a Jewish girl.

If it is more important to you to date this person than it is to them that you NOT, then be honest with yourself and with them. If the future of the Jewish people is now not as important to you as it once was, admit it to yourself. Don't say, "I'm just interdating, it's intermarriage I have to worry about." At least be able to say to yourself, and to your parents, "I am interdating. I am endangering the future of the Jewish people, but the future of the Jewish people is not as important to me as it once was. I may be a perfectly good, compassionate, secular human being, but I am taking the chance that I will no longer be a serious Jew."

If interdating is that important to you, then it is equally important that you acknowledge these things. It may be hard, but it is one way of finding out just how serious you are about your Judaism. The first-class guilt trip your parents, grandparents, and Jewish friends may send you on is better and more honest than living with self-deception and deception of others.

Stuart: Have the parents meet the non-Jew and see that this person is really no different than a Jew. Assure your parents that you don't plan to run away with this person tomorrow, and all you want to do is date. If all else fails, ask your parents if they would want to walk up to this person and tell him or her they can't date you because she or he is not Jewish. This is bound to shake up your parents, but if it doesn't, then cool it with this terrific non-Jew.

If it's only a matter of dating, and you're not going to "run away with this person tomorrow," then con-

(Continued)

ceding to your parents' wish, because it is obviously more important to them that you NOT date this person than it is that you DO, is probably a wise thing to do.

Alisa: If you do decide to interdate, it may hurt your parents a great deal. If they are committed Jews, they will probably feel that what you are doing is a rejection of their most important value in life. If you are interested in dating despite this, but not purely to spite them, there are ways to let them know.

Rona: One thing I think is very important is not to date behind the parents' back. They should know about it right from the start, right from their child.

By doing this, your parents will know that you are not simply out to spite them. You may think that it is better to take the chance of not telling them, because they probably won't find out, and what they don't know, won't hurt them, but you are wrong. If it hurts them that you are interdating, it will hurt them more if you are interdating and being sleazy about it besides.

Alisa: Birds of a feather flock together.

If your primary interest is Judaism, and most of the things you do are affected by the fact that you are Jewish, it is likely that most of your friends, your circle, and the people you date will be too. However, if your main interest is say, photography, and your life revolves around that, you are likely to run around with a lot of photographers. You will probably be running around with a lot of NICE photographers, including nice photographers of the opposite sex, with whom you have a lot in common because of your photography. Unfortunately, NICE photographers of the opposite sex are not always Jewish, and when you become interested in one it becomes very hard to become disinterested just because this photographer is not Jewish. You two have a lot in common, so why should it matter that there is one thing you don't have in common?

CHAPTER FORTY-ONE

AFTER HIGH SCHOOL

Our schools train our kids to go to college. In fact, the headmaster of Akiba Hebrew Academy in Philadelphia reported that one of the most common questions asked of him by parents considering that prestigious private day school is, "What colleges do your graduates get into?" A frequent complaint of high school students in good suburban schools is that too much of their curricula is devoted to preparing them to do well on college board tests. As one bright middle-class teenager told us, "I really *don't* feel that I have any alternatives. I just go to school."

Obviously, we hope that our children will make mature decisions and carefully work through the question What do I want to be when I grow up? We hope that, using all available information, they will stretch their imaginations to consider the consequences of their decisions. We have experienced the difficulty of such decision making, and we can trace in later life the ramifications of decisions we have made. We know that both the process and the end product of decision making rests with our children, but still we want to help. Where can we begin?

First, we have to dispel a painful myth of our culture. That myth has to do with each individual's response to the question "What do you want to be when you grow up?" What underlies that question? First, there is a belief that by finding the single, right answer, everything will be better. This belief in the power of the correct answer does not admit the possibility that for many of us not only does it take years of exploring to find a livable answer but also that the answer may change at different times in our lives. The other difficulty with the myth is the underlying belief that if we work hard enough, we can overcome all odds. Yes, we admire the Israeli-musician-victim of terrorist attack whose hand was so injured that he could not move it and who, through great personal struggle and the help of devoted medical professionals, family, friends, and Heaven, is once again playing the flute. Obviously, we deeply respect those among us who triumph over tremendous adversity. Yet such an attitude can wreak havoc with realistic career planning, with assessing a young person's strengths and weaknesses, with helping and supporting our children in choosing directions for growing and living and earning a livelihood. We want to help our children plan realistically, and that means their learning to pursue impossible dreams but also to know when to quit.

We no longer live in an age when we can assume that the son of the tailor will become a tailor. Nor do we live in a time when we can assume the reverse: that the son of the carpenter must become a doctor. So many stereotypic role functions, both male and female, are changing in our Jewish subculture. In an age characterized by economic and social instability, we must develop skills and specialties in counseling young people who do not want to go from high school to college. Jewish vocational services are beginning to be sensitive to young people who want to apprentice themselves in trades. We must legitimize career planning that excludes college as well as become flexible when a young person tells us that he or she wants to take a year off from college.

In fact, as tuition fees skyrocket, we must begin reevaluation of the role college education has played in not only our own lives but also in the life of the Jewish community. An admissions officer of a prestigious East Coast school told us recently, "Increases in percentages of Jews in the student body are no accident. Jews are among the few minority groups in this country who value college education enough to pay the price. It is also no accident that colleges and universities turn to Jews when fund raising. Jews have never lost their belief in the power of education."

When sending a child to Stanford costs more than ten thousand dollars a year and when Jewish philanthropies compete with our "alma mater" for money, we have to stand back and ask hard questions. In the end, we must admit that high percentages of our children will attend colleges and universities. It behooves us to explore whatever financially beneficial options are available to us. Friends recently told us that their child will be going to university in Israel; even including airfares for vacation visits in America it will be cheaper for them. For those of us whose children might profit from study in Israel, it is to our advantage to explore varieties of programs and ask careful questions about fees, which can vary radically.

Despite its importance, money is not the only factor that we and our children will weigh in choosing what to do after high school. Aware of the important implications for their futures of which college they choose, we have to help our children make that decision. With your concerns for their Jewish futures, you begin by asking what, Jewishly, does any particular school have to offer your child. Are there Jewish studies courses that may raise the level of your child's Hebrew school consciousness? What Jewish services are available on any given campus? Is kosher food available? How is the *Shabbat minyan*? Is it one in which your child might feel comfortable and inspired? Should your child be geographically near or far from you?

So much depends on who you and your child are and how you define your needs and goals. What are your priorities? What is most important to you and what is least important? Try making a list of ten services that you believe any good college should offer your child. Look at the list and number each item, with one being most essential and ten being least. Try making another list of ten values with which you hope your child will graduate college. Order the list. Are there college environments that seem more or less conducive to nurturing these values? Put a star beside each value that you identify as Jewish. Make a check mark beside each value that you believe might be best fostered through some Jewish campus activity. There are no easy answers.

Our best recommendations are, first, to know yourself and your child as well as you can; second, to realize that the decision ultimately rests with your child; and, third, to be as realistic as possible. Visit schools, talk to current students and recent graduates, meet Hillel staff or town rabbis. Learn as much as possible. Know that not to decide is to decide. And then do what thousands of Jewish parents have done before you: hold your breath and pray.

Carl Rogers, a great contemporary thinker-therapist, has pointed out that for learning to occur, risk and security must be in proper balance. Thus, we cannot learn if we are too threatened or frightened; neither can we learn if we are too comfortable or secure. The problem is striking the appropriate balance between challenge and safety.

Some publications that you may find useful:

FISHMAN, SAM, AND SAYPOL, JUDITH. *Jewish Studies at American Colleges and Universities.* B'nai B'rith Hillel Foundations, 1640 Rhode Island Ave., N.W., Washington, DC 20036.
General College Guides by Barrons and Lovejoy.

1938

Dear Editor,

I come to you with my family problem because I think you are the only one who can give me practical advice. I am a man in my fifties, and I came to America when I was very young. I don't have to tell you how hard life was for a "greenhorn" in those times. I suffered plenty.

(Continued)

But that didn't keep me from falling in love with a girl from my home town and marrying her.

I harnessed myself to the wagon of family life and pulled with all my strength. My wife was faithful and she gave me a hand in pulling the wagon. The years flew fast and before we looked around we were parents of four children who brightened and sweetened our lives.

The children were dear and smart and we gave them an education that was more than we could afford. They went to college, became professionals, and are well established.

Suddenly I feel as if the floor has collapsed under my feet. I don't know how to express it, but the fact that my children are well educated and have outgrown me makes me feel bad. I can't talk to them about my problems and they can't talk to me about theirs. It's as if there were a deep abyss that divides us.

People envy me my good, fine, educated children but (I am ashamed to admit it) I often think it might be better for me if they were not so well educated, but ordinary workingmen, like me. Then we would have more in common. I have no education, because my parents were poor, and in the old country they couldn't give me the opportunities that I could give my children. Here, in America, I didn't have time and my mind wasn't on learning in the early years when I had to work hard.

That is my problem. I want to hear your opinion about it. I enclose my full name and address, but please do not print it. I will sign as,

Disappointed

ANSWER:
It is truly a pleasure to have such children, and the father can really be envied. But he must not feel he has nothing in common with them any longer, because they have more education than he. There should be no chasm between father and children, and if there is, perhaps he himself created it.

In thousands of Jewish immigrant homes such educated children have grown up, and many of them remain close to their parents. Also there is no reason why the writer of this letter shouldn't be able to talk to his fine, good children about various problems, even though they are professionals and have outdistanced him in their education.

From Isaac Metzker, ed., *A Bintel Brief*. New York: Doubleday, 1971.

CHAPTER FORTY-TWO

JEWISH LIFE ON CAMPUS

Richard Levy

What is Jewish life on campus like today? Rabbi Richard Levy, West Coast Regional Hillel Director, describes campus life and explains how it got that way.

If we were to define in a phrase the dilemma of the modern Jew, we might characterize it as a struggle between the Jewish heritage of our birth (or conversion) and the Western culture of the society we inhabit. Ever since the French Revolution admitted Jews to participation in Western thought and life, all the religious and secular movements that characterize modern Judaism—from Neo-Orthodoxy to Reform to Zionism—have been trying in some form to integrate these two warring sides of our nature.

But the wars have bruised us all, as anyone involved in Jewish education for college students knows. Ours is a special variety of education for the multiply handicapped. Not only do most college students arrive on campus with precious little Hebraic or Judaic information; far worse, they arrive with misinformation, with a negativity toward the subject and their own Jewishness born of a Jewish school system which segregates the Jewish knowledge of their personal heritage from the Western knowledge of the culture they live in, and which must fight always against the Jewish ambivalence of the homes in which they are raised. Before we discuss methods of Jewish education for college students, therefore, we need first discuss the burden with which Jewish students must deal before they ever set foot inside the college Judaica classroom.

Since Jews started coming to America, we have consistently overestimated our ability to transmit to the next generation a loyalty to Jewish practice in the face of the overwhelming pressures of White Anglo-Saxon Protestant American culture. While many immigrants from Europe welcomed the opportunity America offered to become liberated from the strictures of European Jewish life, others believed that the home was a bulwark impregnable enough to preserve Jewish loyalty on its own. What the home could not provide was what the public school could: a way out of poverty. Serious Jews realized too late that the public school made Faustian bargains, offering access to America only for those who could root out their minority attachments. Roman Catholics realized their inability to compete with this process and established their own school system; it has taken the recent ethnic assertiveness of Jews and other minorities to enlighten us on a broad scale to what Roman Catholics discerned almost a century ago.

Even Jewish day school students are not spared a struggle between their Jewish and Western selves. Too often these students believe they are sufficiently self-motivated Jewishly so as not to need such external influences as Hillel, Yavneh, Zionist activities, university Jewish studies classes, etc. Sometimes students fear that in such pluralistic Jewish settings the Judaism of their upbringing will be diluted. Others merely use the above arguments as an excuse to fulfill a long-held secret yearning to take some deep draughts of non-Jewish air, and flex their muscles in a strangely invigorating non-Jewish environment. Where this motivation for uninvolvement exists, one must suspect that the student's day school (be it Orthodox, Conservative, or Reform) has not really taught integration of the Jewish and Western self, but has rather hidden the beauties of Western culture behind a curtain frayed enough to suggest that unknown glories lie in store for the Jews who immerse themselves in it completely. College offers the opportunity, and a pluralistic Jewish environment often provides the excuse.

Both kinds of students, from day schools and public schools, usually arrive on campus convinced that their Western self and their Jewish self are somehow permanently segregated, and that while in college they must make a choice between them. The majority opts for their Western self, convinced not only by their upbringing but also by the predominant culture of the university that that is the most acceptable, and the most significant, of their two heritages. They study Western history in which the history of the Jews plays a minor, if any, role; they study Western literature in which the Bible—if it is seen as a Jewish document at all—is viewed as a text laundered by Christian interpretations and translations; and if they study Christian literature, the contributions of rabbinic and Jewish philosophic writings to that corpus is not mentioned at all. And of course, if natural science is their field, Jewish views of the cosmos are hardly likely to be mentioned even once.

A number of years ago, under the influence of both the Six-Day War and the black power movement, there began to develop on campuses a growing minority of Jewish students determined that their heritage be given a respected place in their overall university education. Inspired by black students' push for black studies, a number of Jewish students realized that if black Americans had a place in Western culture, so certainly did Jews, and if Asians and Spanish-speaking students could publish newspapers and establish cultural centers on campus, Jews should be able to as well.

As a result student pressure for classes in Jewish studies mounted, and even those professors of Jewish subjects who had disdained any comparison of Jewish studies with "ethnic studies" realized that the time was ripe for an expansion in this field, and a number of them were even willing to use the ethnic argument that the number of Jewish students on the campus alone justified an increase in the Jewish courses—an argument that the university found hard to reject, since it was willing to accept it for black studies and Chicano studies.

Thus, the number of courses, minors, majors, and departments of Jewish studies around the country has grown considerably in the past decade. But the increase has not solved the problem of the Jewish-Western split. Jewish scholars, trained by Western university methods and concerned from the time of their first appointment to demonstrate that Jewish studies were a legitimate form of Western scholarship, embraced the mode of the nineteenth-century *Wissenschaft des Judentums* ("Science of Judaism") which argued that Jewish texts and Jewish history should be taught from the same "objective" stance as other courses in the humanities and social sciences. This allegiance was a very important element in the ultimate acceptance of the claim of Jewish studies to Western legitimacy in the face of claims by many general historians that there was no such thing as Jewish history, or that education in Jewish texts would be a covert form of Jewish proselytizing. The approach was important also for Jewish students—too many of whose prior Jewish education had led them to believe that Jewish studies was only a subject for juveniles—who suddenly saw that Judaica was as respectable, as demanding, as challenging as any other courses in their curriculum. Indeed, in the spring of 1970 when the country was rocked by campus strikes protesting the American incursion into Cambodia, campus after campus reported that large numbers of Jewish students stayed out of all their classes *but* the Jewish ones, convinced that while the university as a whole was an accomplice in the American system which was conducting the Vietnam war, their Jewish studies courses were helping them find an alternative solution to the American way.

But as the initial euphoria over the expansion of Jewish studies in the university curriculum began to wane, more and more students—still influenced by the late '60s doctrine of experimental, person-oriented education—began to perceive that in a religion where the study of Torah was important because it led to the doing of *mitzvot* (God-commanded acts), courses which isolated the teaching of Judaica from a concern about the doing of it was perhaps too slavish to Western modes of education to be "authentically" Jewish. In the critique of university education which pervaded the late '60s and early '70s, the argument that Jewish study should include instruction in the performance of *mitzvot* and the advocacy of various Jewish causes (e.g., the needs of Israel and Soviet Jews) fell on willing ears.

Since the ears did not for the most part belong to the professors of Judaica, alternative modes of practice-oriented Jewish study began to develop. When campus New Leftists were offering alternatives to formal university study through Free Universities, in which faculty members or students were invited to offer courses in their fields of interest to which the university departments may not have been hospitable, Hillel directors and Jewish student leaders initiated Free Jewish Universities (or Jewish Free Universities) on a similar principle: since the university will not offer courses in Jewish studies, or in Jewish practice, take advantage of the courses we offer. Under this rubric courses in Hebrew conversation, biblical or rabbinic texts, Jewish mysticism, Jewish home rituals, Jewish ethics, and Jewish perspectives on such contemporary topics as war and peace, revolution, freedom, and liberation abounded. Students embarrassed at the paucity of their Jewish knowledge compared to their growing Western knowledge, afraid to expose their ignorance in a large university-style credit course, could "bone up" on their past in the informal, nurturing setting of a Hillel director's office, a faculty member's home, a more knowledgeable fellow student's apartment or dorm lounge. While but a few years before, a Hillel director might be lucky to attract five students to a single course in a Jewish subject, he now found dozens—even scores—of students willing to enroll in a selection of as many as fifteen to twenty courses in a single semester's Free Jewish University catalog.

Some Judaica professors supported the Free University principle both as a useful corrective to the *Wissenschaft* method and as a first step in advanced Jewish study which would ultimately lead to enrollment in campus credit courses. Others felt that the informal courses merely perpetuated the sense that Jewish studies were not as serious a discipline as other university subjects, and hence undermined the development of strong programs in academic Jewish study. As more students have enrolled in academic programs in recent years, attendance at Free University classes has tended to fluctuate, and there has been a noticeable increase in classes in Jewish crafts (calligraphy, music, etc.) which could in no way be seen as a conflict with campus offerings. On the other hand, the names of the Free Universities themselves have undergone a change in recent years, indicating perhaps a rejection of both the "Free" New Left model and the Western "university" model. In keeping with the general desire for Jewish authenticity, the new names reflect such traditional Jewish institutions as Beit Midrash, Cheder, or in the spirit of Franz Rosenzweig and Martin Buber's Frankfurt experiment in adult Jewish study, Lehrhaus (itself merely a German translation of Beit Midrash).

This struggle between Academe and informality can be seen as an attempt to force Jewish students and faculty to enlist once again in the great modern struggle between Jewish tradition and Western culture. While the followers of the *Wissenschaft* mode made tremendous contributions to the critical understanding of the historical development of all forms of Jewish literature and history, they also severed the classical literature from its base in Jewish practice. Given both the thoroughly uncritical approach of the traditional *yeshivot* and the growing multiplicity of religious approaches to the classic texts since the inception of the Reform movement, the position of the heirs of *Wissenschaft* was understandable—but not irrefutable. Scientists, after all, study not only theory but experimental method, as do social scientists; and even in the humanities, courses in the practice of writing, music, and art have acquired respectable places in the curriculum of major universities in the past two decades. That the practice of the ideas contained in Jewish religious literature might be conveyed in courses clearly so labeled seems at this stage not such a terrible heresy. No one questions the right of scientists to teach the scientific method; that we ourselves still question the propriety of teaching the *halakhic* method or other variations of a Jewish religious system may reflect our suspicion that there is still more of indisputable "truth" in science than in Jewish religion.

The ban on the teaching of Jewish religious practice may fall harder on some of those who teach than on their students. As scions of the Jewish campus renascence have gradually accepted faculty posts, a growing number of them have found themselves forced to teach texts in isolation from practice in a manner that sometimes seems to violate their understanding of those texts—a manner that, one might say, violates their academic freedom. Perceiving the importance of religious insight, of the necessity of practice to inform texts written to be prayed or studied in fulfillment of a *mitzvah*, a number of them are chafing under a discipline which may well be enforced more by their Judaica colleagues than by the university itself. True, interdenominational departments of religion often hew strictly to the mode of objectivity—but often out of fear that if they teach method like their other colleagues, they will lose what recent legitimacy they have gained from a secular university.

A course in the Siddur is surely as academically respectable as a course in any other major religious corpus; but to teach merely through the historical development of the liturgy and the structure of the prayers threatens to damage a student's understanding of the nature and the purpose of the Siddur, which was compiled not to be read but to guide the mind and heart in the performance of the *mitzvah* of prayer.

Perhaps it is the notion of *mitzvah*, inherent in all traditional forms of Jewish study, that makes the teaching of the texts used in such study or prayer most susceptible to misinterpretation by the *Wissenschaft* mode. If a text reflects only the working of the human mind, one teaches in one way; if it reflects the response of a whole people to a perceived command of God, the dynamic of that response, for the transmitters and the receivers, must be confronted as well as its structure and imagery. When the Bible is studied with the aid of the traditional commentators, the student is introduced not only to a collection of ancient texts, but to the peculiar method of Jewish Bible study with the *m'forshim* as a guide. It is well attested that Jewish thought in the biblical and rabbinic periods cannot be taught in the systematic manner of Christian theology; it may be that the only Judaic disciplines which it is appropriate to teach in the *Wissenschaft* mode are those that developed under the direct tutelage of Western modes, like Jewish history, medieval and modern Jewish philosophy, and modern Hebrew or Yiddish literature.

In short, the expansion in Jewish studies in American universities is not a cause for unmixed celebration. There is a danger that in teaching our students that Judaica is not juvenile, we are still not teaching them that it is spiritually significant, that it can guide them to higher realms of feeling, experience, and insight than they now possess. The natural scientist knows that the discipline of doing science is a special art, a different art from humanities or social science. The manner in which

Jewish studies is taught has yet to convince students that the discipline of Jewish texts is different from the texts of English literature, or French literature, or sociology. To teach them that difference, we shall have to break with some Western traditions of learning, and begin to uncover the source of *mitzvah* in traditional Jewish literature, and the possibility of religious insight. The battle between Judaism and the West must be joined again in this century, by exactly those Jews who teach at what was once the pinnacle of Western culture, the university. That the university has now been revealed as a source of pluralistic cultures makes ours a fortunate time to begin the task.

ADMISSION TO GRADUATE STUDY

Your plans for study in the coming
academic year. (To find out
if the sun grew from the earth,
or if the earth grew from the moon.
Where are we going? Where are we?
Or if there is a reason people
are beginning to carry about
bones, teeth, candiru, bells and clappers,
and whatever else will help them
manage the unknown.)
List other information that will help us
to evaluate your application.
(I do breathing exercises.
I'm a vegetarian, almost,
I do not have a research project,
but I worry very much about the world,
and want to have more knowledge.
I am nauseous, also.
When I was a little kid, I used to get that
   way
before the schoolbus came.)

JOEL ROSENBERG

CHAPTER FORTY-THREE

MY SON THE SWAMI

"We lose our best and our worst sons to conversion," wrote Franz Rosenzweig, the great Jewish theologian and teacher, of his contemporaries in turn-of-the-century Germany. The people to whom he was referring, respectively, were those of his friends and relatives who converted to Christianity out of sincere conviction and those who abandoned Judaism out of expediency, to get ahead in German academic and professional life. Today, in the United States, we are not concerned that our children will convert in order to "make it" in the larger world; in some upwardly mobile segments of our fast-moving society, it is chic to be Jewish. And yet, like Rosenzweig, we have to say that Jews today find their way into other religions for the best and worst of reasons.

It is impossible to talk about young Jews involved in other religions without first considering the process by which adolescents in our society seek out their own independent identities, separate from those of their parents. Examples abound of young people who needed to define their lives differently: the son of Temple-attending Reform Jewish parents who became a Lubavitcher Hasid; the daughter of a Yiddishist family who became a Zionist and lives on a kibbutz; the son of a Jewish Communist who became a rabbi; the child of liberal Orthodox Jews who rejected *halakhah*; the *yeshivah* boy who chose to become a secular Hebrew poet.

Within each of these examples, it is easy to imagine great pain and struggle between parent and child. In each case, there is the issue of acceptance. Can the parent accept the authenticity or legitimacy of what the child is doing? At what point is the child directly rejecting the parents' life-style? To what degree is the child's choice threatening to the parent? To what degree does the parents' position threaten the child's security in his or her decisions? It is never easy. Armchair sociologists and psychologists rightly point out that children often identify with their grandparents' values, thus placing their parents in the odd position of having had similar conversations with both their parents and their children. They also remind us that children will maintain painfully, "But Mom, we are just fulfilling your very own values in our own ways." It does not help that given the average ages at which parents bear children, these adolescent searches for identity often occur at just those points when parents are struggling to deal with their own midlife crises.

Ironically, what for one parent appears to be *meshugana* rebellion may be another parent's dream come true. And yet each of the above examples were of individuals who worked out their identities within the Jewish community. Obviously, no parent wants to lose a child in the process of that child's healthy attempt to establish himself or herself as a separate person. And to be accepting of the child while being honest in reacting to what the child is "into" is no easy task. When does what the child is "into" go "beyond the fringe," far beyond the peripheries of the community?

Here we have to consider the dilemma of Jewish parental responses to other religions and make some important distinctions. Consider, for example, the wide discrepancies between conventional Christian groups; missionary and fundamentalist Christian groups; established Eastern religions; and cults. We have to distinguish between *ways* in which young Jews can pursue other religions. A serious, mature, and stable young man who, after years of search, decides to enter a Benedictine monastery is very different from a sincere but insecure young man seeking meaning and authority in his otherwise empty and confused life who finds himself attracted to Reverend Moon. A young woman who is self-consciously experimenting with ways of enriching her spiritual life through the non-belief-centered physical Yoga or Zen techniques is doing something very different from her sister in Hare Krishna, which demands commitment to a belief system.

No Jewish parent wants his or her child to leave Judaism. On the other hand, the mode of the child's involvement in another religion and the specific nature of the religion affect the ways in which a parent can respond. The issues are serious, but the differences are very real. Regardless of the nature of the young person's involvement or the particular religion, the fact that the individual's needs were not met within the

Jewish community represents a serious criticism of the Jewish community. "Alternative" magazines involved in spiritual renewal through Eastern religions in this country sometimes publish annotated directories of accessible teachers from whom a seeker can learn. Such lists are lengthy, and descriptions of teachers are impressive. A parallel list of spiritual teachers within the Jewish community would be surprisingly short. And yes, there are good reasons for that lack, having to do with secularization and the advocacy of rationalistic elements within Judaism and the cultural inaccessibility of the Hasidic community. But the dilemma for the spiritually seeking Jew remains. We must acknowledge that even in the situation of a truly unhappy person seeking security in a cult whose methods the Jewish community rejects, the fact remains that the young person is there as a result of having found no place within the Jewish community.

Other religions clearly present challenges to the Jewish community. Do they also present threats? The firmness with which a religious order in the Catholic church rejects its missionary past and goes on to enter into constructive dialogue with Jews represents a positive challenge by its very model of willingness to change and grow. Clearly and firmly, we reject any attempt on the part of any other religion to gain converts among Jews. And yet, how serious is that threat? The organizer of the much-publicized Key '73 missionary effort admitted in the *New York Times* that the attempt had been a fiasco; its best advertising came from Jewish groups that organized and publicized their opposition. The horror of Jonestown, combined with other scandals within cults, has led some Jewish communal figures to speak of the "threat of cults." Clearly, membership in a cult is not, from a Jewish point of view, desirable. Neither is passionate overreaction on the part of Jewish public spokespeople.

What are ways in which a parent can respond? The first step is to keep open, to as great an extent as possible, the channels of communication between parent and child. As long as parent and child can talk, it cannot be that bad. Rabbi Richard Israel has prepared a series of questions that a counselor might meaningfully address to a prospective cult member:

Finding the right path

You may have begun to feel that your life has not had sufficient meaning, that you want to reach toward values that are really important. If you are thinking about taking up a totally new life style, or have recently joined a new religious group, these are some questions for you to consider:

1. In the group do you find yourself without enough private time? Enough nourishment? Enough sleep?
2. Does the group make it difficult to place phone calls, receive letters, visit with old friends, or discuss your thoughts with people you trust who are not in the group?
3. Do they demand your entire life, without even small corners left belonging only to you?
4. Is the group reluctant to accept you as you are? Is it essential for you to transform yourself into a totally new person and to suppress thoughts you previously believed acceptable?
5. Does the group view all aspects of your former life as bad?
6. Is it proper to deceive people for the sake of the group?
7. Is it wrong to deviate from the teachings of the leader or the group, even in small ways? If you are to remain within the group, must you view the teacher as always right about everything? Do they make you feel guilty if you have doubts about their teachings?
8. Is the group's teacher reputed to do miracles? Are they revealed only to the initiated?
9. Are you uncomfortable with the group's attitudes to women?

10. Are the rules for the group's leaders different from the rules for its followers?

Breaking with your past in some significant ways could mean a healthy change for the better. Joining a new group may help, and all groups try to impose some values on their members. But if you answer yes to more than a few of these questions, you should think hard about what you are doing. You should be particularly careful if you became interested when you were lonely, depressed, or detached from your family. You may be losing control of yourself to people who have *their* interest in mind more than yours. Though Truth may be absolute, our knowledge of it seldom is. Those who claim to have it all should be suspected.

It is right to try to make yourself into a better person. You may be far from perfect, but you aren't all bad either. Neither are your friends, family, or former values, even if you now feel that you need some distance from them.

As you continue your new explorations, try not to dig yourself into a deeper hole than you can climb out of. Don't irrevocably sever relationships that you may one day want to restore.

For additional copies of this questionnaire (B'nai B'rith Hillel Foundations, 1640 Rhode Island Ave., N.W., Washington, DC 20036.)

The questions provide some helpful insights into what a young person might be "getting into." On the other hand, a parent must use such questions with subtlety and sensitivity in dialogue with a child, lest the already vulnerable child feel threatened or judged or attacked by the parent—feelings that only further impede discussion.

Furthermore, as former cult members recount their sojourns, we sometimes see them as naive young people who were the victims of "brain washing" or "mind control." This leads us to want to warn our children and makes us see as a plausible response creating courses in Jewish high schools which will equip them to be more sophisticated in their reactions to airport solicitations.

There is a temptation to present a prescription or formula for "good Jewish living" and recommend it as a kind of vaccination against future involvement in non-Jewish religions. We might suggest that a good Jewish education when the child is young *might* help to immunize the child against attraction to other religions when the child grows older. Yet the problem is more thoroughgoing. No matter how sincerely we may struggle to do the "right thing" Jewishly for our children, no matter how open we are to sharing their explorations, no matter how empathetically we let them know where we stand, we cannot control all aspects of their lives. Nothing guarantees that children will not become involved in other religions. As we have said elsewhere in this volume, we live as American Jews in at least two cultures. A single Jew's involvement in another religion represents grave difficulties not only for the individual but also for the whole network of the individual's family.

Clearly, we support all informal and formal efforts to help not only the individual but the entire family deal with these issues. We must also think of the dimensions of the problem that go beyond the individuals. Obviously, we oppose any attempt to convert us, yet we are challenged to rethink traditional Jewish attitudes toward other religions and the *goyim*. We raise questions here not in order to suggest answers but to encourage communal discussion.

How do we understand other religions? Are they all bad? Can we learn religiously or spiritually from a non-Jew? At what point must we draw back and go no further? Can we not only learn from other religious traditions but also teach and share our wisdom? Such questions deserve careful discussion in our community and have wide-ranging implications that go far beyond our individual children.

As parents, we want to be able to say there is a point at which we are not responsible for the actions of our children, whom we love but who are, in fact, separate and independent from us. As Jews, we must acknowledge that we are all responsible for one another. And in fulfilling that responsibility, we must exercise great care not only for individuals who are attracted to other religions but for our whole community as we interact with other religions in twentieth-century America.

To help you learn more about cults in America, Michael Masch of Philadelphia has compiled the following helpful list.

BOOKS

BOETTCHER, ROBERT. *Gifts of Deceit*. (New York: Holt, Rinehart & Winston, 1980). Boettcher was staff counsel to the Fraser subcommittee on Korean-American relations and reveals here what the committee learned about Sun Myung Moon and the Unification Church.

CONWAY, FLO, AND SIEGELMAN, JIM. *Snapping: America's Epidemic of Sudden Personality Change*. (New York: Lippincott, 1978). Explains how and why the indoctrination methods of the cults and pseudo-therapies work and what their dangers are to those who are subjected to them.

EDWARDS, CHRIS. *Crazy for God: The Nightmare of Cult Life*. (Englewood Cliffs: Prentice-Hall, 1979).

RUDIN, A. JAMES, AND RUDIN, MARCIA. *Prison or Paradise? The New Religious Cults*. (Cleveland: Collins, 1980). The latest and one of the best overall surveys of the rise of the cults and what the rest of us need to know about—and do about it.

SPECIAL COMMITTEE ON EXOTIC CULTS. *The Challenge of the Cults*. 1979 (2nd ed.). An examination of the cult phenomenon in general, and its implications for the Jewish community in particular. Available for $2.50 from the Jewish Community Relations Council of Greater Philadelphia, 260 S. 15th St., Philadelphia, PA 19102.

UNDERWOOD, BARBARA. *Hostage to Heaven*. (New York: Potter, 1979). Two readable and revealing inside accounts of life inside the Unification Church by former members.

NEWSLETTERS

Two excellent publications sponsored by anti-cult citizens' groups on the East and West Coasts are reprinting published information on cults in digest form. They are:

The Advisor. Journal of the American Family Foundation. P.O. Box 343, Lexington, MA. 02173.

Information Service News. Citizens Freedom Foundation, Box 7000-89, 1719 Via El Prado, Redondo Beach, CA. 90277.

A father and his son, traveling together in a wagon,
  came to the edge of a forest.
Some bushes, thick with berries,
  caught the child's eye.
"Father," he asked, "may we stop awhile
  so that I can pick some berries?"
The father was anxious to complete his journey,
  but he did not have it in his heart
  to refuse the boy's request.
The wagon was called to a halt,
  and the son alighted to pick the berries.

After a while,
  the father wanted to continue on his way.
But his son had become so engrossed in
  berry-picking
  that he could not bring himself
  to leave the forest.
"Son!" cried the father, "We cannot stay here all day!
  We must continue our journey!"

Even his father's pleas were not enough
  to lure the boy away.
What could the father do?
Surely he loved his son no less
  for acting so childishly.
He would not think of leaving him behind—
  but he really did have to get going
  on his journey.

Finally he called out:
  "You may pick your berries for a while longer,
  but be sure that you are still able to find me,
  for I shall start moving slowly along the road.
As you work, call out 'Father! Father!'
  every few minutes, and I shall answer you.
As long as you can hear my voice,
  know that I am still nearby.
But as soon as you can no longer hear my answer,
  know that you are lost,
  and run with all your strength to find me!"

TRANSLATED BY ARTHUR GREEN AND BARRY HOLTZ

PART SIX
GROWING

CHAPTER FORTY-FOUR

THE EMPTY NEST

"Abraham grew old, and God blessed him in all ways." In these simple words we sense great dignity and serenity. The rabbis, however, took our peaceful biblical image of Abraham and gave it a twist. They looked at the Hebrew words "in all ways" and discerned a pun or hidden double meaning. Because of the ambiguities of the Hebrew language, it is possible to read the passage not as "and God blessed him in all ways" but as "and God blessed him with a daughter." Our image of Abraham's later years is turned on its head. Rather than by a quiet retirement, Abraham was comforted in his old age by the gift of a "love child" whose energy must have stood in sharp contrast to her father's.

Just as we see two divergent images of Abraham, we may also hold different visions of ourselves and our future lives as we grow older. We have worked and dreamed of the moment when our children will be truly independent adults, able to make their own decisions and mold their own lives. Now they are gone, and the house is suddenly very quiet; we are alone. Mixed with the *nakhas* (pride and joy) of our children's achievements is the very real sadness of being alone. We realize, for example, that our children will never need us as they once did. We try to remind ourselves that we would not like to be needed as parents of infants are, that our children's growing independence has prepared us for this time, that they will continue to need us in new ways. It's all true, we admit, yet we feel a tinge of nostalgic sadness and anxiety about what is coming next. We experience a sense of loss that our children will never again live with us as our children. How will we handle their future visits home? We do not want to admit that we feel some sense of rejection at not being included in all the small ways of our children's daily lives. And the specter of old age hangs over us. What will become of us then? Who will care for us? How will our children relate to us?

Each of us responds differently to the "empty nest syndrome." And we may be confronted with these issues at different points in our lives. Many of our parents, who bore children when they were in their early twenties, were challenged to respond to their newly private home lives when they were really quite young themselves, perhaps in their forties or fifties. Our generation, which is tending to wait longer to have children, will have to deal with our new-found "childlessness" when we are older, probably minimally in our sixties. This fact raises questions about what other life decisions and demands will coincide with our children's departures to college or to establish lives of their own. Will we, for example, be in the process of retiring from a business or a profession when our children graduate from college? Or will it be more likely that as we reach "retirement age," we will just be coming to grips with additional financial burdens incurred by our children's entry into graduate or medical schools? Will some of us be, in fact, nurturing the children of second marriages when our friends are beginning to "rest on their laurels"?

A grandmother who at age seventy-five took on the responsibility of raising her granddaughter after the child's parents' deaths used to say, "Who knows what life brings?" She was right. We remember the English version of a classic Yiddish proverb: "A person proposes, and God disposes" (or "A person plans, and God laughs"). Yet it makes sense to begin to ask questions about our hopes and dreams and fears of this new life stage. Some of us dream of travel unencumbered by children, of renewed intimacies with our spouses, of retirement to resort communities where we can golf, play tennis, and swim. Others dream of the moment when we can stop working in order to begin serious hard work: writing a novel, or researching the biography of a fifteenth-century kabbalist no one else ever heard of. Our fears, however, are also real. What if we do not have a dream around which to organize our lives? What happens when children are no longer present to defuse the intensity between parents? What happens when we discover that the problems we swept under the rug for thirty-five years have emerged now that the rug is gone? We dream of returning to the first years of our marriage only to discover that both partners in the marriage have grown and changed. "When we were first married, we were in college. It was the Depression, and we had no money, and I would dream of eating a good steak. Today, money is no object, but with my dentures and my ulcer, I really wouldn't enjoy that steak very much," reports a friend, a retired ophthalmologist.

"Just because someone is old does not mean that we have the right to deprive that person of the possibility of growth, even if that growth has to happen through conflict," advises Reuven Gold, a contemporary Jewish thinker. Sometimes growing is easy and natural, sometimes painful and frightening.

Some parents wonder after adult children have moved away from home, "What do we do with their remaining possessions?" Scenarios vary, from parents who create virtual shrines in their absent children's room to parents who yearn to call Goodwill or the Salvation Army. These latter parents often find themselves awkwardly trying to convince their children to come and take what they want. They speak of their annoyance at their children's slowness in disposing of belongings. Whichever extreme we are inclined to, it is important to try to be as self-aware as possible in dealing with the issue. Our difficulty with our children's remaining trunk or stuffed closet may, in fact, be a mask for other feelings that are not being confronted. Are we simply angry that the child has left and then using our frustration over the closet as a way of expressing anger? By calling Goodwill, are we striking back at the

child for leaving us? Is calling the Salvation Army the best way of dealing with our feelings? By maintaining the room as it was when the child occupied it, are we nurturing unrealistic fantasies about the child's eventual return? Are we holding on to something that is simply no longer there? For how long will we need to hold on, to mourn the loss? What will help us move on?

Some of these thoughts and feelings have to be worked through within ourselves. Often it helps to talk about these kinds of issues with our friends or peers who have experienced similar problems. Sometimes it can help to talk with professionals: rabbis, psychologists, social workers. When we have a sense of where to begin, we can then discuss the problems with our children. It is much better to tell a child that you want him to remove his skis before next summer than to resent him every time you fall over them in the garage.

Another locus of difficulty has to do with our needs and dreams of children coming back for visits. We have to evaluate whether the dream that one day the entire family will again live together has any basis in reality. Let us look at the pattern of our children's visits home. Do they seem to make only brief visits? Are the visits pleasant for all concerned? Do we have a small feeling of resentment that even though our children no longer live with us, they still feel free to drop in for a visit? Some friends report that they have concluded that one week is the maximum and ideal amount of time for adult children and parents to live in close proximity.

Surely we have some rights in talking with children about our needs, desires, and conveniences. In fact, blunt conversations as preparation for a visit can help avoid later misunderstandings. On the other hand, we remember visiting elderly relatives who, upon seeing us, would greet us with "So why haven't you come to see me more often? Where have you been? When are you coming back?" We learn from such experiences of people whose tremendous needs interfered with their good sense that nobody wants to visit someone who does not take pleasure in being visited. Who wants to keep coming back to be harangued about not having visited sooner? We must remember to ask ourselves and our children, "How is what I am doing or saying making others feel?"

Some older parents speak of walking a tightrope between honesty and risk, and manipulation and self-deception. One classic example of the latter is the vacation invitation. From our children's earliest years, we indulged in bribes. Before drug companies invented children's aspirin, we used to crumble bits of aspirin in jelly or jam to sweeten it for a sick child. Another sweetening found among affluent parents is the invitation to children to join us at the beach house or the ski lodge. Sometimes children who will not spend two days with us in the city will spend two weeks or even two months with us in the country. For some of us, the strategy, quite simply, works. To varying degrees others of us feel demeaned by a sense of bribery. All of us must keep in mind that problems in parent-child communication that exist in the city do not necessarily go away in the country. By spending a summer together we must not be legitimizing an unrealistic fantasy of "how well we all get along together."

Whether a visit is for an hour or a month, with each return home we must work with our children at evolving increasingly mature ways of interaction, for we simply cannot revert to old patterns. And we must confront our sometimes thwarted feelings of need and love for our children.

It is not easy. Many feel that as we grow into new life stages, we take our old personalities with us. Even though we are now over sixty-five does not mean that we will miraculously begin to speak Yiddish! By the same token, family members who related well to one another do not necessarily stop relating well because their living arrangements change. But as we grow older, we encounter new stresses. What once seemed trivial may now take on importance. Interests and hobbies that have been with us all along, perhaps lying dormant because there was no time to pursue them, may now become essential. Just as the benefit of a hobby to children goes beyond the hobby itself, so, too, we can be helped by old or new-found interests. Even crossword-puzzle solving can give us a reason to get out of bed in the morning—if only to bring in the newspaper. Walking a dog can drag the most reluctant exerciser out of the house. Some of us have found that devotion to a morning *minyan* can provide social, physical, and psychological rewards far beyond the religious nature of the activity. New Jewish activities sometimes help build bridges to other family members. We know of several older people who, for the sake of their families, have wrriten their memoirs or have compiled autobiographical statements about their childhoods. (See, for example, the tremendous importance to his granddaughter of the grandfather's memoirs in *The Journey of David Toback* as retold by Carole Malkin [New York: Schocken Books, 1981].) Reluctant writers are sometimes helped by telling family stories into tape recorders. Others have found that being interviewed by a child or grandchild with a tape recorder is useful. Not only can the process be therapeutic, the end product can be of great importance to the family. And the process itself can serve to foster increased and meaningful contact among family members. Creating a family tree or accurately labeling as many pictures as possible in the family album are both time-consuming and important tasks. Carefully planning and visiting our childhood homes with our spouses, children, or grandchildren can prove rewarding. Such visits might be to anywhere from a large city in the Ukraine to a small town in Kansas. Don't dismiss the American Jewish experience as a less fertile source of stories and heritage than its European counterpart. The John and Elaine Frank family of Philadelphia preserves home movies that John's parents took on a visit to eastern European relatives in the 1930s. Beyond the record of the actual visit, the movies are of historical interest and provide a present generation of Frank children with a visual link to their past.

Never rule out the possibility of volunteer work. Of special interest in the Jewish community are the newly developing programs of foster grandparenting. The idea of serving as a substitute grandparent in our highly transient society suggests rewards not only for grandparents and children but for the entire Jewish community. Jewish Y's and centers regularly design wide-ranging recreational and service programs for senior citizens. What about those of us who do not feel that we can comfortably fit into an established program? Our only recourse is to innovate.

Where could we begin? One approach is to consider our skills. Perhaps we are retired accountants or teachers or cooks. Who might profit best from our years of experience? Let's consider the example of retired engineers, who are sometimes reemployed as housing evaluators in national organizations that, for a fee, check out residential real estate that individuals are considering buying. Or remember retired business executives who are organized to consult with young people just starting small businesses. What can we learn from these examples? Under what circumstances could we become nonprofit consultants? Where can a great cook go? To Jewish schools and classroom teachers who want to help their children experience *hallah* baking. We have the free time that the children's parents lack.

Innovation probably demands more of us than fitting ourselves into existing programs. Innovation requires that we have the strength to make phone calls even though we feel embarrassed and dread negative responses from the voice on the other end of the telephone. Whether we are doing something different or not, we have to keep reaching out, making contact with other people, growing through our exposure to others. We remember that Chinese proverb: "A journey of a thousand miles begins with the first step." Just as we helped our children take their first steps, we must now push ourselves to take steps to grow in our new lives. It is never easy. We recall a passage from our Yom Kippur liturgy: "Do not cast us out in our old age." The Ba'al Shem Tov, the founder of Hasidism, interpreted the passage as saying, "Do not condemn us to days that are old but rather help us to make each day new."

From a wise friend in Los Angeles who wishes to remain anonymous:

It can be easier to love your children than your spouse. Especially when children are young, loving them can be much less complicated than loving your spouse. But remember that children grow up and need to develop independent existences. You need to love and be loved. When your children move away from home, your spouse will still be there. Do not invest in one relationship at the expense of another even though at the time it is the course of least resistance.

Some couples find their *ketubah* (marriage contract) can be a useful symbol for helping them to maintain perspective. They create for themselves time for renegotiating the terms of their *ketubah*. This ritual of renewal can be especially valuable when the last child leaves the nest and the couple returns to the original childless state.

Don't be satisfied to dance the *masinka* dance (the dance that some people do in honor of the parents at their last child's wedding). Consider designing a *ketubah* for yourselves when your child gets married. It would be interesting to compare your essential terms in the contract with what your child and his or her spouse would think important.

CHAPTER FORTY-FIVE

ON BECOMING A GRANDPARENT

Max Ticktin, an Anonymous *Bubbe*, and Sidney Greenberg

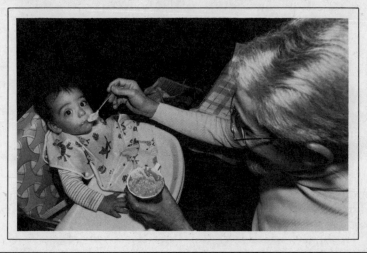

What it is like to become a grandparent? Some grandparents shared with us their thoughts and feelings.

In The Beginning

My wife and I have just concluded our first Hanukah at which Benjamin Elazar, our first grandchild, was with us for the candle lighting and celebration.

Though I am only a first-time grandfather, it seems like an appropriate time, especially in conjunction with a holiday observance, to reflect on grandparenthood.

What joy and happiness! What *nakhas! Derlebt*—blessed to be alive and to enjoy the "interest in the investment" and to be able to look into the future with and through our grandson!

It's a special opening to the future, this grandparenthood. The Hebrew language I so love and that I hope he will love, too, has a single word for the day just beyond the horizon of yesterday and, no less significantly, a single word for the mysterious day after tomorrow, the day that is almost contiguous with my today. That day is an extension of

the tomorrow that I am able to project myself into. So, too, Benjamin has issued from his mother, my daughter. My attachment to him is truly in the realm of the mysterious spirit. The world of the intangible but real spirit has, for me, issued from the world of natural order and creation.

To become a grandfather is to become aware of the possibilities of hoping for and peering into the intangible but real future, the future that, with God's blessing, is his—beyond my death.

And thus, this *zeide* does begin to feel a kinship for "Yisrael Saba," the venerable patriarch Jacob, but also that tradition-laden term for the enduring and eternal Jewish people. Oh, that I may live to have the *nakhas* to see Benjamin learn and grow in the Jewish tradition I have acquired from my grandfathers and grandmothers. Oh, that I may be blessed to see our daughter living the loves and loyalties with her husband and son that she saw in the vibrant Jewishness of her grandparents.

There is something unique in the "Zeide's Berakha" not so different from the tone of the sentimental Yiddish ballad with that name. It's a blessing that comes with the renewed strength and faith in life's possibilities that are part of becoming a grandfather. I have seen this new vigor in the face of Rembrandt's Jacob as he is blessing his grandsons; indeed, the painter succeeds in his interpretation by the expressions on the faces of Joseph and his wife in that same painting. Giving the blessing bestows power on the grandfather as well as on the recipients. Experience and understanding are transferred with the blessing, and, in expressing this wisdom and hope, the grandfather is himself reinvigorated and vindicated.

Becoming a grandfather is for me, then, a new vindication of the continuity of the Jewish people and the Jewish tradition. And I have waited for the day, fully aware that, in our day, for most of us, we will become grandparents some ten or fifteen years later in life than was the case a generation ago. Esther and I are also aware of the special blessing, unusual in our day, of having Benjamin and his parents living in the same community as we do. For now, at least, it's not a long-distance telephonic grandparenthood—God be thanked for that, too.

I am ready to learn a new kind of play, one I really need to know, ready to crawl on the floor with my grandson and be the foolish grandfather, as the *midrash* puts it, returning in part to my own childhood innocence.

But I am also ready for the day—may it be soon—when I can dandle him on my lap and in front of the Hanukah *menorah*, the day when I will be able to sing to him, "Oh, you little candles, you tell us tales; without number are the stories. You tell us of the brave, our people they did save, You speak of our past glories."

MAX TICKTIN

Simply Stated

Once I was really sick in the hospital and I prayed, "Please God, just let me live to dance at my daughter's wedding." Well, I recovered; and let me tell you something, a wedding is a wedding, but there is no joy like the joy of seeing your daughter hold your newborn grandchild. I closed my eyes and I could see my little girl holding a doll, and I blinked and opened my eyes and there was this real live baby. And I thanked God for letting me live to see it.

ANONYMOUS BUBBE

A Grandfather Remembers

I had slept fitfully. Periodically, like every fifteen minutes, I checked the luminous dial to see if it was time to get up. Of course I had set the alarm but who can trust a mechanical contraption when a crucial appointment has to be met punctually on the morrow? It was to be one of the biggest assignments I had carried in a long time. I was going to drive Elisha and two of his nursery school classmates to Solomon Schechter. Elisha is special at Solomon Schechter. He is the first student who is a child of a Schechter graduate. With him, Solomon Schechter begins educating a second generation of Jewish youngsters to know and love their heritage. Being Elisha's driver would be no small honor.

After several hours of "wait-watching"—waiting and watching—I finally decided it wasn't worth the struggle and got up. There was enough time to perform all my exercises, physical and spiritual, at a leisurely pace and still ring the door bell of the first five-year-old passenger at 7:30 A.M.

"Who are you?" a mother shouted at me through the window pane of the door she kept suspiciously bolted.

"I'm Elisha's grandfather," I shouted back. "I'm the car pool driver today." Jeremy Schneider whimpered reluctantly, and finally agreed to go with the stranger only when I promised him a special surprise in the car, a surprise that he would be the first to see. I kept my promise to

Jeremy. I showed him an *etrog* that we had kept from the previous year. It had shrunk to one-fifth its size, its skin was wrinkled and shriveled, its color had turned from golden yellow to mournful brown. Jeremy admitted he had never in his "whole life" seen such an *etrog*.

As we moved along toward Elisha's house, I learned a lot about Jeremy. He would rather stay home. He loved his toys. He enjoyed playing with his younger sister, but he also enjoyed playing by himself. "I like myself," he explained matter-of-factly. I could not suppress the silent prayer that he would go through life liking himself. "You're lucky," I said to Jeremy. "It's important to like yourself because wherever you go, you are going to take yourself along with you." "I know," said Jeremy, sounding much older than his years.

Elisha's door was open, announcing to the driver that his arrival was not unexpected. He greeted me with a casual wave of the hand. I tried very hard to be equally casual as though I had been doing this every morning for twelve consecutive years. I tried not to betray the excitement of doing for Elisha for the first time what I had done for his mother not so many years ago. A last-minute check of his lunch bag, a reminder to take along the birthday present for a classmate, a soft hug and kiss from his mother and the second passenger was tucked into the back of the car.

Susie Spodek was the third stop. She was quite surprised to find me at her door so early in the morning. When I told her that I was the driver of the day, a smile broke on her beautiful face and joyously she joined the men in the back of the car. Susie had a lot to tell us about life in India. She had been born there and spent the last two years there. The only problem that Susie could find with India was that there were a lot of kids who didn't speak English, but otherwise it was really nice and friendly and there was even a synagogue there.

The subject quickly changed to little sisters and wonderful to relate, all three passengers had one and were all rather proud of their younger siblings. They took turns in boasting of their sisters' most recent accomplishments.

A little probing revealed that they each knew "*Oseh Shalom*" and the singing of it occupied the rest of the trip. We were in the middle of the fourteenth round when we pulled into the school driveway. I released my passengers and they were quickly swallowed up by their classmates. Elisha never turned around. It was just as well. He wouldn't understand why his grandfather was crying.

SIDNEY GREENBERG

CHAPTER FORTY-SIX

MEETING OUR PARENTS IN NEW WAYS

(In Memory of Ruth Nulman, Z"l)

Some of us have approached our own middle age before we have resolved the complexities of our relationships to our parents. Part of us remembers the pain, the parents' hostility, the nonacceptance of who we were, and this remembering can color our reflexes later. Childhood is a time when children grow from emotional dependence to emotional self-sufficiency, and now, before our parents become increasingly dependent on us, we, as independent middle-aged adults, must work through (preferably *with* our parents) the problems that continue to trouble us in that relationship.

There is a strong predilection in all of us, and a dangerous one, to stop struggling with our relationship to our parents once we have moved out of their home. We may say, "Oh, the hell with it! I see them three or four times a year; I can live with their *mishugas*," or worse yet, we pat ourselves on the back for our tolerance, saying: "OK, so my mother has a need to denigrate my career choice. *I'm* not threatened by that. I don't need her approval anymore. It's *her* problem, and she has to work on it." The truth is, our relationship to our parents is *our* problem. On the one hand, most of us have profound love for our parents and know that they reciprocate that love for us. On the other hand, our relationship to our parents was, is, and will always be the primal relationship for us. There is probably no other relationship that will affect us more deeply.

However, adolescence, as it has developed in our society, leaves us tremendously distanced from our parents. Frequently, except in ways that are extremely superficial, that distance is not bridged until old age, when our attempts to reach out are colored by our parents' new dependency (both physical and emotional) on us and our unresolved problems with them. We would argue for the assumption of a new responsibility—the responsibility at every stage in our lives to be thinking about, working through, and trying to understand and reinterpret that relationship. We want to treat our parents seriously enough so that we invest in our relationship with them. And that investment calls for spending some of our self-analytical reserves on our ongoing relationship with them. Now that we all have some distance from it, do we understand a little better why the fact that both our parents worked full time left us feeling lonely and abandoned for much of our childhood? And do we understand why our mothers *had* to work? Or do they understand how incredibly jarring it was to us when Aunt Anna moved into our home for a year? Or do we understand how betrayed they felt when we chose to go to an out-of-state university?

Why is it valuable to "drag all this old business" out of the closet? Certainly because no matter how hard we try to close the door, the contents will always ooze out through the cracks. Although we can't change these contents, we might be able to understand a little better why we put those things in the closet in the first place.

Yes, our parents may be too old to change. Yes, *we* may be too old to change. Who knows? What we're looking for, though, is understanding rather than change. Sometimes, with greater understanding comes greater peace.

The process never ends. There is always a deeper level, a new, unexplored path. We may discover that at last we accept who our parents are and why we are the way we are. There will still be new things to work out, but we will finally have made some peace with our past. Then it is finally possible to say, "I ask forgiveness from you for the pain I have created in your lives. In turn, I offer you forgiveness, with a full heart, for the pain that you caused me." Speedily, and in our days.

The sages taught: "Seek peace in your own place." Rabbi Bunam added: "You cannot find peace anywhere but in your own self."

CHAPTER FORTY-SEVEN

DEALING WITH ELDERLY PARENTS—NURSING HOMES

"I will never be a grownup, not until I wear bright-red lipstick, roll my hair up in a pompadour, and put on silk stockings. Also to be a grownup, I would have to speak Hungarian." Clearly, the hidden grownup here is not of our generation, the "real" grownup is someone of the speaker's childhood in the late 1940s, someone perhaps not unlike her own mother.

How do we become grownups? Perhaps it happens when we take responsibility for grown-up decisions. Perhaps it happens when we have children and realize that our children are perceiving us as their "real" grownups as they totter around in our high heels and neckties. But what happens when our own grownups, namely our parents, need us in ways in which we used to need them? As adolescents, we wanted nothing more than for our parents to treat us as adults. (See Chapter Thirty-six.) Yet, for many of us, there comes a painful point when we realize that we must fulfill a parenting role for our now-aged parents. Some of us have witnessed the truth of the statement "The child is father of the man" as we have watched that amazing process of aging in

which an old person's physical needs become increasingly like those of an infant. The problems that families and individuals face in such situations are legion. We learn over and over again that difficulties in individual interactions between family members—difficulties that were there when the people were young—do not go away but are often exacerbated as people grow old. (An octogenarian friend commented to us about a contemporary of his: "She was nasty when she was young, and now that she is old, she is still nasty.")

> A man came to the Kotzker *rebbe* to complain of his sons who refused to support him even though he was old and could no longer earn his own livelihood. "I was always ready to do anything I could for them," he said. "And now they won't have anything to do with me!"
>
> In silence, the *rebbe* raised his eyes to heaven. "That is how it is," he said sadly. "The father shares in the sorrows of his sons, but the sons do not share in the sorrows of their father."

Anyone who loves an old person tells us it isn't always easy to deal with the demands of the situation. It is especially hard to keep straight and separate our needs from those of our parents. An elderly parent may be someone whose immediate need of us is purely emotional and not at all physical. Such a person is capable of maintaining an individual and independent life-style. The other extreme is represented by the parent who is now a patient needing full-time medical and nursing care. Between these extremes is room for a variety of children's responses.

Perhaps the most basic decision along the way has to do with sending a parent to some manner of public-care facility (old-age home, nursing home, etc.) or trying to care for the person at home. What should we do? To begin with, we have to do the obvious: assess the situation and consider the consequences. We can recall horror stories either way. We know of situations in which the martyrdom of home care was really only of neurotic benefit to the care giver, where the parent might have been better off in an institution. We also know horror stories about poor care and debilitating costs of nursing homes. A great deal depends on who each of us is, what we can do, and what resources are available to us.

> After Reb Moshe's death, a friend said of him: "If there had been someone to whom he could have talked, he would still be alive."

This is a time in which the adult child needs support—from friends, family members, others in similar situations, and from professionals who understand the options. So much seems to hinge not only on our immediate responses but also on our underlying attitudes toward aging and death and separation because in seeing someone who is very old, we must see that one day we will be separated from that person. In seeing someone old, we are reminded of our own mortality.

Are there uniquely Jewish responses to problems of aging? Perhaps the most basic responses have to do with *kibud av v'aym* (giving respect to one's parents). We find in the Talmud numerous examples of great effort that adult children have gone to in caring for their elderly parents. For example, Rabbi Tarfon is seen as a model of devotion in that he would make himself into a human ladder to help his old mother crawl into bed. According to Jewish law (Kid. 31b-32a and Shulhan Arukh, Yoreh Deah 240:5), a child is obligated to respond to his or her parents' physical needs. In other words, a child must help an indigent parent, supplying him or her with food, drink, clothing, blankets, and other help. The *halakhah* is even so demanding as to insist that we give to the indigent parent with generosity of spirit, not grudgingly. These Jewish sources are concerned with the limits of appropriate behavior for situations all of us hope to avoid. They tell us that we should behave with decency and respect and that we should try to maximize the humane and respectful manner in which our parents are treated.

Sometimes communities have successfully united to relate well to their older members. The Worcester Jewish community has supported and maintained a residential facility for the elderly that seeks to combine involvement on the part of adult children and professional staff. A non-Jewish community in Maine is conducting a wonderful experiment: it has asked its residential home for the elderly to conduct a day nursery for young children, thus providing children with surrogate grandparents.

In Boston, Massachusetts, a feasibility-study commission is exploring ways in which groups of people, teams of professionals and volunteers, can support families in which one family member has chosen to die at home. Work is thus under way to create a Jewish hospice. Possibilities for community support systems for the elderly go beyond Meals-on-Wheels and are only limited by the boundaries of our own imaginations and ingenuity. The challenge will not decrease with time. A generation ago, in more traditional societies, we thought that extended families contained structures that facilitated their coping with elderly family members. Today, we have to wonder if extended families are a thing of the past. Who of a surrogate extended family would be willing to sacrifice personally to care for an elderly individual? Will families, in general, continue to be so mobile geographically? How are we affected by escalating oil prices? Remember listening to Jack Benny on the car radio Sunday night while riding home from visiting grandma? Our children will not recall such car rides, especially if their grandparents live in Florida, Arizona, and California. And what will happen when inevitably those Florida grandparents become infirm? Will they move North? The post-

A story (paraphrased) from Ms. Deborah Shain, director of Family Life Education at Jewish Family Service of Philadelphia:

As a social worker, I visited a home in which the aged mother was being cared for by a middle-aged daughter. The mother was very frail; she lived in a hospital bed that had been set up in the living room to maximize her contact with the family and to make her care easier. The daughter and I were chatting in the living room, and the daughter explained to me that she felt as though she had become a mother to her mother, who had become infant-like in her patterns of sleeping and eating. As we talked, the mother made a faint hand motion, and the daughter got up and gave her a bedpan. After a few moments, as the daughter removed the used bedpan, the mother said in a barely audible voice, "Remember to wash your hands, dear." And the daughter replied, "Yes, Mother."

World War II baby boom has ended. That means that in about forty years from now, a disproportionate fraction of the population will be over seventy. We will increasingly have to confront the needs of a growing elderly population. And we will have to be very clear with ourselves that the decisions we make on their behalf are well-thought-out, sensitive ones.

CHOOSING A CARE FACILITY

If a nursing home, convalescent home, retirement village, or home for the aged becomes a serious option for you, then you will have to weigh options carefully and become something of a detective. We realize that in the aforementioned list different services are offered in each of the named care facilities.

For example, retirement villages sometimes offer private, structured housekeeping units in which an elderly couple can maintain a semblance of home and household while receiving such services as nurses who visit with medication and cafeterias that cook nourishing meals. Another variation of the retirement village is the cluster of plush condominiums that limit sale of apartments to those over fifty. There are nursing homes that limit care to short-term stays. Others accept patients for the rest of their lives. Quality of care can vary radically. Some homes are private money-making institutions. In general, we feel more comfortable with the "public" facilities that are Jewish communal projects. You will have to listen carefully and evaluate the recommendations you receive from gerontologists and health-care professionals. If appropriate, you may want also to investigate rehabilitative programs. For example, Long Island Jewish Hospital has been studying senility and ways of dealing with it as a medical-psychiatric problem; researchers in this area refuse to accept the commonly offered explanation that senility is "where a patient is and will continue forever to be" but try to experiment with ways of dealing with the devastating symptoms.

By better understanding medical assessments of your parent's condition, you become a more realistic investigator when looking for a good care facility. Here are some ways of gaining information as you embark upon your search. Obviously, you will want to visit the home. In fact, you will try to visit the facility more than once, verifying what you first perceived and compensating for misperception engendered by an especially bad or good day. Watch carefully how staff treat patients. Get a sense of whether your parent will fit in socially; a person who knows no Yiddish will not necessarily be comfortable in an exclusively Yiddish-speaking environment. By the same token, a person who has forgotten how to speak English will not be happy if no member of the staff can communicate in the language he or she speaks.

You are concerned not only with the physical care of your parent; it can be helpful to see yourself as a consumer of an expensive service. Be sure you know all the rules and regulations of the institution and understand financial and contractual agreements fully. Inspect the physical plant thoroughly; the more carefully you look into linen closets and bathrooms, the more skillful you will become as a detective. Speak to the families of other patients. Call them at home and find out what they think of the care their parents have received. The families of many of the patients of the Daughters of Miriam Home for the Aged in Clifton, New Jersey, represent an interesting example. Residents of the home generally come from the greater Paterson area. Often, they have known one another for fifty years. Some are even related. Their children often know

one another and went to school together in Paterson. Today, a number of the middle-aged children of residents are friends who not only share convivial moments when they meet in the home but are able to help and support one another in their daily lives.

This situation occurred because of the self-selection process of residents of the home; nobody self-consciously organized a support group, yet the support that some children of residents experience is suggestive for other situations that lack the homogeneity of the Daughters of Miriam. As you explore, discover in what ways a prospective institution can be helpful to you and your family as well as your parent.

Know that entry into homes is not easy. Some have long waiting lists. If you are unsure, try to maximize flexibility and minimize permanence of commitment. Realize also that adjustment to new surroundings can be traumatic and that regardless of the carefulness of your selection, you will not only have to help your parent adjust, but you also will have to deal with your own doubts.

We live in a time when being a grownup is very hard. It would be easier to put up our hair in pompadours and wear bright-red lipstick and silk stockings. It is so hard to know ourselves and our families and our parents. It is so hard to know the "right" thing to do. It might even be easier to learn Hungarian.

SUGGESTIONS FOR FURTHER READING

JURY, MARK, AND JURY, DAN. *Gramp* ("A man ages and dies. The extraordinary record of one family's encounter with the reality of dying"). New York: Grossman Publishers, a division of Viking Press, 1976.

KRAMER, SYDELLE, AND MASUR, JENNY, eds. *Jewish Grandmothers.* Boston: Beacon Press, 1976.

KUBLER-ROSS, ELISABETH. *Death and Dying.* New York: Macmillan, 1970.

MYERHOFF, BARBARA. *Number Our Days.* New York: E. P. Dutton Co., 1978.

PAOLA, TOMIE DE. *Nana Upstairs & Nana Downstairs.* New York: Puffin Books, 1973. For children, on the death of a grandparent.

You and Your Aging Parent, understanding the aging process; needs; resources available. Mount Vernon, NY: Consumers Union, 1976.

CHAPTER FORTY-EIGHT

THINKING IT OVER*

Esther Ticktin

Now that my active years of parenting are over, I should be able to sit back quietly and reflect on what the experience had been like for me. With three grown-up daughters who are capable of and willing to make their own decisions in life, my major responsibilities as a parent are finished, and only Aunt Martha, who is over eighty now, still praises or blames *me* for what my daughters do. But it is still not easy to relinquish parental power, hopes of influence, and responsibility. Even the writing of an article for an anonymous body of readers is difficult to do without looking over my shoulders for its effects on my children. Yet I will resist the temptation (to which so many writers on parenthood succumb) of making this a covert polemic directed at my children. I would like to use this opportunity to look back at my own experience of two or three decades of parenthood and not for a last chance to sway my daughters.

Since I will be dealing here mostly with the early, active years of parenting and with their problems and conflicts, something has to be said about the nonproblematic aspects of those years and about my present relationships with my daughters. Parenthood was—and re-mains—one of the central experiences of my life. Even when I was obsessed with doing the right thing as a parent, the sense of wonder,

*This article was written some time ago. Since that time Esther's daughters have grown and changed. Esther is now the grandmother of Benjamin Elazar Ticktin Nash.

awe, and privilege of parenthood was never out of my awareness. To watch a new being unfold in all of its beauty and complexity and to have a hand in nurturing and guiding it always felt like a gift to me and filled me with amazement and gratitude. Looking at my daughters now, the· amazement and gratitude are still there. They have grown into attractive, interesting, and responsible human beings whom I like, respect, and admire as persons and would want as friends even if they were not my daughters. We are friends, indeed. One of them is married, and all my feelings about my daughters—love, respect, amazement, and gratitude—go out to her husband as well.

All three are in service occupations (nursing, child day care, mental health), are politically aware and involved, and have warm, positive feelings about their Jewishness, all of which is gratifying to me and my husband. On the other hand, they do not go out of their way to practice *Yiddishkeit*, they have not kept up their Jewish studies, and the Jewish community does not seem, at this point, to be their primary identity and focus of responsibility. Since they have as yet to make major lifetime commitments involving some of these issues, it may be too early to judge. But there is some sadness for my husband and myself that we cannot, at this time, fully share our deepest commitment with our children. Perhaps that is why parenthood is still a live issue for me. The questions of what could I or should I have done—though I consider them unproductive if not actually harmful—still gnaw at me and urge me on.

I speak here mainly about myself, though my husband and I shared the major goals and conflicts of Jewish parenthood. Whatever conflicts there were between us, they were insignificant compared with what we had in common. We were both strongly committed to a Jewish life, but what such a life should entail was never a simple matter to us. We were both drawn to the wider world outside the Jewish orbit and believed that through Judaism, God had something to say to us about our responsibilities in that wider world. But what those responsibilities were and how far they should take us from the Jewish community itself, we did not know.

The more I reflect on it, the clearer it becomes that my story as a Jewish parent begins with my story as a child of my parents and that that, in turn, begins with their story as parents and as children of their parents. I was born to conflict. I knew with my first glimmer of social awareness that just as my father had left his Hasidic-Talmudic background and had embraced Western culture, secularism, socialism, etc., I would have to leave the close confines of my traditional upbringing and choose my identity from a broader selection of possibilities in the open society. But whenever I became seriously involved in an outward-bound alternative—whether it was the secular kibbutz in Eretz Yisrael, a radical social-action commune in America, or an individualistic career in a bohemian-socialist context—I was ineluctably drawn back to tradition, family, and warmth and goodness of *Yiddishkeit*.

It was almost never a question of intellect versus emotions, of courage versus a longing for security, or of selfishness versus loyalty. Each time I was in one camp or the other, the whole of myself—intellect and feelings, courage and fear, self-interest and idealism—was involved. It seemed more like two powerful and attractive giants outside of myself, both with bona fide credentials, waging a struggle for my full allegiance, and myself oscillating uneasily from one to the other, each time stopping just short of full commitment but never comfortable with the margin, either.

Two "solutions"—one in my teens, the other in my twenties—were able to command my commitment for some length of time, because I experienced them as compromises between the extremes. One was the religious *halutz* movement with its socialist-Zionist-kibbutz orientation, and the other was Will Herberg's Jewish crisis theology. The religious *halutz* movement offered me the wider world and social experimentation within a Jewish traditional framework, and Will Herberg offered me Judaism within the open society of America. But when it came down to it, the religious kibbutz was a far cry from the open society, and Will Herberg's Judaism, compelling though it was, was not the *Yiddishkeit* I longed for.

It would have helped to recognize and pinpoint the two poles of the conflict and to work on resolving it before we had children, since it was bound to affect our parenting and our children's attitudes toward Judaism. But involved as I was in the struggle, I did not know that at the time. The conflict itself pushed us toward some resolution, and, I imagine, we had children partly because we unconsciously hoped to resolve the conflict through them, just as other parents hope to bolster a tottering marriage with children.

My vision of parenthood excluded conflict. I was going to raise strong, self-confident, graceful, and independent-minded children whose love for and loyalty to God, Torah, and the People Israel were natural and uncomplicated, taken for granted without pressure or apology. My mentors in child development assured me that natural childbirth, breast-feeding on a self-demand schedule, relaxed toilet training, and a realistic balance between structure, order, and discipline, on the one hand, and a wide range of free expression and experimentation, on the other hand, would produce secure and confident adults who would repay the love and respect in which they were raised with love and respect for us and all that was dear to us. Did that include our Jewishness? I believed it would.

Much of Jewish education in the past had been based on fear: fear of God's punishment, of community disapproval and isolation in a hostile world, or the more subtle fear of the loss of parental love and the pangs of guilt. I saw fear as a dangerous crippler of human beings, stunting emotional, intellectual, and spiritual growth by undermining the freedom to experiment, to discover, to play, and to take risks. It was, therefore, enormously comforting to be told by the experts in child development as well as by progressive Jewish educators that reliance on fear or seduction and guilt was no longer necessary. If the home was a warm Jewish home in which Jewish values and the richness of the tradition were lived as well as taught, we did not have to worry about our children's Jewishness. Early and consistent exposure to the tradition in an atmosphere of mutual love and respect would do the trick, and we would not need fearfully to restrict our children's groping for their own understanding of truth or bind them to us and to Jewishness through guilt.

When less sanguine friends or critics of the Jewish scene suggested that at no time in Jewish history have the options for assimilation been as many and as easy as they are today and that parents need all the help and support they can get from homogeneous Jewish neighborhoods, Orthodox day schools, and self-containing congregations, I had some moments of doubt. I usually assuaged them by rereading my optimistic educational theories, by buying another Jewish record, and by spending more time with my children the next *Shabbat*. Since my children seemed to enjoy their Jewish experiences at home, in the synagogue, and in summer camp, and they did not chafe at the Jewish education we imposed, I felt rather confident.

Yet, much as I suppressed the awareness of conflict, it was evident in every decision I made about my children. I wanted them to grow up not only knowing all the basic elements of Jewishness (Bible, Talmud, *halakhah* and *aggadah*, history, modern Yiddish, and Hebrew literature) but also participating in its daily texture, with a concrete knowledge of the categories of *halakhic* decisions and with a traditional outlook on life. I wanted to prepare them to be a creative link in the ongoing process of Jewishness. That meant not only discipline and sacrifice of time and leisure but also a measure of self-segregation. To learn to live and think Jewishly, one had to learn and live with other Jews engaged in the same process.

But I myself also wanted non-Jewish friends and the stimulation of variety and newness. I also wanted my children to have close contact with the wider world and sympathy for all kinds of human experiences. Both the Jewish emphasis and the open-society emphasis presented problems and aroused fears. When I pulled heavy on the Jewish emphasis, there was the danger that my children would grow up with narrow prejudices, with suspicion of everything foreign, different, and new, and seeing the world from a single perspective. There was also the opposite possibility that when they met the wider world in later years, its glamour and opportunity would dazzle them, and they would be enticed by it precisely because they had never known it. Yet did I dare to reestablish my old friendship with the Christian radical activists who had been so important to me before I had a family? Wasn't there a danger that by encouraging intimate sharing and mutuality with non-Jews, all distinctions and boundaries would be dissolved, and my children would find interdating so easy and natural that it would inevitably lead to intermarriage and assimilation?

Since we had decided to live in a small city with a small Jewish community and to send our children to public school, the bulk of their environment pulled in the direction of the open society. I therefore had to make up for the imbalance by weighting the home in the direction of

Jewishness. It was an inordinately heavy load placed on the home and on myself who spent most of my time there. Our home became a center of Jewish life, open to Jewish students and visiting Israelis. Since in addition to all the Jewish intellectual and religious stimulation, we also had to supply all the tastes, and smells and sounds and sights that go into a full Jewish experience for our children, I found myself cooking and baking and decorating the home much of the time; and since we could not sing and dance and toss around Jewish questions all by ourselves, we needed to surround ourselves with interesting and lively Jews much of the time.

Creating a Jewish home in a non-Jewish environment was a full-time job. It kept me so busy that for a long time I did not notice that the unchosen alternatives—a career in the larger world, a greater variety of friends, time for social and political concerns—were pressing to be acknowledged and creating discontent within me. For the time being I was rewarded when out of the blue, while riding on a bus, my fifteen-year-old daughter announced: "The one thing I know, I could never marry a non-Jew, or a nonobservant Jew, either." What more could I ask for? I felt almost smug. Jewishness did not have to be kept up through fear.

However, my children's adolescence wiped away every trace of smugness I had. Of course, my optimism had been unrealistic! How could I have failed to see that? Since our own way of life was but an uneasy compromise between conflicting desires and aspirations (individual growth and development in the open society on the one hand, and an integrated fully Jewish existence on the other hand), and we gave our children the freedom to choose their own way, how could I possibly count on their coming up with the same form of compromise?

Moreover, our own conflict began to assert itself. The previously suppressed and frustrated sides of the conflict emerged into two major decisions. After sixteen years in which we had built our precarious home-centered Jewish environment in a small town, we moved abruptly to a big city. Believing in the public school system and in integration (it was in the years of Martin Luther King's marches), we enrolled our children in schools that were preponderantly black. In both decisions, our own needs—career considerations, social and political convictions, the excitement and stimulation of big city life—weighed more heavily than the need to maintain the balance between Jewishness and the open society that we had built for our children.

When our daughters began making their own individualistic choices, often swinging radically from total involvement in the civil rights movement and black culture to a yearning for Jewish orthodoxy, I had to recognize that we could not take the continuity of our traditions for granted. Since our own life was based on a compromise between conflicting values, even if we succeeded in transmitting the same values and loyalties to our children, the slightest shift could alter the entire configuration. I had to face the possibility that one or another individualistic choice my children made could, through its own inner logic, lead them away from Jewishness and into assimilation.

It was not a comfortable situation, and to say that I didn't like it is a considerable understatement. Yet I had chosen it, and I had to learn to live with it. Over the years, gritting my teeth and becoming humbler from day to day, I worked out my own parenthood-faith.

God expects us to take care of and teach our children, not to create or produce a certain kind of person. Ultimately, each person is responsible for him or herself, and though we may feel sad if our children don't turn out as we planned, we need not feel guilty about it, and as long as they make responsible choices, we need not make them feel guilty, either.

If the Jewish people will remain necessary in the scheme of things (as in my faith and with my limited understanding, I believe it will), then God will do His or Her part in preserving the people—with my children or without. I will do *my* part. I will teach and hand on and ask my children to teach and hand on, but I will not deprive them of their own choice, and I will not assume the ultimate responsibility for their choice.

Giving my children both a good Jewish education and as honest an example of Jewish living as I can, I will expect them to continue and enhance the tradition I have handed down to them. But I have also chosen to live in an open society and to allow them to be influenced by many people and institutions and to experiment with their own combination of things, and I therefore have to be ready for the possibility of their choosing a different road. If I cannot contemplate such a possibility, I have not truly given them freedom at all.

Such is my parenthood-faith. It includes a great deal of renunciation and self-abnegation, and it does not match my vision of happy, serene parenthood. That vision is still "to see children and children's children engrossed in Torah and in *mitzvot*" with myself as part of their life and their community, sharing the same language and interests and references and hopes, sharing their daily cares and triumphs, giving them of my experience and drawing strength from their potentialities, and together dreaming and working toward the Kingdom of God on earth. It is the renewal of pious parenthood in an integrated, holistic community. But can it be combined with the autonomy and individual freedom that have been so necessary for me?

I believe that it can, that a synthesis between continuity as an integrated Jewish community and the freedom and responsibility of citizenship in the open society can be found. It is the same synthesis toward which every generation of Jews since the Emancipation has been striving. To some of us, it seemed easier after the Holocaust. ("How could any decent Jews relinquish the heritage that survived events of such enormity?") To others, it seemed easier in Israel. ("At least, assimilation there does not involve the loss of common language and national bond.") It has turned out not to be easy anywhere. Some of us have tried to face the conflict head on and to make a decision in one direction or the other. Somehow that has not been foolproof, either. Many assimilated parents have found their children turning back to Jewishness, and those who have turned to self-isolated, "total" Jewish communities, like some of the more radical Hasidim, are discovering that their walls are not impervious to the influences of the open society, either.

The solution will have to include both a full confrontation of the conflict—without denial or self-delusion—and a transcendence of the conflict. It will have to do for our situation what Rabbinic Judaism did for the Jews in the Greek and Roman civilizations. It will take more than the heroic attempts of one set of parents here and there and more than one community here and there, though it cannot be done without parents and communities. Until such time when, once again, parents can more serenely expect to share community and holy service in the vineyard of the Lord with their children, parenthood will include renunciation and self-abnegation.

Perhaps such a time will never come. Perhaps freedom necessarily involves the possibility that individuals will choose the good in another community instead of their own, and as long as we hope and work for mutual understanding and appreciation between communities instead of fear and suspicion, parents will always have to allow for their children turning to another good. Today or tomorrow, then, Jewish parenthood is not a task for the timid or the selfish, but it is an expression of faith in God, in Torah, and in the future of the People Israel.

CHAPTER FORTY-NINE

DEAR ALISA

"A Letter to an Unborn Child" began this book, and here we have another letter by the same father writing to his daughter (the unborn child of the first letter) as she departs for college.

September 4, 1979

Dear Alisa:

It is eighteen years now since I wrote you from the waiting room of the New Haven Hospital. Though we have communicated by letter from time to time over the years, this seems like the right occasion to resume that earlier correspondence. The last time I wrote, you were an abstract idea. This time I am writing to a very concrete you. In a few hours, I am going to take you off to college. I don't know about you, but I certainly don't feel old enough for this sort of thing. I am not sure which of us is more nervous, though we probably are not worried about the same things.

I should imagine that you are worried about losing old friends and making new ones, about how you are going to do in your classes, whether it is really difficult to survive in big, bad old New York City, and the distant, but not distant enough question about what you will do with your life four years from now.

I am worried about the same matters but some additional ones as well. (At the time of the last letter, I thought I was worrying more than you.) In addition to worrying about you, I am worried about myself, worrying about my failings, worried about whether I have adequately prepared you for what is to come.

The Talmud says that a father must teach his children three things: Torah, a worldly occupation, and how to swim. It is presumed that with skills in these three areas, you can manage anywhere. You are certainly a splendid swimmer, far better than one who is as ill coordinated as I am had a right to expect. I am very pleased about your cooking and catering abilities. They are formidable and will always give you an occupation if you want one, whatever else happens in your life. Whether it is a skill you will use or only store away in your head doesn't matter. I have always been grateful to my grandfather for teaching me to bind books. I doubt if I am ever going to bind books for a living, but it is comforting to believe that I could if I really had to.

I don't think that I have taught you enough Torah. When I was growing up, Judaism for me was mostly something I found in books. For you and your other three siblings, I wanted it to be more immediate, the sounds you heard, the food you ate, as natural as breathing. As a result, though you know a lot of pieces of the tradition, certainly much more than I knew at your age, I don't know if you have the right set of connections, the ideas that make it all hang together. I wanted you to be both traditional and modern at the same time, and I am not sure that I have given you the tools. I am also concerned about the extent to which I have tried to glue onto you my kind of Jewishness and what that might be doing to your soul.

I think I should try harder to realize that we are different people. Of late, I have taken to counseling parents that they have no more right to take credit for their children's success than they are obligated to blame themselves for their children's failures. The most casual glance at your brothers and sisters makes it clear that kids raised in the same home turn out to be very different people in ways that can hardly be accounted for by position in the family. It may be biology, it may be *mazal* (luck), or even will that has made each of you unique.

That is what I believe in my head. In my gut, however, I and the other parents to whom I dispense this wisdom feel great personal satisfaction from their children's triumphs and great shame from their failure. I secretly say of you: Look what I did (hooray)! or Look what I did (sigh). For both of us, part of the process of our growing up is learning to separate out some of these issues.

I feel comfortable with your political sensibilities, particularly that you have them but also insofar as they incline in the same direction as mine. Then I say to myself, What right have I to be happy about such a thing? They are, after all, your sensibilities, or if they aren't, they have no meaning. But on the other hand, didn't I help give them to you? Do I deserve no credit? How do I give you standards as a parent while at the same time view you with at least as much nonjudgmental compassion that I would want to extend to any other independent adult? I don't yet know.

You haven't made it any easier, either. Whenever I give you the no-adult-privileges-without-adult-responsibilities speech, you always respond by telling me that you are neither an adult nor a child but are something in between. That is true, but also an easy dodge. We are both rather muddled about this issue, and I am aware of no way out except to be aware of it.

You turned out to be named properly. You are certainly a joy and a ray of sunshine for everyone who knows you. But when I expressed the wish that you would be that way those eighteen years ago, I forgot that the energy that gives people like you, especially, good cheer would from time to time be quite depleted. It is reassuring, however, how much better in control of your gloom you are than you once were.

We have had a special closeness, you and I, perhaps because you were a first child or perhaps because so many of our best and worst qualities and even our styles of dealing with the world are so similar. Perhaps it is because of the way we seem to sweep up after each other. It is more than likely that your mother will have a bird tomorrow upon seeing the state in which you will almost inevitably leave your room. To me, it seems the most natural state of affairs in the world that you should be going to visit Eva in the hospital, and if everything doesn't get done, so be it. On the other hand, you should be clear that people like us need people like her to keep our worlds ordered, and our "flexibility" is most often sustained at small cost to her, by her sense of orderliness, resist it though we may.

I do not think I am much better a parent now than I was eighteen years ago when you were born. I have learned much less along the way than I should have supposed. I have far less insight into how I think you should raise our grandchildren than I would have suspected. What I have learned is that as complex and exhausting as I thought raising children would be, I greatly underestimated the measure of effort and time that would be required. I am now more tolerant of other people's styles of child rearing because I have discovered how much more confusing, exhausting, and sometimes even desperate a task parenting is than I imagined. I certainly no longer believe that if you are sincere, everything works out nicely. But though we have had moments together that have been painful, I can honestly say I do not regret any of them. I have come to view even those hard times as part of what it is all about.

And so, Alisa, may you go in peace and come in peace. May you always be both our child and your own independent person even though it will never be very neat. May you find your path to Torah. May you succeed with hard things. Whatever you do in this world, may you do it well, for then you will remain *aliza* ("happy" in Hebrew, pun intended).

> With a love that has been well seasoned,
> Your satisfied father
> *Richard Israel*

RESOURCES: PEOPLE, PLACES, AND THINGS

Audrey Friedman Marcus

ARCHIVES & ARCHIVAL INSTITUTIONS

American Jewish Archives
 3101 Clifton Ave., Cincinnati, OH 45220
 collections that document the history of the Jews in the Western Hemisphere
See also Historical Societies; Museums
American Jewish Historical Society
 2 Thornton Rd., Waltham, MA 02154
 approximately 4 million items that relate to all areas of American Jewish history
Leo Baeck Institute
 129 E. 73rd St., New York, NY 10021
 research on German-speaking Jewry of Europe, essentially from the era of the Emancipation (the latter part of the 18th century) to the destruction of Jewish communal life by the Nazi regime in the 1930s
Bund Archives of the Jewish Labor Movement
 25 E. 78th St., New York, NY 10021
 specializes mostly in materials relating to the history of the Jewish labor movement, particularly in eastern Europe and the Americas, but including other countries. It also contains materials of general socialist and labor interest

Dropsie University
 Broad and York, Philadelphia, PA 19132
 includes the basic tools for Hebrew bibliographical reference, encyclopedias relating to Jewish culture and history, and miscellaneous reference sets in collateral fields
Hebrew Union College–Jewish Institute of Religion Manuscript Library
 3101 Clifton Ave., Cincinnati, OH 45220
 about a quarter of a million books in the fields of Jewish studies, philosophy, education, art, comparative religion, archaeology, Semitics, etc.
Library of the Jewish Theological Seminary of America
 3080 Broadway, New York, NY 10027
 archival material on various aspects of Jewish life in France, Spain, Italy, Morocco, central Europe, north Africa, and the United States. One of the great Judaica Libraries of the United States.
YIVO Institute for Jewish Research
 1048 5th Ave., New York, NY 10028
 records life of east European Jewry in east European countries and other countries where east European Jews resided

ARTS & CRAFTS RESOURCES

Beckelman, Florance, and Dreiblatt, Lorraine. *Some Things Special for Shabbat.* Seattle: Ricwalt Publishing Co., 1977.
Becker, Joyce. *Hanukkah Crafts.* New York and London: Bonim Books, 1978.
———, *Jewish Holiday Crafts.* New York and London: Bonim Books, 1977.
Brinn, Ruth Esrig. *Let's Celebrate! 57 Jewish Holiday Crafts for Young Children.* Silver Spring, MD: Kar-Ben Copies, 1977.
"Drawing on Experience." Column in *Alternatives* magazine. Published by Alternatives in Religious Education, Inc., 1110 Holly Oak Circle, San Jose, CA 95120.
Englander, Lois, Kansky, Gail, and Sacks, Judy. *The Jewish Holiday Do-Book.* New York: Bloch, 1976.
Ginsberg, Ruth S. *Crafts For the Jewish Child.* New York: Shulsinger, 1976.
The Inkling, vol. 3, no. 2 and vol. 5, no. 3. Denver: Alternatives in Religious Education, Inc.
Lazar, Wendy. *The Jewish Holiday Book.* Garden City, NY: Doubleday, 1977.
Rockland, Mae Shafter. *The Hanukkah Book.* New York: Schocken, 1975.
Sharon, Ruth. *Arts and Crafts the Year Around,* vols. 1 and 2. New York: United Synagogue, 1965.
Siegal, Richard, Strassfeld, Michael, and Strassfeld, Sharon. *The Jewish Catalog.* Philadelphia: Jewish Publication Society, 1973.

BIG BROTHER/BIG SISTER ORGANIZATIONS

Big Brother Association of Cincinnati
 1580 Summit Rd., Cincinnati, OH 45237
Big Brothers of Jewish Family Service
 Jewish Federation of Community Services, Bergen County, 170 State St., Hackensack, NJ 07601
Jewish Big Brother Assoc. of Boston
 72 Franklin St., Boston, MA 02110

Jewish Big Brothers Assoc. of Los Angeles County
 590 N. Vermont Ave., Los Angeles, CA 90004
Jewish Big Brother League of Baltimore
 5750 Park Heights Ave., Baltimore, MD 21215
The Jewish Big Brothers and Big Sisters Assoc.
 22001 Fairmount Blvd., Cleveland, OH 44118
Jewish Big Brothers of the Jewish Board of Guardians
 120 W. 57th St., New York, NY 10019

B'NAI B'RITH HILLEL FOUNDATIONS & COUNSELORSHIPS

ALABAMA
Auburn University Hillel
 304 Fern Hill Ct., Mobile 36608
University of Alabama BBHF
 P.O. Box 6304, University 35486

ARIZONA
Arizona State University BBHF
 Baker Center, 213 E. University Dr., Tempe 85281
Phoenix College Hillel
 % A.S.U.—Baker Center, 213 E. University Dr., Tempe 85281
University of Arizona BBHF
 1245 E. 2nd St., P.O. Box 4325, Tucson 85717

CALIFORNIA
University of California at Berkeley BBHF
 2736 Bancroft Way, Berkeley 94704
Claremont Colleges Hillel
 McAlister Center Chaplains Office, Claremont 91711
University of California at Davis BBHC
 328 A St., Davis 95616

California State University at Fresno Hillel
 P.O. Box 1328, Fresno 93715
University of California at Santa Barbara
 % University Religious Conference, 777 Camino Pescadero, Goleta 93017
University of California at Irvine Hillel
 13411 Cromwell Dr., Tustin 92680
California State University at Long Beach BBHF
 3801 E. Willow Ave., Long Beach 90815
Long Beach City College Hillel Council
 3801 E. Willow Ave., Long Beach 90815
Los Angeles City College BBHF
 900 Hilgard Ave., Los Angeles 90024
Los Angeles Hillel Council Extension Program
 900 Hilgard Ave., Los Angeles 90024
 includes:
 California Institute of Technology, Pasadena 91100
 California Poly State University, San Luis Obispo 93401
 California State College, Dominguez Hills 90247
 California State University, Los Angeles 90024

California, University of, Santa Barbara 93101
Cerritos College, Norwalk 90650
Chaffey College, Alta Loma 91701
Chapman College, Orange 92667
Citrus College, Azusa 91702
Claremont Colleges (Claremont Graduate School, Claremont Men's College, Harvey Mudd College, Pitzer College, Pomona College, Scripps College), Claremont 91711
Cypress College, Cypress 90630
East Los Angeles College, Los Angeles 90024
El Camino College, Torrance 90506
Glendale College, Glendale 91202
La Verne College, La Verne 91750
Los Angeles Harbor College, Los Angeles 90024
Loyola Law School, Los Angeles 90024
Loyola Marymount University, Los Angeles 90024
Moorpark College, Moorpark 93021
Northrup Institute of Technology, Inglewood 90310
Occidental College, Los Angeles 90024
Pacific Oaks College, Pasadena 91106
Pepperdine College, Malibu 90265
Pierce College, Los Angeles 90024
Rio Hondo College, Whittier 90605
Santa Monica College, Santa Monica 90405
Southwestern University School of Law, Los Angeles 90024
West Los Angeles College, Culver City 90230
Whittier College, Whittier 90605
Woodbury University, Los Angeles 90024
University of California at Los Angeles BBHF Hillel Council
900 Hilgard Ave., Los Angeles 90024
University of Southern California BBHF
3300 S. Hoover, Los Angeles 90007
California State University at Northridge Hillel Council
17729 Plummer St., Northridge 91324
University of California at Riverside BBHC
2675 Central Ave., Riverside 92506
San Diego State University BBHC
% CSU–San Diego, 5742 Montezuma Rd., San Diego 92115
City College of San Francisco BBHF
Ecumenical House, 190 Denslowe Dr., San Francisco 94132
San Francisco State University Ecumenical House
190 Denslowe Dr., San Francisco 94132
San Jose State University BBHC
1777 Hamilton Ave., San Jose 95125
Stanford University BBHF
The Club House, Stanford 94305
California State University at Fullerton Hillel
212 Buena Vista Dr., Claremont 91711
Fullerton College Hillel
212 Buena Vista Dr., Claremont 91711
Los Angeles Valley College Hillel Council
13162 Burbank Blvd., Van Nuys 91401

COLORADO
University of Colorado BBHF
2795 Colorado Ave., Boulder 80302
Colorado State University BBHC
2258 S. Josephine St. #10, Denver 80208
University of Northern Colorado BBHC
1414 32nd Ave.,Greeley 80639

CONNECTICUT
University of Bridgeport BBHC
% Interfaith House, University Ave., Bridgeport 06602
Quinnipiac College Hillel
% Temple Beth Sholom, 1809 Whitney Ave., Hamden 06517
Yale University BBHF
1904A Yale Sta., New Haven 06520
Connecticut College Jewish Community Council
302 State St., New London 06320
University of Connecticut BBHF
N. Eagleville Rd., Storrs 06268

Trinity College Hillel
Dept. of Religion, Trinity College, Hartford, Conn. 06106

DELAWARE
University of Delaware Hillel
% Temple Beth El, 70 Amstel Ave., Newark 19711

DISTRICT OF COLUMBIA
American University BBHF
A. S. Kay Spiritual Life Center, Massachusetts and Nebraska Aves., N.W., Washington 20016
Gallaudet College BBHC
Chaplain's Office, Washington 20002
George Washington University BBHF
2129 F St., N.W., Washington 20037
Georgetown University BBHF
Campus Ministries Office, 1 Healy Building, Georgetown U., Washington 20057

FLORIDA
Florida Atlantic University
4300 Sheridan St., Hollywood 33021
Miami Area Extension Service
Miami University BBHF, 1100 Miller Dr., Coral Gables 33146
includes:
Broward Community College, Ft. Lauderdale
Florida Atlantic University, Boca Raton
Florida Technological University, Orlando
Miami–Dade Community College, North Campus, Miami
Miami–Dade Community College, South Campus, Coral Gables
Rollins College, Winter Park
University of South Florida, Tampa
Miami–Dade Community College—South Campus BBHF
11011 S.W. 104th St., Bldg. 6—Engineering Dept., Miami 33176
University of Miami BBHF
1100 Miller Dr., Coral Gables 33146
Broward Community College Jewish Student Org.
4300 Sheridan St. #232, Hollywood 33021
University of Florida BBHF
16 N.W. 18th St., Gainesville 32601
Jacksonville University BBHC
2800 University Blvd. N., Jacksonville 32211
Miami–Dade Community College—North Campus Hillel– Jewish Student Org.
4300 Sheridan St. #232, Hollywood 33021
Florida Technological University
% Congregation Ohev Shalom, 915 Goddard St., Orlando 32810
Rollins College Jewish Student Org.
928 Malone Dr., Orlando 32810
Florida State University BBHC
Box 6883, Tallahassee 32306
University of South Florida Jewish Student Union
5014 Patricia Ct., Tampa 33617

GEORGIA
University of Georgia BBHF
1155 S. Milledge Ave., Athens 30601
Emory University BBHF
Drawer A, Atlanta 30322
Georgia Institute of Technology BBHF
% Emory University, Drawer A, Atlanta 30322
Georgia State University BBHF
% Emory University, Drawer A, Atlanta 30322
Oglethorpe College BBHF
% Emory University, Drawer A, Atlanta 30322

ILLINOIS
Illinois State University Hillel
% Moses Montefiore Temple, 102 Robinhood La., Bloomington 61701
Illinois Wesleyan University Hillel
102 Robinhood Lane, Bloomington 61701
Southern Illinois University BBHF
715 S. University, Carbondale 62901

University of Illinois BBHF
    503 E. John St., Champaign 61820
University of Chicago BBHF
    5715 S. Woodlawn Ave., Chicago 60637
University of Illinois at Chicago Circle Hillel
    516 Chicago Circle Center, Chicago 60680
Northern Illinois University Hillel
    % Northern Illinois Jewish Community Center, 820
    Russell Rd., DeKalb 60115
Northwestern University BBHF
    1935 Sherman Ave., Evanston 60201
Bradley University Hillel
    % Dept. of Biology, Olin Hall, Peoria 61609
    INDIANA
Indiana University BBHF
    730 E. 3rd St., Bloomington 47401
Purdue University BBHF
    912 W. State St., West Lafayette 47906
    IOWA
Iowa State University Hillel
    Dept. of Mathematics, Ames 50010
Drake University Hillel
    2932 University Ave., Des Moines 50311
University of Iowa BBHF
    122 E. Market St., Iowa City 52240
    KANSAS
University of Kansas BBHF
    B107 Kansas Union Bldg., Box 4, Lawrence 66044
Kansas State University Hillel
    1509 Wreath Ave., Manhattan 66502
    KENTUCKY
Transylvania University BBHC
    Lexington 40506
University of Kentucky BBHC
    Box 613, University of Kentucky Sta., Lexington
    40506
University of Louisville BBC
    University of Louisville Ecumenical Center, Louis-
    ville 40208
    LOUISIANA
Louisiana State University at Baton Rouge BBHC
    P.O. Box 16420A, University Sta., Baton Rouge 70803
Newcomb College BBHF
    912 Broadway, New Orleans 70118
Tulane University BBHF
    912 Broadway, New Orleans 70118
University of New Orleans BBHF
    912 Broadway, New Orleans 70118
    MAINE
Bates College Hillel
    % Jewish Community Center, 134 College St., Lewis-
    ton 04240
University of Maine Hillel
    63 Forest Ave., Orono 04473
Colby College BBHC
    % Colby College, Waterville 04901
    MARYLAND
University of Maryland BBHF
    7505 Yale Ave., College Park 20704
    MASSACHUSETTS
Wellesley College Hillel
    Campus Ministry, Wellesley 02181
University of Massachusetts BBHF
    302 Student Union Bldg., University of Massachu-
    setts, Amherst 01002
Boston Area Hillel Counselorship & Extension Service
    233 Bay State Rd., Boston 02215
    includes:
    Babson College
    Bentley College
    Boston College
    Boston State College
    Curry College
    Emerson College
    Lesley College
    Nichols College

Northeastern University
Simmons College
University of Massachusetts, Boston
Wellesley College
Boston University BBHF
    233 Bay State Rd., Boston 02215
Northeastern University Hillel
    456 Parker St., Boston 02115
Harvard University BBHF
    1 Bryant St., Cambridge 02138
Massachusetts Institute of Technology BBHF
    312 Memorial Dr., Cambridge 02139
Radcliffe College BBHF
    1 Bryant St., Cambridge 02138
Boston College Jewish Student Alliance
    % Boston College, Chestnut Hill 02167
Lowell Technological Institute
    Lowell 01850
Smith College BBHF
    % Helen Hills Chapel, Elm St. and Round Hill Rd.,
    Northampton 01060
Salem State College Hillel
    % Salem State College, Salem 01970
Tufts University BBHF
    108 Bromfield St., Somerville 02144
Amherst College BBHC
    % Eliot House, Mt. Holyoke College, South Hadley
    01075
Mount Holyoke College BBHC
    % Eliot House, Mt. Holyoke College, South Hadley
    01075
American International College BBHC
    % Springfield Jewish Federation, 1160 Dickinson St.,
    Springfield 01108
Springfield College BBHC
    % Springfield Jewish Federation, 1160 Dickinson St.,
    Springfield 01108
Bentley College
    % Bentley College Campus Ministry, Waltham 02154
Brandeis University BBHF
    % Usdan Student Center, Chaplain's Office, Rm.
    133, Waltham 02154
Babson College Hillel
    % Park Manor Babson College, Wellesley 02181
Clark University Hillel
    % Jewish Federation, 633 Salisbury St., Worcester
    01609
Worcester Polytechnic Institute
    % Jewish Federation, 633 Salisbury St., Worcester
    01609
    MICHIGAN
University of Michigan BBHF
    1429 Hill St., Ann Arbor 48104
Wayne State University BBHF
    667 Charles Grosberg Religious Center, Detroit 48202
Michigan State University BBHF
    402 Linden St., East Lansing 48823
Kalamazoo College
    3420 Pinegrove Lane, Kalamazoo 49008
Western Michigan University Hillel
    3420 Pinegrove Lane, Kalamazoo 49008
Eastern Michigan University Hillel
    Ypsilanti 48197
    MINNESOTA
Carleton College BBHF
    1521 University Ave., S.E., Minneapolis 55414
University of Minnesota BBHF
    1521 University Ave., S.E., Minneapolis 55414
    MISSISSIPPI
University of Mississippi BBHC
    123 Lakeway Gardens, Oxford 38655
    MISSOURI
Stephens College BBHF
    1107 University Ave., Columbia 65201
University of Missouri BBHF
    1107 University Ave., Columbia 65201

St. Louis University BBHF
  6300 Forsyth Blvd., St. Louis 63105
University of Missouri–St. Louis BBHF
  6300 Forsyth Blvd., St. Louis 63105
Washington University BBHF
  6300 Forsyth Blvd., St. Louis 63105

NEBRASKA
University of Nebraska Hillel
  4820 S. 43rd St., Lincoln 68516

NEW HAMPSHIRE
Dartmouth College BBHF
  Hinman, Box 6154, Hanover 03755
University of New Hampshire Hillel
  Memorial Union Hall, Durham 03824

NEW JERSEY
Monmouth College Hillel
  301 Monmouth Rd.,Oakhurst 07755
Fairleigh Dickinson University Hillel
  285 Madison Ave., Madison 07940
Princeton University BBHF
  Murray-Dodge Hall, Princeton 08540
Douglass College BBHF
  Clifton Ave. and Ryder's La., New Brunswick 08901
Rutgers University BBHF
  Clifton Ave. and Ryder's La., New Brunswick 08901
Fairleigh Dickinson University BBHF
  10-13 Ellis Ave., Fairlawn 07410
Rider College Hillel
  499 Greenwood Ave., Trenton 08609
Trenton State College Hillel
  499 Greenwood Ave., Trenton 08609

NEW MEXICO
University of New Mexico Hillel
  Dept. of Anthropology, Albuquerque 87131

NEW YORK
State University of New York (SUNY) at Albany Jewish Student Coalition Hillel
  19 Colvin Ave., Albany 12222
Alfred University Hillel
  Box 545, Alfred 14802
SUNY at Brockport Hillel
  103 Seymour Union, Brockport 14420
Brooklyn College BBHF
  2901 Campus Rd., Brooklyn 11210
Kingsborough Community College Hillel
  Brooklyn 11230
SUNY at Buffalo BBHF
  40 Capen Blvd., Buffalo 14214
Queens College BBHF
  % Student Services Corp., P.O. Box 446, Flushing 11367
SUNY at Fredonia Hillel
  Fredonia 14063
Adelphi University BBHF
  % Adelphi Religious Center, Garden City 11530
SUNY at Geneseo Hillel
  1 Lomb Memorial Dr., Rochester 14623
Hofstra University BBHF
  % Chaplain's Office, Hempstead 11550
Cornell University BBHF
  % Anabel Taylor Hall, Ithaca 14850
Ithaca College BBHC
  Muller Chapel, Ithaca 14850
C. W. Post Center of Long Island University Hillel
  2325 Lindenmere Dr., Merrick 11566
SUNY at New Paltz Hillel
  118 Johnston Ave., Kingston 12404
Bernard M. Baruch College BBHF
  17 Lexington Ave., New York 10010
City College of CUNY BBHF
  475 W. 140th St., New York 10031
Hunter College BBHF
  % Roosevelt Memorial House, 49 E. 65th St., New York 10021
SUNY at Oswego Hillel
  Hewitt Union, Oswego 13126

Vassar College Hillel Society
  Box 488, Poughkeepsie 12601
Monroe Community College BBHC
  Interfaith Chapel, River Campus Station, Rochester 14623
Rochester Institute of Technology BBHC
  % Hillel Chaplain's Office, 1 Lomb Memorial Dr., Rochester 14623
University of Rochester BBHF
  % The Interfaith Chapel, River Campus Sta., Rochester 14627
Pace University—Westchester Campus BBHC
  Hillel Box, Pleasantville 10570
Union College and University of Schenectady Campus Hillel
  1158 Phoenix Ave., Schenectady 12309
SUNY at Stony Brook BBHF
  % Humanities Bldg., 158 SUNY—Stony Brook, Stony Brook 11794
Syracuse University BBHF
  % Hendricks Memorial Chapel, Syracuse 13210
Rensselaer Polytechnic Institute BBHC
  % Rensselaer Polytechnic Institute Chaplain's Office, Troy 12181
Russell Sage College Hillel
  Troy 12100
Utica College of Syracuse University Hillel
  Utica 13500

NORTH CAROLINA
North Carolina State University BBHF
  210 W. Cameron Ave., Chapel Hill 27514
University of North Carolina BBHF
  210 W. Cameron Ave., Chapel Hill 27514
University of North Carolina at Greensboro BBHF
  210 W. Cameron Ave., Chapel Hill 27514
Duke University BBHC
  210 W. Cameron Ave., Chapel Hill 27514
East Carolina University Hillel
  % Dept. of Foreign Languages, Greenville 27834

OHIO
Ohio University BBHF
  21 Mills St., Athens 43201
University of Cincinnati Hillel
  320 Straight St., Cincinnati 45219
Case Western Reserve University BBHF
  11291 Euclid Ave., Cleveland 44106
Cleveland State University BBHC
  11291 Euclid Ave., Cleveland 44106
Cuyahoga Community College BBHF
  11291 Euclid Ave., Cleveland 44106
Hiram College Hillel
  11291 Euclid Ave., Cleveland 44106
John Carroll University BBHF
  11291 Euclid Ave., Cleveland 44106
Northern Ohio Hillel Extension Program
  11291 Euclid Ave., Cleveland 44106
Kent State University Hillel Jewish Center
  202 N. Lincoln, Kent 44240
Miami University (Ohio) BBHC
  11-15 E. Walnut St., Miami 45056
Baldwin-Wallace College BBHC
  % Oberlin College Hillel, Wilder Hall, Oberlin 44074
Oberlin College BBHC
  Wilder Hall, Oberlin 44074
Bowling Green State University Hillel
  3436 Goddard Rd., Toledo 43606
University of Toledo Hillel
  3436 Goddard Rd., Toledo 43606

OKLAHOMA
University of Oklahoma BBHF
  494 Elm Ave., Norman 73069

OREGON
Oregon State University Hillel
  Dept. of Economics, Corvallis 97331

University of Oregon Hillel
1414 Kincaid St., Eugene 97401
Portland State University Hillel
Portland 97212

PENNSYLVANIA
Pennsylvania State University at Ogontz BBHC
202 W. 36th St., Phila 19104
Muhlenberg College Hillel
1702 Hamilton St., or 2227 Chew St., Allentown
18104
Temple University Hillel—Ambler Campus
Ambler 19002
Lehigh University Hillel
% Dept. of Mathematics, Bethlehem 18015
Moravian College Hillel
% Lehigh University, Dept. of Mathematics, Beth-
lehem 18015
Dickinson College Hillel
Box 166, Dickinson College, Carlisle 17013
Lafayette College Hillel
% Lafayette College, Dept. of History, Easton 18042
Bryn Mawr College Hillel
% Haverford-Bryn Mawr Havurah Yarnell Hall,
Haverford College, Haverford 19041
Haverford College Hillel
% Haverford-Bryn Mawr Havurah Yarnell Hall,
Haverford College, Haverford 19041
Beaver College Hillel
440 W. Sedgwick, Philadelphia 19119
Community College of Philadelphia Hillel
34 S. 11th St., Philadelphia 19107
Drexel University Hillel
% Student Activities Center, 32nd and Chestnut Sts.,
Philadelphia 19104
LaSalle College Hillel
440 W. Sedgwick, Philadelphia 19119
Philadelphia Area Hillel Counselorship and Extension
Service
202 S. 36th St., Philadelphia 19104
includes:
Beaver College
Bryn Mawr College.
Community College of Philadelphia
Drexel College
Haverford College
LaSalle College
Penn State—Ogontz Campus
Philadelphia College of Pharmacy & Science
Philadelphia College of Textile & Science
Swarthmore College
Temple University—Ambler Campus
Villanova University
Philadelphia College of Pharmacy & Science Hillel
43rd St. and Woodland Ave., Philadelphia 19104
Philadelphia College of Textile & Science Hillel
School House La. and Henry Ave., Philadelphia
19144
Temple University BBHF
2014 N. Broad St., Philadelphia 19121
University of Pennsylvania BBHF
202 S. 36th St., Philadelphia 19104
Carnegie-Mellon University BBHF
% YM/YWHA, 315 S. Bellefield Ave., Pittsburgh
15213
Chatham College BBHF
% YM/YWHA, 315 S. Bellefield Ave., Pittsburgh
15213
Duquesne University BBHF
% YM/YWHA, 315 S. Bellefield Ave., Pittsburgh
15213
University of Pittsburgh BBHF
% YM/YWHA, 315 S. Bellefield Ave., Pittsburgh
15213
Pennsylvania State University BBHF
224 Locust La., State College 16801
Bucknell University Hillel

% Congregation Beth-El, P.O. Box 211, Sunbury
17801
Swarthmore College Hillel
Park Dr. Manor, Lincoln Dr. & Harvey St., Phil-
adelphia 19119
Villanova University Hillel
Sullivan Hall, Villanova 19085
West Chester State College BBHC
206 N. Church St., West Chester 19380

RHODE ISLAND
University of Rhode Island Hillel
324 Memorial Union, Kingston 02881
Brown University BBHF
80 Brown St., Providence 02906

SOUTH CAROLINA
The Citadel Hillel
86 Hassell St., Charleston 29401
University of South Carolina Hillel
1213 Lady St., Columbia 29201

TENNESSEE
University of Tennessee at Chattanooga Hillel
12 Edgemon Cir., Ringgold, Ga. 30736
University of Tennessee at Knoxville Hillel
P.O. Box 16204, Knoxville 37919
Memphis State University Hillel
% Jewish Community Center, 6560 Poplar Ave.,
Memphis 38138
Southern College of Optometry Hillel
% Jewish Community Center, 6560 Poplar Ave.,
Memphis 38138
Southwestern at Memphis Hillel
% Jewish Community Center, 6560 Poplar Ave.,
Memphis 38138
University of Tennessee at Memphis Hillel
% Jewish Community Center, 6560 Poplar Ave.,
Memphis 38138
George Peabody College Hillel
2410 Vanderbilt Pl., Box 19, Nashville 37235
Vanderbilt University Hillel
2410 Vanderbilt Pl., Box 19, Nashville 37235

TEXAS
University of Texas BBHF
P.O. Box H, University Sta., Austin 78712
Texas Agricultural and Mechanical University BBHF
800 Jersey St., College Station 77840
Southern Methodist University Hillel
Dallas 75235
University of Texas at El Paso Hillel
7206 Majorca Ct., El Paso 79912
Rice University Hillel
3801 Cullen Blvd., Houston 77004
University of Houston Hillel
% United Orthodox Synagogue, 4221 S. Braeswood
Blvd., Houston 77035
San Antonio College Hillel
San Antonio 78216

UTAH
University of Utah Hillel
2425 Heritage Way, Salt Lake City 84109

VERMONT
University of Vermont BBHF
% Living & Learning Center, Box 127, Burlington
05401
Middlebury College Hillel
% Dept. of Political Science, Middlebury 05753

VIRGINIA
Virginia Polytechnic Institute & State University Hillel
1001 University Blvd. N.W., Sturbridge Sq., #H-14,
Blacksburg 24060
Mary Washington College BBHF
1824 University Circle, Charlottesville 22903
University of Virginia BBHF
1824 University Circle, Charlottesville 22903
Washington & Lee University BBHF
1824 University Circle, Charlottesville 22903

Old Dominion University BBHC
7255 Granby St., Norfolk 23508
University of Richmond Hillel
% Jewish Student Service-Hillel Masada Hall, 1103
W. Franklin St., Richmond 23220
Virginia Commonwealth University Hillel
% Jewish Student Service-Hillel Masada Hall, 1103
W. Franklin St., Richmond 23220
College of William & Mary Hillel
% Law School, Williamsburg 23185

WASHINGTON
University of Washington BBHF
4745 17th Ave., N.E., Seattle 98105

WEST VIRGINIA
West Virginia University BBHF
1420 E. University Ave., Morgantown 26505

WISCONSIN
University of Wisconsin BBHF
611 Langdon St., Madison 53703
Marquette University Jewish Student Service-Hillel
3035 N. Stowell Ave., Milwaukee 53211
Milwaukee School of Engineering Hillel
3035 N. Stowell Ave., Milwaukee 53211
University of Wisconsin at Milwaukee Jewish Student Service-Hillel
3035 N. Stowell Ave., Milwaukee 53211

CANADA
Alberta
University of Alberta Hillel
Religious Studies, Edmonton
British Columbia
University of British Columbia BBHF
P.O. Box 43, SUB, Vancouver
Manitoba
University of Manitoba BBHF
149 University Center, Winnipeg

University of Winnipeg BBHF
149 University Center, Winnipeg
Nova Scotia
Dalhousie University Hillel
% Baron de Hirsch Congregation Beth Israel Synagogue, Halifax
Ontario
McMaster University Hillel
Hamilton
Queen's University BBHF
116 Centre St., Kingston
Waterloo Lutheran University Hillel
124 Charles Best Pl., Kitchener
University of Western Ontario Hillel
Student Council Office, London
Carleton University Hillel Federation of Ottawa
151 Chapel St., Ottawa
University of Ottawa Hillel
151 Chapel St., Ottawa
University of Toronto BBHF
604 Spadina Ave., Toronto
York University BBHF
4700 Keele St., Downsview
Quebec
CEGEP's Vanier College & Dawson College
3460 Stanley St., Montreal
Concordia University Hillel Student Society
2130 Bishop St., 2nd Fl., Montreal
Loyola Branch of Concordia University Hillel
7356 Sherbrooke W., Montreal
McGill University BBHF
3460 Stanley St., Montreal
University of Montreal Centre Hillel
5186 Cote des Neiges Rd., Suite #3, Montreal
Saskatchewan
University of Saskatchewan Hillel
417 Bate Crescent, Saskatoon

BOARDS OF JEWISH EDUCATION

NOTE: "Fed." refers to Federation Committees

ALABAMA
Jewish Education Committee (Fed.)
3960 Montclaire Rd., Birmingham 35213

ARIZONA
Jewish Education Council
1718 W. Maryland Ave., Phoenix 15015
Jewish Education Committee (Fed.)
102 N. Plumer, Tucson 85715

CALIFORNIA
Bureau of Jewish Education of the Jewish Federation
Council of Greater Los Angeles
590 N. Vermont Ave., Los Angeles 90004
Jewish Education Council for Alameda and Contra Costa
Counties
3245 Sheffield Ave., Oakland 94602
Bureau of Jewish Education
4079 54th St., San Diego 92105
Bureau of Jewish Education of San Francisco, Marin
County, and the Peninsula
639 14th St., San Francisco 94118

COLORADO
Denver Jewish Education Committee (Fed.)
400 Kittridge Blvd., Denver 80202

CONNECTICUT
Bureau of Jewish Education
1184 Chapel St., New Haven 06511

DELAWARE
Jewish Education Committee (Fed.)
701 Shipley St., Wilmington 19801

DISTRICT OF COLUMBIA
Board of Jewish Education of the Jewish Community of
Greater Washington
1330 Massachusetts Ave., N.W., Washington 20005

FLORIDA
Central Agency for Jewish Education
4200 Biscayne Blvd., Miami 33137

GEORGIA
Bureau of Jewish Education
1753 Peachtree Rd., N.E., Atlanta 30309
Bureau of Jewish Education
5111 Abercorn St., Savannah 31405

ILLINOIS
Assoc. Talmud Torahs
2828 W. Pratt Blvd., Chicago 60645
Board of Jewish Education of Metropolitan Chicago
72 E. 11th St., Chicago 60605

INDIANA
Jewish Educational Assoc.
6711 Hoover Rd., Indianapolis 46260

IOWA
Bureau of Jewish Education
924 Polk Rd., Des Moines 50312
Jewish Federation of Sioux City
524 14th St., Sioux City 51105

KENTUCKY
Bureau of Jewish Education
3600 Dutchmans La., Louisville 40205

LOUISIANA
Jewish Education Committee (Fed.)
211 Camp St., New Orleans 70130

MARYLAND
Board of Jewish Education
5800 Park Heights Ave., Baltimore 21215

MASSACHUSETTS
Bureau of Jewish Education
72 Franklin St., Boston 02110
MICHIGAN
United Hebrew Schools
21550 W. Twelve Mile Rd., Southfield 48076
MINNESOTA
Talmud Torah of Minneapolis
8200 W. 33rd St., Minneapolis 55426
Talmud Torah of St. Paul
636 S. Mississippi River Blvd., St. Paul 55116
MISSOURI
Jewish Education Council of Greater Kansas City
7721 State Line, Suite 127, Kansas City 64114
Central Agency for Jewish Education
225 S. Meramec, Suite 400, St. Louis 63105
NEBRASKA
Bureau of Jewish Education
101 N. 20th St., Omaha 68102
NEW JERSEY
Bureau of Jewish Education
2395 W. Marlton Pike, Cherry Hill 08034
Metropolitan New Jersey (Essex County and Surrounding
Area) Jewish Education Assoc.
120 Halsted St., East Orange 07018
Board of Jewish Education
152 Van Houten St., Paterson 07505
Jewish Education Committee of the Federation of Jewish
Agencies
5321 Atlantic Ave., Ventnor 08406
NEW YORK
Bureau of Jewish Education
787 Delaware Ave., Buffalo 14209
Board of Jewish Education
426 W. 58th St., New York 10019
Bureau of Jewish Education
440 E. Main St., Rochester 14604
OHIO
Bureau of Jewish Education
1580 Summit Rd., Cincinnati 45237
Bureau of Jewish Education
2030 S. Taylor Rd., Cleveland 44118
Jewish Education Committee
United Jewish Fund and Council, 1175 College Ave.,
Columbus 43209
Bureau of Jewish Education
184 Salem Ave., Dayton 45406
Board of Jewish Education
2727 Kenwood Blvd., Toledo 43606
OKLAHOMA
Jewish Education Committee (Fed.)
#200 Plaza Blvd., 8 E. 3rd St., Tulsa 74103

OREGON
Jewish Education Assoc.
6651 S.W. Capitol Hwy., Portland 97219
PENNSYLVANIA
Board of Jewish Education—Philadelphia Branch, United
Synagogue of America
1701 Walnut St., Philadelphia 19103
Gratz College
10th St. and Tabor Rd., Philadelphia 19141
United Hebrew Schools and Yeshivot of Philadelphia
701 Byberry Rd., Philadelphia 19116
Hebrew Institute of Pittsburgh
6401-07 Forbes Ave., Pittsburgh 15217
School of Advanced Jewish Studies
315 S. Bellefield Ave., Pittsburgh 15213
RHODE ISLAND
Bureau of Jewish Education
76 Dorrance St., Providence 02903
TENNESSEE
Jewish Education Study Committee
5325 Lynnland Terrace, Chattanooga 37411
Committee on Jewish Education (Fed.)
81 Madison Bldg., Suite 1200, Memphis 38103
Jewish Education Services
3500 West End Ave., Nashville 37205
TEXAS
Commission for Jewish Education
5601 S. Braeswood Blvd., Houston 77035
UTAH
Jewish Education Committee (Fed.)
2416 E. 1700 S., Salt Lake City 84108
VIRGINIA
Bureau of Jewish Education (Fed.)
7300 Newport Ave., Norfolk 23505
Jewish Education Committee (Fed.)
5403 Monument Ave., Richmond 23226
WASHINGTON
Community Study Committee on Jewish Education (Fed.)
Suite 606, Securities Bldg., Seattle 98101
Jewish Education Committee (Fed.)
P.O. Box 8134, Manito Sta., Spokane 98103
WISCONSIN
Board of Jewish Education
4515 W. Good Hope Rd., Milwaukee 55223
CANADA
Board of Jewish Education
22 Glen Park Ave., Toronto, ON
Winnipeg Board of Jewish Education
370 Hargrave St., Rm. 200, Winnipeg, MB

BOOK CLUBS & SERVICES

Barnes & Noble, Mail Order
245 W. 19th St., New York, NY 10018
B'nai B'rith Paperback Book Service
1640 Rhode Island Ave., N.W., Washington, DC
20036
*monthly list of recommended current paperbacks; located in
the* National Jewish Monthly
Enjoy-A-Book Club, 25 Lawrence Ave., Lawrence,
N.Y. 11559
Hadassah Book Order Service
66 E. 52nd St., New York, NY 10022
Jewish Book Club, 111 Eighth Ave., Suite 1501, New
York, NY 10011
*a full line of books of Jewish interest, all substantially reduced
in price, some up to 99%; monthly brochure*
The Jewish Bookshelf, P.O. Box 434, Teaneck, NJ 07666
Jewish Publication Society
117 S.17th St., Philadelphia, PA 19103

*JPS has a number of subscription plans, which can save you a
considerable amount, they also have a Hanukah sale each year
that lets you buy selected titles at considerable savings*
Stephen L. Maimes, Bookseller
P.O. Box 22043, San Francisco, CA 94122
mail order only; send in and get on the catalog list
Mayan: A Wellspring of Jewish Books
P.O. Box 246 Sudbury, MA 01776
mail service for Jewish books
Yonathon Shultz's Jewish Periodical Subscription Service
7518 Lexington Ave., Los Angeles, CA 90046
United Synagogue Book Service
218 E. 70th St., New York, NY 10021
Yiddish Book Club
Committee for Jewish Culture in Israel
Bnei Ephraim St., Maoz Aviv, Tel Aviv, Israel
Zionist Book Club
788 Marlee Ave., Toronto, ON, Canada

BOOKSTORES

CALIFORNIA
Shalom House Jewish Store
19757 Sherman Way, Canoga Park 91306
Brower's House of Israel
316 Locust Ave., Long Beach 90812
Al's
370 N. Fairfax Ave., Los Angeles 90024
California House of Israel
Box 4825, Los Angeles 90048
Gans Book Store & Gift Shop
427 N. Farfax Ave., Los Angeles 90036
Harelick & Roth Books
1070 S. La Cienega Blvd., Los Angeles 90035
Herskovitz Books & Gifts
428 N. Fairfax Ave., Los Angeles 90007
Jewish American Bookstore
332 N. Fairfax Ave., Los Angeles 90007
Lose the Blues
424¼ N. Fairfax Ave., Los Angeles 90007
carries Jewish student publications
Norty's
436 N. Fairfax, Los Angeles 90007
The Olive Tree
1441 S. Robertson, Los Angeles 90007
The Shtetl
8028 W. 3rd St., Los Angeles 90006
Sojcher's Hebrew Bookstore
450 N. Fairfax Ave., Los Angeles 90036
Solomon's Books, Gifts
477 N. Fairfax Ave., Los Angeles 90036
Universal News Agency
1655 N. Las Palmas Ave., Los Angeles 90007
World Book & News Co.
1652 Cahuenga, Los Angeles 90007
House of David
12826 Victory Blvd., North Hollywood 91606
Hebrew Book & Gift World
5712 El Cajon, San Diego 92155
The Book Shook
2440 Noriega St., San Francisco 94122
Lieber's Hebrew-English Book & Gift Store
5445 Geary Blvd., San Francisco 94121

COLORADO
The Three Mavins
300 Fillmore, Denver 80226

CONNECTICUT
Media Judaica
1363 Fairfield Ave., Bridgeport 06605
Israel Gift Shop & Hebrew Book Shop
262 S. Whitney St., Hartford 06105
Jewish Book Shop
1184 Chapel St., New Haven 06525

DISTRICT OF COLUMBIA
Discount Books
1342 Connecticut Ave., N.W., Washington 20036
not a specifically Jewish bookstore but carries a good selection of English Judaica

FLORIDA
American-Israeli Shop
1357 Washington Ave., Miami 33157
Relgo
1507 Washington Ave., Miami 33157
Hebrew Book Store
417 Washington Ave., Miami Beach 33139
Shalom Judaica
20002 N.E. 164th St., North Miami Beach 33161

GEORGIA
Ansley Mall Book Store
1544 Piedmont Ave., N.E., Atlanta 30320

HAWAII
Sof Maarav Judaica Shop
% The Poppers, 1110 Pueo St., Kahala 96818

ILLINOIS
Hamakor Judaica Book Store
6112 N. Lincoln Ave., Chicago 60659
Israel-Palestine Gift Studio
220 S. State St., Chicago 60604
Jewish Book Mart
127 N. Dearborn St., Chicago 60602
Rosenblum's Hebrew Book Store
3443 W. Lawrence Ave., Chicago 60625
Rosenblum's Hebrew & English Book Store
2906 W. Devon Ave., Chicago 60645
Schwartz's-Goodman Bros. Hebrew Bookstore
2611 W. Devon Ave., Chicago 60645

MARYLAND
Central Hebrew Bookstore
5416 Park Heights Ave., Baltimore 21215
Pern's Hebrew Book & Gift
7012 Reisterstown Rd., Baltimore 21215
Central Hebrew Book Store
228 Reisterstown Rd., Pikesville 21208
Abe's Jewish Bookstore
11250 Georgia Ave., Wheaton 20902
Goodman's Hebrew Book & Gift
2305 University Blvd. W., Wheaton 20902
Jewish Book Store
11250 Georgia Ave., Wheaton 20902

MASSACHUSETTS
Israel Book Shop
410 Harvard St., Brookline 02146
Melvin's
197-199 Main St., Great Barrington 01230
Davidson's Hebrew Book Store
1100 N. Main St., North Randolph 02368
Mayan Jewish Books
P.O. Box 246, Sudbury 01776
Ephraim's Book Store
80 Franklin St., Worcester 01608

MICHIGAN
Borenstein's Book & Music Store
13535 W. Seven Mile Rd., Detroit 48235
Bernstein's Jewish Book Store
25242 Greenfield Rd., Oak Park 48237
Spitzer's Hebrew Books & Gifts
21770 Eleven Mile Rd., Southfield 48036

MINNESOTA
Brochin's Jewish Book & Gift Shop
4813 Minnetonka Blvd., Minneapolis 55416

MISSOURI
Israeli Gift & Book Center
8503 Olive St. Rd., St. Louis 63132
Midwest Jewish Book & Gift Center
8318 Olive St. Rd., St. Louis 63132

NEW JERSEY
C & S Judaica
111 Lakeview Ave., Clifton 08809
Sky Hebrew Book Store
1923 Springfield Ave., Maplewood 07040
The Judaica Shoppe
435 Cedar Lane, Teaneck 07666

NEW YORK
Ballen Booksellers
66 Austin Blvd., Commack 11725
Bennet Rebecca Publications
5409 18th Ave., Brooklyn 11213
Blum's Hebrew Book Store
169A Ross St., Brooklyn 11202
Center of Jewish Books
1660 Ocean Parkway, Brooklyn 11223
Chaim Wissbrot Hebrew Books
167 Rodney St., Brooklyn 11232
Flohr's Gifts & Religious Articles
4603 13th Ave., Brooklyn 11213

Flusberg's Hebrew Book Store
1276 47th St., Brooklyn 11219
Frankel's Hebrew Book Store
4904 16th Ave., Brooklyn 11204
Grunfeld Hebrew Book Store
4412 15th Ave., Brooklyn 11213
wholesale
Kahan's Hebrew Book Store
4408 15th Ave., Brooklyn 11213
Kalman Teitelbaum
648 Bedford Ave., Brooklyn 11211
Miller's Hebrew Book Store
349 Utica Ave., Brooklyn 11235
Sinai Religious Articles
1456 Coney Island Ave., Brooklyn 11230
Pelham Pkwy. Hebrew Bookstore
781 Lydig Ave., Bronx 10467
Little Professor Book Center
University Plaza, 300 Main St., Buffalo 14200
carries a variety of Jewish books
Theodore S. Cinnamon
420 Jerusalem Ave., Hicksville 11801
Central Israeli Supplies Co.
90-50 150th St., Jamaica 11435
Chasen's Hebrew Gift Shop
989 Kenmore Ave., Kenmore 14217
Jonathan David Co.
68-22 Eliot Ave., Middle Village 11379
Behrman House
1261 Broadway, New York 10001
Biegeleisen
83 Division St., New York 10002
Bloch Publishing Co.
915 Broadway, New York 10010
fills mail orders, get on their mailing list for special sales
Central Yiddish Culture Org.—CYCO
25 E. 78th St., New York 10024
makes Yiddish books available to the public
Rabbi Moses Eisenbach Bookstore
13 Essex, New York 10003
Phillip Feldheim
96 E. Broadway, New York 10002
Israeli Gifts & Bookstores
575 7th Ave., New York 10016
Jewish Gift Shop
2404 Broadway, New York 10024
The Jewish Museum Bookshop
1104 5th Ave., New York 10028
Ktav
75 Varick St. New York 10013
Lazer's Sefer Israel
156 5th Ave., New York 10010
Levine Religious Supplies
58 Eldridge St., New York 10002
Morgenstern Books
150 E. Broadway, New York 10002
Paston's Book Shop
18 Eldridge St., New York 10002
Reinman's Seforim Center
29 Essex St., New York 10003
Sepher Hermon Press
175 5th Ave., New York 10010
Shaller's Israel Gift, Book and Record Center
1495 St. Nicholas Ave., New York 10033
Shilo Publishing Co.
73 Canal St., New York 10002
Solomon Rabinowitz
30 Canal St., New York 10002
Stavsky's Book Store
147 Essex St., New York 10002
Wolozin
33 Eldridge St., New York 10002
Ziontalis Book Division
48 Eldridge St., New York 10002
Orgel's Jewish Religious Articles & Israel Giftware
984 Monroe Ave., Rochester 14609

Otisco Book & Gift Shop
549 W. Moreland Ave., Syracuse 13210
Mazel Tov
833 Englewood Ave., Tonawanda Twp. 14150
Long Island Temple Supplies
433 Hempstead Ave., West Hempstead 11552

OHIO
Frank's Hebrew Book Store
1647 Lee Rd., Cleveland 44118
Jewish Book Store Center of Columbus
1125 College Ave., Columbus 43209
Paul's Hebrew Book Store
13962 Cedar Rd., Cleveland 44110

PENNSYLVANIA
Hebrew Book & Art Center
Barclay Bldg., Belmont Ave. and City Line Ave., Bala Cynwyd 19004
Piotrkowski's Judaica Center
289 Montgomery Ave., Bala Cynwyd 19004
Piotrkowski's Judaica Center
115 Old York Rd., Jenkintown 19046
Rosenberg Hebrew Book Store
413 Old York Rd., Jenkintown 19046
Hebrew Book & Art Center
57th St. and Wyndale Ave., Philadelphia 19131
Magold Co.
722 S. 5th St., Philadelphia 19147
Rosenberg Hebrew Book Store
4939 N. Broad St., Philadelphia 19141
Rosenberg Hebrew Book Store
6408 Castor Ave., Philadelphia 19149
Rosen's Hebrew Books & Gifts
6743 Castor Ave., Philadelphia 19149
Milton Pinsker
2028 Murray Ave., Pittsburgh 15217

RHODE ISLAND
Meltzer's Hebrew Book Store
132 Hope St., Providence 02906

TEXAS
Mrs. Fred Glatzer
6630 Northport Dr., Dallas 75230
House of Books
9215 Stella Link Rd., Houston 77060
House of Books
42 Braeswood Sq., Houston 77063

WISCONSIN
Mallin's Hebrew Book Store
5128 W. Center, Milwaukee 53210

CANADA
Ontario
Lieberman's Jewish Book Centre
2509 Bathurst St., Toronto
Miriam's Book Store
2007 Bathurst St., Toronto
David Mirvish Books
597 Markham St., Toronto
Negev Book & Gift Store
3509 Bathurst St., Toronto
Pollock's Jewish Book & Gift Centre
1132 Eglinton Ave. W., Toronto
Zucker Jewish Books & Art
3453 Bathurst St., Toronto

Quebec
Book Centre
5168 Queen Mary Rd., Montreal
Caplansky Book Store
5031 Park Ave., Montreal
Rodal's Hebrew Book Store
4689 Van Home St., Montreal
Victoria Gift Shop & Book Centre
5865 Victoria Ave., Montreal

CALENDARS

Jewish calendars are available from the following sources:
Advertising Corporation of America, Holyoke, MA 01040
Blue Star Book Club, Box 410, Oceanside, NY 11572
Israel Discount Bank, 511 Fifth Ave., New York, NY 10017
The Jewish Museum, 1109 Fifth Ave., New York, NY 10028
Jewish National Fund, 42 East 69th St., New York, NY 10021
Kar-Ben Copies, 11713 Auth Lane, Silver Spring, MD 20902
National Federation of Temple Sisterhoods, 838 Fifth Ave., New York, NY 10021
United Synagogue of America, 155 Fifth Ave., New York, NY 10010
Universe Books, 381 Park Avenue South, New York, NY 10016
World Union of Jewish Students, 247 Gray's Inn Rd., London W.C.1, England
Ziontalis Manufacturing Co., 48 Eldridge St., New York, NY 10002

CAMPS

The following national organizations sponsor their own camps:
American Jewish Society for Service
    15 E. 26th St., Rm. 1302, New York, NY 10010
    a service-oriented camp
Assoc. of Jewish Sponsored Camps
    130 E. 59th St., New York, NY 10017
    for New York camps
Division of Community Services
    Yeshiva University, 185th St., and Amsterdam Ave., New York, NY 10033
    sponsors camps and winter institutes
National Ramah Commission
    3080 Broadway, New York, NY 10027
    sponsors camps across the U.S.
Union of American Hebrew Congregation
    838 5th Ave., New York, NY 10021
    sponsors camps across the U.S.

General Listing
Camps whose locations differ from their winter addresses are listed according to winter mailing addresses, with the summer location in parentheses; check with local synagogues and centers for additional day camps—see also Community Centers. Camps with winterized facilities are marked with asterisks.

ARIZONA
*Camp Charles Perlstein (Prescott)
    % Temple Beth Israel, 3310 N. 10th Ave., Phoenix 85013
Camp Teva (Prescott)
    % Phoenix Jewish Community Center, 1718 W. Maryland, Phoenix 85015
    kosher

CALIFORNIA
*Camp Alonim (Brandeis)
    The Brandeis Institute, Brandeis 93064
    kosher
*Brandeis Camp Institute
    Brandeis 93064
    kosher
*Camp Young Judaea (St. Helen)
    % Northern California Hadassah, 264 Arlington Ave., Kensington 94707
    kosher
*Camp Komaroff (Lake Arrowhead)
    % Long Beach Jewish Community Center, 2610 Grand Ave., Long Beach 90815
    kosher
*Gindling Hilltop Camp (Malibu)
    % Wilshire Boulevard Temple, 3663 Wilshire Blvd., Los Angeles 90010
Habonim Camp Gilboa (Idyllwild)
    % Ichud Habonim, 8339 W. 3rd St., Los Angeles 90048
    kosher

*Camp Hess Kramer (Malibu)
    % Wilshire Blvd. Temple, 3663 Wilshire Blvd., Los Angeles 90010
*Camp JCA—Barton Flats (San Bernardino)
    8455 Beverly Blvd., Los Angeles 90048
    kosher-style
Camp JCA—High Sierras (Mammoth Lakes)
    8455 Beverly Blvd. Los Angeles 90048
*Camp JCA—Malibu
    8455 Beverly Blvd., Los Angeles 90048
    kosher
*Camp Max Straus
    % Jewish Big Brothers Assoc., 6505 Wilshire Blvd., Los Angeles 90048
Camp NCSY (Angelus Oaks)
    % National Conference of Synagogue Youth, 6505 Wilshire Blvd., Los Angeles 90048
    kosher
*Camp Ramah in California (Ojai)
    % University of Judaism, 6525 Sunset Blvd., Los Angeles 90028
    kosher
Camp Young Judaea (Big Bear Lake)
    % Hadassah Zionist Youth Commission, 2365 Westwood Blvd., #22, Los Angeles 90064
    kosher
Camp Arazim (Soquel)
    % United Synagogue of America, P.O. Box 9154, Sacramento 95816
    kosher
Camp Tawonga
    % United Jewish Community Centers—Bay Area, 3200 California St., San Francisco 94118
*UAHC Swig Camp Institute (Saratoga)
    % Union of America Hebrew Congregations, 703 Market St., San Francisco 94103

COLORADO
J Bar Double C Ranch (Elbert)
    % Jewish Community Center, P.O. Box 6196, Cherry Creek Sta., Denver 80206
    kosher

CONNECTICUT
Camp Hadar
    435 Brooklawn Ave., Fairfield 06430
Camp Isabella Freedman (Falls Village)—see New York
Camp Coeur d'Alene (Kent)—see New York
Camp Ella Fohs (New Milford)—see New York
Camp Laurel-Wood (North Madison)
    % Jewish Community Center, 1156 Chapel St., New Haven 06511
    kosher-style

DISTRICT OF COLUMBIA
Camp B'nai B'rith (Pa.)
    1640 Rhode Island Ave., N.W., Washington 20036
    kosher

Camp Tel Shalom (W.Va.)
% Adas Israel Congregation, 2850 Quebec St., N.W.,
Washington 20008
kosher

FLORIDA
*Camp Coleman (Ga.)
% Union of American Hebrew Congregations, 119 E.
Flagler St., Suite 208, Miami 33131
Savage's Mt. Lake (N.C.)
P.O. Box 4450, Normandy Dr., Miami Beach 33141

GEORGIA
*Camp Barney Medintz (Cleveland)
% Jewish Community Center, 1745 Peachtree St.,
N.E., Atlanta 30309
kosher
Camp Judaea (N.C.)
1132 W. Peachtree St., N.W., Rm. 11, Atlanta 30309
kosher
Camp Coleman (Cleveland)—see Florida

INDIANA
Camp Livingston (Bennington)—see Ohio
Union Camp Institute (Zionsville)—see New York

KANSAS
*Kamp Israel
10910 Nall, Overland Park 66204

KENTUCKY
Camp Ben F. Washer (Vine Grove)
% Jewish Community Center, 3600 Dutchmans La.,
Louisville 40205
kosher

MAINE
Camp Kingswood (Bridgton)—see Massachusetts
Camp Joseph (Harrison)—see Massachusetts
Camp Naomi (Raymond)—see Massachusetts

MARYLAND
Camp Airy
% Straus Foundation, 5750 Park Heights Ave., Baltimore 21215

ILLINOIS
*Camp Chi (Wisc.)
% Jewish Community Center, 1 S. Franklin St., Chicago 60606
kosher-style
Harand Camp
410 S. Michigan Ave., Chicago 60605
*Camp Henry Horner (Round Lake)
% Young Men's Jewish Council, 30 W. Washington
St., Chicago 60602
kosher-style
Camp Moshava (Wisc.)
% Bnei Akiva, 6500 N. California Ave., Chicago
60645
*UAHC Olin-Sang-Ruby Camp (Wisc.)
% Union of American Hebrew Congregations, 100
W. Monroe St., Chicago 60603
Camp Ramah (Wisc.)
72 E. 11th St., Chicago 60605
kosher
Camp Ben Frankel (Carbondale)
% Jewish Federation, 327 Missouri Ave., Suite 412,
East St. Louis 62201
kosher-style

Camp Louise (Cascade)
% Straus Foundation, 5750 Park Heights Ave., Baltimore 21215
Camp Moshava (Annapolis)
% Ichud Habonim, 920 Sligo Ave., Silver Spring
20910
kosher

MASSACHUSETTS
Camp Kingswood
% Combined Jewish Philanthropies, 72 Franklin St.,
Boston 02110
kosher-style
*Grossman Camp
% Assoc. Jewish Community Centers, 72 Franklin
St., Boston 02110
day camp
Camp Ramah in New England (Palmer)
1330 Beacon St., Brookline 02146
kosher
Camp Yavneh (N.H.)
% Hebrew College, 43 Hawes St., Brookline 02146
kosher
Pirchai Day Camp/Bais Sarah Day Camp
% New England Chassidic Center, 1710 Beacon St.,

Brookline 02146
kosher
*Camp Bauercrest (Amesbury)
10 Perkins Rd., Chelsea 02150
kosher
Joseph Eisner Camp Institute (Great Barrington)—see
New York
Camp Avoda (Middleboro)
11 Essex St., Lynnfield 01940
strictly kosher
Camp Shalom
Lake Garfield, Monterey 01245
Camp Pembroke (Pembroke)—see New Hampshire
Camp Joseph (Maine)
% Jewish Community Center Camps, 50 Hunt St.,
Watertown 02172
kosher
Camp Naomi (Maine)
% Jewish Community Center Camps, 50 Hunt St.,
Watertown 02172
kosher
Camp Young Judaea (N.H.)
81 Kingsbury St., Wellesley 02181
kosher
Jewish Community Center Day Camp
Manning Hold St., Worcester 01602
day camp

MICHIGAN
*Camp Tamarack (Brighton and Ortonville)
% Fresh Air Society, 6600 W. Maple Rd., West
Bloomfield 48033
Camp Tavor (Three Rivers)
% Habonim Camp Tavor, 2005 Merrill, #5, Ypsilanti
48197
kosher

MINNESOTA
*Camp Tikvah (Aitkin)
% Jewish Community Center of Greater Minneapolis, 4330 Cedar Lake Rd. S., Minneapolis 55416
kosher
Camp Herzl (Wisc.)
790 S. Cleveland, #202, St. Paul 55116
kosher

MISSISSIPPI
UAHC Henry S. Jacobs Camp Institute (Utica)—see New
York

MISSOURI
Barney Goodman Camp–JCC
8201 Holmes Rd., Kansas City 64131
day camp
*Camp Sabra (Rocky Mount)
% Jewish Community Centers Assoc., 11001 Schuetz
Rd., St. Louis 63141
kosher

NEBRASKA
Camp Esther F. Newman (Louisville)
% Jewish Federation of Omaha, 333 S. 132nd St.,
Omaha 68154
kosher

NEW HAMPSHIRE
Camp Young Judaea (Amherst)—see Massachusetts
Camp Tel Noar (Hampstead)
% Cohen Foundation Camps, 66 Prospect St., Man-
chester 03104
kosher
Camp Pembroke (Mass.)
% Cohen Foundation Camps, 66 Prospect St., Man-
chester 03104
kosher
Camp Tevya (Brookline)
% Cohen Foundation Camps, 66 Prospect St., Man-
chester 03104
kosher
Camp Yavneh (Northwood)—see Massachusetts

NEW JERSEY
Camp Vacamas (Butler)—see New York
New Jersey YMHA/YWHA Camps (2 in Pa.)
% New Jersey Federation of Y's, 589 Central Ave.,
East Orange 07018
kosher
YAC Day Camp
W. St. Georges Ave. and Orchard Terrace, Linden
07036
Camp-by-the Sea of the Jewish Community Center of
Atlantic County
501 N. Jerome Ave., Margate 08402
Camp Oakhurst (Oakhurst)—see New York
Camp Louemma (Sussex)—see New York
Camp Sussex (Sussex)—see New York
YM/YWHA of Passaic
Rifle Camp Rd., West Paterson 07424

NEW YORK
Camp Louemma (N.J.)
41-25 Bell Blvd., Bayside 11361
kosher-style
Yeshiva of Flatbush Day Camp
Cross Bay Blvd., Broad Channel 11693
kosher
Bronx House–Emanuel Camps (Copake)
990 Pelham Pkwy. S., Bronx 10461
kosher-style
Camp Boiberik (Rhinebeck)
Sholom Aleichem Folk Institute, 3301 Bainbridge
Ave., Bronx 10467
kosher-style
*Camp Ella Fohs (Conn.)
1130 Grand Concourse, Bronx 10456
kosher
Beer Mordechai School & Day Camp
1670 Ocean Ave., Brooklyn 11212
kosher
Broad Channel Day Camp
Yeshiva of Flatbush, 919 E. 10th St., Brooklyn 11231
Camp Emunah Tiny Tots (Greenfield Park)
% Lubavitch, 824 Eastern Pkwy., Brooklyn 11213
glatt kosher
Camp Gila
1533 48th St., Brooklyn 11219
kosher
Camp Dora Golding (Pa.)
444 E. 45th St., Brooklyn 11203
male; glatt kosher
Camp Hadar Hatorah
1138 43rd St., Brooklyn 11219
kosher
*Camp HASC (Parksville)
% Hebrew Academy for Special Children, 1311 55th
St., Brooklyn 11219
kosher
Camp Hatikvah (Livingston Manor) for boys 14-16
% YM/YWHA, 575 Bedford Ave., Brooklyn 11211
kosher
Camp H.E.S. (Southfields)
% Hebrew Educational Society, 9502 Sea View Ave.,
Brooklyn 11236
kosher
Camp Huntington
1017 E. 80th St., Brooklyn 11236
kosher; for mentally retarded and neurologically impaired
Camp Mogen Avraham (Livingston Manor) for boys 8-14
% YM/YWHA, 575 Bedford Ave., Brooklyn 11211
glatt kosher
Camp Monroe
1330 52nd St., Brooklyn 11213
kosher-style
Camp Morasha (Pa.)
1277 E. 14th St., Brooklyn 11230
kosher
Camp Naarim (Fleischmans)
1726 45th St., Brooklyn 11219
glatt kosher

Camp Raleigh
  1245 Ocean Ave., Brooklyn 11213
  kosher
Camp Sdei Chemed International
  1618 43rd St., Brooklyn 11204
  kosher
Camp Seguiah
Camp Nissiah
  % YM/YWHA of Williamsburg, 575 Bedford Ave.,
  Brooklyn 11211
  day camp in Huntington, Long Island
Camp Spatt (Mountaindale)
  % YM/YWHA, 575 Bedford Ave., Brooklyn 11211
  female; glatt kosher
Camp Sternberg (Mountaindale)
  % YM/YWHA, 575 Bedford Ave., Brooklyn 11211
  glatt kosher
Camp Torah Vodaath (Highland)
  425 E. 9th St., Brooklyn 11218
  kosher
Camp Toras Chesed
  3121 Kings Hwy., Brooklyn 11234
Kings Bay Day Camp
  2611 Ave. Z, Brooklyn 11212
  kosher
Menucha Day Camp
  841-853 Ocean Pkwy., Brooklyn 11230
  Lubavitch sponsored
Noam Day Camp
  % Yeshiva Chsan Sofer, Brooklyn 11232
Ocean Primary School & Day Camp
  904 E. 98th St., Brooklyn 11232
  kosher
Yeshiva Ateres Yisroel
  8101 Ave. K, Brooklyn 11232
  kosher
Yeshiva of Flatbush Broad Channel Day Camp
  919 E. 10th St., Brooklyn 11212
  kosher
Camp Hi-Li
  17-42 Seagirt Blvd., Far Rockaway 11692
Hi-Li Day Camp
  264 Beach 19th St., Far Rockaway 11692
  kosher
Camp Coeur d'Alene (Conn.)
  % YM/YWHA of Greater Flushing, Flushing 11355
  strictly kosher
Camp Edward Isaacs (Holmes)
  % Central Queens YM/YWHA, 108-05 68th Rd.,
  Forest Hills 11375
  kosher
Forest Hills Summer Play Program
  71-02 113th St., Forest Hills 11372
Forest Park Day Camp
  102-35 63rd Rd., Forest Hills 11375
  kosher
Simcha Day Camp
  1170 William St., Hewlett 11557
Camp Hill
  33 Washington Ave., Lawrence 11559
Camp Shalom
  % Aronskind, 60-29 264th St., Little Neck 11363
Camp Kfar Masada (Rensselaerville)
  % Long Island Zionist Foundation, 381 Sunrise
  Hwy., Lynnbrook 11563
  kosher
Camp Ta-Go-La
  Sackett Lake, Monticello 12701
Block Vacation Center (Pa.)
  % Assoc. Camps, 130 E. 59th St., New York 10022
  senior citizens
Camp Agudah (Ferndale)
  5 Beekman St., New York 10038
  glatt kosher
Camp Betar (Neversink)
  55 W. 42nd St., New York 10036

Camp Beth Jacob
  149 E. Broadway, New York 10002
  kosher
Camp Bnos (Liberty)
  5 Beekman St., New York 10038
  glatt kosher
Camp Cummings & Salomon Vacation Centers (Brewster)
  % The Educational Alliance, 197 E. Broadway, New
  York 10002
  kosher kitchen
Camp Hamshekh (Mountaindale)
  % United Survivors of Nazi Persecution, 25 E. 78th
  St., New York 10021
*Camp Isabella Freedman (Conn.)
  1 Union Sq. W., New York 10003
  kosher-style
Camp Leah (Bear Mountain)
  % The Educational Alliance, 197 E. Broadway, New
  York 10002
  kosher
Camp Lewis Village (Pa.)
  % Assoc. Y Camps, 253 W. 72nd St., Suite 211, New
  York 10023
  kosher-style
Camp Mikan-Recro (Arden)
  % Recreation Rooms & Settlement, 12 Ave. D, New
  York 10009
Camp Moonbeam (Putnam Valley)
  15 E. 40th St., New York 10016
  kosher-style
Camp Moshava (Pa.)
  % Bnei Akiva, 25 W. 26th St., New York 10010
  kosher
Camp Naaleh (Red Hook)
  % Habonim, 575 Ave. of the Americas, New York
  10011
  kosher
Camp Oakhurst (N.J.)
  % New York Service for the Handicapped, 853 Broad-
  way, New York 10003
Camp Poyntelle-Ray Hill (Pa.)
  % Assoc. Y Camps, 253 W. 72nd St., Suite 211, New
  York 10023
  kosher-style
*Camp Rainbow (Croton-on-Hudson)
  33 W. 60th St., New York 10023
Camp Ramah in the Berkshires (Wingdale)
  % Jewish Theological Seminary of America, 3080
  Broadway, New York 10027
  kosher
Camp Ramapo Anchorage (Rhinebeck)
  % Jewish Board of Guardians, 120 W. 57th St., New
  York 10019
Camp Shomria (Liberty)
  % Hashomer Hatzair, 150 5th Ave., New York 10011
Camp Sussex (N.J.)
  1140 Broadway, New York 10001
Camp Tel Ari (Hunter)
  % Labor Zionist Youth, 575 Ave. of the Americas,
  New York 10011
Camp Tel Yehudah (Barryville)
  % Hadassah Zionist Youth, 817 Broadway, New York
  10003
  kosher
*Camp Vacamas (N.J.)
  215 Park Ave. S., New York 10003
  kosher-style
*Camp Wildwood (Central Valley)
  % Recreation Rooms and Settlement, 12 Ave. D, New
  York 10009
*Camp Williams (Suffern)
  1133 Broadway, New York 10002
  kosher-style
*Camp Young Judaea—Sprout Lake (Verbank)
  % Hadassah, 817 Broadway, New York 10003
  strictly kosher

*Cejwin (Port Jervis)
  71 W. 23rd St., Suite 502, New York 10010
  kosher
*Dror—Camp Ein Harod
  % Dror-Young Zionist Org., 215 Park Ave. S., New York 10003
  kosher-style
*Joseph Eisner Camp Institute (Mass.)
  % Union of American Hebrew Congregations, 838 5th Ave., New York 10021
Massad Hebrew Camps (Pa.)
  426 W. 58th St., New York 10019
  kosher; 2 camps
*Sunrise Lake Camp (Cold Spring)
  225 Park Ave. S., New York 10003
  kosher
Torah Vaavodah Institute (Pa.)
  % Bnei Akiva, 25 W. 26th St., New York 10010
*UAHC Kutz Camp
  % Union of American Hebrew Congregations, 838 5th Ave., New York 10021
  kosher-style
*UAHC Henry S. Jacobs Camp Institute (Miss.)
  % Union of American Hebrew Congregations, 838 5th Ave., New York 10021
*Union Camp Institute (Indiana)
  % Union of American Hebrew Congregations, 838 5th Ave., New York 10021
*Wel-Met Camps—Barryville Branch (Narrowsburg)
  % Child Study Assoc. of America/Wel-Met, 50 Madison Ave., New York 10010
*Wel-Met Camps—Narrowsburg Branch (Narrowsburg)
  % Child Study Assoc. of America/Wel-Met, 50 Madison Ave., New York 10010
*Wel-Met Camps—Silver Lake Branch (Narrowsburg)
  % Child Study Assoc. of America/Wel-Met, 50 Madison Ave., New York 10010
Camp Eagle Cove
  164 Longacre Rd., Rochester 14621
*Camp Lakeland (Franklinville)
  % The Jewish Center of Greater Buffalo, 2600 N. Forest Rd., West Amherst 14228
Camp Beth Jacob
  Woodbourne 12788
  girls

NORTH CAROLINA
Blue Star Camps
  Kanuga Rd., P.O. Box 1029, Hendersonville 28739
Camp Judaea (Hendersonville)—see Georgia
Savage's Mt. Lake (Hendersonville)—see Florida

OHIO
*Camp Livingston (Indiana)
  % Jewish Community Center, 1580 Summit Rd., Cincinnati 45237
  kosher
Camp Wise (Chardon)
  % Jewish Community Center, 3505 Mayfield Rd., Cleveland Heights 44118
  kosher
Jewish Center Teen Camp
  4296 E. Walnut St., Columbus 43209
  day camp
Young Israel Moshevet Stone (Pa.)
  14141 Cedar Rd., South Euclid 44121
  kosher

OREGON
*Camp Bnei Brith (Neotsu)
  % Portland Jewish Community Center, 6651 S.W. Capitol Hwy., Portland 97219
  kosher-style

PENNSYLVANIA
Camp Kinderland (Beach Lake)—see New York
Torah Vaavodah Institute (Beach Lake)—see New York
Block Vacation Center—see New York

Camp Lewis Village—see New York
Camp Poyntelle-Ray Hill—see New York
Camp Massad Beth (Dingmans Ferry)—see New York
Camp Dora Golding (East Stroudsburg)—see New York
Camp Moshava (Honesdale)—see New York
Camp Morasha (Lake Como)—see New York
New Jersey YM/YWHA Camps (Lake Como)—see New York
New Jersey YM/YWHA Camps (Milford)—see New Jersey
Camp Kvutza Galil (Ottsville)
  % Mid-States Habonim, P.O. Box 64, Merion 19066
  kosher
*Camp Joseph & Betty Harlam (Kunkletown)
  % Union of American Hebrew Congregations, 117 S. 17th St., Philadelphia 19103
*Camp Ramah in the Poconos (Lake Como)
  1701 Walnut St., Philadelphia 19103
  kosher
Camp Saginaw
  Penn Sq. Bldg., 1317 Filbert St., Philadelphia 19107
  kosher
*Golden Slipper Club Camp (Stroudsburg)
  1315 Walnut St., Philadelphia 19107
  kosher-style
*JYC Camps (Beker, Arthur, Reeta Camps) (Zieglersville)
  % Jewish Y's and Centers, 401 S. Broad St., Philadelphia 19147
*Pinemere Camp (Stroudsburg)
  % JWB Middle Atlantic Region, 438 W. Tabor Rd., Philadelphia 19120
  kosher
*S.G.F. Vacation Camp (Collegeville)
  % Federation of Jewish Agencies, 1511 Walnut St., Philadelphia 19102
  kosher
Camp Emma Kaufmann (W.Va.)
  % Jewish Community Center, 315 S. Bellefield Ave., Pittsburgh 15213
  kosher
Camp Council (Phoenixville)
  452 Shallcross Ave., Southampton 18966
  kosher-style
Camp B'nai B'rith (Starlight)—see District of Columbia
Young Israel Camp Stone (Moshevet Bnei Akiva) (Sugar Grove)—see Ohio
Camp Massad Aleph-Gimel (Tannersville)—see New York

RHODE ISLAND
Camp Shalom
  % Temple Ohave Shalom, 305 High St., Pawtucket 02864
  day camp
Camp Jori
  % Jewish Family & Children's Service, 229 Wayland Ave., Providence 02906

TEXAS
Ben G. Barnett Camp Young Judaea (Wimberly)
  10921 Chimney Rock, Houston 77035
  kosher
Klein Camp
  1010 N. Bayshore Dr., La Porte 77571

WASHINGTON
*Camp Benbow (Graham)
  % Seattle Jewish Community Center, 3801 E. Mercer Way, P.O. Box 779, Mercer Island 98040
Gan Israel Camp
  4541 19th Ave., N.E., Seattle 98118
  Lubavitch camp—glatt kosher

WEST VIRGINIA
Camp Tel Shalom (Capon Bridge)—see District of Columbia
Camp Emma Kaufmann (Morgantown)—see Pennsylvania

WISCONSIN
Camp Ramah in Wisconsin (Conover)—see Illinois
Camp Interlaken (Eagle River)
   % Jewish Community Center, 1400 N. Prospect Ave.,
   Milwaukee 53202
   kosher
Camp Chi (Lake Delton)—see Illinois
UAHC Olin-Sang-Ruby Camp
   (Oconomowoc)—see Illinois
Camp Herzl (Webster)—see Minnesota
Camp Moshava (Wild Rose)—see Illinois

CANADA
British Columbia
Camp Hatikvah (Oyama)
   % Zionist Org. of Canada, 950 W. 41st St., Vancouver
   kosher
Camp Miriam
   % Ichud Habonim, 950 W. 41st St., Vancouver
   kosher
Manitoba
B'nai B'rith Camps
   370 Hargrave St., Winnipeg
   kosher
Nova Scotia
Camp Kadimah (Luneburg County)
   % Canadian Young Judaea, 1551 S. Park St., Halifax
   kosher
Camp Machar (Luneburg County)—see Ontario
Ontario
Camp Massad
   4140 Bathurst St., Downsview
Camp Kadima
   57 Delaware Ave., Hamilton
Camp B'nai B'rith of Ottawa (Quebec)
   34 Elm Bank Crescent, Ottawa
   kosher
Camp Shomria (Perth)—see Quebec
Camp Biluim (Quebec)
   % Canadian Young Judaea, 788 Marlee Ave., Toronto
   kosher (no mashgiah)
Camp Gesher (Cloyne)
   % Dror Zionist Org., 272 Codsell, Toronto
   kosher-style
Camp Machar (Nova Scotia)
   % Canadian Young Judaea and Zionist Org. of Can-
   ada, 788 Marlee Ave., Toronto
   kosher

Camp Moshava (Ennismore)
   % Bnei Akiva, 86 Vaughan Rd., Toronto
   kosher
Camps Northland, B'nai B'rith (Junior, Intermediate,
   Senior Divisions) (Parry Sound)
   % Jewish Camp Council of Toronto, 750 Spadina
   Ave., Toronto
   kosher
Camp Ramah in Canada (Utterson)
   % Jewish Theological Society, 3101 Bathurst St.,
   Toronto
   kosher
Camp Shalom (Gravenhurst)
   % Canadian Young Judaea, 788 Marlee Ave., Toronto
   kosher
Camp Solelim (Sudbury)
   % Canadian Young Judaea, 588 Melrose Ave.,
   Toronto
   kosher
Good Fellowship (Barrie)
   % Jewish Camp Council of Toronto, 750 Spadina
   Ave., Toronto
   kosher/senior citizens

Quebec
Camp B'nai B'rith (Lantier)
   5151 Cote Ste. Catherine Rd., #203 Montreal
   kosher
Camp Shomria (Ontario)
   % Hashomer Hatzair Youth Org., 4970 Monpetit,
   #18, Montreal
Camp Wooden Acres (St. Adolphe de Howard)
   % Jewish Community Camps, 5151 Cote Ste. Cather-
   ine Rd., #203, Montreal
   kosher
Jewish Laurentian Fresh Air Camp (St. Hippolyte)
   % Golden Age Assoc., 5151 Cote Ste. Catherine Rd.,
   #203, Montreal
   kosher; age 60 and over
Y Country Camp (Huberdeau)
   % YM/YWHA of Montreal, 5500 Westbury Ave.,
   Montreal
   kosher
Camp B'nai B'rith of Ottawa (Quyan)—see Ontario
Camp Biluim (Lac Mercier, St. Jouite)—see Ontario

CAMPS: EMOTIONALLY HANDICAPPED

Camp Emma Kaufmann (W.Va)
   % Jewish Community Center, 315 S. Bellefield Ave.,
   Pittsburgh, PA 15213
   kosher
Camp HASC
   % Hebrew Academy for Special Children, 1311 55th
   St., Brooklyn, NY 11219
Camp Henry Horner
   % Young Men's Jewish Council, 30 W. Washington
   St., Chicago, IL 60602
Camp Ramah in New England
   1330 Beacon St., Brookline, MA 02146
   kosher

Camp Ramah in Wisconsin
   72 E. 11th St., Chicago, IL 60605
   kosher
Camp Tamarack (Brighton)
   % Fresh Air Society, 6600 W. Maple Rd., West
   Bloomfield, MI 48033
Maimonides Institute
   Monticello, NY 12701
Max Straus
   % Jewish Big Brothers Assoc., 6505 Wilshire Blvd.,
   Los Angeles, CA 90048

CAMPS: ISRAEL

American Zionist Youth Foundation
   515 Park Ave., New York, NY 10022
   numerous camps and tours in Israel
Camp JCA–Israel
   8455 Beverly Blvd., Los Angeles, CA 90048
   kosher
Camp NCSY
   116 E. 27th St., New York, NY 10016

Camp Yaron
   % Geller-Howard Travel, 75 E. 55th St., New York,
   NY 10022
Summer Institute in Israel for Problem Adolescents & Col-
   lege Students
   71-11 112th St., Forest Hills, NY 11375

CAMPS: TOURS

Mesivta Ohr Torah–Western Tour
  % P. Abelow, Tour Director, 4904 Independence
  Ave., Bronx, NY 10471
92nd St. Y Bicycle Tours
  YM/YWHA, 92nd St. and Lexington Ave., New York,
  NY 10028
Noam
  25 W. 26th St., New York, NY 10010

high school and college students' program in Israel sponsored
  by Religious Zionist Youth Movement
Summer in London for American Jewish Teenagers
  200 Pinehurst Ave., Dept. 47, New York, NY 10033
USY on Wheels
  3080 Broadway, New York, NY 10027

CHILDREN'S HOMES & SERVICES

CALIFORNIA
Hamburger Home
  7357 Hollywood Blvd., Los Angeles 90046
  a residential home for adolescent girls
Vista Del Mar Child Care Service
  3200 Motor Ave., Los Angeles 90034
Emanu-El Residence
  300 Page St., San Francisco 94102
  residential home for girls
Homewood Terrace
  540 Arguella Blvd., San Francisco 94118
  *places children in private homes, operates residential facilities,
  and acts as an adoption agency*

CONNECTICUT
Jewish Home for Children
  152 Temple, New Haven 06500

DISTRICT OF COLUMBIA
Jewish Foster Home
  1341 G St., N.W., Washington 20026

ILLINOIS
Jewish Children's Bureau
  1 S. Franklin St., Chicago 60606
  operates private facilities and places in private homes

KENTUCKY
Jewish Home for Convalescent Children
  1135 S. 1st St., Louisville 40203

LOUISIANA
Jewish Children's Home Service
  5342 St. Charles Ave., P.O. Box 15225, New Orleans
  70115
  regional child care agency

MARYLAND
Jewish Social Service Agency
  6123 Montrose Rd., Rockville 20852
  runs a residential facility and places in private homes

NEW JERSEY
Hebrew Benevolent & Orphan Asylum
  161 Milburn Ave., Milburn 07041

MISSOURI
Jewish Children's Home
  9385 Olive St. Rd., St. Louis 63100

NEW YORK
Hebrew Children's Home
  1682 Monroe Ave., Bronx 10457
  temporary shelter for neglected children
Ohel Children's Home
  4907 16th Ave., Brooklyn 11204
  Orthodox Jewish foster home
Hebrew Kindergarten & Infants Home
  310 Beach 20th St., Far Rockaway 11600
Jewish Board of Guardians
  120 W. 57th St., New York 10019
  *multifaceted organization providing residence homes and
  placement services*
Jewish Child Care Assoc.
  345 Madison Ave., New York 10017
  residence homes and placement services
Louise Wise Services
  12 E. 94th St., New York 10028
  placement and residential facilities

OHIO
Jewish Children's Bureau
  21811 Fairmount, Cleveland 44118

PENNSYLVANIA
Assoc. for Jewish Children
  1301 Spencer St., Philadelphia 19141
Jewish Home for Babies & Children
  5808 Forbes Ave., Pittsburgh 15200

WISCONSIN
Milwaukee Jewish Children's Home
  2466 N. 50th St., Milwaukee 53200

CANADA
Jewish Family & Child Service
  150 Beverly St., Toronto, ON
  operates residential facility and placement services
Jewish Child & Family Service
  304-956 Main St., Winnipeg, MB
  operates residential home and placement facilities

COLORING BOOKS: COLOR ME JEWISH

Alpha Beta Circle Press, 4036 Telegraph Rd., Bloomington, MI 48013
B'Ruach HaTorah Publications, 1742 24th Ave., San Francisco, CA 94122
Chai Art, 51 Seaton Pl., Valley Stream, NY 11580
Freedom Colors, P.O. Box 1775, Englewood Cliffs, NJ 07632
Gravette Publishing Co., 2969 Old Tree Drive, Lancaster, PA 17603
Great Graphics, P.O. Box 43085, Las Vegas, NV 89104
Ktav, 75 Varick St., New York, NY 10013

COMMUNITY CENTERS

ALABAMA
Jewish Community Center
3960 Montclair Rd., P.O. Box 7377,
Birmingham 35223

ARIZONA
Jewish Community Center
1718 W. Maryland Ave., Phoenix 85015
Jewish Community Center
102 N. Plumer Ave., Tucson 85719

CALIFORNIA
Peninsula JCC
2440 Carlmont Dr., Belmont 94002
West Park JCC
22046 Van Owen St., Canoga Park 91303
North Valley JCC
16601 Rinaldi St., Granada Hills 91344
Hollywood Los Feliz JCC
1110 Bates Ave., Hollywood 90029
Jewish Community Center
2601 Grand Ave., Long Beach 90815
Community Services Division (LA JCC)
5870 W. Olympic Blvd., Los Angeles 90036
Jewish Centers Assoc.
5870 W. Olympic Blvd., Los Angeles 90036
Westside JCC
5870 W. Olympic Blvd., Los Angeles 90036
Jewish Community Center of Alameda & Conta Costa
Counties
3245 Sheffield Ave., Oakland 94602
South Peninsula JCC
3573 Middlefield Rd., Palo Alto 94306
Jewish Federation of Sacramento
2418 K St., Suite A., Sacramento 95816
Jewish Community Center
4079 54th St., San Diego 92105
Brotherhood Way Center
655 Brotherhood Way, San Francisco 94132
United Jewish Community Centers
3200 California St., San Francisco 94118
Jewish Community Center
3002 Leigh Ave., San Jose 95124
Marin JCC
200 N. San Pedro Rd., San Rafael 94903
Bay Cities JCC
2601 Santa Monica Blvd., Santa Monica 90403
Valley Cities JCC
13164 Burbank Blvd., Van Nuys 91401

COLORADO
Jewish Community Center
4800 E. Alameda Ave., Denver 80222

CONNECTICUT
Jewish Community Center
4200 Park Ave., Bridgeport 06604
Jewish Community Center
335 Bloomfield Ave., Hartford 06117
Jewish Community Center
1156 Chapel St., New Haven 06511
Jewish Community Center
Shorehaven Rd. E., Norwalk 06855
Jewish Center
132 Prospect St., Stamford 06901
Western Connecticut Jewish Community Center
1020 Country Club Rd., Waterbury 06720

DELAWARE
Jewish Community Center
101 Garden of Eden Rd., Wilmington 19803

DISTRICT OF COLUMBIA
Jewish Community Center of Greater Washington
6125 Montrose Rd., Rockville, MD 20852

FLORIDA
Hollywood Extension Service
2838 Hollywood Blvd., Hollywood 33020
Jewish Community Center of Central Florida
851 N. Maitland Ave., Maitland 32751
Jewish Community Centers of South Florida
8500 S.W. 8th St., Miami 33144
South Beach Activities Center
Workmen's Circle Bldg., 25 Washington Ave., Miami
33139
North County Extension Service
20400 N.E. 24th Ave., North Miami Beach 33160
Jewish Community Center
8167 Elbow La. N., St. Petersburg 33733
Jewish Community Center
2808 Horatio St., Tampa 33609

GEORGIA
Jewish Community Center
1745 Peachtree Rd., N.E., Atlanta 30309
Jewish Educational Alliance
5111 Abercorn St., P.O. Box 6546, Savannah 31405

ILLINOIS
Deborah Boys' Club
3401 W. Ainslie St., Chicago 60625
Henry N. Hart JCC
2961 W. Peterson Ave., Chicago 60659
Bernard Horwich JCC
3003 W. Touhy Ave., Chicago 60645
Hyde Park JCC
5307 S. Hyde Park Blvd., Chicago 60615
Jewish Community Centers
1 S. Franklin St., Chicago 60606
Rogers Park JCC
7101 N. Greenview Ave., Chicago 60626
South Shore Community Center
7601 S. Phillips Ave., Chicago 60649
South Suburban JCC
20820 S. Western Ave., Olympia Fields, Chicago 60641
Young Men's Jewish Council
30 W. Washington St., Chicago 60602
Jewish Federation of Southern Illinois
327 Missouri Ave., Suite 412, East St. Louis 62201
North Suburban JCC
1221 County Line Rd., Highland Park 60035
Jewish Community Council
718 Central Bldg., Peoria 61602
Jewish Community Council
1500 Parkview Ave., Rockford 61107
Tri-City Jewish Center
1804 7th Ave., Rock Island 61201
Mayer Kaplan JCC
5050 Church St., Skokie 60076

INDIANA
Jewish Welfare Council
4844 Broadway, Gary 46405
Jewish Community Center Assoc.
6701 Hoover Rd., Indianapolis 46260
Jewish Community Council
312 Commerce Bldg., South Bend 46601

IOWA
Jewish Community Center
954 Commins Pkwy., Des Moines 50312
Jewish Federation
525 14th St., Sioux City 51105

KENTUCKY
Jewish Community Center
3600 Dutchmans La., Louisville 40205

LOUISIANA
Jewish Community Center
5342 St. Charles Ave., New Orleans 70115

MAINE

Jewish Community Center
28 Somerset St., Bangor 04401
Jewish Community Center
134 College St., Lewiston-Auburn 04240
Jewish Community Center
341 Cumberland Ave., Portland 04101

MARYLAND

Jewish Community Center
5700 Park Heights Rd., Baltimore 21215

MASSACHUSETTS

Assoc. Jewish Community Centers of Greater Boston
72 Franklin St., Boston 02110
JCC of Brookline, Brighton, and Newton
50 Sutherland Rd., Boston 02146
Jewish Community Center of Greater Brockton Area
71 Legion Park, Brockton 02401
Jewish Community Center
298 Harvard St., Cambridge 02139
YM/YWHA
19 Crescent St., Chelsea 02150
Jewish Community Center of Greater Framingham
1000 Worcester Rd., Framingham 01701
Temple Emanuel Community Center
514 Main St., Haverhill 01830
Jewish Community Center
580 Haverhill St., Lawrence 01841
North Shore Jewish Community Center
4 Community Rd., Marblehead 01945
Jewish Community Center
1000 Harvard St., Mattapan 02126
South Area Jewish Community Center
10 Merrymount Rd., Quincy 02169
Jewish Community Center
65 Nahant Ave., Revere 02151
Jewish Community Center
1160 Dickinson St., Springfield 01108
Jewish Community Center
633 Salisbury St., Worcester 01609

MICHIGAN

Jewish Community Center
18100 Meyers Rd., Detroit 48235
Oak Park Branch of the Detroit JCC
15110 W. Ten Mile Rd., Oak Park 48237

MINNESOTA

Jewish Educational Center
1602 E. 2nd St., Duluth 55812
Jewish Community Center of Greater Minneapolis
4330 S. Cedar Lake Rd., Minneapolis 55416
Jewish Community Center
1375 St. Paul Ave., St. Paul 55116

MISSOURI

Jewish Community Center
8201 Holmes Rd., Kansas City 64131
Jewish Community Centers Assoc.
Wohl Bldg., 11001 Schuetz Rd., St. Louis 63141
Yalem Bldg. of JCC Assoc.
7400 Olive St. Rd., St. Louis 63130

NEBRASKA

Jewish Community Center
333 S. 132nd St., Omaha 68154

NEW HAMPSHIRE

Jewish Community Center
698 Beech St., Manchester 03104

NEW JERSEY

Jewish Community Center
1050 Kennedy Blvd., Bayonne 07002
Jewish Community Center of Southern New Jersey
2395 W. Marlton Pike, Cherry Hill 08034
Passaic-Clifton YM/YWHA
199 Scoles Ave., Clifton 07012
Monmouth YM/YWHA
100 Grant Ave., Deal Park 07723

Jewish Community Center
153 Tenafly Rd., Englewood 07631
YMHA of Bergen County
211 Essex St., Hackensack 07601
YM/YWHA of Raritan Valley
2 S. Adelaide Ave., Highland Park 08904
Jewish Community Center
604 Bergen Ave., Jersey City 07304
YM/YWHA of Morris-Sussex Counties
500 Rte. 10, P.O. Box 455, Ledgewood 08402
Atlantic County Jewish Community Center
501 N. Jerome Ave., Margate 08402
YM/YWHA of North Jersey
152 Van Houten St., Paterson 07505
YM/YWHA Schneider Branch Bldg.
26 E. 39th St., Paterson 07514
YMHA of Raritan Bay Area
316 Madison Ave., Perth Amboy 08861
Jewish Community Center
403 W. 7th St., Plainfield 07060
Congregation B'nai Israel of Greater Red Bank
Hance and Ridge Rds., Rumson 07760
Jewish Community Center of Somerset County
11 Park Ave., P.O. Box 874, Somerville 08876
Jewish Community Center
999 Lower Ferry Rd., Trenton 08628
Eastern Union County YM/YWHA
Green La., Union 07083
YM/YWHA of Metropolitan N.J.
760 Northfield Ave., West Orange 07052
Burlington County Extension Program of JCC of Southern
New Jersey
Willingboro 07093

NEW YORK

Jewish Community Center
340 Whitehall Rd., Albany 12208
Astoria Center of Israel
27-35 Crescent Ave., Astoria 11102
South Shore YM/YWHA
806 Merrick Rd., Baldwin 11510
Jewish Center
2305 32nd Ave., Bayside 11361
Jewish Community Center of Broome County
500 Clubhouse Rd., Binghamton 13903
Bronx House
990 Pelham Pkwy. S., Bronx 10461
Bronx-Riverdale YM/YWHA
450 W. 250th St., Bronx 10471
Jewish Center of Wakefield and Edenwald
641 E. 233rd St., Bronx 10466
Jewish Center of Williamsbridge
2910 Barnes Ave., Bronx 10467
Kingsbridge Heights Jewish Center
124 Eames Pl., Bronx 10468
Mosholu Jewish Center
2044 Hull Ave., Bronx 10467
Mosholu-Montefiore Community Center
3450 DeKalb Ave., Bronx 10467
Pelham Pkwy. Branch of Bronx House
222 Wallace Ave., Bronx 10467
Jacob H. Schiff Center
2510 Valentine Ave., Bronx 10458
YM/YWHA
1130 Grand Concourse, Bronx 10456
Brooklyn Jewish Center
667 Eastern Pkwy., Brooklyn 11213
Congregation Sheiris Israel
Bay Ridge Jewish Center, 405 81st St., Brooklyn 11209
East Flatbush Rugby YM/YWHA
555 Remsen Ave., Brooklyn 11236
Hebrew Educational Society
9502 Seaview Ave., Brooklyn 11236
Henrietta and Stuart Hirschman YM/YWHA of Coney
Island
3330 Surf Ave., Brooklyn 11224
Jewish Community House of Bensonhurst
7802 Bay Pkwy., Brooklyn 11214

Kings Bay YM/YWHA
3643 Nostrand Ave., Brooklyn 11229
Shorefront YM/YWHA
3300 Coney Island Ave., Brooklyn 11235
YM/YWHA of Boro Park
4912 14th St., Brooklyn 11219
YM/YWHA of Williamsburg
575 Bedford Ave., Brooklyn 11211
Temple Beth El
Broadway and Locust Ave., Cedarhurst 11516
Elmira Jewish Community Center
115 E. Church St., Elmira 14901
Gustave Hartman YM/YWHA
710 Hartman La., Far Rockaway 11691
Hillcrest Jewish Center
183-02 Union Tpke., Flushing 11366
YM/YWHA of Greater Flushing
45-35 Kissena Blvd., Flushing 11355
Jewish Community Center
106-06 Queens Blvd., Forest Hills 11375
Central Nassau YM/YWHA
276 Franklin Ave., Franklin Square 11010
Jewish Community Center of Fulton County
28 E. Fulton St., Gloversville 12078
Central Queens YM/YWHA
155-24 89th St., Howard Beach 11414
Hebrew Congregation of the Huntington Jewish Center
510 Park Ave., Huntington 11743
Jewish Center of Jackson Heights
34-25 82nd St., Jackson Heights 11372
Samuel Field YM/YWHA
58-20 Little Neck Pkwy., Little Neck 11362
Beach YM/YWHA
405 Long Beach Rd., Long Beach 11561
Congregation Temple Israel
70 E. Park Ave., Long Beach 11561
Sunnyside Jewish Center
45-46 43rd St., Long Island City 11104
Merrick Jewish Center
225 Fox Blvd., Merrick 11566
YM/YWHA of Lower Westchester
30 Oakley Ave., Mt. Vernon 10550
Jewish Community Center
260 Powell Ave., Newburgh 12550
Assoc. YM/YWHA's of Greater New York
130 E. 59th St., New York 10022
Educational Alliance
197 E. Broadway, New York 10002
Emanu-El Midtown YM/YWHA
344 E. 14th St., New York 10003
YM/YWHA
Lexington Ave. and 92nd St., New York 10028
YM/YWHA of Washington Heights and Inwood
54 Nagle Ave., New York 10040
Jewish Center of Port Chester and Town of Rye
258 Willet Ave., Port Chester 10573
Jewish Community Center
110 Grand Ave., Poughkeepsie 12603
Rego Park Jewish Center
97-30 Queens Blvd., Rego Park 11004
Jewish Community Center of Greater Rochester
1200 Edgewood Ave., Rochester 14618
YM/YWHA of Westchester County
999 Wilmot Ave., Scarsdale 10583
Jewish Community Center
2565 Balltown Rd., Schenectady 12309
Jewish Community Center
475 Victory Blvd., Staten Island 10301
Jewish Community Center
2223 E. Genesee St., Syracuse 13210
Jewish Community Center
2500 21st St., Troy 12180
Jewish Community Center Assoc.
2310 Oneida St., Utica 13501
Mid-Island YM/YWHA
921 Wantagh Ave., Wantagh 11793

United Jewish Y's of Long Island
921 Wantagh Ave., Wantagh 11793
Jewish Community Center of Greater Buffalo
2600 N. Forest Rd., West Amherst 14228
Jewish Community Center
122 S. Broadway, Yonkers 10701

OHIO
Akron Jewish Center
750 White Pond Dr., Akron 44230
Jewish Community Center
2631 Harvard Ave., N.W., Canton 44709
Jewish Community Center
1580 Summit Rd., Cincinnati 45237
Jewish Community Center
3505 Mayfield Rd., Cleveland Heights 44118
Park Synagogue
3325 Euclid Ave., Cleveland 44118
Jewish Center
1125 College Ave., Columbus 43209
Jewish Center
Community Services Bldg., 184 Salem Ave., Rm. 240,
Dayton 45406
Jewish Community Center
6465 Sylvania Ave., Toledo 43560
Jewish Community Center of the Jewish Federation of
Youngstown
505 Gypsy La., P.O. Box 449, Youngstown 44501

OKLAHOMA
Jewish Community Suite
1100 N. Dewey, Suite 100, Oklahoma City 73103
Jewish Community Council
3314 E. 51st St., Suite T, Tulsa 74135

OREGON
Jewish Community Center
6651 S.W. Capitol Hwy., Portland 97219

PENNSYLVANIA
Jewish Community Center
22nd and Tilghman St., P.O. Box 236, Allentown
18105
Jewish Memorial Center
1308 17th St., Altoona 16601
Jewish Community Center of Easton and Vicinity
660 Ferry St., Easton 18042
Northeast Branch of JYC's
560 E. Church Rd., Elkins Park 19117
Jewish Community Center
100 Vaughn St., Harrisburg 17110
Jewish Community Center
Laurel and Hemlock Sts., Hazleton 18201
Jewish Community Center
2120 Oregon Pike, Lancaster 17601
Jewish Community Center
1541 Powell St., Norristown 19401
Jewish Y's and Centers of Greater Philadelphia
401 S. Broad St., Philadelphia 19147
Multi-Service Center for Older Adults
Marshall and Porter Sts., Philadelphia 19148
Neighborhood Center Branch of JYC
6600 Bustleton Ave., Philadelphia 19149
Vacation Bureau of JYC's
401 S. Broad St., Philadelphia 19147
Western Branch of JYC's
City Line and Haverford Aves., Philadelphia 19151
YM/YWHA Branch of JYC's
401 S. Broad St., Philadelphia 19147
Congregation B'nai Jacob of Jewish Community Center
Starr and Manavon Sts., Phoenixville 19460
Jewish Community Center of Pittsburgh
315 S. Bellefield Ave., Pittsburgh 15213
JCC of Pittsburgh
Squirrel Hill Bldg., Forbes and Murray Aves., Pitts-
burgh 15217
Oheb Zedeck Synagogue-Center
2300 Manhantongo St., Pottsville 17901

Jewish Community Center
1700 City Line St., Reading 19604
Jewish Community Center
601 Jefferson Ave., Scranton 18510
Jewish Community Center
406 W. Main St., Uniontown 15401
Jewish Community Center
60 S. River St., Wilkes-Barre 18701
Jewish Community Center
120 E. Market St., York 17401
RHODE ISLAND
Jewish Community Center of Rhode Island
401 Elmgrove Ave., Providence 02906
SOUTH CAROLINA
Jewish Community Center
1645 Millbrook Dr., P.O. Box 3565, Charleston 29407
Jewish Community Center
4540 Trenholm Rd., Columbia 29206
TENNESSEE
Jewish Community Center
5326 Lynnland Terrace, Chattanooga 37411
Amstein Jewish Community Center
6800 Deane Hill Dr., P.O. Box 10882, Knoxville 37919
Jewish Community Center
6560 Poplar Ave., P.O. Box 38349, Memphis 38138
Jewish Community Center
3500 West End Ave., Nashville 37205
TEXAS
Jewish Community Center
750 Everhart Rd., Corpus Christi 78411
Julius Schepps Community Center
7900 Northaven Rd., Dallas 75230
Jewish Community Center and Jewish Community Council
405 Mardi Gras Dr., P.O. Box 12097, El Paso 79912
Dan Danciger JCC
6801 Granbury Rd., Ft. Worth 76133
Jewish Community Center
5601 S. Braeswood Blvd., Houston 77035
Jewish Community Center
103 W. Rampart Dr., San Antonio 78216
UTAH
Jewish Community Center
2416 E. 1700 S., Salt Lake City 84108
VIRGINIA
Jewish Community Center
2700 Spring Rd., Newport News 23606
Jewish Community Center of Tidewater Virginia
7300 Newport Ave., Norfolk 23505

Jewish Community Center
P.O. Box 8237, Richmond 23226
WASHINGTON
Jewish Community Center
3601 E. Mercer Way, Mercer Island 98040
WISCONSIN
Jewish Welfare Council
Executive Bldg., 4513 Vernon Blvd. Madison 53705
Jewish Community Center
1400 N. Prospect Ave., Milwaukee 53202
CANADA
Alberta
Calgary Jewish Center
102 18th Ave., S.E., Calgary
Jewish Youth Center
305 Mercantile Bldg., Edmonton
British Columbia
Jewish Community Center
950 W. 41st Ave., Vancouver
Manitoba
YMHA Community Center
370 Hargrave Ave., Winnipeg
Ontario
Jewish Community Center
57 Delaware Ave., Hamilton
Jewish Community Center
532 Huron St., London
Jewish Community Center
151 Chapel St., Ottawa
Bloor Branch YM/YWHA
750 Spadina Ave., Toronto
YM/YWHA
4585 Bathurst St., Willowdale
Jewish Community Council
1641 Quellette Ave., Windsor
Quebec
Laval Jewish Community Center
755 du Sablon Chomeday
Snowdon-Davis Branch of Laval JCC
Davis Bldg., 5700 Kellert Ave., Cote St. Luc
Neighborhood House Services
6645 Darlington Ave., Montreal
Saidye Brontman Center
5170 Cote Ste. Catherine Rd., Montreal
Snowdon-Davis Branch of Laval JCC
Snowdon Bldg., 5500 Westbury Ave., Montreal
YM/YWHA & NHS
5500 Westbury Ave., Montreal

CONSULTANTS: ITINERANT *MAVENS* IN JEWISH EDUCATION

Ailene Avner, 313 Oxford Ave., Terrace Park, OH 45174
Bernard DeKoven, 4516 Chester Ave., Philadelphia, PA 19143
Rivka Dori, 19298 Espinoza St., Tarzana, CA 91356
Dov Peretz Elkins, Box 8429, Rochester, NY 14618
Seymour Epstein, 4 Markdale Ave., Apt. 2, Toronto, Ontario, Canada M6C 1S9
Fradle Freidenreich, American Association for Jewish Education, 114 5th Ave., New York, NY 10011
Joel Grishaver, 6346 Orange St., Los Angeles, CA 90048
Vicki Kelman, 1140 S. Alfred, Los Angeles, CA 90035
Cherie Koller-Fox, 89 Abbottsford Rd., Brookline, MA 02146
Joyce Klein, 292 W. 92nd St., #5A, New York, N.Y. 10025
Amy Kronish, 7 Fernside Rd., Worcester, MA 01602
Dr. Joseph Lukinsky, Jewish Theological Seminary, 3080 Broadway, New York, NY 10027
Audrey Friedman Marcus, 1110 Holly Oak Circle, San Jose, CA 95120

Ruth Pinkenson Feldman, 220 W. Horter, Philadelphia, Pa., 19119
Steven Reuben, Union of American Hebrew Congregations, 838 5th Ave., New York, NY 10021
Peninnah Schram, 525 West End Ave., New York, NY 10024
Mel Silberman, 6820 Quincy, Philadelphia, PA 19119
Shoshana Silberman, 6820 Quincy, Philadelphia, PA 19119
Daniel Syme, Union of American Hebrew Congregations, 838 5th Ave., New York, NY 10021
Howard Wasserman, 541 W. Sedgwick St., Philadelphia, PA 19119
Joel Wittstein, Isaac M. Wise Temple, 8329 Ridge Rd., Cincinnati, OH 45236
Ronald Wolfson, University of Judaism, 2845 Casiano Rd., Los Angeles, CA 90024

DANCE: ISRAELI FOLK DANCING

CALIFORNIA
Ashkenaz
1317 San Pablo Ave., Berkeley 90211
Sunday 8-11 p.m.
Hillel
2736 Bancroft Way, Berkeley 90212
Tuesday 8-11 p.m.
Café Danessa
11533 Pico Blvd., Los Angeles 90007
Tuesday, Thursday, Saturday
Café Hadarim
1204 N. Fairfax, Los Angeles 90046
Tuesday 8-11 p.m.
Hillel
Greenway Court Fairfax High School, Los Angeles
90007
Hillel
900 Hilgard Ave., Los Angeles 90024
Wednesday 7:30-11 p.m.
Hillel
3300 S. Hoover Ave., Los Angeles 90024
International Student Assoc.
University of California, 1023 Hilgard Ave., Los
Angeles 90024
Intersection
2735 W. Temple St., Los Angeles 90007
Monday 7:30 p.m.
Hillel
17729 Plummer St., Northridge 91324
Zorba's
17746 Saticoy, Reseda 91335

Café Shalom
c/o Jewish Community Center, 3200 California St.,
San Francisco 94103
Saturday 9 p.m.-1 a.m.
Ner Tamid Congregation
1250 Quintera and 24th Ave., San Francisco 94102
Wednesday 7:30-10:30 p.m.
Los Angeles Valley College
13164 Burbank Blvd., Van Nuys 90024
Webster Junior High Gym
1130 Graham Pl., West Los Angeles 90024
Sunday 8-11 p.m.

MASSACHUSETTS
M.I.T.
Massachusetts Ave., Cambridge 02138
Sunday 8-10:30 p.m.

NEW YORK
Queens Boro Holl Jewish Center
156-03 Horace Harding Exwy., Flushing 11367
Wednesday 8:30-10:30 p.m.
Queens College
Student Union Bldg., Kissena Blvd., Flushing 11367
Tuesday 8:00-10:30 p.m.
Columbia University
Earl Hall, 117th St. and Broadway, New York 10017
Monday 7-10:30 p.m.
Israeli Folk Dance Center
746 Broadway, New York 10023
YM/YWHA
92nd St. and Lexington Ave., New York 10028
Wednesday 8-11 p.m.

DANCE ORGANIZATION

Israeli Folk Dance Institute
515 Park Ave., New York, NY 10022
*publishes books and a magazine on Jewish dance; also provides
information on dance records, institutes, etc.*

DIRECTORIES & GUIDES

(listed by type)

CAMPS
Assoc. of Jewish Sponsored Camps
Dept. T 15, Box 572 FDR Sta., New York, NY 10022
lists 45 camps in NYC area
Directory of Resident Jewish Camps
% Jewish Welfare Board, 15 E. 26th St., New York,
NY 10010
*lists camps and provides information on kashrut, facili-
ties, and other matters*

CITIES
A Guide to Jewish LA
% Jewish Federation Council of Greater LA, 590 N.
Vermont Ave., Los Angeles CA 90004
A Jewish Guide to the Bay Area.
Published by Hillel Academy of the East Bay (% Hillel
Academy, 330 Euclid, Oakland, CA 94610)
Guide to the Jewish Rockies
Center for Judaic Studies of the Rocky Mountain Jew-
ish Historical Society. University of Denver, Denver,
CO 80208
Shaloha: A Handbook of Jewish Resources in Hawaii
% Temple Emanu-El, 2550 Pali Hwy., Honolulu, HI
96817
prepared by Susan Kairys of the Hawaii Chavurah
Guide to Jewish Chicago
% American Jewish Congress, 22 W. Monroe St.,
Suite 2102, Chicago, IL 60603

Jewish Boston: A Guide
233 Bay State Rd., Boston MA 02215
Jewish New York
526 W. 187th St., New York, NY 10033
put together by Chaim Casper, who did the Boston one
The Source: A Guide to Jewish Cleveland for Young Adults
% Jewish Community Federation, 1750 Euclid Ave.,
Cleveland, OH 44115
Directory of Jewish Organizations in Philadelphia
% Jewish Times, 1530 Spruce St., Philadelphia, PA
19102
published as a newspaper supplement each year
Jewish Philadelphia: A Students' Guide
% Philadelphia Union of Jewish Students, 202 S. 36th
St., Philadelphia, PA 19104
edited by Myra Schiffman and Heshi Gorewitz
A Guide to Jewish Philadelphia by Esther Klein (1965)
*is a history of Jews in Philadelphia and sites of Jewish
interest—out of print*
Shalom Rhode Island
% Young Women's Division of the Jewish Federation
of Rhode Island, 130 Sessions St., Providence, RI
02906
a directory of Jewish Rhode Island

COLLEGES & COLLEGE LIFE
Directory of Kosher Kitchens
% Young Israel Institute, 3 W. 16th St., New York,
NY 10003
*lists colleges with kosher facilities and gives information
on setting up kosher facilities on your campus*

Hillel Directory
% B'nai B'rith Hillel Foundations, 1640 Rhode Island Ave., N.W., Washington, DC 20036
lists Hillel foundations and discusses Jewish life on many campuses
Yeshiva University Student Council Directory
500 W. 185th St., New York, NY 10033
everything you always wanted to know about religious life in medical, dental, and law schools

COMMUNITY ORGANIZATIONS

Directory of Jewish Community Centers and Young Men's and Young Women's Hebrew Associations
% Jewish Welfare Board, 15 E. 26th St., New York, NY 10010
available for $2
Jewish Communal Services in the United States. A Selected Bibliography
% Commission on Synagogue Relations, Federation of Jewish Philanthropies of New York, 130 W. 59th St., New York, NY 10022
available for $5
National Jewish Community Relations Advisory Council Directory of Constituent Organizations
55 W. 42nd St., New York, NY 10017

EDUCATION

Directory of Day Schools in the U.S., Canada & Mexico
% National Society for Hebrew Day Schools, 229 Park Ave. S., New York, NY 10003
available for $5
Jewish Education Directory
% American Assoc. for Jewish Education, 114 5th Ave., New York, NY 10011
Jewish Studies at American Colleges & Universities: A Catalogue
% B'nai B'rith Hillel Foundations, 1640 Rhode Island Ave., N.W., Washington, DC 20036
Learning to Learn: A Guide to the New Yeshivot in Israel
% World Union of Jewish Students, 247 Grey's Inn Rd., London WC1, England

EDUCATION/MEDIA

Art in Jewish Life: Bibliography and Resources
% National Council on Art in Jewish Life, 15 E. 84th St., New York, NY 10028
lists sources for slides, films, etc.; 50¢
Audio Tapes for Jewish Education
% UAHC Dept. of Education, 838 5th Ave., New York, NY 10021
available for $1
Guide to Feature & Documentary Films for the Hillel Program
% B'nai B'rith Hillel Foundations, 1640 Rhode Island Ave., N.W., Washington, DC 20036
Israel Productions
% National Curriculum Research, Institute of the American Association for Jewish Education, 114 5th Ave., New York, NY 10011
a list of books, pamphlets, periodicals, cassettes, etc., from Israel
Jewish Audio-Visual Materials
% Jewish Media Service, 15 E. 26th St., New York, NY 10010
Multimedia Resources of the Jewish Community
% American Assoc. for Jewish Education, 114 5th Ave., New York, NY 10011
On Jews & Judaism: A Selected List of Films & Filmstrips by Chayym Zeldis
% American Jewish Committee, 165 E. 56th St., New York, NY 10022
available for 35¢
Soviet Jewry—A Catalog of Media Materials
% Jewish Media Service, 15 E. 26th St., New York, NY 10010
Teacher's Reference Room Loan Collection Catalog
% Board of Jewish Education, 72 E. 11th St., Chicago, IL 60605
subject arrangement of filmstrips, slides, and cassettes available; $2.25

The Yiddish Source Finder—A Guide for the Student
% Yugntruf, 3328 Bainbridge Ave., Bronx, NY 10467
available for $1

ISRAEL

Made in Israel
% American-Israel Chamber of Commerce and Industry, 11 E. 44th St., New York, NY 10017
directory of Israeli products and where they are sold

KASHRUT

Guide to Kashrut
% Student Org. of Yeshiva University, 500 W. 185th St., New York, NY 10033
Kashrut Bulletin
Union of Orthodox Jewish Congregations of America, 116 E. 27th St., New York, NY 10022
Kashrut Directory
% Jewish Community Council of Montreal, 5491 Victoria Ave., Montreal, PQ, Canada
lists butchers, caterers, bakeries, restaurants, etc.

LIBRARIES & ARCHIVES

Directory of Jewish Archival Institutions, edited by Philip P. Mason
% National Foundation for Jewish Culture, 408 Chanin Bldg., 122 E. 42nd St., New York, NY 10017
lists and describes Jewish archival institutions in the U.S.
Assoc. of Jewish Libraries
% Jewish Division, Rm. 84, New York Public Library, 5th Ave. and 42nd St., New York, NY 10018
publishes membership list each year available to members for $5

ORGANIZATIONS

American Jewish Yearbook
% Jewish Publication Society, 117 S. 17th St., Philadelphia, PA 19103
has a section entitled "Directories and Lists," including lists of and information about organizations, periodicals, etc.; $15
Directory of American Jewish Organizations
% Frankel Mailing Service, 14 Rutgers St., New York, NY 10002
listing by zip codes with no explanations, $12.50
Directory of Jewish Organizations Around the World
% American Jewish Committee, 165 E. 56th St., New York, NY 10022
Jewish Organizations: A Worldwide Directory
% International Conference of Jewish Communal Service, 15 E. 26th St., New York, NY 10010

RELIGIOUS

Yearbook Directory and Buyers Guide
% United Synagogue Book Service, 155 Fifth Ave., New York, NY 10010

SENIOR CITIZENS

Directory of Jewish Homes for the Aged
% National Association of Jewish Homes for the Aged, 2525 Centerville Rd., Dallas, TX 75228
selected directory of Jewish homes for the aged

STUDENTS

A Guide to Jewish Student Groups
% North American Jewish Students Network, 15 E. 26th St., New York, NY 10010
has information about national groups, metropolitan unions, campus federations, campus groups, community groups, havurot and garinim, educational and art groups, high school groups

WELFARE ORGANIZATIONS

Directory of Jewish Federations, Welfare Funds and Community Councils
% Council of Jewish Federations, 315 Park Ave. S., New York, NY 10010
Directory of Jewish Health & Welfare Agencies
% Council of Jewish Federations, 315 Park Ave. S., New York, NY 10010

EXHIBITS: EDUCATION ON WHEELS

American Jewish Archives, 3101 Clifton Ave., Cincinnati, OH 45220
ATID, 155 5th Ave., New York, NY 10010 (books)
The Jewish Museum, 1109 5th Ave., New York, NY 10028
Union of American Hebrew Congregations, 838 5th Ave., New York, NY 10021
Art shows from many galleries like the Pucker Safrai Gallery, 171 Newbury St., Boston, MA 02103, which specializes in beautiful, high-quality Israeli or Jewish art.

FILMS

Alden Films, 7820 20th Ave., Brooklyn, NY 11214
Anti-Defamation League, 315 Lexington Ave., New York, NY 10016
Board of Jewish Education, 426 W. 58th St., New York, NY 10019
Bureau of Jewish Education, 6505 Wilshire Blvd., Los Angeles, CA 90048
Contemporary Films/McGraw-Hill, Princeton Rd., Hightstown, NJ 08520; 828 Custer Ave., Evanston, IL 60202; 1714 Stockton St., San Francisco, CA 94133
Films, Inc., 1144 Wilmette Ave., Wilmette, IL 60091
Gratz College, 10th St. and Tabor Rd., Philadelphia, PA 19141
Halcyon Films, 454 Toilsome Rd., Fairfield, CT 06432
Jewish Media Service, Jewish Welfare Board, 15 E. 26th St., New York, NY 10010
Learning Corporation of America, 1350 Ave. of the Americas, New York, NY 10019
Macmillan Audio–Brandon Films, 34 MacQuesten Parkway, Mt. Vernon, NY 10550
Mass Media Ministries, 2116 N. Charles St., Baltimore, MD 21218; 1740 Stockton St., San Francisco, CA 94133
Miller-Brody Productions, 342 Madison Ave., New York, NY 10017
Multi-Media Productions, P.O. Box 5097, Stanford, CA 94305
National Film Board of Canada, 680 5th Ave., New York, NY 10019
New Day Films, P.O. Box 315, Franklin Lakes, NJ 07417
New Jewish Media Project, 15 E. 26th St., New York, NY 10010
The New Media Bible, available from The Genesis Project, Inc., 1271 Ave. of the Americas, New York, NY 10020
Phoenix Films, 470 Park Ave. S., New York, NY 10016
Pyramid Films, Box 1048, Santa Monica, CA 90406
Quad Films, Inc., Box 2086, University City, MO 63130
Rutenberg and Everett Yiddish Film Library, American Jewish Historical Society, 2 Thornton Rd., Waltham, MA 02154

UNIVERSITIES
Indiana University AV Center, Bloomington, IN 47401
Michigan State University, Instructional Media Center, East Lansing, MI 48823
University of California, Extension Media Center, Berkeley, CA 94720
University of Colorado, A/V Department, Folsom Stadium, Boulder, CO 80302
University of Minnesota, Dept. of AV Extension, 2037 University Ave., S.E., Minneapolis, MN 55455
University of Southern California, Division of Cinema, Film Distribution Section, University Park, Los Angeles, CA 90007

FILMOGRAPHY
Jewish Audio-Visual Review, American Association for Jewish Education, 114 5th Ave., New York, NY 10011
Jewish Films in the United States: A Comprehensive Survey and Descriptive Filmography, compiled by Stuart Fox, G. K. Hall & Co., 70 Lincoln St., Boston, MA 02111
Medium, Jewish Welfare Board, 15 E. 26th St., New York, NY 10010
Round Up, National Council on Jewish Audio-Visual Aids, American Association for Jewish Education, 114 5th Ave., New York, NY 10011

FILMSTRIPS
Board of Jewish Education, 426 W. 58th St., New York, NY 10019
Jewish National Fund, 42 E. 69th St., New York, NY 10021
Kol R'ee Associates, 1923 Springfield Ave., Maplewood, NJ 07040
Miller-Brody Productions, Inc., 342 Madison Ave., New York, NY 10017
Neot Kedumim, 501 5th Ave., Suite 1801, New York, NY 10017
Ru-Barb Productions, 608 W. Matson Run Parkway, Wilmington, DE 19802
Shimbal Studios, P.O. Box 313, Flushing, NY 11367
Torah Umesorah Publications, 229 Park Ave. S., New York, NY 10003
Union of American Hebrew Congregations, 838 5th Ave., New York, NY 10021

SLIDES
Ohio Poster Co., 14077 Cedar Rd., Cleveland, OH 44118
Religious Media, Inc., Box 8626, Rochester, NY 14619
Skirball Museum, Hebrew Union College, 3077 University Ave., Los Angeles, CA 90007
Union of American Hebrew Congregations, 838 5th Ave., New York, NY 10021
Union of American Hebrew Congregation Synagogue Architectural Library, Commission on Synagogue Administration, 838 5th Ave., New York, NY 10021
YIVO Slide Bank, Max Weinreich Center for Advanced Jewish Studies, 1048 5th Ave., New York, NY 10028

SONG SLIDES
Hebrew Song Slides, M. Bentsiyon, Box 6543, Tel Aviv 61-060, Israel
Religious Media, Inc., Box 8626, Rochester, NY 14619
Songs of Israel on Slides, 161 Field Rd., Longmeadow, MA 01106
Song Slides, American Zionist Youth Foundation, 515 Park Ave., New York, NY 10022

MAKE YOUR OWN SLIDES WITHOUT A CAMERA!
Vix-X Slide and Filmstrip Kits, Griggs Educational Service, 1731 Barcelona, Livermore, CA 94550

GAMES & SIMULATIONS

"Aleph Bet Bingo." Educational Resources, 24010 Oxnard St., Woodland Hills, CA 91367 (all ages)
"Aliyah." Contemporary Learning Materials, 1414 Glendale Ave., Ames, IA 50010 (all ages)
"Alpaim." Limud Publications, 181 Finchley Rd., Montreal, PQ, Canada (ages 10 up)
"Arab-Israeli War." Avalon-Hill Co., 4517 Harford Rd., Baltimore, MD 21214 (jr. hi up)
"Can of Squirms." Contemporary Drama Service, Box 68, Downers Grove, IL 60515 (set for each age level)
"Dig." Interact, P.O. Box 262, Lakeside, CA 92040 (sr. hi)
"Dilemma." Behrman House, 1261 Broadway, New York, NY 10001 (jr.-sr. hi)
"Expulsion." Cherie Koller-Fox, 89 Abbottsford Rd., Brookline, MA 02146 (middle grades up)
"Gestapo." Alternatives in Religious Education, Inc., 3945 South Oneida, Denver, CO 80237 (jr. hi up)
"Going Up: The Israel Game." Alternatives in Religious Education, Inc. (grade 4 up and families)
Hebrew Games. Ktav, 75 Varick St., New York, NY 10013 (all ages)
"Hebrew Holiday Lotto" (Pesach and *Shabbat*). Alternatives in Religious Education, Inc. (grade 3 up)
"Hebrew Scrabble." Selchow & Righter Co., Bay Shore, NY 11706 (grade 4 up)
"Holiday Game Pak." Alternatives in Religious Education, Inc. (grade K-3)
"The Jewish Values Game." Alternatives in Religious Education, Inc. (grade 4 up)
"Kibbutz." Saga Publications, 4833 Greentree Rd., Lebanon, OH 45036 (grade 6 up)
"Kibbutz Town Meeting." Union Camp Institute, 9349 Moore Rd., Zionsville, IN 46077 (jr.-sr. hi)
"Moses and the Exodus." Griggs Educational Service, 1731 Barcelona, Livermore, CA 94550 (grade 5 up)
"On the Move: Soviet Jewry." Alternatives in Religious Education, Inc. (jr. hi up)
"People of Israel." Graded Press, 1974. Available from Cokesbury Stores (all ages)
"Pioneers of Israel." Educational Resources (ages 5–8)
"The Prayer Book Game." In *Sh'ma Is for Real Teacher's Guide*, Hamakor Judaica, 6112 N. Lincoln, Chicago, IL 60659 (jr. hi up)
"Prophets and the Exile." Griggs Educational Service (grade 5 up)
"Provinceland: A Biblical Simulation of the Judges and Kings Era." Griggs Educational Service (grade 5 up)
"Route to Freedom." Board of Jewish Education of Greater New York, 426 W. 58th St., New York, NY 10019
"The Russian Jewry Simulation Game; Exodus." Behrman House (jr. hi up)
"Siege of Jerusalem." Avalon-Hill Co., 4517 Harford Rd., Baltimore, MD 21214 (jr. hi up)
"Sinai: The Arab-Israeli Wars." Simulations Publications, Inc., 44 E. 23rd St., New York, NY 10010 (grade 9 up)
"The Slave Game." Social Studies Service, 10000 Culver Blvd., Culver City, CA 90230 (grade 8 up)
"Star Power." Simile II, Box 1023, La Jolla, CA 92037 (grade 5 up)
"Value Prompters." Alternatives in Religious Education, Inc. (grades 4–8)
"Valuing Simulation." Mobley and Associates, 5000 Sheppard Lane, Ellicott City, MD 21043 (sr. hi up)

FOR TEACHERS
"Moreh/Morah." Howard Wasserman, 541 W. Sedgwick St., Philadelphia, PA 19119

FOR CAMP COUNSELORS AND STAFF
"Madrich: A Training Simulation Game for Camp Staff." Howard Wasserman

GAMES & TOYS

Many bookstores and gift shops sell Jewish games and toys. The following is a list of toy producers
Dreidel Factory
    2445 Prince St., Berkeley, CA 94705
    redwood dreidels
Torah Toys
    P.O. Box 5416, Beverly Hills, CA 90210
    lovely early childhood puzzles and toys; write for brochure
Judaica Unlimited
    P.O. Box 6394, Orange, CA 92667
    Hebrew Scrabble sets
Alternatives in Religious Education
    1110 Holly Oak, San Jose, CA 95100
    has some classroom games
Jewish Teacher Center
    161 Green Bay Rd., Wilmette, IL 60091
    devises, designs, and produces all sorts of marvelous educational games. They are not in the distribution and retail-sale business but if you go there, they'll provide you with the equipment you need to duplicate their games at a very nominal charge
Alpha Beta Circle Press
    4036 Telegraph Rd., Bloomfield Hills, MI 48013
    Hebrew coloring books

Scrabble
    Selchow & Righter Co., Bay Shore, NY 11706
    produces a Hebrew Scrabble set
Behrman House
    1261 Broadway, New York, NY 10002
    has published and distributed some of Marcia Kaunfer's educational games, including "Dilemma"—a game dealing with the Jewish establishment
Board of Jewish Education
    426 W. 58th St., New York, NY 10019
    has produced a variety of Hebrew educational card games called "Kartison le-Shabbat"; write for information
Israel Educational Material & Games
    % Israel Trade Center, 111 W. 40th St., New York, NY 10018
    large selection of Hebrew and Israeli games for all ages; write for brochure
Ktav
    120 E. Broadway, New York, NY 10002
    produces and distributes large selection of Jewish games, toys, and novelty items; write for brochure
Simulations Publications
    44 E. 23rd St., New York, NY 10010
    produces "Sinai"—a game of the Israel wars

GENEALOGY: ROOTING FOR YOUR ROOTS

HELPFUL RESOURCES

Kaganoff, Benzion C. *A Dictionary of Jewish Names and Their History.* New York: Schocken, 1977
Keeping Posted, September 1977. Union of American Hebrew Congregations, 838 5th Ave., New York, NY 10021
Kurzweil, Arthur. *From Generation to Generation: How to Trace Your Jewish Genealogy and Personal History.* New York: William Morrow, 1980
New York Public Library, 5th Ave. at 42nd St., New York, NY. 10018
Rosen-Bayewitz, Passi, and Novek, Minda. *Shiloah: Discovering Jewish Identity Through Oral/Folk History, A Source Book.* Institute for Jewish Life, 315 Park Ave. S., New York, NY 10010.
Rosenstein, Neil. *The Unbroken Chain: Biographical Sketches and the Genealogy of Illustrious Jewish Families from the 15th-20th Century.* New York: Shengold Publishers, 1976
Rottenberg, Dan. *Finding Our Fathers: A Guidebook to Jewish Genealogy.* New York: Random House, 1977
Saladoff, Jane. "Some Call It Roots, By Us It's Yichus." *Moment,* October 1977. P.O. Box 922, Farmingdale, NY 11737
Singerman, Robert. *Jewish and Hebrew Onomastics: A Bibliography.* New York and London: Garland Publishing, 1977
Stern, Malcolm H. *Tracing Your Jewish Roots.* American Jewish Archives, 3101 Clifton Ave., Cincinnati, OH 45220
Toledot: The Journal of Jewish Genealogy. 155 E. 93rd St., Suite 3C, New York, NY 10028

GENEALOGY SERVICES

Genealogy Service, 380 N. Broadway, Jericho, NY 11753

GIFT SERVICES & MAIL ORDER

Jaffa Gate Imports
    5512 Connecticut Ave. N.W., Dept. SH-2, Washington, DC 20015
sells Hebrew pendants
To Israel with Love
    61-08 218th St., Bayside, NY 11364
gift shopping service of fruit, flowers, candy, cakes, and other items to Israel; write for brochure
Hebraica Record Distributors
    % Alan Bloom, 402 Burns St., Forest Hills, NY 11375
sends mailings with close-out specials on records; can order anything for you
Ben-Ezer
    4 Park Ave., New York, NY 10016
will send gift cartons of supreme-size Jaffa oranges anywhere in the U.S. except California and Arizona
Jewish National Fund
    42 E. 69th St., New York, NY 10021
for $5 they will plant a tree in Israel and send a notice of this gift to the person you designate
Michael Madigan Medallics
    P.O. Box 1903, Dept. H, Grand Central Sta., New York, NY 10017
has Star of David and chai pendants

Pottery by Fern
    65-50 Wetherole St., Rego Park, NY 11374
Meat Service
    % Mrs. Irving Freistal, 1 N. Dawes Ave., Kingston, PA 18704
sends 20 lbs. of kosher meat to family or friends in Israel
Decorative Products Co.
    P.O. Box 11248, Philadelphia, PA 19117
if you buy toaster, percolator, can opener, etc., covers from them, they'll include Hebrew chai appliqués
Tempo Designs
    P.O. Box 42, East Greenwich, RI 02818
mezuzah and miniature Torah shields with chains
Mail Order Maven, Inc.
    R.F.D. Box 375, Norwich, VT 05055
Jerusalem Products Corp.
    Box 76, Dept. K, Waitsfield, VT 05673
order by mail Bar/Bat Mitzvah scrolls and other curio items
Israel Buy Mail
    Horev St., 58, Haifa, Israel
order a tallit—many sizes—by mail

HEBREW LETTERS

RUB-ON

B. Arbit Books, 3134 N. Downer Ave., Milwaukee, WI 53211

TEAR-PRESS

Kohl Jewish Teacher Center, 161 Green Bay Rd., Wilmette, IL 60091
Bureau of Jewish Education, 2030 S. Taylor Rd., Cleveland, OH 44118
Czigler, 331 Beardsley Rd., Dayton, OH 45426

IRON-ON

Hebrew Iron-Ons, P.O. Box 2072, Teaneck, NJ 07666
Ktav Publishers, 75 Varick St., New York, NY 10013

HISTORICAL SOCIETIES

CALIFORNIA

Western Jewish History Center of the Judah L. Magnes Memorial Museum
    2911 Russell Ave., Berkeley 94705
Southern California Jewish Historical Society
    590 N. Vermont Ave., Los Angeles 90004

CONNECTICUT

Jewish Historical Society of Greater Hartford
    335 Bloomfield Ave., West Hartford 06117

DELAWARE

Jewish Historical Society of Delaware
    701 Shipley St., Wilmington 19801

DISTRICT OF COLUMBIA

Jewish Historical Society of Greater Washington
    4501 Connecticut Ave., N.W., Apt. 807, Washington 20008

FLORIDA

Jewish Historical Society of South Florida
    4200 Biscayne Blvd., Miami 33137

ILLINOIS

Israel Historical Society
  1 S. Wacker Dr., Chicago 60606

INDIANA

The Indiana Jewish Historical Society
  215 E. Berry St., Ft. Wayne 46982

MARYLAND

Jewish Historical Society of Annapolis
  24 Romar St., Annapolis 21403
Jewish Historical Society of Maryland
  5800 Park Heights Ave., Baltimore 21215

MASSACHUSETTS

Greater Boston Jewish Historical Society
  2 Thornton Rd., Waltham 02154

MICHIGAN

Jewish Historical Society of Michigan
  163 Madison St., Detroit 48226

NEW JERSEY

Jewish Historical Society of Trenton
  999 Lower Ferry Rd., P.O. Box 7249, Trenton 08628

NEW YORK

Jewish Historical Society of New York
  8 W. 70th St., New York 10023

OREGON

Oregon Jewish Historical Society
  % Oregon Jewish Oral History & Archives Project,
  6651 S.W. Capitol Hwy., Portland 97219

PENNSYLVANIA

Philadelphia Jewish Archives Center
  625 Walnut St., Philadelphia 19106

RHODE ISLAND

Rhode Island Jewish Historical Assoc.
  130 Sessions St., Providence 02926

VIRGINIA

Southern Jewish Historical Society
  % Congregation Beth Ahabah, 1111 W. Franklin St.,
  Richmond 23220

CANADA

Canadian Jewish Congress
  150 Beverly St., Toronto, ON

INFORMATION BUREAUS

Jewish Information Bureau
  250 W. 57th St., New York, NY 10017
Jewish Statistical Bureau
  1182 Broadway, New York, NY 10023
Jewish Information Bureau
  234 McKee Pl., Pittsburgh, PA 15213

Jewish Information Service
  22 Glen Park, Toronto, ON, Canada
Jewish Information Service
  150 Beverly St., Toronto, ON, Canada
Israel Information Centre
  P.O. Box 13010, Jerusalem, Israel

LEARNING DISABILITY PROGRAMS & FACILITIES

CALIFORNIA

Gateways Hospital & Community Mental Health Center
  1891 Effie St., Los Angeles 90026
Julia Ann Singer Pre-School Psychiatric Center
  4737 Fountain Ave., Los Angeles 90029
Emanu-El Residence (for Girls)
  300 Page St., San Francisco 94102

COLORADO

Hope Center for the Retarded
  3601 E. 32nd Ave., Denver 80205

ILLINOIS

Jewish Children's Bureau
  1 S. Franklin St., Chicago 60606
Michael Reese Hospital & Medical Center
  29th St. and Ellis Ave., Chicago 60616

MASSACHUSETTS

Temple Kehilath Israel Day Care/Educational Services for
  Retarded Children
  384 Harvard St., Brookline 02146

NEW JERSEY

Day Treatment Center for Emotionally Disturbed Children
  337 S. Harrison St., East Orange 07018
Torah Workshop Day Care/Educational Service for Retarded Children
  120 Halsted St., East Orange 07018

NEW YORK

Shield Institute for Retarded Children
  1800 Andrews Ave., Bronx 10453
Brooklyn Hebrew School for Special Children
  376 Bay 44th St., Brooklyn 11214

Camp Huntington
  % Dr. Kurtzer, 1017 E. 80th St., Brooklyn 11236
Community School Beth Moshe
  913 49th St., Brooklyn 11219
Pride of Judea Children's Services
  1000 Dumont Ave., Brooklyn 11208
National Commission on Torah Education
  500 W. 185th St., New York 10035
  Orthodox
Shalayim
  United Synagogue Dept. of Education, 155 5th Ave.,
  New York 10010
  organization for parents of exceptional children
Tikvah Program
  National Ramah Commission, 3080 Broadway, New
  York 10027
  summer camp program for learning disabled teenagers

OHIO

Suburban East School of PVA—Day Care/Educational Service for Retarded Children
  3031 Monticello Blvd., Cleveland 44118

PENNSYLVANIA

Philadelphia Psychiatric Center (operates Irving Schwartz
Institute for Children & Youth)
  Ford Rd. and Monument Ave., Philadelphia 19131

CANADA

Camp Wooden Acres
  % Jewish Community Camps, 5151 Cote Ste. Catherine Rd., #203, Montreal, PQ
  integrates retarded children into regular groups
Miriam Home for the Exceptional
  4321 Guimont, Montreal, PQ

MAPS & MAP TRANSPARENCIES: JEWISH GEOGRAPHY

The American Map Co., 1929 Broadway, New York, NY 10023
B. Arbit Books, 3134 Downer Ave., Milwaukee, WI 53211
Board of Jewish Education, 426 W. 58th St., New York, NY 10019
The Defense Mapping Agency Topographic Center, Attention 55500, Washington, DC 20015
El Al Israel Airlines, 1225 Connecticut Ave., N.W., Washington, DC 20006
Israel Office of Information, 11 E. 70th St., New York, NY 10021
National Geographic Society, P.O. Box 2806, Washington, DC 20013
Superintendent of Documents, Washington, DC 20402

MUSEUMS

B'nai B'rith Klutznick Exhibit Hall, 1640 Rhode Island Ave., N.W., Washington, DC 20036
Ferkauf Museum of International Synagogue, John F. Kennedy International Airport, Jamaica, NY 11430
Gallery of Art and Artifacts, Hebrew Union College–Jewish Institute of Religion, 3101 Clifton Ave., Cincinnati, OH 45220
Hebrew Union College Skirball Museum, 3077 University Ave., Los Angeles, CA 90007
Jewish Museum, 1109 Fifth Ave., New York, NY 10028
Judah Magnes Museum, 2911 Russell St., Berkeley, CA 94705
Museum of American Jewish History, Independence Mall East, Philadelphia, PA 19106
Rebecca and Gershon Fenster Gallery of Jewish Art, 1719 S. Owasso Ave., Tulsa OK 74120
Spertus Museum of Judaica, 618 S. Michigan Ave., Chicago, IL 60605
Yeshiva University Museum, Amsterdam and 186th St., New York, NY 10033
YIVO, 1048 Fifth Avenue, New York, NY 10028

SYNAGOGUE MUSEUMS

Beth Yeshurun Jewish Museum, 4525 Beechnut, Houston, TX 77000
Beth Zedek Museum, 1700 Bathurst, Toronto, ON, Canada
Chizuk Amuno Congregation, 8100 Stevenson Rd., Baltimore, MD 21208
Congregation Emanu El Museum, 1 E. 65th St., New York, NY 10021
The Morton Weiss Memorial Museum of Judaica, K.A.M. Isaiah Israel Congregation, 1100 Hyde Park Blvd., Chicago, IL 60615
Temple Beth Israel, 3310 N. 10th Ave., Phoenix, AZ 85031
Temple B'rith Kodesh Museum, 2131 Elmwood Ave., Rochester, NY 14618
The Temple-Congregation B'nai Jehuda Museum, 712 E. 69th St., Kansas City, MO 64131
The Temple Museum of Religious Art, Temple Emanuel, 4100 Sherbrooke St. W., Montreal, PQ, Canada
The Temple Museum of Religious Art, University Circle & Silver Park, Cleveland, OH 44106

MUSIC

SONG BOOKS OF NOTE

"The American Experience in Song." Produced by the Board of Jewish Education of Metropolitan Chicago. Available from Tara Publications, 29 Derby Ave., Cedarhurst, NY 11516.
"Bekol Ram." American Zionist Youth Foundation, 515 Park Ave., New York, NY 10022
Coopersmith, Harry. *Companion Volume to the Songs We Sing.* New York: United Synagogue, 1950
———. *The Songs We Sing.* New York: United Synagogue, 1950
———. *More of the Songs We Sing.* New York: United Synagogue, 1971
"Especially Jewish Symbols." Alternatives in Religious Education, Inc., 3945 S. Oneida, Denver, CO 80237 (tape and song book)
"Especially Wonderful Days." Alternatives in Religious Education, Inc. (tape and song book)
"Great Songs of Israel." Tara Publications, 29 Derby Ave., Cedarhurst, NY 11516
"Hassidic Favorites." Tara Publications, 29 Derby Ave., Cedarhurst, NY 11516
"Hassidic-Israeli Club Date." Tara Publications, 29 Derby Ave., Cedarhurst, NY 11516
"Israel in Song." Tara Publications, 29 Derby Ave., Cedarhurst, NY 11516
"Rejoice! Songs in Modern Hasidic Style." Tara Publications, 29 Derby Ave., Cedarhurst, NY 11516
"Shiron." UAHC Camp Institute, 100 W. Monroe St., Chicago, IL 60603
"Shiron Hashachar." Hadassah Zionist Youth Committee, 817 Broadway, New York, NY 10003
"Shlomo Carlebach Songbook." Oak Publishing Co. Available at Jewish book stores
"Sing for Fun I and II." Union of American Hebrew Congregations, 838 5th Ave., New York, NY 10021
"Songs NFTY Sings." National Federation of Temple Youth, 838 5th Ave., New York, NY 10021 (four records and the words to the songs)
"Songs of the Chassidim." Tara Publications, 29 Derby Ave., Cedarhurst, NY 11516

BOOKS ABOUT JEWISH MUSIC

Coppersmith, Harry, and Neumann, Richard. *Music for the Jewish School.* Board of Jewish Education, 426 W. 58th St., New York, NY 10019
Eisenstein, Judith Kaplan. *Heritage of Music.* New York: UAHC, 1972
Idelsohn, A. *Jewish Music.* New York: Tudor, 1929
———. *Jewish Music in its Historical Development.* New York: Schocken, 1967
Neumann, Richard. *Jewish Music Guide for Teachers.* Board of Jewish Education, 426 W. 58th St., New York, NY 10019
Rubin, Ruth. *A Treasury of Jewish Folksong.* New York: Schocken, 1976
———. *Voices of a People: The Story of Yiddish Folksong.* New York: McGraw-Hill Book Co., 1973
MUSIC ORGANIZATIONS: Jewish Music Council, Jewish Welfare Board, 15 E. 26 St., New York, NY 10010

NEWSPAPERS: ANGLO-JEWISH

ALABAMA
Jewish Monitor
   P.O. Box 491, Tuscaloosa, 35401
monthly

ALASKA
Alaskan Jewish Bulletin
   7-730H J St., Anchorage 99506

ARIZONA
Phoenix Jewish News
   1530 W. Thomas Rd., Phoenix 85015
fortnightly

Arizona Post
   102 N. Plumer Ave., Tucson 85719
bimonthly

CALIFORNIA
B'nai B'rith Messenger, incorporating the *California Jewish Voice*
   2510 W. 7th St., Los Angeles 90057
weekly
Heritage Southwest Jewish Press
   2130 S. Vermont Ave., Los Angeles 90007
weekly

Israel Today
 10340½ Reseda Blvd., Northridge, 91326
 bi-weekly
Jewish Observer for the East Bay
 3245 Sheffield Ave., Oakland 94602
 monthly
Jewish Star
 693 Mission St., #305, San Francisco 94105
 monthly
San Francisco Jewish Bulletin
 870 Market St., Suite 504, San Francisco 94102
 weekly

COLORADO
Intermountain Jewish News
 1275 Sherman St., Denver 80203
 weekly

CONNECTICUT
Connecticut Jewish Ledger
 P.O. Box 1923, Hartford 06101
 bimonthly

DELAWARE
Jewish Voice
 701 Shipley St., Wilmington 19801
 bimonthly

FLORIDA
Jewish Floridian
 P.O. Box 2973, Miami 33101
 weekly
Southern Jewish Wekly
 P.O. Box 3297, Jacksonville, CA 32206

GEORGIA
Southern Israelite
 P.O. Box 77388, 188-15 St. N.W., Altanta 30357
 weekly

ILLINOIS
Chicago Jewish Post & Opinion
 6350 N. Albany, Chicago 60659
 weekly
Sentinel
 323 S. Franklin St., Chicago 60606
 weekly
Southern Illinois Jewish Community News
 6464 W. Main, Belleville 62223
 monthly

INDIANA
Indiana Jewish Post & Opinion
 611 N. Park Ave., Indianapolis 46204
 weekly

KENTUCKY
Kentucky Jewish Post & Opinion
 1551 Bardstown Rd., Louisville 40205
 weekly

LOUISIANA
The Jewish Civic Press
 P.O. Box 15500, New Orleans 70175
 monthly
Jewish Times
 211 Camp St., New Orleans, 70130

MARYLAND
Baltimore Jewish Times
 2104 N. Charles St., Baltimore 21218
 weekly
Jewish Week
 8630 Fenton St., Silver Spring, 20910

MASSACHUSETTS
Jewish Advocate
 251 Causeway St., Boston 02114
 weekly
Jewish Times
 118 Cypress St., Brookline 02146
 weekly
Jewish Reporter
 1000 Worcester Rd., Framingham 01701
 monthly

Jewish Weekly News
 P.O. Box 1569, Springfield 01101
 weekly
Jewish Civic Leader
 340 Main St., Worcester 01608
 weekly

MICHIGAN
Detroit Jewish News
 17515 W. Nine Mile Rd., Suite 865, Southfield 48075
 weekly

MINNESOTA
American Jewish World
 9 N. 4th St., Minneapolis 55401
 weekly

MISSOURI
Kansas City Jewish Chronicle
 P.O. Box 8709, Kansas City 64114
 weekly
Missouri Jewish Post & Opinion
 8235 Olive St., St. Louis 63132
 weekly
St. Louis Jewish Light
 611 Olive St., Rm. 1541, St. Louis 63101
 fortnightly

NEBRASKA
Jewish Press
 333 S. 132 St., Omaha 68154
 weekly

NEVADA
Las Vegas Israelite
 P.O. Box 14096, Las Vegas 89114
 weekly

NEW JERSEY
Jewish Record
 1537 Atlantic Ave., Atlantic City 08401
 weekly
Voice
 2393 W. Marlton Pike, Cherry Hill 08002
 semimonthly
Jewish News
 60 Glenwood Ave., East Orange 07017
 weekly
Jewish Journal
 2 S. Adelaide Ave., Highland Park 08904
 fortnightly
Jewish Standard
 40 Journal Sq., Jersey City 07306
 weekly
Morris/Sussex Jewish News
 500 Rte. 10, Ledgewood 07852
 monthly

NEW YORK
Jewish Press
 338 3rd Ave., Brooklyn 11215
 weekly
Buffalo Jewish Review
 110 Pearl St., Buffalo 14202
 weekly
Jewish Current Events
 430 Keller Ave., Elmont, LI 11003
 bi-weekly
Jewish Post & Opinion
 101 5th Ave., New York 10003
 weekly
Jewish Telegraphic Agency Community News Reporter
 165 W. 46th St., Rm 511, New York 10036
 weekly
Jewish Telegraphic Agency Daily News Bulletin
 165 W. 46th St., Rm. 511, New York 10036
 daily
Jewish Week
 1 Park Ave., New York 10016
 weekly
Jewish Ledger
 721 Monroe Ave., Rochester 14607
 weekly

Albany Jewish World
416 Smith St., Schenectady 12305
weekly

NORTH CAROLINA
American Jewish Times
P.O. Box 10674, Charlotte 28234
monthly

OHIO
The American Israelite
906 Main St., Cincinnati 45202
weekly
Cleveland Jewish News
3637 Bendemeer Rd., Cleveland 44118
weekly
Ohio Jewish Chronicle
2831 E. Main St., Columbus 43209
weekly
Dayton Jewish Chronicle
118 Salem Ave., Dayton 45406
weekly
The Stark Jewish News
P.O. Box 9120, Canton 44711
monthly
Toledo Jewish News
2506 Evergreen St., Toledo 43606
monthly
Youngstown Jewish Times
P.O. Box 777, Youngstown 44501
fortnightly

OKLAHOMA
Southwest Jewish Chronicle
324 N. Robinson St., Rm. 313, Oklahoma City 73102
quarterly
Tulsa Jewish Review
2205 E. 51st St., Tulsa 74105
monthly

PENNSYLVANIA
Jewish Exponent
226 S. 18th St., Philadelphia 19102
weekly
Jewish Times
2417 Welsh Rd., Philadelphia 19116
weekly
Jewish Chronicle of Pittsburgh
315 S. Bellefield Ave., Pittsburgh 15213
weekly

RHODE ISLAND
Rhode Island Herald
99 Webster St., Pawtucket 02861
weekly

TENNESSEE
Hebrew Watchman
227 Jefferson, Memphis 38103
Observer
Wilson Pike Circle, Brentwood 37027
weekly

TEXAS
Texas Jewish Post
P.O. Box 742, Ft. Worth 76101; 11333
N. Central Exwy., Dallas 75243
weekly
Jewish Herald-Voice
P.O. Box 153, Houston 77001
weekly

VIRGINIA
UJF News
P.O. Box 9776., Norfolk 23505
weekly

WASHINGTON
Jewish Transcript
Securities Bldg., Rm. 929, Seattle 98101
fortnightly

WISCONSIN
Wisconsin Jewish Chronicle
1360 N. Prospect Ave., Milwaukee 53202
weekly

CANADA
British Columbia
Jewish Western Bulletin
3268 Heather St., Vancouver
weekly
Manitoba
Jewish Post
P.O. Box 3777, Sta. B, Winnipeg
weekly
Western Jewish News
P.O. Box 87, Winnipeg
weekly
Ontario
Ottawa Jewish Bulletin & Review
151 Chapel St., Ottawa
Canadian Jewish News
562 Eglinton Ave. E. Ste. 401, Toronto, Ontario M4P 1P1
weekly
Canadian Jewish Outlook
P.O. Box 65, Sta. B, Toronto
Windsor Jewish Community Council Bulletin
1641 Quellette Ave., Windsor
Quebec
Your Community News
5151 Cote Ste. Catherine Rd., Montreal

NEWSPAPERS: HEBREW & ISRAELI

Haaretz
575 Lexington Ave., New York, NY 10016
Hebrew daily or weekly
Hadoar
1841 Broadway, New York, NY 10023
Hebrew weekly
The Jerusalem Post
110 E. 59th St., New York 10022
English weekly

Maariv
575 Lexington Ave, New York, NY 10016
Hebrew daily or weekly
Omer
150 5th Ave., New York, NY 10011
Hebrew (vocalized daily or weekly)
Yediot Ahronot
% M. Dworkin & Co., 150 5th Ave., New York, NY 10011
weekly

NEWSPAPERS: YIDDISH & FOREIGN LANGUAGE

Der Algemeiner Journal
979 42nd St., Brooklyn, NY 11219
Yiddish weekly
Der Yid
260 Broadway, Brooklyn NY 11214
Yiddish weekly

Yiddishe Zeitung
150 Marcy Ave., Brooklyn, NY 11211
Yiddish weekly
Aufbau
2121 Broadway, New York, NY 10023
German weekly

Jewish Daily Forward
45 E. 33rd St., New York, NY 10016
Yiddish daily
Morning Freiheit
22 W. 21st St., New York, NY 10003
Yiddish daily

Yiddisher Kempfer
575 Ave. of the Americas, New York, NY 10011
Yiddish weekly
Canadian Jewish Weekly-Vochenblatt
379 Spadina Ave., Toronto, ON, Canada
fortnightly

NEWSPAPERS & NEWS SYNDICATES

Der Algemeiner Journal
979 42nd St., Brooklyn, NY 11219
Yiddish Lubavitch weekly
Jewish Press
338 3rd Ave., Brooklyn, NY 11215
Orthodox weekly
Aufbau
2121 Broadway, New York, NY 10023
German weekly
Jewish Daily Forward
45 E. 33rd St., New York, NY 10016
Yiddish daily
Jewish Post & Opinion
101 5th Ave., New York, NY 10003
weekly

Jewish Telegraphic Agency Daily & Weekly News
165 W. 46th St., Rm. 511, New York, NY 10036
daily and weekly editions
Jewish Student Press Service
15 E. 26th St., New York, NY 10010
monthly feature service
Jewish Week & American Examiner
3 E. 40th St., New York, NY 10016
weekly
Morning Freiheit
22 W. 21st St., New York, NY 10003
Yiddish daily
Seven Arts Feature Syndicate and World Wide News Service
165 W. 46th St., Rm. 511, New York, NY 10036
semiweekly

ORGANIZATIONS: SOCIAL SERVICE

American Jewish Society for Service, 15 E. 26th St., Room 1302, New York, NY 10010
Mitzvah Corps, National Federation of Temple Youth, 838 5th Ave., New York, NY 10021
Project Areivim, Network, 15 E. 26th St., New York, NY 10010

ORGANIZATIONS: STUDENT/YOUNG ADULT/YOUTH

The following are the main addresses of organizations. Write to them for the addresses of local affiliates
Lubavitch Youth Org.
770 Eastern Pkwy., Brooklyn, NY 11213
American Zionist Youth Foundation
515 Park Ave., New York, NY 10022
Atid
155 5th Ave., New York, NY 10010
Betar
116 Nassau St., New York, NY 10038
affiliated with Revisionist ideology
B'nai Akiva
25 W. 26th St., New York, NY 10010
affiliated with religious kibbutz movement
Dror Young Zionist Org.
215 Park Ave. S., New York NY 10003
Zionist programs with emphasis on aliyah to Kibbutz Hameuchad
Habonim
575 Ave. of the Americas, New York, NY 10011
affiliated with the Labor party of Israel and the kibbutz movement
Hamagshimim
817 Broadway, New York, NY 10003
affiliated with the general Zionist movement
Hashachar
817 Broadway, New York, NY 10003
promotes Jewish and Zionist values with aliyah as goal
Hashomer Hatzair
150 5th Ave., New York, NY 10011
affiliated with the Mapam party of Israel and the left wing kibbutz movement
Ichud Habonim Labor Zionist Youth
575 Ave. of the Americas, New York, NY 10011
fosters identification with pioneering in Israel
Israel Students Organization
515 Park Ave., New York, NY 10022
Jewish Student Appeal
15 E. 26th St., New York, NY 10010
fund-raising mechanism for national independent Jewish student organizations

Jewish Student Press Service
15 E. 26th St., New York, NY 10010
provides information to editors and those interested in starting papers; also sends out monthly packets of original features and graphics to its member publications
National Conference of Synagogue Youth
116 E. 27th St., New York, NY 10016
Orthodox youth organization
National Federation of Temple Youth
838 5th Ave., New York, NY 10021
Reform youth organization
Network
15 E. 26th St., New York, NY 10010
the major national student coordinating body; publishes a Guide to Jewish Student Groups that is well worth owning
New Jewish Media Project
15 E. 26th St., New York, NY 10010
Noar Mizrachi
26 W. 26th St., New York, NY 10003
religious Zionist organization
North American Jewish Youth Council
515 Park Ave., New York, NY 10022
coordinates and exchanges programs among youth organizations, principally about Israel and Zionism
ORT Youth Fellowship
1250 Broadway, New York, NY 10001
provides vehicle for high school students to strengthen their Jewish identity
Student Struggle for Soviet Jewry
220 W. 72nd St., New York, NY 10023
initiator of the entire Soviet Jewry movement
United Synagogue Youth
155 5th Ave., New York, NY 10010
Conservative student organization
Yavneh
25 W. 26th St., New York, NY 10010
Orthodox college student organization
Zeirei Agudath Israel
5 Beekman St., New York, NY 10038
Orthodox youth organization

PEOPLE TO VISIT OR INVITE AS GUESTS

Rabbi
Cantor
Funeral director
Baker
Social worker with Family Service
Group worker at Jewish community center or youth group
Professor of Jewish Studies
Member Chevra Kadisha
Jewish artist
Doctor
Bride and groom
New mother or father
Grandparent
Jewish teacher
Shaliach
Shofar blower
Mashgiach
Mohel
Executive director of federation
Principal of Jewish school
Federation director
Israeli
Soviet Jew
Holocaust survivor
Immigrant from eastern Europe
Israeli dancer

Sofer
Calligrapher
Schochet
Jewish filmmaker
Volunteer in Jewish agency or organization
President of federation or agency
Hillel director
Sports figure
Jewish author
Jewish musician
Tefillin checker
Jewish politician
Jewish business person
Engineer
Beneficiary of Jewish agency
Member or officer of Jewish youth group
Traveler to Israel
Synagogue officer or board member
Sisterhood/men's club officer or board member
Someone active in Tay Sachs testing
Jewish feminist
Ketubah designer
A convert
Jewish librarian
A day-school student and/or teacher
Lubovitcher Hasid
A secular Jew

PERIODICALS

FOR EVERYONE

American Jewish Historical Quarterly, American Jewish Historical Society, 2 Thornton Rd., Waltham, MA 02154

Biblical Archaeology Review, 1819 H St., N.W., Washington, DC 20006

Commentary, American Jewish Committee, 165 E. 56th St., New York, NY 10022

Conservative Judaism, 155 5th Ave., New York, NY 10010

Hadassah, 65 E. 52nd St., New York, NY 10022

Jerusalem Post, 110 E. 59th St., New York, NY 10022

Jewish Digest, P.O. Box 57, Heathcote Station, Scarsdale, NY 10583

Jewish Spectator, P.O. Box 2016, Santa Monica, CA 90406

Journal of Reform Judaism, 790 Madison Ave., New York, NY 10021

Judaism, American Jewish Congress, 15 E. 84th St., New York, NY 10028

Lilith, 250 W. 57th St., New York, NY 10023

Midstream, Theodor Herzl Foundation, Inc., 515 Park Ave., New York, NY 10022

Moment, P.O. Box 922, Farmingdale, NY 11737

National Jewish Monthly, B'nai B'rith, 1640 Rhode Island Ave., N.E., Washington, DC 20005

Near East Report, 1341 G. St., Washington, DC 20005

Network: A Forum of the Jewish Student Movement, 15 E. 26th St., New York, NY 10010

Options, The Jewish Resources Newsletter, Box 311, Wayne, NJ 07470

Present Tense, American Jewish Committee, 165 E. 56th St., New York, NY 10022

Reconstructionist, Jewish Reconstructionist Foundation, Inc., 15 W. 86th St., New York, NY 10024

Reform Judaism, Union of American Hebrew Congregations, 838 5th Ave., New York, NY 10021

Response, 610 W. 113th St., New York, NY 10025

Sh'ma, P.O. Box 567, Port Washington, NY 11050

Toledot: The Journal of Jewish Genealogy, 155 E. 93rd St., Suite 3C, New York, NY 10028

Tradition, 220 Park Ave. S., New York, NY 10003

FOR TEACHERS

Jewish

Alternatives Magazine. Alternatives in Religious Education, Inc., 3945 S. Oneida, Denver, CO 80237

Compass. Union of American Hebrew Congregations, 838 5th Ave., New York, NY 10021

The Inkling. Alternatives in Religious Education, Inc.

Jewish Education. National Council for Jewish Education, 114 5th Ave., New York, NY 10011

Medium. Jewish Welfare Board, 15 E. 26th St., New York, NY 10010

The Melton Research Center Newsletter. The Melton Research Center, 3080 Broadway, New York, NY 10027

Pedagogic Reporter. American Association for Jewish Education, 114 5th Ave., New York, NY 10011

Christian

Church Teachers Journal. National Teacher Education Project, 6947 E. MacDonald Dr., Scottsdale, AZ 85253

JED Share. 287 Park Ave. S., New York, NY 10010

Probe. Department of Communications, Christian Association of Southwest Pennsylvania, 401 Wood St., 1800 Arrott Bldg., Pittsburgh, PA 15222

Recycle. P.O. Box 12811, Pittsburgh, PA 15241

Scan. P.O. Box 12811, Pittsburgh, PA 15241

Cross-denominational

Religious Education. Religious Education Association of the United States and Canada, 400 Prospect St., New Haven, CT 06510

Secular

Learning. 530 University Ave., Palo Alto, CA 94301

Media & Methods. 401 N. Broad St., Philadelphia, PA 19103

Media Mix. 145 Brentwood, Palatine, IL 60067

FOR STUDENTS

Keeping Posted. Union of American Hebrew Congregations, 838 5th Ave., New York, NY 10021

Tom Thumb, The Israeli Children's Magazine. % Gottex Industries, 1411 Broadway, New York, NY 10018

World Over. 426 W. 58th St., New York, NY 10019

Young Judean. 817 Broadway, New York, NY 10002

Zionist Comments. American Zionist Youth Foundation, 515 Park Ave., New York, NY 10022

PLACES TO VISIT WITH CHILDREN

HaBaD Houses (for the address of your local HaBaD House write to Lubavitch, 770 Eastern Parkway, Brooklyn, NY 11213)
Jewish book store
Synagogue gift shop
Jewish school
Synagogue
Federation office
Jewish agency
Mikvah
Jewish museum
Synagogue museum
Kosher bakery
Bagel factory
Cemetery
Home for the aged
Hillel house
Jewish community center
Jewish camp
Mortuary
Jewish community library
Synagogue library
Rabbi's study
Jewish Studies Department or course at a university

Kosher restaurant
Jewish hospital
Jewish youth organization
Old jewish neighborhood
Former synagogue building
Streimel store
Jewish play or concert

If you live in New York, or visit there, add

The Lower East Side
Williamsburg
Jewish theater for children
Publisher of a Yiddish paper
Museum at the Statue of Liberty
Ellis Island
The Jewish Museum, 1109 5th Ave., New York, NY 10028
Yeshiva University Museum, Amsterdam & 186th St., New York, NY 10033
Temple Emanu El, 1 E. 65th St., New York, NY 10028
Jewish Theological Seminary, 3080 Broadway, New York, NY 10025
Hebrew Union College–Jewish Institute of Religion, 1 W. 4th St., New York, NY 10003

POSTERS

American Jewish Archives, 3101 Clifton Ave, Cincinnati, OH 45220
American Zionist Youth Foundation, 515 Park Ave., New York, NY 10022
Argus Communications, 7440 Natchez Ave., Niles, IL 60648
Educational Resources, 24010 Oxnard, Woodland Hills, CA 91367
Jewish National Fund, 42 E. 69th St., New York, NY 10021
Keshet, P.O. Box 20, Wayland, MA 01778
Options Publishing Co., Box 311, Wayne, NJ 07470
Religious Media, Inc., Box 8626, Rochester, NY 14619
Teachers Press, P.O. Box 3105, Orange, CA 92665
Union of American Hebrew Congregations, 838 5th Ave., New York, NY 10021
Words of Wisdom, P.O. Box 8172, Jerusalem, Israel
Ya-El Imports, 72 Lake Ave., Danbury, CT 06810

BOOKS ABOUT POSTERS AND DISPLAY

Caprio, Betsy. *Poster Ideas for Personalized Learning.* Niles, IL: Argus Communications, 1974 (For Christian settings, can be adapted)
Dester, Kerry. *The Display Book.* Wilton, CT: Morehouse-Barlow, 1977

PUBLISHERS

Prayer Book Press/Media Judaica
    1363 Fairfax Ave., Bridgeport, CT 06605
Ahavath Torah
    1630 50th St., Brooklyn, NY 11212
Arista Press
    332 Empire Blvd., Brooklyn, NY 11232
Behrman House
    1261 Broadway, New York 10010
Bennet Rebecca Publications
    5409 18th Ave., Brooklyn, NY 11238
Goldstein Press
    4602 16th Ave., Brooklyn, NY 11212
    Hebrew
P. Shalom Publications
    5409 18th Ave., Brooklyn, NY 11238
Bloch Publishing Co.
    915 Broadway, New York, NY 10010
Philipp Feldheim
    96 E. Broadway, New York, NY 10002
Hermon Press
    175 5th Ave., New York, NY 10002
Israel Science Services
    440 Park Ave. S., New York, NY 10019
    scientific and other translations
Keter Publishing House
    104 E. 40th St., New York, NY 10016

Ktav
    75 Varick St., New York, NY 10013
J. Levine Co.
    58 Eldridge St., New York, NY 10002
    Hebrew religious books and texts
Leon Mandell
    185 Madison Ave., New York, NY 10016
    medical publications
M. Monderer
    320 Riverside Dr., New York, NY 10024
    technical and scientific works
Otzer Seforim
    33 Canal St., New York, NY 10002
Schocken Books
    200 Madison Ave., New York, NY 10016
Sefer Israel
    156 5th Ave., New York, NY 10010
    books, maps
Sheingold Publishers
    45 W. 45th St., New York, NY 10036
    manuscripts
Shulsinger Bros.
    121 W. 17th St., New York, NY 10011
    books and greeting cards
Jewish Publication Society
    117 S. 17th St., Philadelphia, PA 19103

PUBLISHERS OF JEWISH EDUCATIONAL MATERIALS

Alternatives in Religious Education, Inc., 3945 S. Oneida, Denver, CO 80237

American Association for Jewish Education, 114 5th Ave., New York, NY 10011

American Zionist Youth Foundation, 515 Park Ave., New York, NY 10022

Ani Po, 11805 Monticello Ave., Silver Spring, MD 20902

B. Arbit Books, 3134 N. Downer Ave., Milwaukee, WI 53211

Behrman House, 1261 Broadway, New York, NY 10001

Bloch Publishing Co., 915 Broadway, New York, NY 10010

Blue Star Book Club, P.O. Box 410, Oceanside, NY 11572

Board of Jewish Education, 426 W. 58th St., New York, NY 10019

Board of Jewish Education of Metropolitan Chicago, 72 E. 11th St., Chicago, IL 60605

Brocha Puzzles, P.O. Box 305, Station C, Flushing, NY 11367

B'Ruach HaTorah, 1742 24th Ave., San Francisco, CA 94122

Bureau of Jewish Education, 6505 Wilshire Blvd., Los Angeles, CA 90048

Central Agency for Jewish Education, 4200 Biscayne Blvd., Miami, FL 33137

Cherie Koller-Fox, 89 Abbottsford Rd., Brookline, MA 02146

Contemporary Jewish Learning Materials, Inc., 1414 Glendale, Ames, IA 50010

Czigler, 331 Beardsley, Dayton, OH 45426

Educational Resources, 24010 Oxnard, Woodland Hills, CA 91367

Eric Feldheim, 86 Wooley Lane, Great Neck, NY 11023

Griggs Educational Service, 1731 Barcelona, Livermore, CA 94550

Growth Associates, P.O. Box 8429, Rochester, NY 14608

Hadassah Education Dept., 267 W. 25th St., New York, NY 10010

Howard Wasserman, 541 W. Sedgwick St., Philadelphia, PA 19119

Jaffe Publications, 18401 Shaker Blvd., Cleveland, OH 44120

Jewish Educational Materials, Temple Emanu-El, 99 Taft Ave., Providence, RI 02906

Jewish National Fund, 42 E. 69th St., New York, NY 10021

Jewish Publication Society, 117 S. 17th St., Philadelphia, PA 19103

Jewish Welfare Board, 15 E. 26th St., New York, NY 10010

Jonathan David Publishers, Inc., 6822 Eliot Ave., Middle Village, NY 11379

Kar-Ben Copies, 11713 Auth Lane, Silver Spring, MD 20902

Kohl Jewish Teacher Center, 161 Green Bay Rd., Wilmette, IL 60091

Ktav, 75 Varick St., New York, NY 10013

J. Levine's, 58 Eldridge St., New York, NY 10003

Limud, 181 Finchley Rd., Montreal, PQ, Canada

Machat, 20 Burton Woods Lane, Cincinnati, OH 45229

Media Judaica, 1363 Fairfield Ave., Bridgeport, CT 06605

Melton Research Center, 3080 Broadway, New York, NY 10027

Resler Publication Fund, 5419 E. Broad St., Columbus, OH 43212

Rocket Press, 3101 Clifton Ave., Cincinnati, OH 45220

Simulations Publications, Inc., 44 E. 23rd St., New York, NY 10010

Steven Rittner, 345 Marlborough St., Boston, MA 02115

Teacher's Press, P.O. Box 3105, Orange, CA 92665

Torah Umesorah Publications, 229 Park Ave. S., New York, NY 10003

Union of American Hebrew Congregations, 838 Fifth Ave., New York, NY 10021

United Synagogue, 155 5th Ave., New York, NY 10010

PUPPETS AND PUPPETEERS

Lynn Gottlieb, 126 E. 27th St., New York, NY 10016

Earl Kaplan, University Synagogue, 11960 Sunset Blvd., Los Angeles, CA 90049

Marily Price Puppets, 2430 Prairie Ave., Evanston, IL 60201

Ya-El Imports, 72 Lake Ave., Danbury, CT 06810

RECORDS, SHEET MUSIC, TAPES OF SONGS

Elite Records, 214-18 Whitehall Terrace, Queens Village, NY 11427

Hataklit, 436 N. Fairfax, Los Angeles, CA 90036

Hebraica Record Distributors, 50 Andover Rd., Roslyn Heights, NY 11577

Lyron Music Enterprises, P.O. Box 6103, Beverly Hills, CA 90212

Nama Records, 2367 Glendon Ave., Los Angeles, CA 90064

Tara Publications, 29 Derby Ave., Cedarhurst, NY 11516

SCHOOLS: DAY

C = Conservative
N = Nondenominational
O = Orthodox
R = Reform
B = Boys only
G = Girls only

ALABAMA
Birmingham Day School
   3960 Montclair Rd., Birmingham 35223   N

ARIZONA
Phoenix Hebrew Academy
   515 E. Bethany Home Rd., Phoenix 85012   O
Tucson Hebrew Academy
   5550 E. 5th St., Tucson 85711   O

CALIFORNIA
Hillel Hebrew Academy
   9120 Olympic Blvd., Beverly Hills 90212   O
Rambam High School for Girls
   8844 Burton Way, Beverly Hills 90211   OG
Kadima Hebrew Day School
   7401 Shoup Ave., Canoga Park 91307   C
Long Beach Hebrew Academy
   3981 Atlantic Ave., Long Beach 90807   O
Akiba Academy
   10400 Wilshire Blvd., Los Angeles 90024   C
Bais Yaakov
   7561 Melrose Ave., Los Angeles 90046   OG
Herzl Academy
   1039 S. La Cienega Blvd., Los Angeles 90035   N

Institute of Jewish Education Yiddish & Hebrew School
    8339 W. 3rd St., Los Angeles 90048   N
Rambam Torah Institute
    9017 W. Pico Blvd., Los Angeles 90036   OB
Samuel Fryer Yavneh Academy
    7353 Beverly Blvd., Los Angeles 90036   O
Sephardic Magen David Yeshiva
    7454 Melrose Ave., Los Angeles 90046   O
West Coast Talmudical Seminary
    851 N. Kings Rd., Los Angeles 90069   OB
Yeshiva Torath Emeth
    1071 S. Fairfax Ave., Los Angeles 90019   O
San Diego Hebrew Day School
    520 E. 8th St., National City 92050   N
Emek Hebrew Day School
    12732 Chandler Blvd., North Hollywood 91607   O
Hillel Academy of East Bay
    3778 Park Blvd., Oakland 94610   N
South Peninsula Hebrew Day School
    4175 Manuela Ave., Palo Alto 94306   O
Hebrew Laboratory School
    4605 Alice St., San Diego 92115   N
Brandeis Day School
    2266 California St., San Francisco 94115   N
Brandeis Day School
    601 14th Ave., San Francisco 94118   N
Hebrew Academy of San Francisco
    766 26th Ave., San Francisco 94121   N
Ezra Torah Institute
    1525 Clearview Rd., Santa Barbara 93101   O

COLORADO
Beth Jacob High School
    5100 W. 14th Ave., Denver 80204   OG
Hebrew Educational Alliance School
    1555 Stuart St., Denver 80204   O
Hillel Academy
    450 S. Hudson St., Denver 80222   N
Yeshivas Toras Chaim
    1400 Quitman St., Denver 80204   OB

CONNECTICUT
Yeshiva Hebrew Academy of Greater Hartford
    53 Gabb Rd., Bloomfield 06002   O
Hillel Academy
    4200 Park Ave., Bridgeport 06601   N
Hillel Academy
    1571 Stratfield Rd., Fairfield 06430   N
Solomon Schechter of New London County
    P.O. Box 807, New London 06320   C
Hebrew Day School
    151 Washington St., Norwich 06360   N
Beth Chana Academy
    261 Derby Ave., Orange 06477   OG
New Haven Hebrew Day School
    261 Derby Ave., Orange 06477   OB
Bi-Cultural Day School
    159 Colonial Rd., Stamford 06906   O
Solomon Schechter Day School
    160 Mohegan Dr., West Hartford 06117   C
Ezra Academy
    Rimmon Rd., Woodbridge 06525   C

DELAWARE
Albert Einstein Hebrew Academy
    300 Lea Blvd., Wilmington 19802   O

DISTRICT OF COLUMBIA
Agudath Achim Academy
    6343 13th St., N.W., Washington 20011   N
Hebrew Academy of Greater Washington
    6045 16th St., N.W., Washington 20011   O

FLORIDA
Solomon Schechter Day School
    P.O. Box 3235, Jacksonville 32206   C
Greater Miami Hebrew Academy
    2400 Pine Tree Dr., Miami 33140   N
Lehram Day School
    727 77th St., Miami 33141   C

Oholei Torah Day School
    1200 Alton Rd., Miami 33139   O
    boys and girls separate
Solomon Schechter School
    7500 S.W. 120th St., Miami 33156   C
South Dade Hebrew Academy
    118-01 S.W. 74th St., Miami 33156   O
Greater Miami Hebrew Academy for Girls
    2525 Pinetree Dr., Miami Beach 33140   OG
Menorah Day School
    620 75th St., Miami Beach 33139   C
Yeshiva Day School
    990 N.E. 171st St., North Miami Beach 33162   O
Hillel School
    2713 Bayshore Blvd., Tampa 33609   C
Jewish Community Day School of Palm Beach
    2815 N. Flagler Dr., West Palm Beach 33407   O

GEORGIA
Hebrew Academy of Atlanta
    1892 N. Druid Hills, N.E., Atlanta 30319   O
Solomon Schechter Day School
    600 Peachtree Battle Ave., N.W., Atlanta 30327   C
Yeshiva High School
    1787 Lavista Rd., N.E., Atlanta 30329   O
Savannah Hebrew Day School
    5111 Abercorn St., Savannah 31405   O

ILLINOIS
Arie Crown Hebrew Day School
    5101 N. Kimball Ave., Chicago 60625   N
Bais Yaakov Hebrew School
    2447 W. Granville Ave., Chicago 60659   OG
Bais Yaakov Hebrew School, Boys Division
    6526 N. California, Chicago 60659   OB
Hamasmid Center High School
    4721 N. Bernard, Chicago 60625   N
Hillel Torah North Suburban Day School
    3003 W. Touhy Ave., Chicago 60645   O
Ida Crown Jewish Academy
    2828 W. Pratt Blvd., Chicago 60645   OG
Ida Crown Jewish Academy
    6350 N. Whipple St., Chicago 60659   OG
Sholem Aleichem School
    2100 W. Devon Ave., Chicago 60645   N
Solomon Schechter Day School
    5200 Hyde Park Blvd., Chicago 60615   C
Telshe Yeshiva Chicago Branch
    3535 W. Foster Ave., Chicago 60625   OB
Yeshiva Brisk
    6043 N. California Ave., Chicago 60659   OB
Sager Solomon Schechter Day School
    350 Lee Rd., Northbrook 60062   C
Peoria Hebrew Day School
    3616 N. Sheridan Rd., Peoria 61604   N
Hillel Torah North Suburban Day School
    7120 Laramie Ave., Skokie 60076   O
Yeshiva High School Preparatory Division
    7135 N. Carpenter Rd., Skokie 60076   OB
North Shore School of Jewish Studies
    2834 Birchwood, Wilmette 60091   C

INDIANA
Hebrew Academy of Indianapolis
    6510 Hoover Rd., Indianapolis 46260   N
South Bend Hebrew Day School
    3610 S. Miami Rd., South Bend 46614   OG

KANSAS
Hebrew Academy of Greater Kansas City
    5311 W. 75th St., Prairie Village 66208   N

KENTUCKY
Louisville Jewish Day School
    3600 Dutchmans La., Louisville 40205   N

LOUISIANA
Lake Shore Hebrew Day
    7000 Canal Blvd., New Orleans 70124   O

MAINE

Hebrew Academy of Bangor
  28 Somerset St., Bangor 04401   O
Hillel Academy
  76 Noyes St., Portland 04103   O

MARYLAND

Bais Yaakov School for Girls
  Seven Mile La., Baltimore 21208   OG
Bais Yaakov School for Girls
  4901 Greenspring Ave., Baltimore 21209   OG
Beth Tefiloh Day School
  3300 Old Court Rd., Baltimore 21208   O
Greenspring Valley Synagogue School
  6214 Pimlico Rd., Baltimore 21209   O
Ner Israel High School
  400 Mt. Wilson La., Baltimore 21208   OB
Talmudical Academy of Baltimore
  4445 Old Court Rd., Baltimore 21208   OB
Yeshiva Shearith Hapleta
  6612 Biltmore Ave., Baltimore 21215   OB
Solomon Schechter Day School
  8402 Freyman Dr., Chevy Chase 20015   C
Bais Yaakov School for Girls
  8729 Church La., Randalstown 21133   OG
Silver Spring Jewish Center School
  1401 Arcola Ave., Silver Spring 20902   O
Weizmann Yiddish-Hebrew School
  11724 Auth La., Silver Spring 20902   N
Yeshiva High School of Greater Washington
  813 University Blvd. W., Silver Spring 20901   OG
Yeshiva High School of Greater Washington,
Boys Division
  11801 Kemp Mill Rd., Silver Spring 20902   OB
Shaare Tikvah School
  5405 Old Temple Rd., Temple Hills 20031   C

MASSACHUSETTS

South Shore Hebrew Academy
  144 Belmont Ave., Brockton 02401   O
Brookline I. L. Peretz School of the Workmen's Circle
  1762 Beacon St., Brookline 02146   N
Maimonides School
  Philbrick Rd., Brookline 02146   O
New England Academy, Lubavitch Yeshiva
  9 Prescott St., Brookline 02146   O
Chelsea Hebrew Academy
  48 Washington Ave., Chelsea 02150   O
Montefiore Day School
  460 Westford St., Lowell 01851   O
Shaloh House Day School
  68 Smith Rd., Milton 02168   O
Solomon Schechter Day School
  385 Ward St., Newton 02159   C
I. L. Peretz Yiddish Center
  51 N. Main St., Randolph 02368   N
Hebrew Academy
  89 Randolph St., Springfield 01108   N
Heritage Academy Beth Morasha
  302 Maple St., Springfield 01105   N
Lubavitcher Yeshiva
  29 Oakland St., Springfield 01108   O
Hillel Academy of North Shore
  140 Atlantic Ave., Swampscott 01907   N
Yeshiva Achei Tmimim
  22 Newton Ave., Worcester 01602   O

MICHIGAN

Hillel Day School
  32200 Middlebelt Rd., Farmington 48024   C
Beth Jacob School
  15400 W. Ten Mile Rd., Oak Park 48237   OG
Akiva Hebrew Day School
  Rohlick Bldg. 21550 W. Twelve Mile Rd.,
  Southfield 48076   O
Yeshiva Beth Yehuda
  15751 W. 10½ Mile Rd., Southfield 48075   O

MINNESOTA

Torah Academy of Minneapolis
  8200 W. 33rd St., Minneapolis 55426   O

MISSOURI

Rabbi H. F. Epstein Hebrew Academy
  1138 N. Warson Rd., St. Louis 63132   O
Yeshiva Rabbi Zachariah Joseph
  1236 North and South Rd., St. Louis 63130   OB
Torah Academy for Girls
  8630 Olive Blvd., University City 63130   OG

NEBRASKA

Omaha Jewish Day School
  12604 Pacific St., Omaha 68154   O

NEW JERSEY

Talmudical High School of Central N.J.
  Adelphia-Farmingdale Rd., P.O. Box 7,
  Adelphia 07710   OB
Harry B. Kellman Academy
  2901 W. Chapel Ave., Cherry Hill 08034   C
Moriah Yeshiva Academy
  2 Harrison St., Edison 08817   O
Bruria High School for Girls
  35 North Ave., Elizabeth 07208   OG
Yeshiva & Mesivta of Elizabeth
  330 Elmora Ave., Elizabeth 07208   O
Moriah School
  53 S. Woodland St., Englewood 07631   O
Bergen Hebrew Institute
  2-8 Oxford Ave., Jersey City 07304   N
Rogosin Yeshiva High School
  25 Cottage St., Jersey City 07306   O
Hebrew Academy of Morris County
  Lincoln Ave., Lake Hiawatha 07034   C
Bazalel Hebrew Day School
  419 5th St., Lakewood 08701   O
Lakewood Cheder School
  601 Private Way, Lakewood 08701   O
Solomon Schechter Academy
  P.O. Box 461, Lakewood 08701   C
Yeshiva Yetev Lev Satmar
  405 Forest Ave., Lakewood 08701   O
  boys and girls separate
Hebrew Academy of Atlantic City
  501 N. Jerome Ave., Margate 08402   N
Workmen's Circle School
  73 Woodbridge Ave., New Brunswick 08904   N
Frisch School—Yeshiva High School of North N.J.
  243 E. Frisch Court, Paramus 07652   O
Hillel Academy
  565 Broadway, Passaic 07055   O
Yavneh Academy
  413 12th Ave., Paterson 07514   O
Hillel Academy
  100 1st St., Perth Amboy 08861   O
Plainfield Hebrew Day School
  532 W. 7th St., Plainfield 07060   O
Hebrew Youth Academy
  457 Center St., South Orange 07079   O
Solomon Schechter Day School
  70 Sterling Pl., Teaneck 07666   C
Trenton Hebrew Academy
  1201 W. State St., Trenton 08618   N
Solomon Schechter Day School
  Vauxhall Rd. and Cedar Ave., Union City 07083   C
Yeshiva of Hudson County
  2501 New York Ave., Union City 07087   O
Yeshiva Sanz of Hudson County
  3400 New York Ave., Union City 07087   OB
Jewish Day School
  N. Orchard Rd., Vineland 08360   O
Kadimah Torah School of South N.J.
  321 Grape St., Vineland 08360   O
Hillel School
  Logan Rd. and Park Blvd., Wanamassa 07712   O

NEW YORK

Max & Rose Heller Hebrew Academy
    203-05 32nd Ave., Bayside 11361   O

Yeshiva of Belle Harbor
    134-01 Rockaway Beach Blvd., Belle Harbor 11694

HHANC Mid-Island Hebrew Day School
    42 Locust Ave., Bethpage 11714   O

Hillel Academy of Broome County
    Deerfield Pl., Binghamton 13903   O

Academy for Jewish Religion
    250th St. and Henry Hudson Pkwy., Bronx 10471   N

Beth Jacob–Beth Leah
    1301 St. Lawrence Ave., Bronx 10472   OG

Beth Jacob–Beth Miriam School
    1570 Walton Ave., Bronx 10452   OG

Beth Jacob High School of the Bronx
    2058 Wallace Ave., Bronx 10462   OG

Beth Jacob School for Girls of East Bronx
    2126 Barnes Ave., Bronx 10462   OG

Edenwald School
    1250 E. 229th St., Bronx 10466   N

Hebrew Academy of Pelham Pkwy.
    900 Pelham Pkwy. S., Bronx 10462   C

Hebrew Day Nursery
    5720 Mosholu Ave., Bronx 10471   O

Lubavitcher Yeshiva Achei Tmimim
    3880 Sedgwick Ave., Bronx 10463   OG

Lubavitcher Yeshiva Achei Tmimim
    3415 Olinville Ave., Bronx 10467   OB

Manhattan Hebrew High School—Mesivta Ohr Torah
    3700 Independence Ave., Bronx 10463   OB

N.Y. Institute for the Education of the Blind
    999 Pelham Pkwy., Bronx 10469   N

Salanter Akiba Riverdale Academy
    655 W. 254th St., Bronx 10471   O

Yeshiva Torah Ve'Emunah
    1779 E. 172nd St., Bronx 10472   OB

Yeshiva Zichron Moshe
    2060 Wallace Ave., Bronx 10462   OB

Achiezer Yeshiva
    2433 Ocean Pkwy., Brooklyn 11235   O

Achiezer Yeshiva Branch
    293 Neptune Ave., Brooklyn 11235   O

Bais Chana High School
    187 Hooper St., Brooklyn 11211   OG

Bais Chana School for Girls
    204 Keap St., Brooklyn 11211   OG

Bais Isaac Zvi
    1019 46th St., Brooklyn 11219   O

Bais Isaac Zvi
    867 50th St., Brooklyn 11220   O

Bais Yaacov D'Khal Yereim
    563 Bedford Ave., Brooklyn 11211   OG

Bais Yaacov of Brooklyn
    1362 49th St., Brooklyn 11219   OG

Bais Yaacov of Brooklyn High School
    1315 43rd St., Brooklyn 11219   OG

Beer Mordechai
    1670 Ocean Ave., Brooklyn 11230   O

Beth Jacob
    143 S. 8th St., Brooklyn 11211   OG

Beth Jacob Day School for Girls
    550 Ocean Pkwy., Brooklyn 11218   OG

Beth Jacob Elementary School of Flatbush
    1302 Ave. I, Brooklyn 11230   OG

Beth Jacob High School
    4421 15th Ave., Brooklyn 11219   OG

Beth Jacob of Boro Park
    1371 46th St., Brooklyn 11219   OG

Beth Medrash Shaarei Yosher
    4102 16th Ave., Brooklyn 11204   OB

Beth Rachel School for Girls
    125 Heyward St., Brooklyn 11206   OG

Beth Rachel School for Girls
    225 Patchen Ave., Brooklyn 11233   OG

Beth Rachel School for Girls
    960 49th St., Brooklyn 11219   OG

Beth Rivka High School for Girls
    2301 Snyder Ave., Brooklyn 11229   OG

Beth Rivka School
    310 Crown St., Brooklyn 11225   OG

Beth Rivka School for Girls
    2270 Church Ave., Brooklyn 11226   OG

Beth Sarah School for Girls
    5801 16th Ave., Brooklyn 11204   OG

Bialik School of Flatbush Jewish Center
    500 Church Ave., Brooklyn 11218   C

Bnos Israel of East Flatbush
    9214 Ave. B, Brooklyn 11236   OG

Bnos Jacob School for Girls
    174 Pacific St., Brooklyn 11201   OG

Bnos Zion of Bobov
    5220 13th Ave., Brooklyn 11219   OG

Bobover Yeshiva Bnei Zion
    1533 48th St., Brooklyn 11219   OB

Hadar Hatorah
    875 Eastern Pkwy., Brooklyn 11213   OB

Hebrew Institute of Boro Park
    5000 13th Ave., Brooklyn 11219   OB

Kingsway Academy
    2810 Nostrand Ave., Brooklyn 11229   O

Magen David Yeshiva
    50 Ave. P, Brooklyn 11204   O

Mesivta Bnei Torah
    4722 18th Ave., Brooklyn 11204   OB

Mesivta Eitz Chaim of Bobov
    1533 48th St., Brooklyn 11219   OB

Mesivta Haichel Hatorah
    2025 64th St., Brooklyn 11204   OB

Mesivta Nachlas Yaakov
    185 Wilson St., Brooklyn 11211   OB

Mesivta Rabbi Chaim Berlin
    1593 Coney Island Ave., Brooklyn 11230   OB

Mesivta Shaarei Emunah
    661 Linden Blvd., Brooklyn 11203   OB

Mesivta Torah Vodaath
    425 E. 9th St., Brooklyn 11218   OB

Mesivta Torah Emes Kamenitz, Joseph S. Gruss H.S.
    1651 57th St., Brooklyn 11204   OB

Mirrer Yeshiva H.S.
    1795 Ocean Pkwy., Brooklyn 11223   OB

Ohel Soroh
    771 Crown St., Brooklyn 11213   O

Oholei Torah
    667 Eastern Pkwy., Brooklyn 11213   OB

Oholei Torah Branch
    1267 Eastern Pkwy., Brooklyn 11213   OB

Oholei Torah Branch
    417 Troy Ave., Brooklyn 11213   OB

Philip Hirth Academy of Brooklyn
    4419 18th Ave., Brooklyn 11204   OB

Prospect Park Yeshiva
    1202 Ave. P, Brooklyn 11229   O

Prospect Park Yeshiva High School for Girls
    1609 Ave. R, Brooklyn 11229   OG

Rabbi Harry Halpern Day School
    1625 Ocean Ave., Brooklyn 11230   C

Rabbinical Seminary of Munkacs
    1377 42nd St., Brooklyn 11219   OB

Sara Schenirer High School
    4622 14th Ave., Brooklyn 11219   OG

Sephardic Institute
    511 Ave. R, Brooklyn 11223   OB

Shulamith School for Girls
    1353 50th St., Brooklyn 11219   OG

Skwere Mosdow
    1301 49th St., Brooklyn 11219   OG

Talmud Torah Toldos Yakov Yosef
    94 Wilson St., Brooklyn 11211   OB

Tomer Dvorah School for Girls
    4500 9th Ave., Brooklyn 11219   OG

United Lubavitcher Yeshivoth
  841-853 Ocean Pkwy., Brooklyn 11230   OB
United Talmudical Academy Torah Vyirah
  176 Degraw St., Brooklyn 11231   OB
United Talmudical Academy Torah Vyirah
  167 Sands St., Brooklyn 11201   OB
United Talmudical Academy Torah Vyirah Branch
  212 Williamsburg St. E., Brooklyn 11211   OB
United Talmudical Academy Torah Vyirah Branch
  235-238 Marcy Ave., Brooklyn 11211   OB
United Talmudical Academy Torah Vyirah of Boro Park
  1350 53rd St., Brooklyn 11219   OB
Yeshiva Ahavas Yisroel
  6 Lee Ave., Brooklyn 11211   OB
Yeshiva & Beth Jacob School of Canarsie
  904 E. 98th St., Brooklyn 11236   O
Yeshiva & Mesivta Arugath Habosem
  171-173 Hooper St., Brooklyn 11211   OB
Yeshiva & Mesivta Bais Yitzchok
  1301 49th St., Brooklyn 11219   OB
Yeshiva & Mesivta Beer Shmuel
  1363 50th St., Brooklyn 11219   OB
Yeshiva & Mesivta Beer Shmuel
  4407 12th Ave., Brooklyn 11219   OB
Yeshiva & Mesivta Karlin Stolin
  1818 54th St., Brooklyn 11204   OB
Yeshiva & Mesivta Zichron Meilech of Eastern Pkwy.
  418 E. 45th St., Brooklyn 11203   OB
Yeshiva & Mesivta Zichron Meilech of Eastern
Pkwy. Branch
  1604 Ave. R, Brooklyn 11229   OB
Yeshiva Ateres Yisroel
  8101 Ave. K, Brooklyn 11236   O
Yeshiva Bais Yitzchok D'Spinka
  192 Keap St., Brooklyn 11211   OB
Yeshiva Bais Yitzchok D'Spinka Branch
  191 Rodney St., Brooklyn 11211   OB
Yeshiva Beth Hatalmud
  2127 82nd St., Brooklyn 11214   OB
Yeshiva Beth Hillel D'Krasna
  1364-66 42nd St., Brooklyn 11219   OB
Yeshiva Beth Jehudo
  1383 44th St., Brooklyn 11219   OB
Yeshiva Harama
  Yeshiva High School for Girls, 875 Ave. Z,
  Brooklyn 11235   OG
Yeshiva Hasode Hatorah
  131 Lee Ave., Brooklyn 11211   OB
Yeshiva Imrei Yosef Spinka
  1460 56th St., Brooklyn 11219   OB
Yeshiva Kehilath Yaakov
  206 Wilson St., Brooklyn 11211   OB
Yeshiva Machzikei Hadas Belz
  1601 42nd St., Brooklyn 11204   OB
Yeshiva Machzekei Torah D'Chassidei Belz
  630 Bedford Ave., Brooklyn 11211   OB
Yeshiva of Brooklyn
  1470 Ocean Pkwy. Brooklyn 11230   OG
Yeshiva of Brooklyn
  1210 Ocean Pkwy., Brooklyn 11230   OB
Yeshiva of Crown Heights
  963 E. 107th St., Brooklyn 11236   O
Yeshiva of Flatbush
  919 E. 10th St., Brooklyn 11230   O
Yeshiva of Flatbush High School
  1609 Ave. J, Brooklyn 11230   O
Yeshiva of Kings Bay
  2611 Ave. Z, Brooklyn 11235   O
Yeshiva of Mill Basin
  2114 E. 66th St., Brooklyn 11234   O
Yeshiva Ohel Moshe
  7914 Bay Pkwy., Brooklyn 11214   O
Yeshiva Ohel Yaakov
  1480 43rd St., Brooklyn 11219   OB
Yeshiva Rabbi Chaim Berlin
  321 Ave. N, Brooklyn 11230   OB

Yeshiva Rabbi Chaim Berlin Branch
  1750 E. 4th St., Brooklyn 11230   OB
Yeshiva Rabbi David Leibowitz
  9102 Church Ave., Brooklyn 11236   O
Yeshiva Rabbi Solomon Kluger
  Mesivta Chasan Sofer, 1876 50th St., Brooklyn
  11204   OB
Yeshiva Rambam
  3121 Kings Hwy., Brooklyn 11234   O
Yeshiva R'Tzahd
  Rabbi Hirsh Dachowitz Day School, 1800 Utica
  Ave., Brooklyn 11234   O
Yeshiva Sharei Zedek in Sea Gate
  3701 Surf Ave., Brooklyn 11224   O
Yeshiva Shevet Yehudah
  Resnick Institute of Technology, 670
  Rockaway Pkwy., Brooklyn 11236   OB
Yeshiva Torah Vodaath
  425 E. 9th St., Brooklyn 11218   OB
Yeshiva Torah Vodaath
  5202 13th Ave., Brooklyn 11219   OB
Yeshiva Torah Vodaath of Flatbush
  150 Ocean Pkwy., Brooklyn 11218   OB
Yeshiva Toras Emes Kaminetz
  1650 56th St., Brooklyn 11204   OB
Yeshiva Tores Emes Kamenitz
  Flatbush Annex, 1167 E. 13th St., Brooklyn 11230 O
Yeshiva Tores Emes Kamenitz Branch
  Boro Park Annex, 53rd St. and 14th Ave., Brooklyn
  11219   O
Yeshiva University High School of Brooklyn
  1277 E. 14th St., Brooklyn 11230   OBG
Yeshiva Yagdil Torah
  5110 18th Ave., Brooklyn 11204   OB
Yeshiva Yesode Hatorah Adas Yereim
  505 Bedford Ave., Brooklyn 11211   OB
Yeshiva Yesode Hatorah Adas Yereim (Weiner Yeshiva)
  5402 14th Ave., Brooklyn 11219   OB
Yeshivat Mikdash Melech
  1616 Ocean Pkwy., Brooklyn 11223   OB
High School of Jewish Studies
  787 Delaware Ave., Buffalo 14209   N
I. L. Peretz Jewish School
  574 Newbridge Ave., East Meadow 11554   N
Bnos Israel Institute
  612 Beach 9th St., Far Rockaway 11691   O
Hebrew Institute of Long Island
  1742 Seagirt Blvd., Far Rockaway 11691   O
Torah Academy for Girls
  444 Beach 6th St., Far Rockaway 11691   OG
Yeshiva of Far Rockaway
  1126 Virginia St., Far Rockaway 11691   O
Bais Yaakov
  Bais Yaakov Campus, Ferndale 12734   OG
Beth Shoshana Academy of Queens
  75-09 Main St., Flushing 11367   O
Solomon Schechter Day School of Queens
  76-16 Parsons Blvd., Flushing 11366   C
Yeshiva of Central Queens
  147-37 70th Rd., Flushing 11367   O
Young Israel of Kew Garden Hills Primary School
  150-04 70th Rd., Flushing 11367   O
Max & Dorothy Cohn High School
  66-35 108th St., Forest Hills 11375   OG
Rabbi Dov Revel Yeshiva of Forest Hills
  71-02 113th St., Forest Hills 11375   O
Yeshiva & Mesivta Ohr Yisroel
  66-20 Thornton St., Forest Hills 11374   OB
Yeshiva Chofetz Chaim—Mesivta of Forest Hills
  68-54 Kessel St., Forest Hills 11375   OB
North Shore Hebrew Academy
  26 Old Mill Rd., Great Neck 11023   O
Linden Hill School
  500 Linda Ave., Hawthorne 10532   N

Yeshiva & Mesivta Toras Chaim of South Shore
    Maidenbaum Prep School, 1170 Williams, St.
    Hewlett 11557   OB
Yeshiva High School of Queens
    86-86 Palo Alto St., Holliswood 11423   OBG
Hebrew Academy of West Queens
    34-25 82nd St., Jackson Heights 11372   O
Bais Yaacov Academy for Girls
    124-15 Metropolitan Ave., Kew Gardens 11415   OG
Yeshiva Tifereth Moshe
    83-06 Abingdon Rd., Kew Gardens 11415   OB
Hebrew Day School for Sullivan & Ulster County
    Kiamesha Lake 12751   OBG
Brandeis School—Irving Miller Elementary School
    25 Frost La., Lawrence 11559   C
Hillel High School
    44 Frost La., Lawrence 11559   O
Hillel School
    33 Washington Ave., Lawrence 11559   O
Hebrew Academy of Long Beach
    530 W. Broadway, Long Beach 11561   O
Yeshiva of Long Beach
    205 W. Beech St., Long Beach 11561   OB
Yeshiva Kehilath Yaakov
    33-23 Greenpoint Ave., Long Island City 11101   OB
Westchester Day School
    856 Orienta Rd., Mamaroneck 10543   O
Beth Jacob High School for Girls
    Smolley Dr., P.O. Box 116, Monsey 10952   OG
Beth Rochel School for Girls
    Maple Ave., P.O. Box 27, Monsey 10952   OG
Hebrew Institute of Rockland County
    70 Highview Rd., Monsey 10952   O
Mesivta Beth Shraga
    20 Saddle River Rd., Monsey 10952   OB
Monsey Mesivta
    221 Viola Rd., Monsey 10952   OB
Yeshiva Bais Yitzchok
    184 Maple Ave., Monsey 10952   O
Yeshiva Beth David
    P.O. Box 136, Monsey 10952   OB
Yeshiva of Spring Valley
    229 Maple Ave., Monsey 10952   OBG
Yeshiva Viznitz
    P.O. Box 446, Monsey 10952   OB
Yeshivat Hadar High School
    70 Highview Rd., Monsey 10952   OG
Talmud Torah Bais Yechiel
    Pines Bridge Rd., Mt. Kisco 10549   OB
Yeshiva Farm Settlement School
    Mt. Kisco 10549   OB
Ohr Hameir Theological Seminary & H.S.
    3 Boulevard, New Rochelle 10801   OB
Gruss Girls School of New Square
    Village Hall, New Square 10977   OG
Beth Hillel Hebrew Institute
    124 W. 95th St., New York 10025   N
Beth Jacob Parochial School of the Lower East Side
    142 Broome St., New York 10002   OG
B'nai Jeshurun Day School
    270 W. 89th St., New York 10024   C
Darche Shalom School
    344 E. 14th St., New York 10003   N
East Side Hebrew Institute
    295 E. 8th St., New York 10001   O
Esther Schoenfeld High School
    142 Broome St., New York 10002   OG
Jewish Folk Schools
    575 Ave. of the Americas, New York 10011   N
Manhattan Day School
    310 W. 75th St., New York 10023   O
Mesivta Rabbi Jacob Joseph School
    165 Henry St., New York 10002   OB
Mesivta Rabbi Samson R. Hirsch
    85-93 Bennett Ave., New York 10033   OB
Mesivta Tifereth Jerusalem
    145 E. Broadway, New York 10002   OB

Ramaz School
    125 E. 85th St., New York 10028   O
Sholom Aleichem Folk Institute
    41 Union Sq., New York 10003   N
Yeshiva & Mesivta Chofetz Chaim
    346 W. 89th St., New York 10024   OB
Yeshiva Haichel Hatorah
    630 Riverside Dr., New York 10031   OB
Yeshiva Rabbi Joseph Konvitz
    313 Henry St., New York 10002   O
Yeshiva Rabbi Moses Soloveichik
    560 W. 185th St., New York 10033   O
Yeshiva Rabbi Samson Raphael Hirsch
    85-93 Bennett Ave., New York 10033   O
Yeshiva Rabbi Samson Raphael Hirsch Beth Jacob
High School
    85-93 Bennett Ave., New York 10033   OG
Yeshiva U. H.S. for Boys of Manhattan
    186th St. and Amsterdam Ave., New York 10033 OB
Yeshiva U. H.S. for Girls of Manhattan
    462 W. 58th St., New York 10019   OG
Sholom Aleichem School
    3480 Weidener Ave., Oceanside 11572   N
Yeshiva Day School of South Queens
    107-01 Cross Bay Blvd., Ozone Park 11417   O
First Hebrew Day School of Westchester & Putnam
    First Hebrew Congregation, 1821 E. Main
    St., Peekskill 10566   O
Pleasantville Cottage School
    Pleasantville 10570   N
Mid Hudson Hebrew Day School
    110 Grand Ave., Poughkeepsie 12590   C
Nursery of Yeshiva of Central Queens
    % Young Israel of Hillcrest, 170th St. and Jewel
    Ave., Queens 11375   O
Ezra Academy of Queens
    88-01 102nd St., Richmond Hill 11418   O
Hillel School of Rochester
    2131 Elmwood Ave., Rochester 14618   O
Talmudical Institute of Upstate New York
    144 Pinnacle Rd., Rochester 14618   O
Robert Gordis Day School
    445 Beach 135th St., Rockaway Park 11694   C
Solomon Schechter Day School of Nassau County
    Roslyn Road and Northern State Pkwy., Roslyn
    Heights 11577   C
Hebrew Academy of the Capitol District
    3489 Carman Rd., Schenectady 12303   C
Hebrew Academy of Suffolk County
    525 Veterans Hwy., Smithtown 11787   O
Molinoff High School
    B'nai Akiva Yeshiva, 495 Veterans Hwy.,
    Smithtown 11787   OB
Yeshiva Gedolah Limtzuyonim Zichron Moshe
High School
    South Fallsburg 12779   O
Solomon Schechter Day School
    250 N. Main St., Spring Valley 10977   C
Yeshiva of New Square
    91 Washington Ave., Spring Valley 10977   OB
Jewish Foundation School of Staten Island
    20 Parkhill Circle, Staten Island 10304   O
Jewish Foundation School of S.I. Nursery
    835 Forest Hill Rd., Staten Island 10314   N
Mesivta of Staten Island
    1870 Drumgoole Rd. E., Staten Island 10309   OB
Yeshiva of Willowbrook
    61 Rupert Ave., Staten Island 10314   O
Max Gilbert Hebrew Academy
    450 Kimber Rd., Syracuse 13224   O
Kibutz Tashbar
    24 Highview Rd., Tallman 10952   OB
Kadimah School of Buffalo
    2368 Eggert Rd., Tonawanda 14510   O
Hebrew Academy of Nassau City Moses
Hornstein Jr. H.S. & Brookdale H.S.
    215 Oak St., Uniondale 11553   O

Hillel School of Greater Utica
    14 Clinton Pl., Utica 13501   O
Hebrew Academy of Nassau County
    609 Hempstead Ave., West Hempstead 11552   O
Solomon Schechter School
    20 Soundview Ave., White Plains 10804   C
Hebrew Academy H.S. of Westchester
    700 McLean Ave., Yonkers 10704   O

NORTH CAROLINA
Michael & Jonathan Baron Hebrew Academy
    1006 Sardis La., Charlotte 28211   C

OHIO
Hillel Academy of Akron
    750 White Pond Dr., Akron 44320   O
Cincinnati Hebrew Day School
    7855 Dawn Rd., Cincinnati 45237   O
Yavneh Day School
    1636 Summit Rd., Cincinnati 45237   N
Akiva High School
    2030 S. Taylor Rd., Cleveland 44118   N
Hebrew Academy of Cleveland
    1860 S. Taylor Rd., Cleveland 44118   O
Jewish Day Nursery
    22201 Fairmount Blvd., Cleveland 44106   N
Mesivta High School of Hebrew Academy
    1975 Lyndway, Cleveland 44121   O
Yeshiva Adat B'nai Israel
    2308 Warrensville Center Rd., Cleveland 44118   O
Columbus Torah Academy
    5419 E. Broad St., Columbus 43213   O
Hillel Academy of Dayton
    6560 N. Amin St., Dayton 45415   O
Hebrew Academy
    2727 Kenwood, Toledo 43606   O
Telshe Yeshiva High School
    28400 Euclid Ave., Wickliffe 44092   OB

OREGON
Hillel Academy
    920 N.W. 25th Ave., Portland 97210   O

PENNSYLVANIA
Jewish Day School
    2313 Pennsylvania St., Allentown 18104   O
Beth Jacob School of Philadelphia
    Church and Stahr Rds., Elkins Park 19117   O
Forman Day School
    York and Foxcroft Rds., Elkins Park 19117   C
Yeshiva Academy
    100 Vaughn St., Harrisburg 17110   O
Israel Ben Zion Academy
    3rd Ave. and Institute La., Kingston 18704   O
Akiba Hebrew Academy
    223 N. Highland Ave., Merion 19072   N
Akiba Hebrew Academy
    2280 Georges La., Philadelphia 19131   N
Beth David Nursery School
    5220 Wynnefield Ave., Philadelphia 19131   R
Beth Jacob Nursery School
    701 Bayberry Rd., Philadelphia 19120   O
George Friedland Institute of Beth Jacob School
    Penway and Friendship Sts., Philadelphia 19111
Talmudical Yeshiva
    6063 Drexel Rd., Philadelphia 19131   OB
Torah Academy of Greater Philadelphia
    5337 Wynnefield Ave., Philadelphia 19131   O
Hebrew Institute of Pittsburgh
    6401-07 Forbes Ave., Pittsburgh 15217   N
Hillel Academy
    5685 Beacon St., Pittsburgh 15217   O
Nechama Minsky High School
    2100 Wightman St., Pittsburgh 15217   OG
Talmudical Institute & Mesivta
    5751 Bartlett St., Pittsburgh 15217   O
Yeshiva Achei Tmimim
    2410 5th Ave., Pittsburgh 15213   O
Milton Eisner Yeshiva High School
    538 Monroe Ave., Scranton 18510   O

Scranton Hebrew Day School
    520 Monroe Ave., Scranton 18510   O
Solomon Schechter Day School
    410 Montgomery Ave., Wynnewood 19096   C

RHODE ISLAND
Providence Hebrew Day School
    450 Elmgrove Ave., Providence 02906   O

SOUTH CAROLINA
Charleston Hebrew Institute
    182 Rutledge Ave., Charleston 29403   O

TENNESSEE
Chattanooga Jewish Day School
    5326 Lynnland Terrace, Chattanooga 37411   O
Bais Yaacov
    392 Cokwell Rd., Memphis 38117   OG
Memphis Hebrew Academy
    390 S. White Station Rd., Memphis 38117   O
Yeshiva of the South
    5255 Meadowcrest La., Memphis 38117   OB
Akiva School
    3600 West End Ave., Nashville 37205   O

TEXAS
Akiba Academy
    6210 Churchill Way, Dallas 75230   O
Beth Yeshurun Day School
    4525 Beechnut, Houston 77035   C
South Texas Hebrew Academy
    4221 S. Braeswood Blvd., Houston 77035   O
San Antonio Solomon Schechter
    1201 Donaldson, San Antonio 78228   C

VIRGINIA
Jewish Academy of Richmond
    4811 Patterson Ave., Richmond 23226   O
Richmond Hebrew Day School
    6300 Patterson Ave., Richmond 23226   O
Richmond Hebrew Day School
    6801 Patterson Ave., Richmond 23226   O
Hebrew Academy of Tidewater
    1244 Thomkins La., Virginia Beach 23462   O

WASHINGTON
Seattle Hebrew Academy
    1617 Interlaken Dr. E., Seattle 98112   O

WISCONSIN
Hillel Academy
    4650 N. Port Washington Rd., Milwaukee 53212   O

CANADA
Alberta
Calgary Hebrew School
    1415 Glenmore Trail, Calgary   N
I. L. Peretz School
    1915 36th Ave., S.W., Calgary   N
Edmonton Hebrew Day School
    133rd St. and 106th Ave., Edmonton   O

British Columbia
School of Jewish Education
    3476 Oak St., Vancouver   N
Vancouver Talmud Torah School
    998 W. 26th Ave., Vancouver   N

Manitoba
Herzalia Academy
    620 Brock St., Winnipeg   O
I. L. Peretz School
    600 Jefferson Ave., Winnipeg   N
Ramah Hebrew School
    Grant and Lanark Sts., Winnipeg   N
Winnipeg Hebrew School
    427 Matheson Ave., Winnipeg   N

Ontario
Borochov School
    272 Codsell Ave., Downsview   N
Hamilton Hebrew Academy Zichron Meir
    60 Dow Ave. S., Hamilton
London Community Hebrew Day School
    534 Huron St., London   O

Hillel Academy	
453 Rideau St., Ottawa	O
Ulpanat Orot	
8308 Bathurst St., Box 610, Thorn Hill	OG
Assoc. Hebrew Schools	
3630 Bathurst St., Toronto	O
Bais Yaakov School	
85 Stormont Ave., Toronto	OG
Beth Jacob High School	
410 Lawrence Ave. W., Toronto	OG
Etz Chaim School	
1 Viewmount Ave., Toronto	O
Or Chaim B'nai Akiva Yeshiva	
86 Vaughn Rd., Toronto	OB
United Synagogue Day School	
1700 Bathurst St., Toronto	C
Workmen's Circle School	
471 Lawrence Ave. W., Toronto	N
Yeshiva Torah Chaim	
475 Lawrence Ave. W., Toronto	O
Yeshiva Yesodei Hatorah	
367 Lawrence Ave. W., Toronto	O
Assoc. Hebrew Schools	
252 Finch Ave., Willowdale	O
Etz Chaim Yeshiva	
475 Patricia Ave., Willowdale	O
New Israel Yeshiva College	
625 Finch Ave., Willowdale	O
Sephardic Religious School	
464 Ellerslie Ave., Willowdale	O
United Hebrew Day School	
3080 Bayview Ave., Willowdale	C
Windsor Hebrew Day School	
1661 Quellette Ave., Windsor	O
Quebec	
Hebrew Academy Nursery	
6519 Baily Rd., Cote St. Luc	O
Hebrew Foundation School	
2 Hope Dr., Dollard Des Ormeaux	O
Akiva School	
5500 Westbury Ave., Montreal	O
Beis Esther	
5214 St. Urbain St., Montreal	OG

Beth Jacob School	
1750 Glendale Ave., Montreal	OG
Beth Rivka Academy	
5001 Vezina Ave., Montreal	OG
Beth Zion Hebrew School	
5740 Hudson Ave., Montreal	O
First Mesivta of Canada	
2325 Ekers St., Montreal	OB
Hebrew Academy	
1500 Ducharme Ave., Montreal	O
Herzliah High School	
4840 St. Kevin Ave., Montreal	O
Jewish People's School	
5170 Van Horne, Montreal	N
Maor Hagola Rabbinical College	
5815 Jeanne Mance St., Montreal	OB
Rabbinical College of Canada	
6405 Westbury Ave., Montreal	OB
Sephardic Academy of Montreal	
805 Gougeon, Montreal	O
Solomon Schechter Academy	
5555 Cote St. Luc Rd., Montreal	C
United Jewish Teachers Seminary	
5237 Clanranaid, Montreal	O
United Talmud Torahs	
4894 St. Kevin Ave.—Snowdon, Montreal	O
Yeshiva Chasiedei Belz	
5336 Jeanne Mance St., Montreal	OB
Yeshiva Gedola of Montreal	
6155 Deacon Rd., Montreal	OB
Yeshiva Toras Moshe	
5402 Park Ave., Montreal	O
Herzliah High School	
805 Dorals, St. Laurent	O
MEXICO	
Escuela Israelita Yavneh	
Agrarism 221, Mexico City 18, D.F.	O
Instituo Femenino Beth Jacob A.C.	
Platon 439, Esquina Dickens, Mexico City 5, D.F.	OG
Instituo Scientifico Educacion y Cultura	
Yeshiva D'Mexico, Anatole France 13 Planco,	
Mexico City 7, D.F.	O
Yeshiva Keter Torah	
331 La Fontaine, Mexico City, D.F.	OB

SCHOOLS: SPECIAL

C = Conservative
N = Nondenominational
O = Orthodox
Brooklyn Hebrew School for Special Children
376 Bay 44th St., Brooklyn, NY 11214   N
Community School Beth Moshe
913 49th St., Brooklyn, NY 11219   N
Hebrew Academy for Special Children
1311-55th St., Brooklyn, NY 11219   O
Hebrew Institute for the Deaf
2025 67th St., Brooklyn, 11204   N

Maimonides Day School and Residential Center for Exceptional Children
Monticello, NY 12701   N
Shallaym
155 5th Ave., New York, NY 10010   C
hopes to establish a village for exceptional children
Hebrew Academy for Special Children
Parksville, NY 12768   N
Pennsylvania School for the Deaf
7500 Germantown Ave., Philadelphia, PA 19119   N

SCHOOLS: TEACHER TRAINING

CALIFORNIA
Hebrew Union College–Jewish Institute of Religion
3077 University Mall, Los Angeles 90007
University College of Jewish Studies
University of Judaism, 6525 Sunset Blvd., Los Angeles 90028
ILLINOIS
Spertus College of Judaica
618 S. Michigan Ave., Chicago 60625
MARYLAND
Baltimore Hebrew College
5800 Park Heights, Baltimore 21215
MASSACHUSETTS
Hebrew College
43 Hawes St., Brookline 02146

MICHIGAN
Detroit Midrasha College of Jewish Studies
21550 W. Twelve Mile Rd., Southfield 48075

NEW YORK
Hebrew Union College–Jewish Institute of Religion
40 W. 68th St., New York 10023
Herzliah Hebrew Teachers Institute and Jewish Teachers Seminary and People's University
69 Bank St., New York 10014
Teachers Institute—Seminary College of Jewish Studies
3080 Broadway, New York 10027
Yeshiva University
500 W. 185th St., New York 10033
Stern College for Women of Yeshiva University
253 Lexington Ave., New York 10016

Teachers Institute for Women of Yeshiva University
253 Lexington Ave., New York 10016
Ferkauf Graduate School of Humanities and Social
Sciences of Yeshiva University
55 5th Ave., New York 10003

OHIO
Cleveland College of Jewish Studies
2030 S. Taylor Rd., Cleveland 44118

PENNSYLVANIA
Gratz College
10th St. and Tabor Rd., Philadelphia 19141

SUPPLIES AND IDEAS: WHERE TO SCROUNGE

Jewish book stores
Christian book stores
Teacher supply stores
Secular stores (old wallpaper, books, boxes, scraps, etc.)
Industry (carpet scraps, rubber scraps, wood scraps, etc.)
Printers (cardboard and paper scraps, pads, punched holes for mosaics, etc.)
Rummage sales
Garage sales
Truck lettering companies (magnet scraps)
Education magazines—Jewish, secular, and Christian

For ideas on recycling, read *Recyclopedia* by Robin Simons (Boston: Houghton Mifflin Co., 1976) and send for a catalog from The Teacher Shop, The Children's Museum, Boston, MA 02130. Better yet, visit the museum and take any and all available youngsters along!

TAPE RECORDINGS

Adventures in Judaism Tapes, UAHC, 838 5th Ave., New York, NY 10021
Butterfly Media Dimensions, 8817 Shirley Ave., Northridge, CA 91324
Caedmon Records, 505 8th Ave., New York, NY 10018
The Center for the Study of Democratic Institutions, P.O. Box 4446, Santa Barbara, CA 93103

TAPE REPAIR SERVICE
Tape Repair Service, P.O. Box 7368, Milwaukee, WI 53226

TEACHER CENTERS

Associated Talmud Torah, 8200 W. 33rd, Minneapolis, MN 55426
Board of Jewish Education of Greater Washington, 7961 Eastern Ave., Silver Spring, MD 20910
Central Agency for Jewish Education, 225 S. Meramec, Suite 400, St. Louis, MO 63105
Commission for Jewish Education, P.O. Box 35097, Houston, TX 77035
Jewish Teacher Center, 1580 Summit Rd., Room 206, Cincinnati, OH 45237
Jewish Teacher Center, Board of Education of Greater New York, 426 W. 58th St., New York, NY 10019
Ha Moreh, Beit Rassco—Building 2, No. 33, Beersheva, Israel
Ha Moreh, 3 Dorot Rishonim, Jerusalem, Israel
The Kohl Jewish Teacher Center, 161 Green Bay Rd., Wilmette, IL 60091
The Learning Center, Hirsch School of Education, Hebrew Union College, 3077 University Ave., Los Angeles, CA 9000?
Philadelphia Jewish Teacher Center, Gratz College, 10th St. and Tabor Rd., Philadelphia, PA 19141
Teacher Creativity Center, Milwaukee Board of Jewish Education, 4650 N. Port Washington Rd., Milwaukee, WI 5321
Toronto Board of Jewish Education, 22 Glen Park Ave., Toronto, ON, Canada
United Hebrew Schools, 21550 W. Twelve Mile Rd., Southfield, MI 48076

TEACHER TRAINING PROGRAMS: SUMMER

Hebrew Union College, 3077 University Ave., Los Angeles, CA 90007
Hebrew Union College, 40 W. 68th St., New York, NY 10023
Union of American Hebrew Congregation Ulpan in Israel, 838 5th Ave., New York, NY 10021
University of Judaism, 2845 Casiano Rd., Los Angeles, CA 90024

TOYS

Alpha Beta Circle Press, 4036 Telegraph Rd., Bloomfield Hills, MI 48013
Alternatives in Religious Education, 1110 Holly Oak Circle, San Jose, CA 95100
Behrman House, 1261 Broadway, New York, NY 10002
Board of Jewish Education, 426 W. 58th St., New York, NY 10019
Brocha Puzzles, P.O. Box 305, Station C, Flushing, NY 11367
Dreidel Factory, 2445 Prince St., Berkeley, CA 94705
Israel Educational Material & Games, % Israel Trade Center, 111 W. 40th St., New York, NY 10018
Jewish Teacher Center, 161 Green Bay Rd., Wilmette, IL 60091
Judaica Unlimited, P.O. Box 6394, Orange, CA 92667
Ktav, 75 Varick St., New York, NY 10013
Machat, 20 Burton Woods Lane, Cincinnati, OH 45229
Simulations Publications, 44 E. 23rd St., New York, NY 10010
Torah Toys, 3838 Pine Ave., Long Beach, CA 90807

TYPEWRITERS: HEBREW

All Languages Typewriter Co., 119 W. 23rd St., New York, NY 10011
The Office Machine, 2109 Murray Ave., Pittsburgh, PA 15217

INDEX

ABOUT THE AUTHORS

SHARON STRASSFELD co-edited the enormously popular *Jewish Catalog* along with her husband, Michael, and Richard Siegel. Published in 1973, the *Catalog* provided American Jews with a "how to" kit to enrich their Jewish life styles. The Strassfelds alone continued the innovative approach in *The Second* and *Third Jewish Catalogs*. Sharon, along with Arthur Kurzweil, edited *Behold a Great Image* (Philadelphia: Jewish Publication Society, 1978). An early member of Havurat Shalom in Boston, Sharon is active in Minyan Miat and in communal affairs on the Upper West Side of New York City, where she lives with her husband and two children.

KATHY GREEN has served as a Jewish teacher and school administrator working with students who vary in age from eighteen-month-old toddlers to senior citizens. She has master's degrees in educational psychology and early childhood education and is the author of a variety of articles relating to Jewish education. Kathy was one of the founders of Havurat Shalom in Boston, the first attempt at an alternative Jewish community in the 1960s. She lives with her husband and daughter in Philadelphia, where she is a member of the Germantown Minyan.

ABOUT THE PHOTOGRAPHER

BILL ARON has had recent one-man photographic exhibitions at the Pucker/Safrai Gallery in Boston, the Skirball Museum in Los Angeles, The Museum of the Diaspora in Tel Aviv, and the Milton Weil Gallery in New York City. He teaches photography at the Otis Art Institute of the Parsons School of Design in Los Angeles, and Visual Anthropology at the University of Southern California. He is represented by the Pucker/Safrai Gallery, which features his work both in Boston and as travelling exhibitions.